THE CLASSIC 1000
QUICK & EASY RECIPES

by

Carolyn Humphries

with contributions from:

Fiona Williams

Susan Crook

Veena Chopra

Chrissie Taylor

foulsham
LONDON · NEW YORK · TORONTO · SYDNEY

foulsham

The Oriel, Thames Valley Court, 183-187 Bath Road,
Slough, Berkshire, SL1 4AA, England

ISBN 978-0-572-02909-8

Photographs by Carol and Terry Pastor
Cover photograph by Peter Howard Smith

With thanks to the following companies for providing items for the photographs:
Tiles from **Smith and Wareham Tile Merchants**, Unit 2, Autopark,
Eastgate Street, Bury St Edmunds, Suffolk, IP33 1YQ. Tel: 01284 704188.
Web site: www.kitchendesign.co.uk.

Turquoise measuring cup (opposite page 32) from a set of four from the Nigella Lawson
Living Kitchen Range. Available from **Bliss**, Paradise Works, Arden Forest
Estate, Alcester, Warwickshire, B49 6HN. Tel: 01789 400077.
Web site: www.blisscatalogue.co.uk.

Cuisipro Accutec graters used in the preparation of the food from **Cuisipro**, 4 The
Waterhouse, Hemel Hempstead, Hertfordshire, HP1 1EN. Tel: 01442 261199.

Printed in Great Britain by Printwise (Haverhill) Ltd, Haverhill

CONTENTS

INTRODUCTION

Even with the busy lives we lead today, eating should be a pleasure. This book is designed to help you cook anything and everything that looks great, tastes terrific and is quick and easy to prepare. You can dip into it for everyday meals, quick snacks, complete feasts for entertaining in style, a whole variety of vegetarian dishes and the best and easiest breads, biscuits and cakes in the business!

Notes on the Recipes

- When following a recipe, use EITHER imperial, metric or American measures; never swap from one to another.

- All spoon measurements are level: 1 tsp = 5 ml; 1 tbsp = 15 ml.

- Eggs are medium (size 3) unless otherwise stated.

- All preparation and cooking times are approximate.

- Always wash and peel, if necessary, all fresh produce before use.

- Wherever possible use fresh herbs, unless dried are specifically called for. You can substitute dried herbs, but use only half the quantity stated in the recipe as they are very pungent.

- Always preheat the oven and cook on the centre shelf unless otherwise stated.

SOUPS

Soups are a good choice before a less substantial main course. But they also make a delicious light meal, served with crusty bread and followed by a cheese board and fresh fruit.

Moreish Onion Soup

SERVES 6

1 kg/1¹/₄ lb onions, thinly sliced
45 ml/3 tbsp olive oil
900 ml/1¹/₂ pts/3³/₄ cups beef stock, hot
Croûtons (see page 17)

Fry (sauté) the onions gently in the oil for 15 minutes, covered, until soft. Remove the lid and increase the heat, letting the onions caramelise to a rich brown, stirring regularly to dissolve the deposits on the base of the pan. Continue like this for 30 minutes; it may seem excessive, but the more caramelised the onions are, the better the flavour will be. Pour in the stock, bring to the boil, then simmer for 20 minutes. Garnish with croûtons.

Leek and Potato Soup

SERVES 4

3 leeks, sliced
25 g/1 oz/2 tbsp unsalted (sweet) butter
225 g/8 oz potatoes, diced
600 ml/1 pt/2¹/₂ cups chicken or vegetable stock
Salt and freshly ground black pepper
A little double (heavy) cream or plain yoghurt
Snipped chives or grated orange rind

Fry (sauté) the leeks in the butter for 5 minutes. Add the potato, stock and seasoning, bring to the boil, cover and simmer for 20 minutes. Leave to cool slightly, then purée in a blender or food processor until smooth. Reheat and ladle into warm soup bowls. Garnish each with a swirl or cream or yoghurt and a sprinkling of chives or grated orange rind and serve.

Courgette, Tomato and Basil Soup

SERVES 4

25 g/1 oz/2 tbsp butter
1 onion, finely chopped
350 g/12 oz courgettes (zucchini),
 coarsely grated
1 garlic clove, crushed
600 ml/1 pt/2¹/₂ cups vegetable stock
400 g/14 oz/1 large can chopped
 tomatoes
15 ml/1 tbsp tomato purée (paste)
30 ml 2 tbsp chopped basil
Salt and freshly ground black pepper
60 ml/4 tbsp double (heavy) cream or
 a drizzle of olive oil
A few basil leaves

Melt the butter in a large pan. Add the onion and cook until soft. Add the courgettes and garlic and cook for 3–4 minutes. Add the stock, tomatoes and their juice and the tomato purée. Bring to the boil. Cover and simmer for 15 minutes. Add the chopped basil, salt and pepper. Ladle into warm soup bowls and serve garnished with a swirl of cream or a drizzle of olive oil and a few basil leaves.

Egg and Watercress Soup

SERVES 6

1 onion, finely chopped
30 ml/2 tbsp olive oil
350 g/12 oz watercress
15 ml/1 tbsp plain (all-purpose)
 flour
1 litre/1³/₄ pts/4¹/₄ cups chicken
 stock
Salt and freshly ground black pepper
60 ml/4 tbsp double (heavy) cream
2 hard-boiled (hard-cooked) eggs,
finely chopped

Fry (sauté) the onion in the oil in a saucepan for 2 minutes until soft. Roughly chop the watercress, reserving a few small sprigs for garnish. Add the chopped watercress to the onion and cook for 2 minutes. Stir in the flour, then gradually stir in the stock and seasoning and simmer for 30 minutes. Purée the soup in a processor so that it is smooth but still speckled. Add the cream and reheat gently. Serve garnished with the chopped egg and tiny watercress sprigs.

Tomato and Carrot Soup

SERVES 4

400 g/14 oz/1 large can chopped
tomatoes
2 large carrots, grated
1 small onion, finely chopped
300 ml/¹/₂ pt/1¹/₄ cups chicken or
 vegetable stock
5 ml/1 tsp dried oregano
Grated nutmeg
Salt
1 bay leaf
5 ml/1 tsp light brown sugar
15 ml/1 tbsp chopped parsley

Put all the ingredients except the parsley in a saucepan and bring to the boil, stirring all the time. Cover and simmer for 30 minutes. Remove the bay leaf, ladle into warm soup bowls, garnish with the parsley and serve.

8

Tuna and Sweetcorn Bisque

1 small onion, finely chopped
25 g/1 oz/2 tbsp butter
5 ml/1 tsp mild curry powder
5 ml/1 tsp turmeric
5 ml/1 tsp paprika
25 g/1 oz/¹/₄ cup plain (all-purpose)
* flour*
450 ml/³/₄ pt/2 cups chicken stock
450 ml/³/₄ pt/2 cups milk
¹/₂ lemon
350 g/12 oz/1 large can sweetcorn
(corn), drained
185 g/6¹/₂ oz/1 small can tuna,
* drained*
Chopped parsley

Cook the onion in the butter until soft. Stir in the curry powder, turmeric, paprika and flour. Cook for 1 minute, stirring all the time. Gradually stir in the stock and bring to the boil, stirring constantly. Add the milk, lemon and sweetcorn. Simmer for a further 5 minutes. Stir in the tuna. Simmer for a further 5 minutes. Serve sprinkled with parsley to garnish.

Tuna, Prawn and Sweetcorn Bisque

Prepare as for Tuna and Sweetcorn Bisque, but use 100 g/4 oz/1 small can tuna and 100 g/4 oz/1 cup peeled prawns (shrimp) instead of all tuna.

Carrot and Coriander Soup

1 small onion, finely chopped
1 garlic clove, crushed
450 g/1 lb carrots, finely chopped
30 ml/2 tbsp olive oil
5 ml/1 tsp coriander (cilantro)
* seeds, crushed*
5 ml/1 tsp ground coriander
900 ml/1¹/₂ pts/3³/₄ cups vegetable
* stock*
50 g/2 oz/¹/₃ cup sultanas (golden
* raisins), chopped*
Salt and freshly ground black pepper
20 ml/4 tsp double (heavy) cream
15 ml/1 tbsp chopped coriander
* leaves*

Fry (sauté) the onion, garlic and carrots in the oil in a large pan for 10 minutes. Stir in the crushed and ground coriander and cook for 1 minute. Add the stock. Cover and simmer for 15 minutes until the carrots are tender. Let the soup cool slightly. Liquidise in a blender or food processor, return to the pan, add the sultanas, salt and pepper and reheat gently. Ladle into warm soup bowls and garnish with a swirl of cream and chopped coriander.

Spiced Carrot Soup

SERVES 4

Finely grated rind of 1 orange
1 onion, finely chopped
450 g/1 lb carrots, chopped
5 mm/^{1}/$_4$ in piece fresh root ginger,
*   peeled and crushed*
5 cm/2 in piece cinnamon stick
750 ml/1^1/$_4$ pts/3 cups chicken stock
200 ml/7 fl oz/scant 1 cup fresh
*   orange juice*
Salt and freshly ground black pepper
60 ml/4 tbsp plain yoghurt
1 egg yolk
Orange rind, cut into thin strips

Place all the ingredients, except the yoghurt, egg yolk and strips of orange rind, in a saucepan. Bring to the boil and simmer for 25 minutes. Cool the soup slightly, remove the cinnamon stick, and liquidise in a blender or food processor until smooth. Return to the rinsed-out pan. Beat the yoghurt and egg yolk, add a little of the soup and stir, then return all this mixture to the pan. Heat through gently, but do not boil. Serve hot, garnished with the orange rind.

Creamy Cauliflower Soup

SERVES 4

1 onion, diced
50g/2 oz/^{1}/$_4$ cup butter
750 ml/1^1/$_4$ pts/3 cups hot chicken
stock
350 g/12 oz cauliflower florets
30 ml/2 tbsp plain (all-purpose)
*   flour*
Salt and freshly ground black pepper
30 ml/2 tbsp single (light) cream
Chopped parsley

In a saucepan, fry (sauté) the onion in the butter for 2 minutes until soft but not brown. Stir in the stock and the cauliflower, cover and simmer for about 10 minutes until the cauliflower is tender. Purée in a processor or blender and return to the pan. Blend the flour with a little water until smooth. Stir into the purée. Bring to the boil and simmer for 2 minutes, stirring. Season to taste. Stir in the cream and heat through but do not boil. Ladle into warm soup bowls, garnish with parsley and serve hot.

Creamy Broccoli and Cauliflower Soup

SERVES 4

Prepare as for Creamy Cauliflower Soup but use half broccoli and half cauliflower and serve with grated Cheddar cheese to sprinkle over.

Bortsch

SERVES 6

2 celery sticks
2 carrots
1 onion
350 g/12 oz cooked beetroot (red
*   beets)*
900 ml/1^1/$_2$ pts/3^3/$_4$ cups beef stock
15 ml/1 tbsp wine vinegar
Salt and freshly ground black pepper
Soured (dairy sour) cream or plain
*   yoghurt*

Grate the vegetables into a pan. Add the stock and vinegar, bring to the boil, reduce the heat, cover and simmer for 20 minutes or until the vegetables are tender. Season to taste. Ladle into soup bowls and garnish each with a spoonful of soured cream or yoghurt. Alternatively, chill before garnishing.

Provençal Fish Chowder

60 ml/4 tbsp olive oil
1 small onion, finely chopped
1 leek, trimmed and finely sliced
2 garlic cloves, crushed
350 g/12 oz ripe tomatoes,
skinned and diced
1 bouquet garni
1 bay leaf
225 g/8 oz potatoes, diced
1.5 litres/2¹/₂ pts/6 cups fish stock
15 ml/1 tbsp tomato purée (paste)
750 g/1¹/₂ lb white fish, skinned and
boned
5 ml/1 tsp dried basil
50 g/2 oz/¹/₃ cup small black olives,
stoned (pitted) and halved
(optional)
Salt and freshly ground black pepper

In a large pan heat the oil and cook the onion, leek and garlic gently for 5 minutes until soft. Add the tomatoes and cook for about 10 minutes. Add the bouquet garni, bay leaf, potatoes, stock and tomato purée. Cover and simmer for 15 minutes until the potatoes are cooked. Cut the fish into 4 cm/1¹/₂ in pieces and add to the soup with the basil and olives. Cook until the fish is just tender, season, and remove the bouquet garni and bay leaf. Serve immediately.

Light Tomato Soup

1 onion, finely chopped
30 ml/2 tbsp olive oil
500 ml/17 fl oz/2¹/₄ cups passata
(sieved tomatoes)
Juice and coarsely grated rind of 1
orange
Juice of ¹/₂ lemon
250 ml/8 fl oz/1 cup water
Salt and freshly ground black pepper
Pinch of sugar

Fry (sauté) the onion in the oil until soft, but not brown. Add the passata, orange and lemon juices and water. Simmer for 20 minutes. Season to taste with a little salt, pepper and the sugar and serve garnished with the grated orange rind.

Chilled Cucumber Soup with Dill

1 cucumber
Salt
10 ml/2 tsp dried dill (dill weed)
30 ml/2 tbsp cider or wine vinegar
Freshly ground black pepper
300 ml/¹/₂ pt/1¹/₄ cups plain yoghurt
300 ml/¹/₂ pt/1¹/₄ cups cold milk

Cut 4 thin slices from the cucumber and reserve for garnish. Grate the remainder into a bowl. Sprinkle with salt, stir and leave to stand for 10 minutes. Squeeze out all the moisture and drain off. Stir in the dill, vinegar and a little pepper, and then add the yoghurt. If time allows, chill, then stir in the milk just before serving in soup bowls. Garnish with the reserved slices of cucumber.

Curried Parsnip Soup

450 g/1 lb parsnips, sliced
1 onion, chopped
25 g/1 oz/2 tbsp butter or margarine
15 ml/1 tbsp curry powder
600 ml/1 pt/2¹/₂ cups vegetable stock
300 ml/¹/₂ pt/1¹/₄ cups milk
Salt and freshly ground black pepper
15 ml/1 tbsp chopped parsley

Put the parsnips, onion and butter or margarine in a pan. Fry (sauté) gently, stirring for 3 minutes. Add the curry powder and fry for 1 minute. Stir in the stock, bring to the boil, reduce the heat, cover and simmer for 15 minutes or until the parsnips are really tender. Purée in a blender or food processor. Return to the pan. Stir in the milk, season to taste and add the parsley. Heat through. Serve ladled into soup bowls.

Curried Yam Soup

Prepare as for Curried Parsnip Soup, but use yams instead of parsnips and chopped coriander instead of parsley.

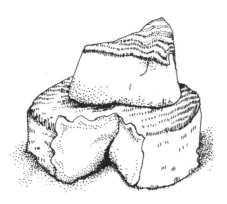

Golden Cheddar Soup

1 large potato, diced
1 large onion, chopped
1 carrot, chopped
1 celery stick, chopped
600 ml/1 pt/2¹/₂ cups vegetable or chicken stock
100 g/4 oz/1 cup grated Cheddar cheese
150 ml/¹/₄ pt/²/₃ cup milk or single (light) cream
30 ml/2 tbsp chopped parsley

Simmer all the vegetables in the stock for 15 minutes or until soft. Blend or purée in a food processor and return to the pan. Stir in the cheese, milk or cream and parsley. Heat through but do not boil. Serve hot.

Greek Egg and Lemon Soup

900 ml/1¹/₂ pts/3³/₄ cups chicken or lamb stock (preferably fresh)
50 g/2 oz/¹/₄ cup long-grain rice
2 eggs
1 small lemon
15 ml/1 tbsp water
Salt and freshly ground black pepper
Chopped parsley

Put the stock and rice in a pan. Bring to the boil and simmer for 10–12 minutes until the rice is cooked. Break the eggs into a bowl. Squeeze in the juice from the lemon and add the water. Whisk to blend. Whisk in one ladleful of the hot stock. Then whisk in two more. Remove the hot stock from the heat and stir in the egg mixture. Taste and season if necessary. Serve in soup bowls, garnished with chopped parsley.

Green Velvet Soup

SERVES 6

450 g/1 lb spinach
15 g/¹/₂ oz/1 tbsp butter
1 onion, chopped
175 g/6 oz/1¹/₄ cups broad (lima)
beans, shelled
Pinch of grated nutmeg
600 ml/1 pt/2¹/₂ cups vegetable stock
300 ml/¹/₂ pt/1¹/₄ cups milk
Salt and freshly ground black pepper
Croûtons (see page 17)

Wash the spinach well, removing any thick stalks. Tear the leaves into pieces. Melt the butter in a pan. Add the onion and fry (sauté) gently for one minute. Add the spinach and stir until it cooks down a little. Add the beans, nutmeg and stock. Bring to the boil, reduce the heat, cover and simmer for 15 minutes until the beans are soft. Purée in a blender or food processor until smooth. Return to the pan and add the milk. Season if necessary. Reheat and serve in soup bowls, garnished with croûtons.

Mediterranean Summer Soup

SERVES 4

1 slice fresh bread
15 ml/1 tbsp oil
15 ml/1 tbsp lemon juice
30 ml/2 tbsp water
¹/₂ small onion, chopped
1 small garlic clove, chopped
1 red (bell) pepper, roughly diced
¹/₂ cucumber, roughly chopped
400 g/14 oz/1 large can tomatoes
15 ml/1 tbsp tomato purée (paste)
5 ml/1 tsp caster (superfine) sugar
Salt and freshly ground black pepper
150 ml/¹/₄ pt/²/₃ cup iced water
Chopped parsley

Break up the bread and place in a bowl with the oil, lemon juice and water. Leave to soak for 5 minutes. Place in a blender or food processor with the remaining ingredients, except the iced water and parsley. Run the machine until smooth. Stir in the iced water and season. Ladle into soup bowls and garnish with chopped parsley.

Minted Pea Soup

SERVES 6

900 g/2 lb fresh peas (unshelled
weight) or 450 g/1 lb/4 cups
frozen peas
900 ml/1¹/₂ pts/3³/₄ cups chicken
stock
10 ml/2 tsp caster (superfine) sugar
1 large sprig of mint
Salt and freshly ground black pepper
1 egg yolk
60 ml/4 tbsp single (light) cream

Shell the peas, if using fresh. Place the peas in a pan with the stock, sugar, mint and a little salt and pepper. Bring to the boil, reduce the heat, cover and simmer for 15 minutes. Discard the mint sprig. Purée in a blender or food processor until smooth. Return to the pan. Blend the egg yolk and half the cream together and stir into the soup. Reheat but do not boil, or chill. Serve in soup bowls, garnished with a swirl of the remaining cream.

Mushroom and Corn Chowder

SERVES 4

*225 g/8 oz/4 cups button mushrooms,
  chopped*
1 onion, chopped
*40 g/1¹/₂ oz/3 tbsp butter or
margarine*
*25 g/1 oz/¹/₄ cup plain (all-purpose)
  flour*
300 ml/¹/₂ pt/1¹/₄ cups chicken stock
300 ml/¹/₂ pt/1¹/₄ cups milk
*320 g/12 oz/1 large can sweetcorn
(corn)*
30 ml/2 tbsp single (light) cream
Snipped chives

Fry (sauté) the mushrooms and onion gently in a pan with the butter or margarine for 3 minutes, stirring. Add the flour and cook, stirring, for a further minute. Remove from the heat, blend in the stock, milk and corn. Return to the heat and bring to the boil, stirring. Reduce the heat and simmer gently for 10 minutes. Remove from the heat. Season to taste and stir in the cream. Serve straight away in soup bowls, garnished with chives.

Peanut Soup

SERVES 6

1 small onion, chopped
1 celery stick, chopped
25 g/1 oz/2 tbsp butter
*20 g/³/₄ oz/3 tbsp plain (all-purpose)
  flour*
1 litre/1³/₄ pts/4¹/₄ cups chicken stock
*225 g/8 oz/1 cup smooth peanut
  butter*
*200 ml/7 fl oz/scant 1 cup single
  (light) cream*
Chopped peanuts
Chopped parsley

Fry (sauté) the onion and celery in the butter in a pan until soft, but not brown. Sprinkle in the flour and cook, stirring for 1 minute. Gradually blend in the stock, bring to the boil and simmer for 5 minutes. Purée in a blender or food processor. Return to the pan and blend in the peanut butter and cream. Reheat, but do not boil. Serve in soup bowls garnished with chopped peanuts and parsley.

Quick Minestrone

SERVES 6

1 small onion, grated
15 ml/1 tbsp olive oil
1 carrot, grated
1 small parsnip or turnip, grated
¹/₄ small cabbage, shredded
50 g/2 oz/¹/₂ cup frozen peas
*25 g/1 oz/¹/₄ cup quick-cook
  macaroni*
*400 g/14 oz/1 large can chopped
  tomatoes*
1 vegetable stock cube
2.5 ml/¹/₂ tsp dried oregano
Salt and freshly ground black pepper
Grated Parmesan cheese

Fry (sauté) the onion in the oil in a large pan for 1 minute, stirring. Add the remaining ingredients except the cheese. Fill the tomato can with cold water and add to the pan. Add a further canful of water. Bring to the boil, reduce the heat and simmer for 10 minutes, or until the vegetables and pasta are soft. Taste and re-season if necessary. Serve in soup bowls with Parmesan cheese to sprinkle over.

Noodle Soup

SERVES 4

*1.75 litres/3 pts/7^1/$_2$ cups vegetable
    stock*
Salt
5 ml/1 tsp lemon grass, chopped
5 ml/1 tsp soy sauce
*175 g/6 oz/1^1/$_2$ cups vermicelli,
    broken into small pieces*

Bring the stock to the boil with the
salt, lemon grass and soy sauce. Add
the vermicelli and simmer for 5 minutes
until just tender. Check and adjust the
seasoning if necessary.

Speedy Green Pea and Ham Soup

SERVES 4

1.2 litres/2 pts/5 cups ham stock
225 g/8 oz/2 cups frozen peas
*50 g/2 oz/1^1/$_2$ cup cooked ham,
    chopped*
60 ml/4 tbsp milk
Salt and freshly ground black pepper
Pinch of grated nutmeg

Bring the stock to the boil. Add the
peas and simmer for 2–3 minutes.
Purée in a blender or food processor or
rub through a sieve (strainer). Return to
the pan, add the remaining ingredients
and reheat gently.

Chilled Tomato Soup

SERVES 4

*400 g/14 oz/1 large can chopped
    tomatoes*
15 ml/1 tbsp red wine vinegar
15 ml/1 tbsp olive oil
45 ml/3 tbsp crème fraîche
2.5 ml/1^1/$_2$ tsp made mustard
5 ml/1 tsp dried basil
Salt and freshly ground black pepper

Rub the tomatoes through a sieve
(strainer) or purée in a blender or
food processor, then sieve. Add all the
remaining ingredients and mix well.
Season to taste and chill before serving.

Welsh Soup

SERVES 4–6

100 g/4 oz/^{2}/$_3$ cup red lentils
1.2 litres/2 pts/5 cups water
2 leeks, chopped
4 potatoes, chopped
3 carrots, chopped
1 parsnip, chopped
2 small turnips, chopped
1 small swede (rutabaga), chopped
1 vegetable stock cube
Salt and freshly ground black pepper

Place the lentils in a large pan with the
water. Bring to the boil, then skim off
any scum. Add the vegetables and stock
cube, return to the boil, then simmer for
about 20 minutes until the soup is thick
and the vegetables soft. Season to taste.

Red Lentil Soup

15 ml/1 tbsp oil
1 onion, chopped
2 garlic cloves, crushed
175 g/6 oz/1 cup red lentils
900 ml/1¹/₂ pts/3³/₄ cups vegetable
*   stock*
10 ml/2 tsp chopped marjoram
Salt and freshly ground black pepper

Heat the oil and fry (sauté) the onion and garlic until soft. Drain off the oil. Add the remaining ingredients, bring to the boil, then simmer for 30 minutes. Adjust the seasoning to taste.

Herby Garlic Soup

900 ml/1¹/₂ pts/3³/₄ cups vegetable
*   stock*
4 garlic cloves, crushed
5 ml/1 tsp dried sage
3 bay leaves
4 whole cloves
Salt and freshly ground black pepper

Bring all the ingredients to the boil in a saucepan, then simmer for 45 minutes. Discard the bay leaves and cloves. Serve hot.

Spanish Almond Soup

100 g/4 oz/1 cup ground almonds
2 garlic cloves, crushed
900 ml/1¹/₂ pts/3³/₄ cups water
75 g/3 oz/1¹/₂ cups fresh breadcrumbs
75 ml/5 tbsp olive oil
15 ml/1 tbsp sherry vinegar
Salt and freshly ground black pepper

Purée the almonds and garlic with a little water in a blender or food processor to make a paste. Mix in the breadcrumbs, then gradually beat in the oil. Add the vinegar and enough water to make the consistency you prefer. Season with salt and pepper. Chill well before serving.

Winter Swede and Cauliflower Soup

1 cauliflower, cut into tiny florets
1 swede (rutabaga), finely diced
1 onion, sliced
1.2 litres/2 pts/5 cups vegetable
*   stock*
Salt and freshly ground black pepper
15 ml/1 tbsp tomato purée (paste)
15 ml/1 tbsp chopped thyme

Place the vegetables and stock in a saucepan, bring to the boil, then simmer for at least 30 minutes until the vegetables are soft. Season with salt and pepper, add the tomato purée and thyme and continue to simmer over a low heat until ready to serve.

Soft Fruit Soup

450 g/1 lb/4 cups soft fruit such as
*   raspberries, strawberries,*
*   blackcurrants*
100 g/4 oz/¹/₂ cup sugar
900 ml/1¹/₂ pts/3³/₄ cups milk

Heat the fruit gently until soft. Mash and whisk with the sugar. Rub through a sieve to remove any pips, if you wish. Bring the milk to the boil, then allow it to cool before slowly stirring into the fruit. Chill before serving.

Milk Soup with Croûtons

1 slice bread, cubed
Butter, for frying
300 ml/¹/₂ pt/1¹/₄ cups milk
Salt
1 egg, beaten
5 ml/1 tsp curry powder
Freshly ground black pepper
Pinch of dried basil

To make the croûtons, fry (sauté) the bread in some butter until crisp. Drain on kitchen paper. Heat the milk with a pinch of salt. Slowly add the egg and curry powder. Stir and heat until thickened, without allowing the soup to boil. Season with salt, pepper and the basil. Serve sprinkled with the croûtons.

Chilled Minted Pea Potage

225 g/8 oz/2 cups frozen peas
600 ml/1 pt/2¹/₂ cups vegetable or
*   chicken stock*
5 ml/1 tsp dried mint
Pinch of freshly ground black pepper
30 ml/2 tbsp instant mashed potato
powder
150 ml/¹/₄ pt/²/₃ cup single (light)
*   cream*

Cook the peas in the stock with the mint for 5 minutes. Purée in a blender or food processor, or pass through a sieve (strainer), and return to the saucepan. Season with a little pepper and whisk in the potato. Stir in all but 30 ml/2 tbsp of the cream. Chill and serve in soup bowls, garnished with a swirl of the reserved cream.

Tangy Carrot and Tomato Soup

275 g/10 oz/1 small can carrots
400 g/14 oz/ 1 large can tomatoes
150 ml/¹/₄ pt/²/₃ cup pure orange
*   juice*
5 ml/1 tsp dried basil or mixed
*   herbs*
Salt and freshly ground black pepper
20 ml/4 tsp plain yoghurt or a little
*   cream (any will do)*

Drain the carrots and place in a food processor or blender. Add the contents of the can of tomatoes and blend until smooth. Alternatively, pass through a sieve (strainer). Add the orange juice, herbs and seasoning to taste. Heat through or chill, and serve in bowls with 5 ml/1 tsp of yoghurt or cream spooned over each portion.

Crab Bisque

SERVES 6

1 onion, very finely chopped
25 g/1 oz/2 tbsp butter or margarine
45 g/1³/₄ oz/1 small can dressed crab
45 ml/3 tbsp plain (all-purpose)
*   flour*
900 ml/1¹/₂ pts/3³/₄ cups fish,
*   chicken or vegetable stock*
5 ml/1 tsp celery salt
30 ml/2 tbsp dry sherry
150 ml/¹/₄ pt/²/₃ cup milk
150 ml/¹/₄ pt/²/₃ cup single (light)
*   cream*
170 g/6 oz/1 small can white
*   crabmeat*
Croûtons (see page 17)

Fry (sauté) the onion gently in the butter in a saucepan for 3 minutes until soft but not brown. Stir in the dressed crab and the flour and cook for 1 minute. Remove from the heat and gradually blend in the stock. Bring to the boil, stirring until thickened. Simmer for 15 minutes. Stir in the remaining ingredients. Reheat, but do not boil. Serve in soup bowls garnished with croûtons.

Chicken and Corn Chowder

SERVES 4

298 g/10¹/₂ oz/1 small can condensed
*   cream of chicken soup*
Milk
200 g/7 oz/1 small can sweetcorn
*   (corn)*
Pinch of cayenne
30 ml/2 tbsp single (light) cream
*   (optional)*
Chopped parsley

Empty the soup into a saucepan. Fill the empty soup can with milk and gradually blend it in. Add the contents of the can of corn and season with the cayenne. Heat through gently, stirring occasionally. Serve in soup bowls, garnished with a little cream, if liked, and some chopped parsley.

Chinese Egg Flower Soup

SERVES 4

900 ml/1¹/₂ pts/3³/₄ cups chicken
*   stock*
15 ml/1 tbsp soy sauce
30 ml/2 tbsp dry sherry
Pinch of ground ginger
25 g/1 oz/¹/₄ cup frozen peas, thawed
1 egg, beaten
Prawn crackers

Put all the ingredients except the egg and crackers in a saucepan and heat to boiling point. Remove from the heat and pour the egg in a thin stream through the prongs of a fork, so it solidifies in 'flowers'. Let the soup stand for 10 seconds for the egg to set, then ladle into soup bowls. Serve with prawn crackers.

Italian-style Consommé

40 g/1¹/₂ oz/¹/₃ cup conchiglietti or other soup pasta
298 g/10¹/₂ oz/1 small can condensed consommé
30 ml/2 tbsp red wine or port
Grated Parmesan cheese

Cook the pasta in plenty of boiling salted water until tender. Drain and rinse with hot water. Empty the consommé into a saucepan. Add water as directed and heat through. Stir in the wine or port and the pasta. Reheat. Ladle into soup bowls and serve with grated Parmesan cheese.

Monday Mulligatawny

225 g/ 8 oz/ 2 cups cooked leftover mixed vegetables, chopped (or frozen)
1 garlic clove, crushed
5–10 ml/1–2 tsp curry paste
15 ml/1 tbsp oil
600 ml/1 pt/2¹/₂ cups vegetable stock
15 ml/1 tbsp tomato purée (paste)
15 ml/1 tbsp instant mashed potato powder (optional)
Salt and freshly ground black pepper
Lemon slices

Fry (sauté) the vegetables, garlic and curry paste in the oil for 1 minute. Add the stock and tomato purée, bring to the boil and simmer for 5 minutes. Purée in a liquidiser or food processor. Thicken, if liked, with mashed potato and season to taste. Reheat. Serve in warm soup bowls with a slice of lemon on top.

French Mushroom and Herb Soup

2 × 298 g/2 × 10¹/₂ oz/2 small cans condensed cream of mushroom soup
Milk
15 ml/1 tbsp chopped tarragon
45 ml/3 tbsp cognac
A little single (light) cream

Empty the cans of soup into a saucepan. Blend in 4 canfuls of milk, 10 ml/2 tsp of the tarragon and the cognac. Heat through, stirring, until almost boiling. Ladle into soup bowls and garnish each with a swirl of cream and a sprinkling of the remaining tarragon.

Salmon and Prawn Bisque

300 g/11 oz/1 can creamed sweetcorn (corn)
300 ml/¹/₂ pt/1¹/₄ cups chicken stock
300 ml/¹/₂ pt/1¹/₄ cups milk
200 g/7 oz/1 small can pink salmon
50 g/2 oz/¹/₂ cup peeled prawns (shrimp)
15 ml/1 tbsp brandy
60 ml/4 tbsp double (heavy) cream
15 ml/1 tbsp chopped parsley
Salt and freshly ground black pepper

Blend the corn with the stock and milk in a saucepan. Drain in the salmon liquid. Discard the skin and bones from the salmon, then add the fish with the prawns to the saucepan. Stir in the brandy, cream and half the parsley. Heat through gently until piping hot. Season to taste. Ladle into warm bowls and top each with a sprinkling of the remaining parsley.

Frankfurter Speciality

SERVES 4

1 onion, finely chopped
15 g/¹/₂ oz/1 tbsp butter
¹/₄ small white cabbage, finely
*   shredded*
900 ml/1¹/₂ pts/3³/₄ cups chicken
*   stock*
5 ml/1 tsp caraway seeds
400 g/14 oz/1 large can frankfurters,
*   drained and cut into small*
*   chunks*
Salt and freshly ground black pepper
Grated Cheddar cheese

Fry (sauté) the onion in the butter in a saucepan for 3 minutes until softened and lightly golden. Stir in the cabbage, stock and caraway seeds. Bring to the boil, reduce the heat and simmer gently for about 15 minutes until the cabbage is really soft. Stir in the frankfurters and season to taste. Ladle into warm soup bowls and serve with a bowl of grated Cheddar cheese handed separately.

Bangers, Beans 'n' Bacon Chowder

SERVES 4

2 onions, sliced
4 streaky bacon rashers (slices),
*   rinded and diced*
25 g/1 oz/2 tbsp butter
300 ml/¹/₂ pt/1¹/₄ cups passata
*   (sieved tomatoes)*
600 ml/1 pt/2¹/₂ cups beef or pork
*   stock*
2.5 ml/¹/₂ tsp mixed dried herbs
425 g/15 oz/1 large can baked beans
*   with pork sausages*
Salt and freshly ground black pepper
5 ml/1 tsp caster (superfine) sugar
Hot crusty rolls

Fry (sauté) the onions and bacon in the butter for 3 minutes, stirring. Add the remaining ingredients except the rolls. Bring to the boil, reduce the heat and simmer gently for 10 minutes. Ladle into warm bowls and serve with the rolls.

Peanut and Corn Chowder

SERVES 6

¹/₂ bunch of spring onions
*   (scallions), chopped*
15 g/¹/₂ oz/1 tbsp butter
45 ml/3 tbsp smooth peanut butter
600 ml/1 pt/2¹/₂ cups vegetable stock
45 ml/3 tbsp dried milk (non-fat
*   milk powder)*
50 g/2 oz/¹/₄ cup light brown sugar
100 g/4 oz/1 cup salted roasted
*   peanuts*
200 g/7 oz/1 small can Mexican
*   sweetcorn (corn with bell*
*   peppers)*
Salt and freshly ground black pepper
225 g/8 oz/2 cups grated Cheddar
*   cheese*
2 slices white bread, cubed
Oil for shallow-frying

Fry (sauté) the onions in the butter for about 3 minutes until soft and lightly golden. Stir in the peanut butter and a little of the stock and stir until smooth. Blend in the dried milk and remaining stock, the sugar, nuts and sweetcorn. Bring to the boil, stirring, then reduce the heat. Season to taste and simmer for 10 minutes. Meanwhile, fry the cubes of bread in hot oil until golden, then drain on kitchen paper. Stir the cheese into the soup until melted. Ladle into warm bowls and sprinkle the croûtons over before serving.

Chinese Chicken, Prawn and Sweetcorn Soup

SERVES 4

100 g/4 oz/1 cup cooked chicken, diced
100 g/4 oz/1 cup peeled prawns (shrimp)
900 ml/1¹/₂ pts/3³/₄ cups chicken stock
5 ml/1 tsp grated fresh root ginger
200 g/7 oz/1 small can sweetcorn (corn)
15 ml/1 tbsp soy sauce
Salt and freshly ground black pepper
15 ml/1 tbsp cornflour (cornstarch)
30 ml/2 tbsp dry sherry
2 spring onions (scallions), finely chopped

Place all the ingredients except the cornflour, sherry and spring onions in a saucepan. Bring to the boil and simmer for 1 minute. Blend the cornflour with the sherry. Stir into the soup and simmer for 1 minute until slightly thickened. Ladle into warm bowls and sprinkle with the spring onions before serving.

Creamy White Onion Soup

SERVES 4

2 large onions, chopped
1 large potato, diced
50 g/2 oz/¹/₄ cup butter
450 ml/³/₄ pt/2 cups chicken stock
1 bouquet garni sachet
45 g/1¹/₂ oz/¹/₃ cup plain (all-purpose) flour
300 ml/¹/₂ pt/1¹/₂ cups milk
150 ml/¹/₄ pt/²/₃ cup single (light) cream
Salt and white pepper
Snipped chives

Fry (sauté) the onions and potato gently in the butter for 3 minutes until softened but not browned, stirring all the time. Stir in the stock and add the bouquet garni sachet. Bring to the boil, reduce the heat, cover and simmer gently for 10 minutes or until the vegetables are tender. Cool slightly. Discard the bouquet garni, then purée in a blender or food processor. Return to the saucepan. Blend the flour with a little of the milk. Stir in the remaining milk, then add to the pan. Bring to the boil and cook for 2 minutes, stirring all the time. Stir in the cream and season to taste. Ladle into soup bowls and garnish with snipped chives.

Baked Garlic and Egg Soup

SERVES 4

45 ml/3 tbsp olive oil
1 large garlic clove, finely chopped
225 g/8 oz/4 cups white breadcrumbs
15 ml/1 tbsp paprika
250 ml/8 fl oz/1 cup chicken stock
Salt and freshly ground black pepper
4 eggs
Grated Parmesan cheese (optional)

Heat the oil in a frying pan (skillet). Add the garlic and fry (sauté) gently until brown. Stir in the breadcrumbs and cook gently over a low heat until lightly golden. Stir in the paprika and chicken stock. Season to taste and simmer for 2 minutes. Ladle into 4 individual ovenproof dishes. Break an egg into each and bake in the oven at 180°C/350°F/gas mark 4 for about 10 minutes or until the eggs are cooked. Serve sprinkled with grated Parmesan if liked.

Garlic, Egg and Pancetta Soup

Prepare as for Baked Garlic and Egg Soup but add 50 g/2 oz/^{1}/$_2$ cup chopped pancetta with the breadcrumbs and sprinkle the eggs with a little chopped basil before baking.

Chilled Beetroot and Orange Refresher

4 small cooked beetroot (red beet), grated
600 ml/1 pt/2^1/$_2$ cups cold chicken or vegetable stock
15 ml/1 tbsp cider vinegar
2 oranges
300 ml/^{1}/$_2$ pt/1^1/$_4$ cups crème fraîche
Snipped chives

Mix the beetroot with the stock and vinegar in a bowl. Grate the rind and squeeze the juice from one of the oranges. Remove and discard all the rind and pith from the second orange and cut the fruit into 6 slices. Stir the grated rind and juice into the beetroot mixture, then blend in the crème fraîche. Chill well, then ladle into bowls, add a slice of orange to each and top with a sprinkling of chives. Serve immediately.

Chilled Avocado and Pimiento Soup

2 ripe avocados, peeled and stoned (pitted)
10 ml/2 tsp lemon juice
450 ml/^{3}/$_4$ pt/2 cups cold vegetable stock
2 spring onions (scallions), roughly chopped
300 ml/^{1}/$_2$ pt/1^1/$_4$ cups Greek-style plain yoghurt
15 ml/1 tbsp Worcestershire sauce
2 canned pimiento caps
Salt and freshly ground black pepper
1.5 ml/^{1}/$_4$ tsp chilli powder (optional)
Cold milk
Snipped chives

Place all the ingredients except the milk and chives in a blender or food processor. Blend until smooth. Thin to taste with cold milk. Chill in the refrigerator, then ladle into bowls and garnish with snipped chives.

Creamy Cheese and Cucumber Soup

SERVES 4

15 g/¹/₂ oz/1 tbsp butter
15 g/¹/₂ oz/2 tbsp plain (all-purpose) flour
300 ml/¹/₂ pt/1¹/₄ cups milk
1 bay leaf
50 g/2 oz/¹/₂ cup grated Cheddar cheese
50 g/2 oz/¹/₂ cup grated Parmesan cheese
300 ml/¹/₂ pt/1¹/₄ cups chicken stock
¹/₂ cucumber, roughly chopped
Salt and freshly ground black pepper
150 ml/¹/₄ pt/²/₃ cup single (light) cream

Melt the butter in a saucepan. Stir in the flour, then gradually blend in the milk and add the bay leaf. Bring to the boil and cook for 2 minutes, stirring all the time. Stir in the cheeses, then blend in the stock. Leave to cool, then remove the bay leaf. Turn the mixture into a blender or food processor and add the cucumber, a little salt and pepper and all but 15 ml/1 tbsp of the cream. Run the machine until smooth. Taste and re-season if necessary. Chill. Ladle into soup bowls and garnish each with a swirl of the remaining cream before serving.

English Summer Soup

SERVES 4

600 ml/1 pt/2¹/₂ cups Passata (sieved tomatoes)
10 ml/2 tsp caster (superfine) sugar
Grated rind and juice of ¹/₂ lemon
5 ml/1 tsp grated onion
Salt and freshly ground black pepper
2 tomatoes, skinned, seeded and chopped
¹/₄ cucumber, skinned and finely diced
3 slices ham, finely chopped
1 hard-boiled (hard-cooked) egg, finely chopped
15 ml/1 tbsp chopped parsley

Blend all the ingredients except the egg and parsley in a bowl. Chill. Just before serving, ladle into bowls and garnish each with a little chopped egg and parsley.

Creamed Summer Soup

SERVES 4

Prepare as for English Summer Soup but add 120 ml/4 fl oz/¹/₂ cup double (heavy) cream to the passata before adding the remaining ingredients. Omit the chopped egg.

STARTERS

A sumptuous starter will set the scene for a truly memorable meal. It should be filling enough to stave off the first hunger pangs, but not so substantial as to dull the appetite for the main course. Remember to keep portions small and beautifully presented. Many of these dishes also make excellent light lunch or supper dishes, simply served with crusty bread.

Asparagus with Fresh Herb Hollandaise

SERVES 4

750 g/1¹/₂ lb asparagus
1 bunch of watercress
4 parsley sprigs
8 marjoram leaves
2 eggs
30 ml/2 tbsp lemon juice
100 g/4 oz/¹/₂ cup butter, melted

Wash the asparagus. Trim off about 5 cm/2 in from the base of the stems. Tie the spears in a bundle. Stand the bundle in a pan of lightly salted water. Cover with a lid (or foil if the pan is not deep enough). Bring to the boil, reduce the heat and cook over a moderate heat for 10 minutes. Turn off the heat and leave for 5 minutes. Drain and untie. Meanwhile, make the sauce. Cut off the watercress stalks, wash the leaves and chop finely with the parsley and marjoram. Whisk the eggs in a pan with the lemon juice. Gradually whisk in the melted butter. Cook over a gentle heat, whisking all the time until thickened. Do not allow to boil. Stir in the herbs. Lay the asparagus on warm plates, spoon a little sauce in a line over the stalks just below the heads. Serve straight away.

Aubergine Pâté

SERVES 6

1 large aubergine (eggplant)
5 ml/1 tsp lemon juice
30 ml/2 tbsp plain yoghurt
1 small onion, finely chopped
175 g/6 oz/³/₄ cup low-fat soft cheese
5 ml/1 tsp snipped chives
Salt and freshly ground black pepper
French bread

Cut the stalk off the aubergine and discard. Boil in water for 10 minutes until tender. Drain. Peel off the purple skin and purée the flesh in a blender or food processor with the lemon juice and yoghurt. Beat in the onion, cheese and chives and season to taste. Spoon into small pots. Chill, then serve with French bread.

Brittany Artichokes

SERVES 4

4 globe artichokes
30 ml/2 tbsp lemon juice
50 g/2 oz/¹/₄ cup butter
100 g/4 oz/¹/₂ cup soft cheese with garlic and herbs
60 ml/4 tbsp milk

Twist off the artichoke stalks and trim the bases level so they will stand up. Trim off the points of the outer leaves with scissors, if preferred (this is not strictly necessary). Cook in boiling water to which the lemon juice has been added for about 20 minutes or until a leaf pulls away easily. Drain and turn upside-down on kitchen paper for a few minutes. Transfer to serving plates. Meanwhile, melt the butter and cheese in a pan, stirring over a moderate heat. Gradually blend in the milk and heat through, stirring until smooth. Pour into 4 individual dishes and serve with the artichokes. To eat: pull off each leaf in turn, dip the base in the sauce and draw through the teeth to remove the fleshy part; when the hairy choke is revealed, cut or pull it off and eat the heart with a knife and fork and any remaining sauce.

Calamares à la Plancha

SERVES 4

1 onion, chopped
2 garlic cloves, finely chopped
60 ml/4 tbsp olive oil
450 g/1 lb small squid, cleaned and
    sliced into rings
Salt and freshly ground black pepper
30 ml/2 tbsp chopped parsley
10 ml/2 tsp lemon juice
Lemon wedges
Crusty bread

Gently fry (sauté) the onion and garlic in the oil for 2 minutes until soft but not brown. Add the squid (including the tentacles) and toss gently until the rings turn pinky-white. Season with salt and pepper, cover the pan with lid and cook over a very gentle heat for 5–10 minutes. The squid will now be bathed in lots of

delicious juice. Sprinkle with chopped parsley and stir in the lemon juice, then spoon into warm shallow dishes. Garnish with lemon wedges and serve with crusty bread to mop up the juices.

Chinese-style Salad

SERVES 4–6

175 g/6 oz/1¹/₂ cups bean sprouts
¹/₂ red (bell) pepper, chopped
100 g/4 oz/1 cup peeled prawns
    (shrimp)
10 ml/2 tsp soy sauce
10 ml/2 tsp white wine vinegar
5 ml/1 tsp caster (superfine) sugar
30 ml/2 tbsp olive or sesame oil
Salt and freshly ground black pepper
Lettuce leaves
2 spring onions (scallions), chopped

Wash the bean sprouts and put in a bowl with the chopped pepper and prawns. Blend together the remaining ingredients, except the lettuce and spring onions, and pour over the salad. Toss well. Pile on to lettuce leaves and garnish with the chopped spring onions.

Creamy Cucumber with Crab

1 large cucumber, diced
50 g/2 oz/¹/₄ cup butter
225 g/8 oz/4 cups button mushrooms,
*   sliced*
10 ml/2 tsp plain (all-purpose) flour
150 ml/¹/₄ pt/²/₃ cup fish stock
15 ml/1 tbsp dry vermouth
90 ml/6 tbsp single (light) cream
170 g/6 oz/1 small can crabmeat
Salt and freshly ground black pepper
Chopped parsley
Hot Walnut Bread (see page 291)

Cook the cucumber in lightly salted boiling water for 3 minutes. Drain, rinse with cold water and drain again. Melt the butter in a pan, add the mushrooms and cook, stirring, for 2 minutes. Add the cucumber, cover with a lid and cook gently for 2 minutes. Blend in the flour, then gradually stir in the stock, vermouth and cream until smooth. Bring to the boil, stirring. Add the crabmeat and heat through. Season to taste. Spoon into scallop shells or ramekins (custard cups), garnish with chopped parsley and serve with Hot Walnut Bread.

Garlicky Mushrooms

8 large flat mushrooms
25 g/1 oz/2 tbsp butter
1 large garlic clove, finely chopped
Salt and freshly ground black pepper
150 ml/¹/₄ pt/²/₃ cup dry white wine
150 ml/¹/₄ pt/²/₃ cup single (light)
*   cream or plain yoghurt*
Chopped parsley
French bread

Wash the mushrooms, pat dry on kitchen paper. Peel if necessary. Grease a large ovenproof dish with the butter. Lay the mushrooms in the dish, stalks up. Scatter the garlic over, season with a little salt and pepper, and pour over the wine and cream. Cover with foil. Bake in the oven at 190°C/375°F/gas mark 5 for about 20 minutes until the mushrooms are tender. Transfer the mushrooms to serving plates, spoon the sauce over and sprinkle with chopped parsley. Serve with French bread to mop up the juices.

Golden Camembert with Cranberry Sauce

6 individual Camembert portions
2 eggs, beaten
50 g/2 oz/1 cup fresh white
*   breadcrumbs*
Oil for deep-frying
Salad, to garnish
Cranberry sauce

Dip the cheese portions in the beaten egg, then the breadcrumbs. Repeat to coat thoroughly. Heat the oil until a cube of day-old bread browns in 30 seconds. Deep-fry the cheeses for 2 minutes or until crisp and golden brown. Drain on kitchen paper and transfer to serving plates. Add an attractive salad garnish and spoon a little cranberry sauce to the side of each cheese. Serve immediately.

Golden Goat's Cheese with Redcurrant and Orange

Prepare as for Golden Camembert with Cranberry Sauce but substitute goat's cheese for the Camembert. Use redcurrant jelly (clear conserve) instead of cranberry and add a twist of orange to the side of each with the salad garnish.

Jellied Eggs and Bacon

4 eggs
4 streaky bacon rashers (slices)
298 g/10¹/₂ oz/1 small can
*   condensed beef consommé,*
*   chilled*
Chopped parsley
Hot crusty bread

Boil the eggs for 4 minutes for soft yolks and firm whites (or cook for 6 minutes if you prefer hard yolks). Drain and place in cold water immediately to prevent further cooking. Meanwhile grill (broil) or fry (sauté) the bacon until crisp. Cut into bite-sized pieces. Carefully shell the eggs and place in 4 ramekins (custard cups). Add the bacon. Spoon the jellied consommé over each and decorate with chopped parsley. Chill if you have time before serving with hot crusty bread.

Moorish Mushrooms

450 g/1 lb/8 cups button mushrooms
1 onion, chopped
1 garlic clove, crushed
60 ml/4 tbsp olive oil
400 g/14 oz/1 large can chopped
*   tomatoes*
5 ml/1 tsp caster (superfine) sugar
150 ml/¹/₄ pt/²/₃ cup red wine
Chopped parsley

Put the mushrooms, onion, garlic and oil in a pan and cook gently, stirring, for 3 minutes. Add the tomatoes, sugar and wine. Bring to the boil, reduce the heat and simmer for 15 minutes or until the liquid is well reduced. Season to taste and serve hot or chilled, sprinkled with chopped parsley.

Melon and Clementine Cocktail

1 honeydew melon
3 clementines
2 pieces of stem ginger in syrup,
*   chopped*
45 ml/3 tbsp medium-dry sherry

Cut the melon in half, remove the seeds, then scoop out the flesh with a melon baller or cut into dice. Place in a bowl. Peel and segment the clementines, discarding any pith. Add to the bowl. Mix in the ginger, 30 ml/ 2 tbsp of the ginger syrup and the sherry. Toss well, Chill, if time, before serving in individual glass dishes.

Melon with Westphalian Ham

1 honeydew melon
4 Westphalian ham slices
4 pickled gherkins (cornichons)
4 pumpernickel slices, buttered

Halve the melon, scoop out the seeds, cut each half into 4 wedges and peel them. Cut each slice of ham in half lengthways and wrap each round a wedge of melon. Lay these on 4 individual serving plates. Using a sharp knife, make four slices down each gherkin from the round end almost down to the stalk, then gently ease the slices apart to form a fan. Lay one on each plate to garnish. Cut the pumpernickel into quarters and lay attractively on the plates.

Moules Marinières

1.75 kg/4 lb fresh mussels
40 g/1¹/₂ oz/3 tbsp butter
1 large onion, chopped
2 wineglasses dry white wine or
vermouth
1 wineglass water
Freshly ground black pepper
30 ml/2 tbsp chopped parsley

Scrub the mussels and scrape off the beards and barnacles. Discard any that are damaged or do not close immediately when tapped. Rinse well in cold running water. Heat the butter in a large saucepan. Fry (sauté) the onion gently for one minute without browning. Add the mussels, wine and water and a good grinding of pepper. Bring to the boil, cover the pan and shake over a moderate heat for 5 minutes. Discard any mussels that have not opened. Ladle into soup bowls with the liquor and sprinkle liberally with chopped parsley.

Mozzarella and Tomatoes with Basil

4 beefsteak tomatoes, sliced
225 g/8 oz Mozzarella cheese, sliced
16 basil leaves
60 ml/4 tbsp olive oil
Freshly ground black pepper

Arrange the tomato and Mozzarella slices attractively on 4 serving plates. Tear up the basil leaves and sprinkle over. Drizzle with the oil and add a good grinding of black pepper.

Mushroom Pâté

25 g/1 oz/2 tbsp butter
1 small onion, finely chopped
350 g/12 oz/ 6 cups button
mushrooms, finely chopped
15 ml/1 tbsp lemon juice
225 g/8 oz/1 cup low-fat soft cheese
30 ml/2 tbsp chopped parsley
Hot buttered toast

Melt the butter in a pan. Fry (sauté) the onion until pale golden. Add the mushrooms and fry until no liquid remains, stirring all the time. Add the lemon juice, turn into a bowl and allow to cool. Beat in the cheese and parsley. Chill before serving with hot buttered toast.

Pâté-stuffed Peppers

1 green (bell) pepper
1 red or yellow (bell) pepper
225 g/8 oz/1 cup smooth liver pâté
25 g/1 oz/¹/₂ cup soft white
breadcrumbs
50 g/2 oz/¹/₄ cup butter, melted
15 ml/1 tbsp snipped chives
Freshly ground black pepper
Salad, to garnish

Cut the stalk ends off the peppers and remove the seeds. Blend the pâté with the breadcrumbs, melted butter, chives and a little black pepper until smooth. Pack into the peppers, wrap in cling film (plastic wrap) and chill for at least 30 minutes until the filling has firmed up. Cut each pepper into 6 slices, carefully transfer one of each colour to individual serving plates and garnish with a little salad before serving.

Pears with Creamy Tarragon Dressing

SERVES 6

6 ripe pears
Lettuce leaves
150 ml/^{1}/$_4$ pt/^{2}/$_3$ cup crème fraîche
30 ml/2 tbsp sunflower oil
10 ml/2 tsp lemon juice
30 ml/2 tbsp chopped tarragon
5 ml/1 tsp caster (superfine) sugar
Salt and freshly ground black pepper
Small tarragon sprigs

Peel, halve and core the pears. Place cut-side down on a bed of lettuce on individual serving plates. Beat together the remaining ingredients, except the tarragon sprigs, and spoon over the pears. Chill, if time, before serving garnished with small tarragon sprigs.

Pears with Stilton Mayonnaise

SERVES 6

550 g/1 lb 4 oz/1 large can pear halves
Lettuce leaves
100 g/4 oz blue Stilton cheese, crumbled
60 ml/4 tbsp double (heavy) cream
45 ml/3 tbsp mayonnaise
5 ml/1 tsp lemon juice
Milk
Paprika

Drain the pears and arrange the fruit, cut-side down, on lettuce leaves on serving plates. Mash the cheese, then beat in half the cream until fairly smooth. Beat in the remaining cream, the mayonnaise and lemon juice. Thin with a little milk if necessary to give a coating consistency. Spoon over the pears and garnish with paprika.

Asian Pears with Blue Cheese Mayonnaise

SERVES 6

100 g/4 oz Danish blue cheese, crumbled
60 ml/4 tbsp mayonnaise
45 ml/3 tbsp double (heavy) cream
5 ml/1 tsp lemon juice
Freshly ground black pepper
4–6 Asian pears
Paprika
Parsley sprigs

Mash the cheese well with 15 ml/ 1 tbsp of the mayonnaise. When fairly smooth, beat in the remaining mayonnaise, the cream and lemon juice. Add a good grinding of pepper. Quarter, core and slice the pears, but do not peel. Arrange the pear slices attractively on individual serving plates and spoon the mayonnaise to one side of the slices. Dust the mayonnaise with paprika and garnish each plate with a sprig of parsley.

Pineapple Boats

SERVES 4

1 small fresh pineapple
225 g/8 oz/1 cup cottage cheese
50 g/2 oz/^{1}/$_2$ cup walnuts, chopped
Salt and freshly ground black pepper

Cut the pineapple into quarters, lengthways, leaving the green leaves on. Cut most of the flesh off the skin, leaving a thin border of fruit. Roughly chop, discarding any core. Mix the fruit with the cottage cheese and walnuts. Season to taste and spoon back into the skins. Chill, if time, before serving.

Rosy Eggs

4 hard-boiled (hard-cooked) eggs
15 ml/1 tbsp mayonnaise
10 ml/2 tsp tomato purée (paste)
Salt and freshly ground black pepper
4 canned anchovy fillets
1 stuffed olive, sliced
Lettuce

Shell the eggs, cut into halves, scoop out the yolks and place in a bowl. Mash the yolks, then beat in the mayonnaise, tomato purée and salt and pepper to taste. Pile back into the egg whites. Garnish each with a rolled anchovy fillet and a slice of stuffed olive. Serve on a bed of lettuce.

Royal Grapefruit

3 grapefruit
30 ml/2 tbsp caster (superfine)
  sugar
30 ml/2 tbsp port or sweet sherry
75 g/3 oz Stilton cheese, crumbled

Cut the grapefruit into halves. Loosen the segments with a serrated edged knife, removing any pips. Place in 6 individual flameproof dishes. Sprinkle with the sugar, then the port or sherry. Scatter some cheese over each half. Place under a hot grill (broiler) for about 4 minutes until the cheese has melted and is turning golden.

Smoked Mackerel with Horseradish Mayonnaise

60 ml/4 tbsp mayonnaise
15 ml/1 tbsp olive oil
15 ml/1 tbsp creamed horseradish
4 smoked mackerel fillets
Lemon wedges
Parsley sprigs

Beat the mayonnaise with the olive oil and horseradish to taste. Lay the mackerel fillets on 4 individual serving plates. Spoon the mayonnaise in a band across each fillet and garnish with a lemon wedge and parsley sprig.

Smoked Salmon Pâté

225 g/8 oz/2 cups smoked salmon
  pieces
150 ml/¹/₄ pt/²/₃ cup double (heavy)
  cream
50 g/2 oz/¹/₄ cup butter, softened
30 ml/2 tbsp lemon juice
Pinch of cayenne
Lemon wedges
Parsley sprigs
Hot toast

Discard any skin and bones from the salmon. With the blender or food processor running, drop in the salmon pieces, a few at a time, with the cream. Add the butter, a knob at a time, and blend until smooth. Add the lemon juice and cayenne and run the machine briefly again. Chill. Spoon on to individual serving plates, garnish each with a wedge of lemon and a sprig of parsley and serve with hot toast.

Sweet and Sour Runner Beans

SERVES 6

900 g/2 lb runner beans
6 streaky bacon rashers (slices),
diced
100 g/4 oz/2 cups button mushrooms,
sliced
30 ml/2 tbsp olive oil
30 ml/2 tbsp Worcestershire sauce
15 ml/1 tbsp soy sauce
30 ml/2 tbsp light brown sugar
30 ml/2 tbsp wine vinegar

String and slice the beans and cook in boiling salted water for about 5 minutes until just tender. Drain. In a large pan quickly fry (sauté) the bacon and mushrooms in the oil until golden. Remove from the pan with a draining spoon. Add the remaining ingredients to the juices in the pan. Stir until the sugar dissolves, then bring to the boil. Add the bacon, mushrooms and beans. Toss over a gentle heat until heated through. Serve straight away.

Tangy Whiting Goujons

SERVES 6

750 g/1¹/₂ lb whiting fillets, skinned
25 g/1 oz/¹/₄ cup plain (all-purpose)
flour
Salt and freshly ground black pepper
2 eggs, beaten
175 g/6 oz/3 cups fresh breadcrumbs
150 ml/¹/₄ pt/²/₃ cup mayonnaise
Grated rind and juice of 1 lime
Oil for deep-frying
Lime wedges

Cut the fish into strips, discarding any bones. Toss in the flour, seasoned with salt and pepper. Coat in the beaten egg, then the breadcrumbs. Reserve a pinch of lime rind for garnish, then blend the mayonnaise with the rest of the lime rind and juice. Spoon into a small pot and sprinkle with the reserved rind. Heat the oil until a cube of day-old bread browns in 30 seconds and deep-fry the fish for 4 minutes until golden. Drain on kitchen paper, arrange on a dish around the pot of mayonnaise and garnish with lime wedges.

Marinated Mozzarella and Olives

SERVES 4

450 g/1 lb Mozzarella cheese, cut
into chunks
75 g/3 oz/¹/₂ cup stoned (pitted)
black olives
120 ml/4 fl oz/¹/₂ cup dry white wine
120 ml/4 fl oz/¹/₂ cup olive oil
30 ml/2 tbsp lemon juice
50 g/2 oz/¹/₂ cup sun-dried tomatoes
in oil, chopped
2–3 garlic cloves, crushed
30 ml/2 tbsp chopped parsley
30 ml/2 tbsp chopped basil
Pinch of cayenne
Salt and freshly ground black pepper
Crusty bread
Tomato salad

Place the cheese and olives in a large wide-mouthed jar or bowl. Blend together the remaining ingredients except the bread and salad and pour over the cheese and olives. Marinate in the fridge for at least 3 hours, preferably longer. Serve with crusty bread and a fresh tomato salad.

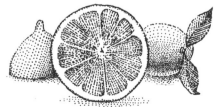

Sweet and Sour Tofu

SERVES 4

275 g/10 oz firm tofu
60 ml/4 tbsp sunflower oil
150 ml/¹/₄ pt/²/₃ cup soy sauce
30 ml/2 tbsp red wine vinegar
60 ml/4 tbsp light brown sugar
1.5 ml/¹/₄ tsp mustard powder
15 ml/1 tbsp grated fresh root ginger
2 garlic cloves, crushed

Drain the tofu and cut into bite-sized cubes. Mix together the remaining ingredients and pour over the tofu. Cover and chill for 24 hours, turning occasionally. Serve on cocktail sticks (toothpicks).

Fake Foccaccia

SERVES 4

45 ml/3 tbsp olive oil
6 onions, sliced
3 garlic cloves, chopped
4 pitta breads
Salt and freshly ground black pepper

Heat the oil and fry (sauté) the onions and garlic until softened but not browned. Brush the pitta breads on one side with a little more oil. Pile the onion and garlic mixture on top and season generously with salt and pepper. Grill (broil) under a hot grill (broiler) for about 5 minutes until browned on top.

Grilled Avocado

SERVES 4

2 avocados
15 ml/1 tbsp lemon juice
45 ml/3 tbsp butter or margarine,
   melted
Salt and freshly ground black pepper
30 ml/2 tbsp chopped parsley

Peel and stone (pit) the avocados and sprinkle with lemon juice. Cut into thick slices. Brush generously with butter or margarine and season with salt and pepper. Grill (broil) for about 2 minutes on each side until lightly browned. Serve sprinkled with parsley.

Breaded Button Mushrooms

SERVES 4

450 g/1 lb/8 cups button mushrooms
30 ml/2 tbsp plain (all-purpose)
   flour
Salt and freshly ground black pepper
1 egg, beaten
50 g/2 oz/1 cup fresh breadcrumbs
Oil for deep-frying
Cocktail Sauce (see page 245)
   (optional)

Dust the mushrooms in seasoned flour, shaking off any excess. Dip in the beaten egg, then in the breadcrumbs, until well covered. Deep-fry in hot oil for about 4 minutes until golden brown. Drain well before serving either plain or with Cocktail Sauce.

Photograph opposite: **Courgette, tomato and basil soup (page 8)**

Artichoke and Prawn Moscova

SERVES 4

425 g/15 oz/1 large can artichoke
  hearts
175 g/6 oz/1¹/₂ cups peeled prawns
  (shrimp)
45 ml/3 tbsp olive oil
15 ml/1 tbsp white wine vinegar
Salt and freshly ground black pepper
150 ml/¹/₄ pt/²/₃ cup soured (dairy
  sour) cream
50 g/2 oz/1 small jar Danish
  lumpfish roe

Drain the artichokes and roughly chop them. Mix with the prawns. Sprinkle over the oil, vinegar and a little salt and pepper and toss lightly. Spoon into 4 wine goblets. Top each with a spoonful of the soured cream. Chill. Just before serving, top the cream with a spoonful of Danish lumpfish roe.

Flageolets Vinaigrette

SERVES 4

400 g/14 oz/1 large can flageolet
  beans
1 garlic clove, crushed
45 ml/3 tbsp olive oil
15 ml/1 tbsp white wine vinegar
2.5 ml/¹/₂ tsp dried thyme
Salt and freshly ground black pepper
15 ml/1 tbsp chopped parsley
Lettuce

Drain the beans, rinse with cold water and drain again. Place in a bowl with the remaining ingredients, except the lettuce. Toss well. Cover and chill until ready to serve on individual plates on a bed of lettuce.

Tuna Cheese

SERVES 4–6

185 g/6¹/₂ oz/1 small can tuna,
  drained
200 g/7 oz/scant 1 cup low-fat soft
cheese
15 ml/1 tbsp lemon juice
1.5 ml/¹/₄ tsp cayenne
Salt and freshly ground black pepper
15 ml/1 tbsp chopped parsley
Paprika
Lemon wedges
Parsley sprigs

Mash the tuna in a bowl with the cheese. Add the remaining ingredients, except the paprika, lemon wedges and parsley sprigs, and mix well. Either shape into a sausage on greaseproof (waxed) paper and roll up, or pack into 4 ramekin dishes (custard cups). Chill. Cut the roll into 12 slices. Place the slices or ramekins on individual plates and garnish with paprika, lemon wedges and parsley.

Photograph opposite: **Smoked salmon salad (page 41)**

Pilchard Creams

SERVES 4

425 g/15 oz/1 large can pilchards in
*   tomato sauce*
30 ml/2 tbsp mayonnaise
15 ml/1 tbsp tomato purée (paste)
100 g/4 oz/1 small can cream
5 ml/1 tsp red wine vinegar
Salt
1.5 ml/¹/₄ tsp cayenne
Cucumber slices

Empty the pilchards into a bowl. Discard the bones, then mash well. Add the mayonnaise and tomato purée and beat well with a wooden spoon. Drain the whey from the can of cream and beat the cream into the fish with the vinegar and seasonings. Pack into ramekin dishes (custard cups) and chill, if time. Garnish with cucumber slices before serving.

Sardine Pâté

SERVES 6

2 × 125 g/2 × 5 oz/2 small cans
*   sardines in oil*
75 g/3 oz/¹/₃ cup butter, melted
150 ml/¹/₄ pt/²/₃ cup plain yoghurt
5 ml/1 tsp lemon juice
1.5 ml/¹/₄ tsp cayenne
Salt and freshly ground black pepper
3 hard-boiled (hard-cooked) eggs
2 small onions, sliced into rings
Chopped parsley

Drain the sardines and place in a food processor or blender with the butter, yoghurt, lemon juice and cayenne. Run the machine until smooth. Add salt and pepper to taste, then pack into a small pot and chill for about 2 hours until quite firm. Spoon on to individual plates. Garnish with wedges of egg, onion rings and chopped parsley.

Marinated Kipper Fillets

SERVES 6

2 × 175 g/2 × 6 oz/2 small packets
frozen kipper fillets, thawed
1 small onion, sliced into rings
1 bay leaf
90 ml/6 tbsp olive oil
30 ml/2 tbsp red wine vinegar
5 ml/1 tsp Dijon mustard
1.5 ml/¹/₄ tsp caster (superfine)
*   sugar*
Salt and freshly ground black pepper
Parsley sprigs
Buttered brown bread

Pull the skin off the kipper fillets and lay the fish in a large shallow dish. Arrange the onion rings over and add the bay leaf. Whisk together the remaining ingredients, except the parsley sprigs and bread, and pour over the fish. Leave in a cool place to marinate for several hours until the fish feels tender when pierced with the point of a knife. Turn over in the marinade occasionally. Remove the bay leaf. Fold the fillets and arrange decoratively on shallow individual serving dishes. Spoon the marinade and onion rings over. Garnish with parsley and serve with brown bread and butter.

Ham and Pineapple Cocktail

75 g/3 oz/¹/₃ cup long-grain rice
30 ml/2 tbsp olive oil
10 ml/2 tsp lemon juice
5 ml/1 tsp soy sauce
¹/₂ small onion, finely chopped
215 g/7¹/₂ oz/ 1 small can ham
225 g/8 oz/1 small can pineapple
chunks in natural juice
12 stoned (pitted) black olives
30ml/2 tbsp mayonnaise

Cook the rice in plenty of boiling, salted water for 10 minutes until tender. Drain, rinse with cold water and drain again. Mix the olive oil, lemon juice, soy sauce and onion together. Add to the rice, toss well and divide between 6 plates, forming a ring of rice on each plate. Dice the ham, discarding any jelly. Drain the pineapple, reserving 15 ml/ 1 tbsp of the juice. Quarter 6 of the olives and mix with the ham and pineapple. Pile into the rice rings. Mix the mayonnaise with the reserved pineapple juice and spoon a little over each. Garnish with the remaining whole olives.

Sicilian Peppers

Prepare as for Sicilian Pimientos but use 6 red (bell) peppers, seeded and quartered, instead of canned pimientos and fry (sauté) for about 6 minutes until they are just tender.

Mulled Florida Cocktail

300 g/11 oz/1 small can mandarin
oranges in syrup
410 g/14¹/₂ oz/1 large can grapefruit
segments in syrup
60 ml/4 tbsp white wine
1 piece of cinnamon stick
2 whole cloves
6 maraschino cherries

Drain the syrup from both fruits into a saucepan. Add the wine, cinnamon stick and cloves. Bring to the boil, reduce the heat and simmer very gently for 3 minutes. Remove the cinnamon and cloves, add the fruit and heat through gently but do not boil. Spoon into wine goblets. Top each with a maraschino cherry and serve straight away.

Sicilian Pimientos

2 × 400 g/2 × 14 oz/2 large cans
whole pimientos
45 ml/3 tbsp olive oil
Coarse sea salt
A few black or green olives
(optional)
Hot ciabatta bread

Drain the pimientos and dry on kitchen paper. Heat the oil in a large frying pan (skillet) and fry (sauté) the pimientos for 1–2 minutes on each side until sizzling. Transfer to warm serving plates, drizzle over the oil from the pan. Sprinkle with coarse sea salt, garnish with olives, if using, and serve straight away with hot ciabatta bread.

Corn Fritters with Peanut Sauce

SERVES 6

300 g/11 oz/1 large can coconut
milk
75 ml/5 tbsp crunchy peanut butter
10 ml/2 tsp sugar
1.5 ml/¹/₄ tsp chilli powder
5 ml/1 tsp lemon juice
1 garlic clove, crushed
90 ml/6 tbsp plain (all-purpose)
flour
2 eggs
60 ml/4 tbsp milk
300 g/11 oz/1 large can sweetcorn
(corn), drained
Salt and freshly ground black pepper
Oil for shallow-frying

To make the sauce, put the coconut milk, peanut butter, sugar, chilli, lemon juice and garlic in a pan and heat through gently, stirring occasionally, until boiling. To make the fritters, put the flour in a bowl. Beat the eggs and milk together. Add to the flour and beat well until smooth. Add the corn and a little seasoning. Mix well. Heat the oil in a large frying pan (skillet), fry (sauté) spoonfuls of the corn batter until golden on the base, turn and fry the other side. Drain on kitchen paper. Spoon the sauce into 4 individual dishes on serving plates, arrange the fritters around and serve hot.

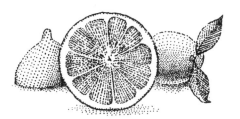

Pâté Nests

SERVES 4

4 slices bread, from sliced loaf
Butter or margarine
100 g/4 oz/¹/₂ cup smooth liver pâté
15 ml/1 tbsp mayonnaise
1 hard-boiled (hard-cooked) egg,
finely chopped
4 cocktail gherkins (cornichons),
finely chopped
Paprika

Cut off and discard the crusts and spread the bread liberally with butter or margarine. Press firmly into 4 sections of a tartlet tin (patty pan). Bake in the oven at 190°C/375°F/gas mark 5 for about 25 minutes or until golden brown. Transfer to a wire rack to cool. Mash the pâté with the mayonnaise. Stir in the chopped egg and gherkins. Pile into the bread cases and garnish with paprika. Serve straight away.

Anytime Melon Cocktail with Herby Cheese Slices

SERVES 4–6

410 g/14¹/₂ oz/1 large can melon
balls
300 g/11 oz/1 small can mandarin
oranges
60 ml/4 tbsp ginger wine
1 small French stick
80 g/3¹/₂ oz/scant 1 cup soft cheese
with garlic and herbs
25 g/1 oz/2 tbsp butter or margarine

Put the contents of the cans of melon and mandarins into a glass bowl. Pour over the ginger wine, stir, then chill until ready to serve. Cut the French stick into 12 slices. Toast on one side under a grill (broiler). Mash the soft cheese and butter or margarine together and spread over the untoasted sides of the bread. Just before serving, grill (broil) until the cheese mixture is melted and bubbling. Serve straight away with the fruit cocktail.

Creamy Mussels

SERVES 6

1 onion, finely chopped
15 g/¹/₂ oz/1 tbsp butter or margarine
2 × 250 g/2 × 9 oz/ 2 small cans
*   mussels in brine*
150 ml/¹/₄ pt/²/₃ cup white wine or
*   dry vermouth*
150 ml/¹/₄ pt/²/₃ cup water
15 ml/1 tbsp cornflour (cornstarch)
150 ml/¹/₄ pt single (light) cream
Freshly ground black pepper
30 ml/2 tbsp chopped parsley
French bread

Fry (sauté) the onion in the butter or margarine for 2 minutes until soft, but not brown. Drain one of the cans of mussels and add them to the onions with the complete contents of the other can. Add the wine or vermouth. Blend the water with the cornflour and stir in. Bring to the boil, stirring until thickened. Stir in the cream, some pepper to taste and the chopped parsley. Heat through, but do not boil. Spoon into bowls and serve with French bread.

Herring and Potato Salad

SERVES 6

4 rollmop herrings
275 g/10 oz/1 small can new
*   potatoes, drained*
30 ml/2 tbsp mayonnaise
15 ml/1 tbsp plain yoghurt
5 ml/1 tsp dried dill (dill weed)
Freshly ground black pepper
Lettuce leaves
A little extra dill

Using a sharp knife, slice each rollmop into 6 pinwheels. Cut the potatoes into quarters or sixths. Mix the mayonnaise, yoghurt and dill together and season with pepper. Add to the potatoes and toss lightly. Put a small pile of potato on to lettuce leaves on each of 6 serving plates. Arrange 4 slices of rollmop alongside attractively. Dust the potato with a little more dill. Chill, if time, before serving.

Nutty Cheese Peaches

SERVES 4

430 g/15¹/₂ oz/1 large can peach
*   halves*
Lettuce leaves
225 g/8 oz/1 cup cottage cheese
50 g/2 oz/¹/₂ cup walnut pieces,
*   chopped*
2.5 ml/¹/₂ tsp grated onion
Freshly ground black pepper
Paprika

Drain the peaches and dry on kitchen paper. Arrange cut-sides up on lettuce leaves on 4 individual plates. Mix the cheese, nuts and onion together and season with a little pepper. Pile into the centres of the peaches. Dust with paprika and chill, if time, before serving.

Smoked Salmon on Horseradish Butter

SERVES 4

4 slices rye bread
40 g/1¹/₂ oz/3 tbsp butter or
margarine, softened
30 ml/2 tbsp horseradish sauce
A few drops of lemon juice
Salt and freshly ground black pepper
100 g/4 oz smoked salmon, cut into
slivers
15 ml/1 tbsp chopped parsley

Cut the bread into about 2.5 cm/1 in squares. Blend or beat together the butter or margarine, horseradish, lemon juice, salt and pepper. Spread on the bread squares. Arrange the salmon on top and garnish with parsley.

Prawns in Garlic Butter

SERVES 4

100 g/4 oz/¹/₂ cup unsalted (sweet)
butter
24 unshelled prawns (shrimp)
2 garlic cloves, crushed
30 ml/2 tbsp chopped parsley
Crusty French bread

Melt the butter in a large shallow frying pan (skillet). Add the prawns and garlic at the same time. Gently heat the prawns through and sprinkle on the parsley. Serve with fresh French bread to mop up the buttery sauce.

Piri Piri Prawns

SERVES 4

750 g/1¹/₂ lb large prawns (jumbo
shrimp)
4–5 ml/³/₄–1 tsp chilli powder
4–5 ml/³/₄–1 tsp salt
Juice of 1 small lemon or lime
Oil for shallow-frying
Lime or lemon wedges

Remove the heads and body shells of the prawns, but leave the tails on. Combine the chilli powder, salt and lemon or lime juice. Pour over the prawns and marinate for 1 hour. Fry (sauté) in oil for 3–4 minutes. Do not overcook. Serve hot, garnished with lemon or lime wedges.

Pepper Provençale

SERVES 4

1 onion, finely chopped
2 red (bell) peppers, sliced
2 green (bell) peppers, sliced
30 ml/2 tbsp olive oil
1 garlic clove, crushed
400 g/14 oz/1 large can tomatoes
45 ml/3 tbsp dry white wine
5 ml/1 tsp sugar
15 ml/1 tbsp tomato purée (paste)
5 ml/1 tsp herbes de Provence (or
mixed dried herbs)
15 ml/1 tbsp chopped parsley
Crusty French bread

Fry (sauté) the onion and peppers in the oil until soft. Add the garlic and fry for a further 2–3 minutes. Add the tomatoes, wine, sugar, tomato purée and herbs. Bring to the boil and simmer until the peppers are tender and the sauce is reduced and pulpy. Turn into 4 ramekins (custard cups) and top with parsley. Serve with crusty French bread.

Prawn Provençale

Make as for Pepper Provençale, but omit the peppers, herbs and tomato purée. Make the sauce in the same way, but thicken with 5 ml/1 tsp cornflour (cornstarch) blended with a little water. Add 350 g/12 oz/3 cups peeled prawns (shrimp), heat through and serve in ramekins or on a side plate in a ring of plain boiled rice.

Tuna Pâté

30 ml/2 tbsp mayonnaise
3 × 185 g/3 × 6¹/₂ oz/3 small cans
*   tuna, drained*
100 g/4 oz/¹/₂ cup butter
30 ml/2 tbsp double (heavy) cream
*   or thick yoghurt*
Salt and freshly ground black pepper
Few drops of Tabasco sauce
10 ml/2 tsp lemon juice

Put the mayonnaise, tuna, butter and cream or yoghurt in a blender or food processor. Run the machine until well blended. Season to taste with salt and pepper and add the Tabasco and lemon juice. Taste again. Add a little more seasoning if required. Chill until ready to serve.

Smoked Mackerel Pâté

4 smoked mackerel fillets, skinned
150 ml/¹/₄ pt/²/₃ cup soured (dairy
*   sour) cream or thick yoghurt*
100 g/4 oz/¹/₂ cup cottage cheese
Juice of ¹/₂ large lemon
Salt and freshly ground black pepper
Grated nutmeg
Cayenne
Hot toast

Put the fish, soured cream or yoghurt, cottage cheese and lemon juice in a blender or food processor. Run the machine until well blended. Season to taste with salt, pepper and nutmeg. Chill. Spoon on to small plates, sprinkle with cayenne and serve with hot toast.

Spanish Prawns

25 g/1 oz/2 tbsp butter
30 ml/2 tbsp olive oil
25 g/1 oz/¹/₄ cup ground almonds
1 red chilli, seeded and finely
*   chopped*
1 garlic clove, finely chopped
350 g/12 oz/3 cups peeled prawns
*   (shrimp)*
Grated rind and juice of ¹/₂ lemon
30 ml/2 tbsp chopped coriander
*   (cilantro)*

Melt the butter in a frying pan (skillet) with the oil, add the almonds, chilli and garlic. Cook for 2 minutes. Add the prawns and lemon rind and juice and cook over a moderate heat, stirring until the prawns are heated through. Spoon on to warm plates and garnish with chopped coriander.

Eggs with Tuna Fish Mayonnaise

SERVES 4

4 hard-boiled (hard-cooked) eggs
100 g/4 oz/1 small can tuna,
drained
Juice of ¹/₂ lemon
6 anchovy fillets
150 ml/¹/₄ pt/²/₃ cup mayonnaise
Freshly ground black pepper
Crisp lettuce leaves
Chopped parsley

Shell the eggs. Mash the tuna and blend in the lemon juice. Chop and add 2 of the anchovy fillets. Place in a blender or food processor with the mayonnaise. Blend until smooth. Season to taste. Cut the eggs in half lengthways (easy with a wet knife). Arrange the halves in pairs, rounded sides up, on lettuce leaves on individual plates. Coat with the mayonnaise mixture. Cut the remaining anchovies in half lengthways and arrange over the eggs. Sprinkle with parsley.

Avocado with Prawns and Seafood Sauce

SERVES 4

2 avocados, halved and stoned
(pitted)
A little lemon juice
100 g/4 oz/1 cup peeled prawns
(shrimp)
120 ml/4 fl oz/¹/₂ cup mayonnaise
15 ml/1 tbsp tomato purée (paste) or
ketchup (catsup)
10 ml/2 tsp brandy
Drop of Tabasco sauce
Pinch of curry powder
5 ml/1 tsp lemon juice
2 spring onions (scallions), finely
chopped
Lemon twists
Cayenne

Brush the cut surfaces of the avocados with lemon juice. Place in individual dishes. Drain the prawns on kitchen paper. Mix together all the remaining ingredients except the lemon twists and cayenne. Stir in the prawns. Fill up the avocados with the mixture. Garnish with lemon twists and a sprinkling of cayenne before serving.

Smoked Salmon or Trout Salad

SERVES 4

1 crisp lettuce
50 g/2 oz smoked salmon or trout,
thinly sliced
40 ml/8 tsp crème fraîche or thick
Greek yoghurt
50 g/2 oz/1 small jar Danish
lumpfish roe
4 tomatoes, skinned, seeded and
very finely chopped
1/2 onion, finely chopped
5 cm/2 in piece cucumber, finely
chopped
1 celery stick, finely chopped

Cut the lettuce into thin strips and
put on each plate. Cut the salmon or
trout into strips and arrange on the
lettuce. Put a spoonful of crème fraîche
in the centre and top with a little lumpfish
roe. Arrange the salad ingredients over
the lettuce between the fish strips and
serve.

Mushrooms in Cumin and Coriander Sauce

SERVES 2 OR 3

1 garlic clove, crushed
15 g/1/2 oz/1 tbsp butter
298 g/10 1/2 oz/1 small can sliced
mushrooms, drained
2.5 ml/1/2 tsp ground cumin
2.5 ml/1/2 tsp ground coriander
(cilantro)
5–10 ml/1–2 tsp cornflour
(cornstarch)
150 ml/1/4 pt/2/3 cup whipping cream
Salt and freshly ground black pepper
Hot French bread

Fry (sauté) the garlic in the butter
until soft. Add the mushrooms, cumin
and coriander. Cook gently for 2 minutes.
Mix the cornflour and cream and add to
the pan. Bring to the boil gently and
simmer for 5 minutes. Taste and add more
spices or cream (if too thick) and salt and
pepper to taste. Serve with hot French
bread.

Piquant Mushrooms on Garlic Toasts

SERVES 6

90 ml/6 tbsp olive oil
Pinch of mixed dried herbs
1 garlic clove, crushed
12 French bread slices
450 g/1 lb button mushrooms,
halved
10 ml/2 tsp coriander (cilantro)
seeds, crushed
1 red onion, sliced
90 ml/6 tbsp red wine
15 ml/1 tbsp red wine vinegar
30 ml/2 tbsp clear honey
2 or 3 spring onions (scallions),
finely chopped

Prepare the toasts by mixing together
30 ml/2 tbsp of the oil, the herbs and
garlic. Brush over the slices of bread and
toast under a hot grill (broiler), then keep
warm while preparing the mushrooms. Fry
(sauté) the mushrooms, coriander and
onion in the remaining oil over a high heat
for 2 minutes. Cover the pan and cook for
2 minutes, then add the wine, vinegar and
honey. Stir, uncovered, for a further 2
minutes until the sauce is reduced and the
mushrooms are just tender. Spoon on to
the hot toasts and serve garnished with
finely chopped spring onion.

Bacon and Onion Slice

SERVES 6

100 g/4 oz back bacon, finely
  diced
25 g/1 oz/2 tbsp unsalted (sweet)
  butter
3 large onions, sliced
100 g/4 oz/$1\frac{1}{2}$ cup low-fat soft cheese
100 g/4 oz Feta cheese, crumbled
5 ml/1 tsp French mustard
5 ml/1 tsp dried tarragon
Freshly ground black pepper
350 g/12 oz frozen puff pastry
  (paste), thawed
Beaten egg, to glaze

Gently fry (sauté) the bacon in the butter for 5 minutes. Add the onion and cook until both begin to brown. Drain on kitchen paper and cool. Mix together the two cheeses, the mustard and tarragon and season with salt and pepper. Roll out the pastry and cut into 2 rectangles each measuring 25 × 30 cm (10 × 12 in) and put one of them on a dampened baking sheet. Spoon the onion and bacon into the centre, leaving a small border all the way round. Top with the cheese mixture. Brush the border with beaten egg and cover with the other piece of pastry. Seal well and trim. Make two holes in the top to let the steam escape, then glaze with beaten egg. Bake in the oven at 230°C/450°F/gas mark 8 for 15 minutes, then reduce the heat to 220°C/425°F/gas mark 7, cover loosely with foil and bake for a further 15 minutes. Serve warm, cut into slices.

Lardon Salad

SERVES 6

225 g/8 oz streaky bacon rashers
  (slices), cut into narrow strips
45 ml/3 tbsp olive oil
1 garlic clove, crushed
15 ml/1 tbsp red wine vinegar
350 g/12 oz mixed salad leaves
Salt and freshly ground black pepper
2 plum tomatoes, chopped
6 spring onions (scallions), finely
  chopped

Fry (sauté) the bacon pieces in the oil until nearly crisp. Add the garlic, continue cooking and remove from the heat when the bacon is crisp. Add the vinegar and stir, then pour over the salad leaves in a bowl. Season and scatter over the tomatoes and onions, toss and serve at once.

Chorizo Salad

SERVES 6

Prepare as for Lardon Salad but substitute Chorizo sausage for the bacon, add 2 hard-boiled (hard-cooked) eggs, cut into wedges, and 25 g/1 oz/$\frac{1}{4}$ cup toasted whole almonds.

Cajun Wings

SERVES 8

20 ml/4 tsp paprika
10 ml/2 tsp ground coriander
   (cilantro)
5 ml/1 tsp celery salt
5 ml/1 tsp ground cumin
2.5 ml/^{1}/$_2$ tsp cayenne
2.5 ml/^{1}/$_2$ tsp salt
15 ml/1 tbsp sunflower oil
30 ml/2 tbsp red wine vinegar
1 garlic clove, crushed
16 chicken wings, wing tips
removed
Extra oil
Lettuce

Mix the spices and salt together with the oil, vinegar and garlic. Rub this into the wings. Chill for at least 1 hour. Place in a roasting tin (pan). Pour over a little extra oil and cook in the oven at 200°C/400°F/gas mark 6 for 15–20 minutes. Baste with the juices several times. Serve on a bed of lettuce.

Fried Goat's Cheese

SERVES 8

2 round goat's cheeses (size and
   shape of Camemberts)
120 ml/4 fl oz/^{1}/$_2$ cup apricot jam
   (conserve)
60 ml/4 tbsp plain (all-purpose)
   flour
Salt and freshly ground black pepper
50 g/2 oz/^{1}/$_2$ cup walnuts, chopped
100 g/4 oz/2 cups fresh white
   breadcrumbs
30 ml/2 tbsp snipped chives
30 ml/2 tbsp chopped parsley
1 egg, lightly beaten
50 g/2 oz/^{1}/$_4$ cup butter
90 ml/6 tbsp oil
Salad

Spread each cheese with jam and coat with seasoned flour. Mix the walnuts, breadcrumbs and herbs. Dip the cheeses in the egg and then the breadcrumb mixture. Chill for at least 15 minutes. Fry the cheeses in the butter and oil until golden brown on both sides. Cut into quarters and serve on a bed of salad.

Grilled Goat's Cheese Salad

SERVES 6

225 g/8 oz goat's cheese roll
12 baguette slices
45 ml/3 tbsp olive oil
45 ml/3 tbsp walnut oil
30 ml/2 tbsp balsamic vinegar
25 g/1 oz/^{1}/$_4$ cup walnuts, chopped
Salt and freshly ground black pepper
12 cherry tomatoes, halved
Crisp lettuce leaves

Cut the cheese into 12 slices and put on top of the slices of bread. Grill (broil) for 3–4 minutes until bubbling and golden. Meanwhile, mix together the remaining ingredients, except the tomatoes and lettuce. Serve two hot toasts on each plate surrounded by the lettuce and tomatoes and with the dressing drizzled over.

Deep-fried Stuffed Mushrooms

SERVES 4

16 button mushrooms, stalks
  removed
50 g/2 oz/¹/₄ cup smooth liver pâté
65 ml/2¹/₂ fl oz/4¹/₂ tbsp plain
  yoghurt
Pinch of mustard powder
5 ml/1 tsp salt
40 g/1¹/₂ oz/¹/₃ cup gram or plain
  (all-purpose) flour
Pinch of chilli powder
15 ml/1 tbsp lemon juice
Oil for deep-frying

Stuff each of the mushroom cavities with pâté. Mix together thoroughly all the remaining ingredients, except the oil. Leave to stand for about 30 minutes. Heat the oil and when hot dip the stuffed mushrooms into the batter, then deep-fry until golden. Drain on kitchen paper.

Cheesy Stuffed Mushrooms

SERVES 4

85 g/3¹/₂ oz/1 packet stuffing mix
  (any flavour)
4 large flat mushrooms
175 g/6 oz/1¹/₂ cups Stilton cheese,
  crumbled

Make up the stuffing as directed on the packet. Remove and chop the mushroom stalks and mix them into the stuffing. Arrange the mushroom caps in a shallow ovenproof dish, gills upwards. Spoon the stuffing mix into the mushroom caps and sprinkle with cheese. Bake in the oven at 190°C/375°F/gas mark 5 for 15–20 minutes.

Melon Balls with Prawns and Sauce

SERVES 4

¹/₂ honeydew melon
100 g/4 oz/1 cup peeled prawns
  (shrimp)
45 ml/3 tbsp mayonnaise
15 ml/1 tbsp tomato purée (paste)
Pinch of chilli powder
5 ml/1 tsp sugar

Scoop the melon into about 24 balls, using a melon baller. Mix with the prawns. Spoon into 4 wine goblets. Mix together the remaining ingredients. Spoon over the melon and prawns and serve.

Scrambled Egg and Smoked Salmon

SERVES 4

15 g/¹/₂ oz/1 tbsp butter
4 eggs, beaten
150 ml/¹/₄ pt/²/₃ cup single (light)
  cream
100 g/4 oz/1 cup smoked salmon
  pieces, cut into tiny strips
Freshly ground black pepper
4 slices wholemeal toast, buttered
Chopped parsley

Melt the butter in a saucepan. Add the eggs and cream and whisk lightly. Stir over a gentle heat until scrambled but still creamy. Stir in the salmon and a good grinding of black pepper. Pile on to the buttered toast and sprinkle with chopped parsley before serving.

Scottish Turkey Liver Pâté

SERVES 6

75 g/3 oz/¹/₃ cup butter
225 g/8 oz/2 cups turkey livers,
*   diced*
50 g/2 oz streaky bacon
rashers (slices), rinded and diced
1 garlic clove, crushed
2.5 ml/¹/₂ tsp dried thyme
Salt and freshly ground black pepper
15 ml/1 tbsp whisky
Parsley sprig
Lemon slices
Hot toast

Melt 50 g/2 oz/¹/₄ cup of the butter in a saucepan. Add the turkey livers, bacon, garlic, thyme and a little salt and pepper. Stir well, cover and cook over a gentle heat, stirring occasionally, for 6 minutes or until the turkey livers are just cooked but not hardening. Stir in the whisky. Purée in a blender or processor, turn into a small pot and level the surface. Cool, then chill until firm. Melt the remaining butter and pour over. Chill until set, then garnish with the parsley sprig and lemon slices. Serve with hot toast.

Spicy Crab Pots

SERVES 4

200 g/7 oz/1 small carton low-fat
*   soft cheese*
30 ml/2 tbsp crème fraîche
¹/₂ small green chilli, seeded and
*   chopped or 1.5 ml/¹/₄ tsp chilli*
*   powder*
15 ml/1 tbsp tomato ketchup (catsup)
170 g/6 oz/1 small can crabmeat,
*   drained*
Lemon juice
Salt and freshly ground black pepper
¹/₄ cucumber, finely chopped
Tortilla chips

Mash the cheese with the crème fraîche until smooth. Stir in the chilli, tomato ketchup and crab. Add lemon juice, salt and pepper to taste. Spoon into small pots and chill until ready to serve. Cover each with a layer of chopped cucumber and serve surrounded by tortilla chips.

Crab and Avocado Cocktail

SERVES 4

1 large ripe avocado, peeled and
*   stoned (pitted)*
Lemon juice
170 g/6 oz/1 small can crabmeat,
*   drained*
45 ml/3 tbsp mayonnaise
10 ml/2 tsp Worcestershire sauce
15 ml/1 tbsp tomato purée (paste)
30 ml/2 tbsp single (light) cream
Salt and freshly ground black pepper
Shredded lettuce
Paprika
4 lemon slices

Dice the avocado and toss in lemon juice to prevent browning. Add the crab and toss gently. Blend the mayonnaise with the Worcestershire sauce, tomato purée, cream and a little salt and pepper until smooth. Place some lettuce in 4 wine goblets. Top with the crab and avocado mixture. Spoon the dressing over and sprinkle each with a little paprika. Place a lemon slice on the side of each glass and chill, if time, before serving.

Nutty Cheese and Olive Roll

SERVES 6

225 g/8 oz/2 cups grated Cheddar
    cheese
25 g/1 oz/^{1}/$_6$ cup stuffed olives,
    chopped
3 hard-boiled (hard-cooked) eggs,
chopped
2.5 ml/^{1}/$_2$ tsp Dijon mustard
30 ml/2 tbsp single (light) cream
30 ml/2 tbsp mayonnaise
30 ml/2 tbsp snipped chives
Salt and freshly ground black pepper
45 ml/3 tbsp toasted chopped mixed
    nuts
Lettuce leaves
Tomato wedges
Cucumber slices
Crackers or crisp toast

Mix all the ingredients except the nuts, lettuce, tomato, cucumber and crackers in a bowl until well blended. Shape into a cylinder on a sheet of baking parchment, roll up firmly and chill for 2 hours. Unwrap and roll in the chopped nuts to coat. Cut in slices and arrange on lettuce leaves. Garnish with tomato wedges and cucumber slices before serving with crackers or crisp toast.

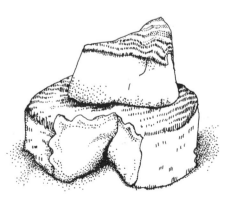

Avocado and Pepper Salad

SERVES 6

2 ripe avocados, peeled and stoned
    (pitted)
1 red (bell) pepper, cut into rings
1 yellow (bell) pepper, cut into rings
1 green (bell) pepper, cut into rings
1 small onion, sliced into rings
45 ml/3 tbsp olive oil
15 ml/1 tbsp white wine vinegar
Salt and freshly ground black pepper
15 ml/1 tbsp chopped parsley
6 black olives
Hot ciabatta bread

Slice the avocados. Place in a bowl with the peppers and onion. Whisk the oil and vinegar with a little salt and pepper and pour over. Toss gently. Spoon on to small plates and sprinkle with parsley. Garnish each with an olive before serving with hot ciabatta bread.

Prawn Pâté

SERVES 4

2 slices white bread, crusts removed
100 g/4 oz/1 cup peeled prawns
    (shrimp)
150 ml/^{1}/$_4$ pt/^{2}/$_3$ cup sunflower oil
10 ml/2 tsp anchovy essence
    (extract)
Lemon juice
Salt and freshly ground black pepper
Chopped parsley
Lemon wedges
Warm pitta bread

Soak the bread in water for 1 minute. Squeeze out the excess water and place the bread in a blender or food processor. Add the prawns and run the machine until smooth. With the machine still running, add the oil in a thin trickle, stopping to scrape down the sides from time to time until a thick, smooth paste is formed. Add the anchovy essence and lemon juice to taste. Season lightly. Spoon on to plates, sprinkle with parsley and garnish with lemon wedges. Serve with warm pitta bread.

Avocado Chicken Tikka

SERVES 4

2 ripe avocados, halved and stoned
    (pitted)
Lemon juice
225 g/8 oz/1 tub cottage cheese with
    chicken tikka
20 ml/4 tsp mango chutney
15 ml/1 tbsp chopped coriander
    (cilantro)
4 lemon wedges
Mini popadoms

Place the avocado halves in avocado dishes or small bowls. Brush with lemon juice to prevent browning. Spoon the cheese into the cavities and top each with a teaspoon of mango chutney. Sprinkle with the coriander. Add a wedge of lemon to the side of each and serve with a dish of mini popadoms.

Cheesy Salmon Avocados

SERVES 4

Prepare as for Avocado Chicken Tikka but substitute cottage cheese with salmon for the cottage cheese with chicken tikka. Top with cucumber relish and serve with a dish of prawn crackers.

Baby Bel-lissimo

SERVES 6

6 Baby Bel cheeses, rinds removed
A little plain (all-purpose) flour
2 eggs, beaten
100 g/4 oz/2 cups fresh breadcrumbs
Oil for deep-frying
Cucumber slices
Curried peach chutney
French bread

Dust the cheeses in flour, then dip in the egg, then the breadcrumbs. Repeat the dipping in turn until they are well coated. Chill. When ready to serve, heat the oil and deep-fry the cheeses until crisp and golden. Drain on kitchen paper, then transfer to small serving plates. Garnish with cucumber slices and a spoonful of curried peach chutney and serve with French bread.

Neapolitan Bagels

SERVES 4

30 ml/2 tbsp tomato purée (paste)
5 ml/1 tsp water
2 bagels, split in half and toasted
50 g/2 oz Mozzarella cheese, grated
4 cherry tomatoes, sliced
50 g/2 oz/1 small can anchovies,
    drained
5 ml/1 tsp dried oregano

Blend the tomato purée with the water and spread over the cut sides of the bagels. Place on the grill (broiler) rack. Sprinkle the cheese over. Arrange the slices of tomato on top, then lay the anchovies in a criss-cross pattern over. Sprinkle with the oregano. Grill (broil) until the cheese melts and bubbles and serve straight away.

Cheesy Egg and Tomato Concertinas

2 hard-boiled (hard-cooked) eggs
4 beefsteak tomatoes
2 small whole Mozzarella cheeses,
*   each cut into 6 slices*
Olive oil
15 ml/1 tbsp chopped basil
4 small basil sprigs

Slice off and discard the ends of both eggs, then slice the remainder of each into 4. Stand the tomatoes stalk-side down on a board. With a sharp knife make a cut down through the centre but not quite through to the base. Make 2 cuts at an angle either side of the first in the same way, so the tomatoes are divided into 6 equal portions with a slit between each. Place a slice of cheese in each centre slit, a slice of egg in the slits either side, and the remaining mozzarella in the outer slits. Transfer to small serving plates. Drizzle over the olive oil, sprinkle with basil and garnish with basil sprigs on the side.

Grilled Somerset Oranges

SERVES 4

2 large oranges
75 g/3 oz/³/₄ cup grated Cheddar
*   cheese*
30 ml/2 tbsp orange liqueur
4 walnut halves

Halve the oranges, then loosen the segments as if preparing grapefruit. Place in flameproof dishes then stand them in the grill (broiler) pan. Mash the cheese with the liqueur and spoon on to the oranges. Place under a hot grill until the cheese melts and bubbles. Serve straight away, each garnished with a walnut half.

Salami and Melon Antipasto

SERVES 6

100 g/4 oz/1 packet mixed salami
*   selection*
1 small honeydew melon, peeled,
*   seeded and cut into 6 wedges*
6 stoned (pitted) black olives, sliced
6 stuffed green olives, sliced

Arrange the salami slices attractively on 6 small serving plates with a wedge of melon to one side. Scatter the olive slices over and serve chilled.

French-style Mushrooms with Eggs

SERVES 4

1 onion, chopped
15 ml/¹/₂ oz/1 tbsp butter
225 g/8 oz/4 cups button mushrooms,
*   sliced*
1 garlic clove, crushed
150 ml/¹/₄ pt/²/₃ cup chicken stock
10 ml/2 tsp chopped tarragon
15 ml/1 tbsp chopped parsley
Salt and freshly ground black pepper
4 eggs
45 ml/3 tbsp single (light) cream
French bread

Fry (sauté) the onion in the butter in a large frying pan (skillet) for 3 minutes until soft but not brown. Add the mushrooms, garlic and stock. Bring to the boil and simmer gently for 10 minutes. Stir in the herbs and a little salt and pepper. Make 4 wells in the mushroom mixture and break an egg into each. Drizzle the crcam over. Cover with foil or a lid and cook for 5–10 minutes or until the eggs are cooked to your liking. Serve straight from the pan with lots of crusty French bread.

Potted Garlic Mushrooms

SERVES 4

100 g/4 oz/¹/₂ cup butter
1 onion, chopped
450 g/1 lb open mushrooms, peeled
*   and sliced*
15 ml/1 tbsp chopped parsley
1 large garlic clove, crushed
Salt and freshly ground black pepper

Melt half the butter in a saucepan. Add the onion and fry (sauté) for 2 minutes, stirring. Stir in the mushrooms, parsley and garlic and season lightly. Cover and cook gently for 10 minutes, stirring occasionally, until the mushrooms are really tender and the juices have run. Turn the whole mixture into a blender or food processor and run the machine briefly to chop the mushrooms and onion finely. Do not purée. Taste and re-season if necessary. Turn into 4 ramekin dishes (custard cups) and level the surfaces. Leave to cool, then chill until firm. Melt the remaining butter and pour over the mushroom mixture. Chill until the butter is firm.

Mixed Greek Starter

SERVES 6

200 g/7 oz/1 small tub tzatziki
*   (minted cucumber and yoghurt*
*   dip)*
200 g/7 oz/1 small tub hummus
*   (chick pea (garbanzo) pâté)*
200 g/7 oz/1 small tub taramasalata
*   (smoked cods' roe pâté)*
A few pickled chillies
A few Greek black olives
Lemon wedges
Pitta bread

Arrange a spoonful of each of the three dips attractively on serving plates. Arange pickled chillies and olives around and place a lemon wedge on each plate. Serve with pitta bread.

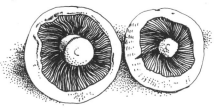

Golden-topped Ratatouille

SERVES 4

425 g/15 oz/1 large can ratatouille
15 ml/1 tbsp red wine
75 g/3 oz/³/₄ cup grated Cheddar
  cheese
Crusty bread

Heat the ratatouille in a saucepan with the wine. Spoon into 4 individual gratin dishes. Top with the cheese and place under a hot grill (broiler) until the cheese is melted and bubbling. Serve straight away with crusty bread.

Italian Aubergines

SERVES 4

1 aubergine (eggplant), sliced
30 ml/2 tbsp plain (all-purpose)
  flour
Salt and freshly ground black pepper
Olive oil
120 ml/4 fl oz/¹/₂ cup passata
  (sieved tomatoes)
5 ml/1 tsp dried basil
100 g/4 oz Mozzarella cheese,
  grated

Dip the aubergine slices in seasoned flour then fry (sauté) in hot oil until golden on both sides. Drain on kitchen paper, then arrange in 4 individual gratin dishes. Spoon the passata over and sprinkle with the basil. Top with the Mozzarella and grill (broil) until the cheese is melted and bubbling. Serve straight away.

Pastrami Slices

SERVES 6

6 slices pumpernickel
Butter
6 thin slices pastrami
150 ml/¹/₄ pt/²/₃ cup double (heavy)
  cream
15 ml/1 tbsp creamed horseradish
Lemon juice
Black pepper
Lettuce
Tomato slices
Cucumber slices

Spread the pumpernickel thinly with butter. Top with a slice of pastrami, trimming to fit the bread. Place on serving plates. Whip the cream until peaking, then fold in the horseradish. Spike with lemon juice to taste. Put a spoonful on top of the pastrami and add a good grinding of pepper. Garnish the plates with lettuce, tomato and cucumber before serving.

Mock Blinis

SERVES 6

100 g/4 oz/1 cup plain (all-purpose)
  flour
Pinch of salt
2 eggs, separated
300 ml/¹/₂ pt/1¹/₄ cups milk
Oil for shallow-frying
50 g/2 oz/1 small jar Danish
  lumpfish roe
1 onion, finely chopped
150 ml/¹/₄ pt/²/₃ cup soured (dairy
  sour) cream
Lemon wedges

Sift the flour and salt into a bowl. Add the egg yolks and half the milk and beat well until smooth. Stir in the remaining milk. Whisk the egg whites until stiff and fold in with a metal spoon. Heat a little oil in a frying pan (skillet). Add 30 ml/2 tbsp of the batter and swirl with the back of the spoon to a round about 10 cm/ 4 in in diameter. Cook until golden underneath. Flip over and cook the other side. Keep warm in a clean napkin on a plate over a pan of hot water while cooking 11 more pancakes in the same way. Arrange the lumpfish roe, onion, soured cream and lemon wedges to one side of 6 serving plates. Place two pancakes on each plate and serve straight away.

Easy Hot Finger Foods

Roll half rashers (slices) of bacon round mushrooms, dried apricots or stoned (pitted) prunes and grill (broil) until crisp.

Thread large prawns (shrimp) on to soaked wooden skewers, brush with oil, flavoured with garlic if liked, and grill (broil) for a few minutes.

Grill (broil) kebabs made with cubes of salami and pineapple.

Spread slices of bread with mustard and sprinkle with slivers of ham. Top with grated cheese and grill until sizzling and browned, then cut into fingers and serve.

Wrap cubes of cheese in squares of filo pastry and brush with oil. Do this in advance, then chill until required. Bake in a hot oven at 220°C/425°F/gas mark 7 for a few minutes until the pastry is crisp and golden.

Bite-sized sausage rolls may seem uninspired, but they are a good filler or back-up starter and are so easy – cook them straight from the freezer. And remember, most people never cook sausage rolls at home; they only eat them when they come to parties! Serve with a bowl of dip (see pages 249–251) or flavoured mayonnaise (see page 229) to turn them into something extra special.

Grill (broil) frozen 'mini Kiev' balls and serve on cocktail sticks (toothpicks).

Roast whole baby potatoes in their skins, in a little olive oil. Serve on cocktail sticks with a bowl of flavoured mayonnaise (see page 229) to dip into.

Serve hot cocktail sausages with a bowl of mayonnaise flavoured with grainy mustard or tomato ketchup (catsup).

BEEF

Apart from mince, for quick-cooking, you need to use the more expensive cuts. But the saving on fuel and the lack of waste make them a better buy than you would think... And they taste fantastic.

Spaghetti with Spicy Meatballs

SERVES 4

350 g/12 oz spaghetti
450 g/1 lb/4 cups minced (ground)
*   lamb or beef*
1 onion, finely chopped
1 garlic clove, crushed (optional)
50 g/2 oz/1 cup fresh breadcrumbs
1.5 ml/¹/₄ tsp chilli powder
1.5 ml/¹/₄ tsp ground coriander
*   (cilantro)*
1.5 ml/¹/₄ tsp ground cumin
Salt and freshly ground black pepper
1 size 4 egg, beaten
Oil for frying
600 ml/1 pt/2¹/₂ cups passata (sieved
*   tomatoes)*
5 ml/1 tsp dried oregano
Freshly grated Parmesan cheese

Cook the spaghetti according to the packet directions, drain. Meanwhile, mix the meat, onion, garlic, breadcrumbs, spices and a little salt and pepper thoroughly in a bowl. Add the beaten egg and mix well to bind. Shape into small balls. Fry (sauté) in hot oil for about 3 minutes until golden brown. Drain on kitchen paper. Heat the passata and oregano in a pan. Add the meatballs and simmer gently for 10 minutes. Pile the spaghetti on to serving plates. Top with the meatballs and sauce and serve with Parmesan cheese.

Spaghetti with Italian Meatballs

SERVES 4

Prepare as for Spaghetti with Spicy Meatballs but omit the three spices and add 5 ml/1 tsp dried oregano to the meat mixture in addition to that in the tomato sauce.

Beef and Noodle Stir-fry

SERVES 4

100 g/4 oz/1 slab quick-cook
*   Chinese egg noodles*
225 g/8 oz fillet or tenderised
*   minute steak*
30 ml/2 tbsp oil
1 onion, sliced
1 carrot, cut into matchsticks
1 celery stick, cut into matchsticks
1 small red (bell) pepper, cut into
*   thin strips*
50 g/2 oz/1 cup mushrooms, sliced
¹/₄ cucumber, cut into matchsticks
30 ml/2 tbsp sherry
30 ml/2 tbsp soy sauce
15 ml/1 tbsp light brown sugar
5 ml/1 tsp ground ginger
Salt and freshly ground black pepper

Cook the noodles according to the packet directions. Drain. Cut the steak diagonally into thin strips. Heat the oil in a large pan or wok. Add the steak and fry (sauté) for 2 minutes, stirring.

Add the onion, carrot and celery and continue frying, for a further 3 minutes. Add the pepper, mushrooms and cucumber and continue cooking, stirring for 2 minutes. Add the noodles and the remaining ingredients. Toss well until heated through. Serve straight away.

Burgundy-style Steak

SERVES 4

25 g/1 oz/2 tbsp butter
30 ml/2 tbsp olive oil
1 onion, sliced
100 g/4 oz button mushrooms
2 streaky bacon rashers (slices), diced
450 g/1 lb fillet or rump steak, cubed
15 ml/1 tbsp cornflour (cornstarch)
2.5 ml/¹/₂ tsp mixed dried herbs
15 ml/1 tbsp brandy
150 ml/¹/₄ pt/²/₃ cup red wine
150 ml/¹/₄ pt/²/₃ cup beef stock
Salt and freshly ground black pepper
Chopped parsley

Melt half the butter and oil in a pan. Add the onion, mushrooms and bacon and fry (sauté) for 3 minutes until soft and lightly brown. Remove from the pan with a draining spoon. Toss the meat in the cornflour and herbs. Heat the remaining butter and oil in the pan and fry the meat quickly for about 5 minutes until browned and cooked through. Add the brandy and set alight. When the flames subside, add the mushroom mixture, the wine and stock. Bring to the boil, stirring all the time. Season to taste. Spoon on to plates and sprinkle with chopped parsley.

Fillet Steaks Wyrardisbury

SERVES 4

4 thin slices French bread
40 g/1¹/₂ oz/3 tbsp butter
50 g/2 oz/¹/₄ cup smooth liver pâté
4 fillet steaks
90 ml/6 tbsp red wine
15 ml 1 tbsp tomato purée (paste)
2.5 ml/¹/₂ tsp caster (superfine) sugar
2.5 ml/¹/₂ tsp dried marjoram
Salt and freshly ground black pepper
Parsley sprigs

Spread the bread on both sides with a little of the butter. Fry (sauté) until golden on each side. Spread with the pâté and set aside. Melt the remaining butter and fry the steaks for 2–3 minutes on each side for rare, 5–6 minutes each side for well done (depending on thickness). Place a steak on each slice of bread and pâté on warm serving plates and keep warm. Stir the wine, tomato purée, sugar and marjoram together in a pan. Bring to the boil, stirring, and season to taste. Spoon the sauce over the steaks. Garnish with parsley sprigs and serve.

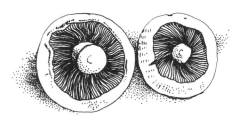

Minute Steak Diane

SERVES 4

4 tenderised minute steaks
10 ml/2 tsp lemon juice
25 g/1 oz/2 tbsp butter
15 ml/1 tbsp olive oil
¹/₂ small onion, grated
10 ml/2 tsp chopped parsley
30 ml/2 tbsp Worcestershire sauce
Cherry tomatoes, sliced

Brush the surfaces of the steaks with lemon juice. Heat the butter and oil in a frying pan (skillet) and fry (sauté) the steaks for 2–3 minutes on each side until cooked through (do not attempt to cook them rare). Transfer to warm serving plates. Keep warm. Add the onion, parsley and Worcestershire sauce to the pan juices. Cook gently for one minute then spoon over the steaks. Garnish with sliced cherry tomatoes and serve.

Pasta Grill

SERVES 4

225 g/8 oz/2 cups pasta shapes
1 onion, chopped
1 garlic clove, crushed
225 g/8 oz/2 cups minced (ground) beef
400 g/14 oz/1 large can tomatoes
2.5 ml/¹/₂ tsp mixed dried herbs
Salt and freshly ground black pepper
75 g/3 oz/³/₄ cup grated Cheddar cheese

Cook the pasta according to the packet directions, drain. Meanwhile, fry (sauté) the onion, garlic and beef in a pan and stir until browned and the meat grains are separate. Add the tomatoes, break up with a wooden spoon. Stir in the herbs and a little salt and pepper. Bring to the boil, reduce the heat and simmer for 10 minutes until cooked through and the sauce is reduced. Stir in the pasta. Turn into a 1.5 litre/2¹/₂ pt/6 cup flameproof dish. Sprinkle with the cheese and place under a hot grill (broiler) until the cheese is melted and golden.

Pied-à-terre Pie

SERVES 4

1 onion, finely chopped
450 g/1 lb/4 cups minced (ground) beef
15 ml/1 tbsp plain (all-purpose) flour
300 ml/¹/₂ pt/1¹/₄ cups beef stock
Gravy salt or browning
75 g/3 oz/³/₄ cup frozen peas
450 g/1 lb potatoes, thinly sliced
Salt and freshly ground black pepper
75 g/3 oz/³/₄ cup grated Cheddar cheese

Fry (sauté) the onion and beef in a pan until the meat is browned and the onion is softened. Stir to break up the meat. Add the flour and cook for 1 minute. Pour in the stock, gravy salt or browning and add the peas. Bring to the boil, stirring. Reduce the heat and simmer for 10 minutes. Meanwhile, cook the sliced potatoes in boiling salted water for about 4 minutes until cooked. Drain. Taste and season the meat mixture, then turn into a 1.5 litre/2¹/₂ pt/6 cup flameproof dish. Top with sliced potato then sprinkle with the grated cheese. Place under a hot grill (broiler) until golden brown.

Popovers

40 ml/8 tsp sunflower oil
50 g/2 oz/¹/₂ cup plain (all-purpose)
  flour
Pinch of salt
1 egg
75 ml/5 tbsp milk
75 ml/5 tbsp water
45 ml/3 tbsp roast beef, finely
  diced
45 ml/3 tbsp cooked, leftover
  vegetables, chopped
Gravy

Put 5 ml/1 tsp oil into each of eight sections of a bun tin (muffin pan). Place in the oven at 230°C/450°F/gas mark 8. Put the flour and salt in a bowl. Add the egg and half the milk and water and beat until smooth. Stir in the remaining milk and water. Divide the meat and vegetables between the tins. Spoon the batter over and cook towards the top of the oven for 15–18 minutes until puffy and golden. Serve hot with gravy.

Quick Chilli

1 onion, chopped
1 garlic clove, crushed
350 g/12 oz/3 cups minced (ground)
  beef
2.5 ml/¹/₂ tsp hot chilli powder
5 ml/1 tsp ground cumin
5 ml/1 tsp dried oregano
400 g/14 oz/1 large can tomatoes
425 g/15 oz/1 large can red kidney
  beans, drained
15 ml/1 tbsp tomato purée (paste)
Salt and freshly ground black pepper
Cornmeal Pancakes (see page 295)
Grated Cheddar cheese
Shredded lettuce

Put the onion, garlic and beef in a pan and fry (sauté) until browned and the grains of meat are separate. Add the chilli powder and cumin and fry for a further minute. Stir in the oregano and tomatoes and break up with a wooden spoon, then add the beans, tomato purée and seasoning to taste. Bring to the boil, reduce the heat and simmer for 10–15 minutes until reduced and a good rich colour. To serve: spoon the chilli on to cornmeal pancakes, top with cheese and lettuce, roll up and eat.

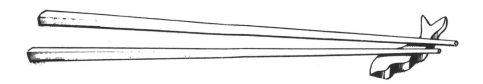

Speedy Beef in Wine

SERVES 4–6

1 onion, finely chopped
15 ml/1 tbsp oil
2 × 425 g/2 × 15 oz/2 large cans
  stewed steak without gravy
300 ml/¹/₂ pt/1¹/₄ cups red wine
300 g/11 oz/1 small can button
  mushrooms
275 g/10 oz/1 small can sliced
  carrots
2.5 ml/¹/₂ tsp mixed dried herbs
Pinch of caster (superfine) sugar
20 ml/4 tsp cornflour (cornstarch)
Salt and freshly ground black pepper

Fry (sauté) the onion in the oil for 3 minutes until soft, but not brown. Add the steak and wine and heat through, stirring to break up the meat. Drain the mushrooms and carrots, reserving 30 ml/ 2 tbsp of the mushroom liquid. Add the vegetables, herbs and sugar to the pan and continue to heat through gently until bubbling. Blend the cornflour with the reserved mushroom liquid. Stir gently into the pan and cook until thickened. Taste and season if necessary. Serve hot.

International Beef Pot

SERVES 4–6

2 × 425 g/2 × 15 oz/2 large cans
  stewed steak, with or without
  gravy
225 g/8 oz/1 small can water
  chestnuts
298 g/10¹/₂ oz/1 small can
  condensed mushroom soup
450 g/1 lb potatoes, thinly sliced and
  par-boiled

Empty the meat into a large, shallow ovenproof dish and break up with a wooden spoon. Drain and slice the water chestnuts and scatter over. Spoon over half the can of soup. Arrange the sliced potatoes neatly in a single layer over the top. Thin the remaining soup slightly with water and spoon over. Bake in the oven at 200°C /400°F /gas mark 6 for about 35 minutes until the potatoes are cooked and the top is golden brown.

Dashing Beef in Beer

SERVES 4–6

2 × 425 g/2 × 15 oz/2 large cans
  stewed steak in gravy
60 ml/4 tbsp beer
15 ml/1 tbsp brandy
30 ml/2 tbsp instant mashed potato
  powder
6–8 French bread slices
25 g/1 oz/2 tbsp butter
15 ml/1 tbsp wholegrain mustard

Empty the cans of meat into a saucepan with the beer and brandy. Stir well. Head through until bubbling. Sprinkle the instant mashed potato over and stir in to thicken. Turn into a flameproof casserole (Dutch oven). Toast the slices of French bread on one side. Mash the butter and mustard together and spread on the untoasted sides. Arrange around the top of the dish, toasted sides down. Place under a hot grill (broiler) until toasted and bubbling. Serve straight away.

Quick Mexican Meal

*425 g/15 oz/1 large can minced
(ground) steak with onions
15 ml/1 tbsp tomato purée (paste)
2.5 ml/¹/₂ tsp chilli powder
1 garlic clove, crushed
425 g/15 oz/1 large can red kidney
beans, drained
Taco shells
Shredded lettuce
Chopped tomato
Soured (dairy sour) cream
Grated Cheddar cheese*

Put the mince in a pan with the tomato purée, chilli powder, garlic and beans. Heat through, stirring until bubbling. Warm the taco shells in a hot oven or in the microwave according to the packet directions. Spoon the chilli into the shells and serve with shredded lettuce, chopped tomato, soured cream and cheese to spoon on top of the meat.

Instant Town House Pie

*425 g/15 oz/1 large can minced
(ground) steak with onion
225 g/8 oz/1 small can baked beans
in tomato sauce
10 ml/2 tsp Worcestershire sauce
2.5 ml/¹/₂ tsp dried thyme
4 instant mashed potato servings
50 g/2 oz/¹/₂ cup grated Cheddar
cheese*

Put the meat, beans, Worcestershire sauce and thyme in a saucepan and heat through until piping hot, stirring occasionally. Turn into a flameproof dish (or put in a dish and heat in the microwave). Meanwhile make up the potato according to the packet directions. Pile on top of the meat mixture and sprinkle with the cheese. Place under a hot grill (broiler) until golden and bubbling.

Savoury Strudel

*4 filo pastry (paste) sheets
25 g/1 oz/2 tbsp butter, melted
425 g/15 oz/1 large can minced
(ground) steak with onions
Pinch of grated nutmeg
90 ml/6 tbsp passata (sieved
tomatoes)*

Brush a sheet of filo pastry lightly with butter and lay another sheet on top. Continue layering in this way. Gently spread the meat mixture over the pastry to within 1 cm/¹/₂ in of the edge all round. Sprinkle with a little grated nutmeg. Fold in the short sides of the pastry, then roll up from a long end. Carefully transfer the strudel to a lightly buttered baking sheet and shape it into a curve. Brush with a little more butter. Bake in the oven at 200°C/400°F/gas mark 6 for about 20 minutes or until crisp and golden brown. Carefully transfer to a warm serving platter. Heat the passata and spoon around. Serve hot.

Potato Maybe Moussaka

SERVES 4

450 g/1 lb potatoes, scrubbed and
  sliced (not peeled) (or a large
  can)
425 g/15 oz/1 large can minced
  (ground) steak with onions
1 garlic clove, crushed
15 ml/1 tbsp tomato purée (paste)
5 ml/1 tsp ground cinnamon
150 ml/¹/₄ pt/²/₃ cup plain yoghurt or
  single (light) cream
1 egg
Salt and freshly ground black pepper
50 g/2 oz/¹/₂ cup grated Cheddar
  cheese

Boil the potatoes in salted water for
about 5 minutes until tender. Drain.
Alternatively, drain and slice the canned
potatoes. Mix the mince with the garlic,
tomato purée and cinnamon. Layer the
potatoes and meat mixture in an
ovenproof serving dish, finishing with a
layer of potatoes. Beat the yoghurt or
cream with the egg and a little salt and
pepper. Stir in the cheese. Pour over the
potatoes. Bake in the oven at 190°C/
375°F/gas mark 5 for about 35 minutes
until bubbling, golden and the top has set.
Alternatively, cook in the microwave and
brown under the grill (broiler).

Speedy Pasta Supper

SERVES 4

225 g/8 oz/2 cups pasta shapes
425 g/15 oz/1 large can minced
  (ground) steak with onions
5 ml/1 tsp mixed dried herbs
50 g/2 oz/¹/₂ cup grated Cheddar
  cheese
Sliced tomatoes, to garnish

Cook the pasta according to the
packet directions. Drain, rinse with
hot water and drain again. Return to the
saucepan and add the contents of the can
of mince and the herbs. Heat through,
stirring gently until piping hot. Turn into
a flameproof dish, sprinkle the cheese
over and arrange the tomato slices around
the edge. Brown under a hot grill (broiler)
for about 3 minutes.

Pan Hash

SERVES 4

2 onions, chopped
30 ml/2 tbsp oil
450 g/1 lb cooked potatoes, diced
350 g/12 oz/1 large can corned beef,
  diced
425 g/15 oz/1 large can baked beans
  in tomato sauce
15 ml/1 tbsp brown table sauce
Salt and freshly ground black pepper

Fry (sauté) the onion in the oil for 3
minutes until soft, but not brown. Mix
together the remaining ingredients. Add
to the pan and fry for 5 minutes, turning
the mixture over occasionally. Press down
with a fish slice and continue frying for a
further 5 minutes without disturbing until
crisp and brown underneath. Loosen, then
turn out on to a hot plate and serve cut
into wedges.

Everyday Bolognese

350 g/12 oz/3 cups minced (ground)
beef or lamb
1 onion, chopped
1 garlic clove, crushed
400 g/14 oz/1 large can chopped
tomatoes
15 ml/1 tbsp tomato purée (paste)
Salt and freshly ground black pepper
5 ml/1 tsp dried oregano
Pinch of caster (superfine) sugar
350 g/12 oz spaghetti
Freshly grated Parmesan cheese

Put the meat, onion and garlic in a saucepan. Cook, stirring, until the meat is browned and in separate grains. Add the remaining ingredients except the pasta and cheese. Stir well. Bring to the boil, reduce the heat, part-cover and simmer gently for 15–20 minutes until a rich sauce has formed. Stir gently from time to time. Cook the pasta according to the packet directions. Drain and pile on serving plates. Spoon the sauce over. Serve with grated Parmesan cheese.

Simple Lasagne

Put a spoonful of the Everyday Bolognese mixture in the base of a fairly shallow ovenproof dish. Top with strips of no-need-to-precook lasagne. Add half the remaining sauce, more lasagne, the rest of the sauce then a final layer of lasagne. Top with Basic Cheese Sauce (see page 245) and bake at 190°C/375°F/gas mark 5 for 35 minutes until cooked through and golden brown, or microwave for about 15 minutes until the lasagne feels tender when a knife is inserted down through the centre, then place under a hot grill (broiler) to brown the top.

Cannelloni Al Forno

Cook 8 cannelloni tubes (if necessary). Put the bolognese in a piping bag fitted with a large plain tube (tip) (or use a spoon). Fill the pasta tubes with the sauce. Lay in a shallow ovenproof dish. Cover with Basic Cheese Sauce (see page 245) and bake as for Lasagne.

Sesame Beef

30 ml/2 tbsp sesame seeds
3 garlic cloves, crushed
120 ml/4 fl oz/¹/₂ cup dry white wine
75 ml/5 tbsp soy sauce
10 ml/2 tsp red wine vinegar
10 ml/2 tsp sesame oil
Salt and freshly ground black pepper
450 g/1 lb good quality steak, such
as rump

Toast the sesame seeds in a dry pan until golden. Mix the seeds with the garlic, wine, soy sauce, vinegar and sesame oil and season with salt and pepper. Cut the steak into thin strips about 3 × 1 cm/1¹/₄ × ¹/₂ in. Marinate the steak in the mixture for 2 hours. Thread the steak on to soaked wooden skewers and grill (broil) for about 5 minutes, turning occasionally.

Corned-ish Pasties

SERVES 4

350 g/12 oz shortcrust pastry (basic pie crust)
185 g/6¹/₂ oz/1 small can corned beef, finely diced
275 g/10 oz/1 small can mixed vegetables, drained
Freshly ground black pepper
1 egg, beaten, to glaze

Cut the pastry into quarters, roll out each one to an 18–20 cm/7–8 in circle, using a plate or saucepan lid as a guide. Divide the meat and vegetables between the centres of the four pastry circles. Season with pepper. Brush the edges with beaten egg and draw up over the filling, pressing the edges together firmly to seal. Crimp between finger and thumb. Transfer to a baking sheet. Brush with beaten egg to glaze and bake in the oven at 200°C /400°F /gas mark 6 for about 15–20 minutes until golden brown. Serve hot or cold.

Midweek Beef Wellington

SERVES 4–6

1 large onion, chopped
15 ml/1 tbsp sunflower oil
300 g/11 oz/1 small can sliced mushrooms, drained
15 ml/1 tbsp sweet pickle
450 g/1 lb frozen puff pastry (paste), thawed
350 g/12 oz/1 large can corned beef
Beaten egg, to glaze
Passata (sieved tomatoes)

Fry (sauté) the onion in the oil for 3 minutes until soft, not brown. Stir in the mushrooms and sweet pickle and leave to cool. Roll out the pastry to a rectangle about 25 cm × 18 cm/10 in × 7 in. Spoon the onion mixture into the centre of the pastry. Remove the corned beef from the tin and place on top. Brush the edges of the pastry with beaten egg, fold over the filling and press the edges together firmly to seal. Place sealed side down on a dampened baking sheet. Make a criss-cross pattern over the top of the pastry with a sharp knife and brush all over with beaten egg. Bake in the oven at 220°C/425°F/gas mark 7 for 30 minutes, covering lightly with foil if over browning. Serve hot with a sauceboat of hot passata as a sauce.

Beef Stroganoff

SERVES 4

350 g/12 oz fillet steak
75 g/3 oz/¹/₃ cup butter
2 onions, thinly sliced
100 g/4 oz/2 cups button mushrooms, sliced
Salt and freshly ground black pepper
15 ml/1 tbsp brandy
150 ml/¹/₄ pt/²/₃ soured (dairy sour) cream
225 g/8 oz ribbon noodles
Chopped parsley

Cut the steak into thin strips about 2.5 cm/1 in long. Heat a third of the butter in a large frying pan (skillet). Add the onions and fry (sauté) for 2–3 minutes until softened and lightly golden. Add the mushrooms and continue cooking, stirring for 2–3 minutes until cooked through. Remove from the pan and reserve. Heat half the remaining butter and add the beef. Season well with salt and pepper and fry, stirring, for about 3 minutes until just cooked through. Add the brandy, ignite, and shake the pan until the flames subside. Return the onions and mushrooms to the pan with any cooking juices. Stir in the cream and heat through. Meanwhile, cook the noodles according to the packet directions. Drain and toss in the remaining butter. Pile on to plates and spoon the Stroganoff mixture to one side. Garnish with parsley before serving.

Rich Steak and Spaghetti

SERVES 4–6

2 onions, finely chopped
25 g/1 oz/2 tbsp dripping or lard
450 g/1 lb/4 cups lean top rump
*   steak, minced (ground)*
450 ml/³/₄ pt/2 cups beef stock
A little gravy salt or browning
25 g/1 oz/¹/₄ cup plain (all-purpose)
*   flour*
Salt and freshly ground black pepper
350 g/12 oz spaghetti
Warmed passata (sieved tomatoes) or
*   ketchup (catsup)*
Chopped parsley

Fry (sauté) the onion in the dripping until softened and lightly golden. Add the steak and fry, stirring, until browned and the grains are separate. Add the stock and a little gravy salt or browning. Part-cover and simmer gently for 30–40 minutes until really tender (or cook in a pressure cooker for 20 minutes or a slo-cooker for up to 6 hours). Blend the flour with a little water until smooth. Stir into the meat and bring to the boil. Simmer, stirring for 2 minutes. Season to taste with salt and pepper. Cook the spaghetti according to the packet directions. Drain. Pile on to serving plates. Spoon the sauce over. Drizzle with a little warmed passata or ketchup and sprinkle with chopped parsley.

Corned Beef Stuffed Pancakes

SERVES 4

350 g/12 oz/1 large can corned beef
30 ml/2 tbsp tomato ketchup
*   (catsup)*
15 ml/1 tbsp sweet pickle
1 packet pancake batter mix, or 1
*   quantity Basic Pancake Mix (see*
*   page 267)*
1 egg (if necessary)
600 ml/1 pt/2¹/₂ cups milk or water
*   (according to packet)*
Oil
1 packet cheese sauce mix, or 1
*   quantity Basic Cheese Sauce (see*
*   page 245)*

Chop the corned beef and mix with the tomato ketchup and pickle. Heat through gently until piping hot. Meanwhile, make up the pancake batter mix, if using, with egg, if necessary, and 300 ml/¹/₂ pt/ 1¹/₄ cups of liquid. Heat a little oil in a frying pan (skillet) and pour off the excess. Add about 30 ml/2 tbsp of the batter and swirl around to coat the base of the pan. Fry (sauté) until the underside is golden, turn over and brown the other side. Slide out of the pan and keep warm while cooking the remaining pancakes in the same way. Spread a little of the filling on each pancake, roll up and place in a warmed serving dish. Keep hot while making the sauce according to the packet directions with the remaining liquid or according to the recipe. Pour over the centre of the pancakes and serve hot.

Quick Beefburgers

SERVES 4

450 g/1 lb/4 cups minced (ground)
beef
1 onion, chopped
1 garlic clove, crushed
5 ml/1 tsp mustard powder
5 ml/1 tsp tomato purée (paste)
5 ml/1 tsp Worcestershire sauce
Salt and freshly ground black pepper
1 egg, beaten

Mix together the meat, onion, garlic, mustard, tomato purée and Worcestershire sauce, seasoning to taste with salt and pepper. Bind the mixture with the egg (you may not need to use all of it). Press the mixture together firmly into patties and chill before cooking. Grill (broil) for about 6 minutes on each side, depending on the thickness, until cooked through.

Cumin Kebabs

SERVES 4

450 g/1 lb lean rump or fillet steak,
cubed
15 ml/1 tbsp red wine vinegar
45 ml/3 tbsp milk
15 ml/1 tbsp ground ginger
5 ml/1 tsp ground coriander
(cilantro)
2.5 ml/¹/₂ tsp turmeric
2.5 ml/¹/₂ tsp cumin seeds
5 ml/1 tsp lemon juice
Salt and freshly ground black pepper
45 ml/3 tbsp melted butter or
margarine

Place the meat in a shallow bowl and sprinkle with the vinegar. Mix together all the remaining ingredients except the butter or margarine and pour over the meat. Leave to marinate for 30 minutes. Thread the meat on to soaked wooden skewers and brush with the butter or margarine. Grill (broil) for about 15 minutes, turning frequently and basting with butter or margarine as it cooks.

Pineapple Steaks

SERVES 4

4 fillet steaks
400 g/14 oz/1 large can pineapple in
juice
2 garlic cloves, crushed
5 ml/1 tsp ground coriander
(cilantro)
Pinch of chilli powder
60 ml/4 tbsp sunflower oil
Salt and freshly ground black pepper
30 ml/2 tbsp double (heavy) or
whipping cream
25 g/1 oz/2 tbsp butter or margarine

Arrange the steaks in a shallow dish. Drain the pineapple. Coarsely purée the pineapple with the garlic, coriander and chilli in a blender or food processor. Pour over the steaks and leave to marinate for at least 2 hours, longer if possible. Lift the steaks from the marinade and wipe off any excess. Brush with oil. Grill (broil) the steaks for 5–8 minutes each side until cooked to your liking. Season with salt and pepper. Meanwhile, heat the marinade and stir in the cream. Dot the steaks with butter or margarine and serve with the pineapple sauce.

Beef with Creamy Walnut Sauce

SERVES 4

100 g/4 oz/1 cup walnuts, chopped
2 spring onions (scallions), finely
*   chopped*
60 ml/4 tbsp chicken stock
45 ml/3 tbsp lemon juice
1.5 ml/¹/₄ tsp ground ginger
Salt and freshly ground black pepper
450 g/1 lb sirloin steak, cut into
*   strips*
250 ml/8 fl oz/1 cup fromage frais

B lend the walnuts, spring onions, stock, lemon juice, ginger, salt and pepper in a food processor or blender. Thread the meat on to soaked wooden skewers. Brush generously with the walnut sauce. Mix the remaining sauce with the fromage frais. Grill (broil) the kebabs for about 8 minutes each side, turning frequently. Serve with the fromage frais sauce.

Steak with Peppers

SERVES 4

1 garlic clove, crushed
10 ml/2 tsp chopped parsley
10 ml/2 tsp chopped basil
60 ml/4 tbsp sunflower oil
Salt and freshly ground black pepper
450 g/1 lb frying steak, cut into
*   strips*
1 red (bell) pepper, cut into thick
*   strips*
1 green (bell) pepper, cut into thick
*   strips*
1 yellow (bell) pepper, cut into thick
*   strips*
2 onions, thickly sliced into rings

M ix the garlic, parsley and basil into the oil and season with salt and pepper. Brush over the steak, peppers and onions in the grill (broiler) pan. Grill (broil) the meat and vegetables for about 15 minutes until lightly browned on the outside, brushing frequently with the herb oil while cooking and turning once or twice.

Tangy Spiced Beef Casserole

SERVES 4

750 g/1¹/₂ lb stewing beef, cubed
175 g/6 oz button mushrooms
2 carrots, diced
30 ml/2 tbsp sunflower oil
40 g/1¹/₂ oz/3 tbsp plain (all-purpose)
*   flour*
300 ml/¹/₂ pt/1¹/₄ cups beef stock
300 ml/¹/₂ pt/1¹/₄ cups orange juice
10 ml/2 tsp red wine vinegar
10 ml/2 tsp light brown sugar
2.5 ml/¹/₂ tsp ground cinnamon
1 bay leaf
Grated rind of ¹/₂ orange
Salt and freshly ground black pepper
15 ml/1 tbsp rum

F ry (sauté) the meat, mushrooms and carrots in the oil until browned. Add the flour and cook for a further minute, stirring continuously. Gradually blend in the stock and orange juice. Stir in the remaining ingredients and bring to the boil. Transfer to a casserole dish (Dutch oven), cover and cook in the oven at 180°C/350°F/gas mark 4 for 2¹/₂ hours. Remove the bay leaf, taste and re-season if necessary.

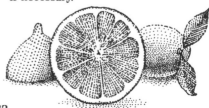

Steak Madeira

SERVES 2

2 × 175 g/2 × 6 oz fillet steaks
7.5 ml/1¹/₂ tsp mixed peppercorns
(green, pink and black)
30 ml/2 tbsp sunflower oil
2 shallots, chopped
60 ml/4 tbsp Madeira
Salt
25 g/1 oz/2 tbsp butter

Lightly score the steaks, crush the peppercorns and press into the surfaces. Fry (sauté) them in the oil, turning once, for between 5–10 minutes depending on your taste. Remove from the pan and keep warm while you make the sauce. Add all the remaining ingredients to the pan plus 90 ml/6 tbsp water. Bring to the boil, stirring occasionally, and let it boil until slightly reduced. Check the seasoning. Serve the steaks with the sauce spooned over.

Carpaccio con Salsa Verdi

SERVES 6

450 g/1 lb beef fillet
250 ml/8 fl oz/1 cup olive oil
30 ml/2 tbsp soy sauce
Freshly ground black pepper
3 canned anchovy fillets, drained
2 garlic cloves, crushed
2.5 ml/¹/₂ tsp balsamic vinegar
15 ml/1 tbsp capers
60 ml/4 tbsp chopped parsley

The beef has to be sliced really thinly and I have found the best way to do this is to freeze it until it's fairly solid, then you can slice it quite easily with a sharp knife. Put the thin slices under cling film (plastic wrap) and beat them with a rolling pin or meat mallet so they are nearly transparent. Mix together 90 ml/6 tbsp of the olive oil, the soy sauce and plenty of black pepper and pour this marinade over the meat. Leave for a minimum of 2 hours, but preferably overnight. Turn the meat over occasionally to ensure even coating of the marinade. Meanwhile, make the salsa by puréeing all the remaining ingredients, except the remaining oil, in a blender or food processor until well blended. Gradually add the remaining oil, running the machine all the time, and season with pepper. Lay the drained beef slices on two large baking sheets (it must be a single layer only). Bake in a very hot oven 240°C/475°F/gas mark 9 for between 1 and 2 minutes until the slices are just turning brown. Serve immediately on warmed plates dressed with a little of the salsa.

Redcurrant Beef

SERVES 6

20 pink peppercorns, or plenty of
coarse ground black pepper
600 g/1¹/₄ lb beef fillet, cut into 6
equal slices
30 ml/2 tbsp olive oil
5 shallots, finely chopped
3 streaky bacon rashers (slices),
rinded and cut into strips
175 ml/6 fl oz/³/₄ cup red wine
50 ml/2 fl oz/3¹/₂ tbsp beef stock
15 ml/1 tbsp lemon juice
Good pinch of grated nutmeg
30 ml/2 tbsp redcurrant jelly (clear
conserve)
Salt and freshly ground black pepper

Photograph opposite: **Steak with Peppers (page 63)**

Tightly crush the pink peppercorns if using and use to season both sides of the beef slices. Heat the oil and seal the beef on each side. When browned, remove from the pan and keep warm. Add the shallots and bacon pieces to the pan and sauté for 4–5 minutes. Mix in the wine, stock, lemon juice and nutmeg. Bring to the boil, stir in the redcurrant jelly until dissolved and season. Replace the meat and simmer for about 5–10 minutes until the meat is tender. Serve hot.

Creamy Mushroom Steaks

SERVES 4

1 onion, finely chopped
60 ml/4 tbsp olive oil
175 g/6 oz/3 cups button mushrooms,
 sliced
200 ml/7 fl oz/scant 1 cup white wine
4 × 175 g/4 × 6 oz fillet steaks
150 ml/¹/₄ pt/²/₃ cup double (heavy)
 cream
1 garlic clove, crushed
15 ml/1 tbsp chopped tarragon
10 ml/2 tsp French mustard
Salt and freshly ground black pepper
Tarragon sprigs

Fry (sauté) the onion in half the oil until softened. Add the mushrooms and cook for a further 2 minutes. Add the wine and simmer for 5 minutes. Meanwhile, flatten the steaks slightly with a mallet or rolling pin and fry in another pan in the remaining oil for 4–12 minutes depending on your taste. Stir the cream, garlic, tarragon and mustard into the onion and mushroom mixture and heat gently for 4–5 minutes. Season to taste. Place the steaks on top of the mushroom and tarragon sauce on warmed plates. Garnish with sprigs of tarragon and serve.

Alpine Beef Stroganoff

SERVES 6

750 g/1¹/₂ lb fillet or rump steak
50 g/2 oz/¹/₄ cup unsalted (sweet)
 butter
1 onion, finely chopped
100 g/4 oz/2 cups button mushrooms,
 finely sliced
10 ml/2 tsp tomato purée (paste)
10 ml/2 tsp French mustard
20 ml/4 tsp plain (all-purpose) flour
150 ml/¹/₄ pt/²/₃ cup soured (dairy
 sour) cream
Salt and freshly ground black pepper
Lemon juice

Beat the steak flat between clingfilm (plastic wrap) or greaseproof (waxed) paper with a rolling pin. Cut into narrow, short strips. Heat half the butter and fry (sauté) the onion and mushrooms gently until soft and just beginning to colour. Stir in the tomato purée, mustard and enough flour to absorb the fat. Continue frying over a very low heat for 2–3 minutes, then blend in the cream. In another pan, fry the meat in the remaining butter until browned. Add to the other pan and season with salt and pepper and lemon juice. Serve immediately.

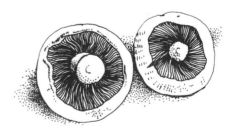

Photograph opposite: **Pork chops with orange and wine sauce (page 84) with mashed potatoes**

Peppered Steak

60 ml/4 tbsp green peppercorns,
*   crushed*
4 fillet or entrecôte steaks
50 g/2 oz/¹/₄ cup unsalted (sweet)
*   butter*
15 g/1 tbsp olive oil
30 ml/2 tbsp brandy
150 ml/¹/₄ pt/²/₃ cup double (heavy)
*   cream*
Salt

Press the peppercorns into all sides of the steaks. Cook them in the butter and oil for 2 minutes over a high heat, turning once. Lower the heat and cook for 5 minutes for rare, 8–9 minutes for medium rare and 12 minutes for well done. Remove from the pan and keep warm on a serving dish. Add the brandy to the juices in the pan and set alight. Shake the pan and when the flames die down, stir in the cream, season with salt and pour over the steaks.

Carbonnades à la Flamande

1.5 kg/3 lb lean braising steak, cut
*   into neat, wide strips*
350 g/12 oz/1¹/₂ cups unsalted
*   (sweet) butter*
15 ml/1 tbsp olive oil
3 large onions, sliced
7 garlic cloves, crushed
Salt and freshly ground black pepper
30 ml/2 tbsp plain (all-purpose)
*   flour*
15 ml/1 tbsp light brown sugar
300 ml/¹/₂ pt/1¹/₄ cups strong beef
*   stock*
450 ml/³/₄ pt/2 cups brown ale
15 ml/1 tbsp red wine vinegar
1 bouquet garni
1 bay leaf
1 French stick

Brown the beef quickly in a third of the butter and the oil and put aside. Cook the onions until golden and add half the garlic. Layer the onions and beef in a deep casserole dish (Dutch oven) beginning with the onions. Lightly season the layers. Add the flour and sugar to the pan juices and cook for 1 minute, stirring. Stir in a little of the stock until the mixture is smooth. Bring to the boil and add the remaining stock, the ale and vinegar. Bring the mixture to the boil again. Put the bouquet garni and bay leaf into the casserole, pour the sauce over the meat and cook for 2¹/₂ hours in the oven at 160°C/325°F/gas mark 3. For the garlic crust, melt the remaining butter in a frying pan (skillet) and add the remaining garlic. Slice the bread into 2.5 cm/1 in thick slices and soak in the garlic butter. Put the bread on top of the casserole, buttered side up. Cook for a further 15 minutes uncovered until the garlic crust is golden.

Stifado

SERVES 6

1 kg/2¹/₄ lb lean braising steak or shin beef, cut into cubes
50 g/2 oz/¹/₂ cup seasoned plain (all-purpose) flour
75 ml/5 tbsp olive oil
1.5 ml/¹/₄ tsp cumin seeds
5 cm/2 in piece of cinnamon stick
45 ml/3 tbsp tomato purée (paste)
30 ml/2 tbsp herb vinegar
Salt and freshly ground black pepper
900 ml/1¹/₂ pts/3¹/₄ cups beef stock
A small handful of thyme sprigs
450 g/1 lb small onions, peeled
100 g/4 oz Feta cheese, cubed

Toss the meat in the flour, fry (sauté) in the oil and transfer to a casserole (Dutch oven). Add the cumin, cinnamon stick and tomato purée to the remaining juices. Stir in the vinegar, salt and pepper, stock and thyme, reserving a few sprigs for garnish. Bring to the boil and pour over the meat. Cover and cook in the oven for 2¹/₂ hours at 160°C/325°F/gas mark 3 or in a slow cooker for about 6 hours. Discard the thyme sprigs. Plunge the onions into boiling water, drain and add to the casserole and cook for a further 30 minutes. Add the cubed cheese and return to the oven until the cheese begins to melt. Garnish with the reserved thyme and serve.

Deep-fried Spiced Meatballs

SERVES 3 OR 4

Pinch of ground cumin
5 ml/1 tsp ground coriander (cilantro)
Pinch of chilli powder
5 ml/1 tsp garlic powder
5 ml/1 tsp mild curry powder
350 g/12 oz/3 cups minced (ground) beef
15 ml/1 tbsp finely chopped coriander
5 ml/1 tsp salt
Oil for deep-frying

Put all the ground spices, the garlic powder and curry powder in a cup and add 15 ml/ 1 tbsp water. Put the mince in a bowl and add the spices from the cup and the remaining ingredients, except the oil. Knead well with your hands or process in a food processor for about 15 seconds. Form into 12 balls and deep-fry in hot oil until golden brown. Drain on kitchen paper.

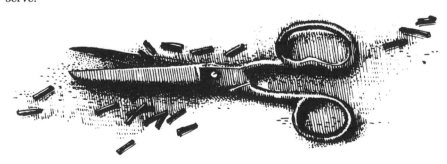

Crumble-topped Beef Bake

SERVES 4

1 onion, finely chopped
1 carrot, finely chopped
450 g/1 lb/4 cups minced (ground)
*   beef*
75 g/3 oz/³/₄ cup plain (all-purpose)
*   flour*
600 ml/1 pt/2¹/₂ cups beef stock
5 ml/1 tsp yeast extract
Salt and freshly ground black pepper
1 × 85 g/1 × 3¹/₂ oz/1 small packet
country herb stuffing mix
100 g/4 oz/¹/₂ cup butter
75 g/3 oz/³/₄ cup grated Cheddar
*   cheese*

Put the onion, carrot and beef in a flameproof casserole (Dutch oven). Fry (sauté), stirring until all the grains of meat are brown and separate. Stir in 25 g/1 oz/¹/₄ cup of the flour and cook for 2 minutes. Remove from the heat and blend in the stock. Add the yeast extract, return to the heat, bring to the boil stirring, then simmer gently for 10 minutes. Season to taste. Meanwhile, put the stuffing mix and remaining flour in a bowl. Add the butter and rub in with the fingertips until the mixture looks like breadcrumbs, then stir in the cheese. Sprinkle over the meat and bake in the oven at 190°C/375°F/gas mark 5 for 35–40 minutes until golden brown.

Steak and Potato Kebabs

SERVES 4

450 g/1 lb rump steak, cubed
30 ml/2 tbsp olive oil
10 ml/2 tsp red wine vinegar
5 ml/1 tsp mixed dried herbs
Salt and freshly ground black pepper
16 whole baby waxy new potatoes,
*   scrubbed*
4 cherry tomatoes

Place the meat in a dish and sprinkle on the oil, vinegar, herbs and a little salt and pepper. Toss gently, then leave to marinate for at least 1 hour. Meanwhile, cook the potatoes in plenty of boiling, salted water until just tender. Drain, rinse with cold water and drain again. Thread the meat and potatoes on to 4 skewers, ending with a cherry tomato. Brush with the marinade. Grill (broil) until golden brown and the steak is to your liking, turning occasionally and basting all over with the marinade.

Oriental Steak Kebabs

SERVES 4

450 g/1 lb rump steak, cubed
45 ml/3 tbsp soy sauce
45 ml/3 tbsp sesame or sunflower oil
5 ml/1 tsp grated fresh root ginger
15 ml/1 tbsp medium-dry sherry
8 button (pearl) onions
¹/₄ cucumber
8 cherry tomatoes
8 button mushrooms
250 g/9 oz/1 packet Chinese egg
*   noodles, cooked*

Put the meat in a bowl. Mix together the soy sauce, oil, ginger and sherry and pour over. Toss gently, then leave to marinate for at least 1 hour. Meanwhile, cook the onions in boiling water for 3 minutes. Drain, rinse with cold water and drain again. Cut the cucumber into four thick slices, then quarter each slice. Thread the ingredients onto skewers, starting and finishing with cucumber. Brush with marinade and grill (broil) for about 6–8 minutes until golden brown and just cooked, turning and brushing with the marinade occasionally during cooking. Serve on a bed of Chinese egg noodles.

Chuck-it-together Meat Loaf

SERVES 4

450 g/1 lb/4 cups minced (ground) beef
1 onion, finely chopped
15 ml/1 tbsp chopped parsley
15 ml/1 tbsp chopped thyme
Grated rind and juice of ¹/₂ lemon
10 ml/2 tsp Worcestershire sauce
45 ml/3 tbsp red wine
10 ml/2 tsp tomato purée (paste)
Salt and freshly ground black pepper
1 egg, beaten
Hot passata (sieved tomatoes) and vegetables, or salad

Mix together all the ingredients except the passata and vegetables or salad and press into a greased 450 g/ 1 lb loaf tin (pan). Cover with foil and bake at 180°C/350°F/gas mark 4 for 1 hour. Cool slightly, then turn out and serve hot with passata and vegetables, or cold in slices with salad.

Keema

SERVES 4

1 onion, finely chopped
1 garlic clove, crushed
15 ml/1 tbsp sunflower oil
5 ml/1 tsp grated fresh root ginger
15 ml/1 tbsp garam masala
2.5 ml/¹/₂ tsp chilli powder
5 ml/1 tsp ground cumin
5 ml/1 tsp turmeric
450 g/1 lb/4 cups minced (ground) beef
200 g/7 oz/1 small can chopped tomatoes
30 ml/2 tbsp tomato purée (paste)
150 ml/¹/₄ pt/²/₃ cup beef stock
150 ml/¹/₄ pt/²/₃ cup plain yoghurt
Salt and freshly ground black pepper
Plain boiled rice
Chopped coriander (cilantro)

Put the onion and garlic in a saucepan with the oil. Fry (sauté), stirring, for 3 minutes. Stir in the ginger and other spices and cook for 1 minute. Stir in the beef and cook, stirring until all the grains of meat are brown and separate. Add the remaining ingredients except the rice and coriander, seasoning with a little salt and pepper. Bring to the boil, cover, reduce the heat and simmer gently for 40 minutes. Remove the cover half-way through cooking and stir from time to time. Spoon over plain boiled rice and sprinkle with chopped coriander.

Rooty-tooty

SERVES 6

1 onion, grated
1 large carrot, grated
1 parsnip, grated
450 g/1 lb/4 cups minced (ground)
beef
50 g/2 oz/1 cup fresh breadcrumbs
Salt and freshly ground black pepper
1 egg, beaten
330 ml/12 fl oz/scant 1¹/₂ cups mixed
vegetable juice
15 g/¹/₂ oz/1 tbsp butter
15 g/¹/₂ oz/2 tbsp plain (all-purpose)
flour
15 ml/1 tbsp chopped parsley

Mix the onion, carrot, parsnip, meat and breadcrumbs thoroughly with the hands. Season well. Stir in the egg and 60 ml/4 tbsp of the vegetable juice. Mix well, then turn into a greased 900 g/2 lb loaf tin (pan). Press down well. Bake in the oven at 190°C/375°F/gas mark 5 for 1¹/₄ hours. Meanwhile, melt the butter. Remove from the heat and whisk in the flour, then the remaining vegetable juice until smooth. Return to the heat, bring to the boil and simmer for 3 minutes, stirring all the time. Stir in the parsley. Leave the Rooty-tooty to cool in the tin for 5 minutes, then loosen the edges, turn out and cut into 6 thick slices. Spoon the sauce on to 6 serving plates, lay a slice of the meat loaf in the centre and serve hot.

Blue Cheese Steak Roll

SERVES 4

450 g/1 lb/4 cups minced (ground)
steak
75 g/3 oz/1¹/₂ cups wholemeal
breadcrumbs
10 ml/2 tsp Dijon mustard
¹/₂ bunch of spring onion (scallions),
finely chopped
30 ml/2 tbsp chopped parsley
Salt and freshly ground black pepper
2 eggs, beaten
15 ml/1 tbsp plain (all-purpose)
flour
100 g/4 oz blue cheese, crumbled
30 ml/2 tbsp melted butter

Mix the steak with the breadcrumbs, mustard, spring onions, parsley and a little salt and pepper. Add the eggs to bind. Cut a piece of foil 40 × 25 cm/16 × 10 in. Dust with the flour. Press the meat mixture out on the foil to within 1 cm/¹/₂ in of the edges all round. Sprinkle with the cheese and roll up, using the foil as a guide. Wrap in the foil and chill for 30 minutes. Unwrap the foil on a baking sheet so the meat is lying, rolled side down, on the open foil. Brush with the melted butter and bake for 1 hour at 180°C/350°F/gas mark 4. Serve hot, cut into slices.

American-style Cheeseburgers

450 g/1 lb/4 cups minced (ground) steak
2.5 ml/¹/₂ tsp steak seasoning (optional)
Salt and freshly ground black pepper
4 sesame seed buns
12 slices dill pickle
Shredded lettuce
4 slices tomato
4 slices processed cheese
20 ml/4 tsp hamburger or tomato relish
10 ml/2 tsp American or French mustard
Chips (fries)

Mix the steak with the seasoning, if using, and a little salt and pepper. Shape into 4 thick patties about the size of the buns. Grill (broil) or fry (sauté) for about 4–6 minutes until cooked to your liking. Split the buns and toast on the cut sides if liked. Place a burger on the bottom half of each bun. Top each with 3 slices of dill pickle, a little lettuce, a tomato slice and a cheese slice. Grill until the cheese begins to melt. Spread a little relish and mustard on the underside of the tops of the buns. Place over the cheese and serve with chips.

PORK

Pork is one of the richest and most flavoursome of meats. The danger is cooking it to death when it becomes dry and stringy. All these dishes will give you succulent, tender results. But don't keep prodding it with a fork as it cooks or all the juice will run out. There are wonderful ham, bacon and sausage recipes too.

Austrian Pork Chops

SERVES 4

4 thin boneless pork chops
15 ml/1 tbsp olive oil
1 onion, thinly sliced
1 garlic clove, crushed
¹/₂ small cabbage, shredded
150 ml/¹/₄ pt/²/₃ cup vegetable or
  pork stock
15 ml/1 tbsp caraway seeds
Salt and freshly ground black pepper
Chopped parsley

Fry (sauté) the chops in the oil in a deep frying pan (skillet) for 3 minutes on each side to brown. Remove from the pan. Add the onion and garlic and fry for 2 minutes. Stir in the cabbage and cook, stirring, for about 3 minutes until it softens slightly. Add the stock. Lay the chops on top, sprinkle with the caraway seeds and a little salt and pepper. Cover with foil or a lid, reduce the heat and simmer for 20 minutes until tender. Garnish with chopped parsley and serve.

Barbecued Pork

SERVES 4

15 g/¹/₂ oz/1 tbsp butter or margarine
4 pork shoulder steaks
15 ml/1 tbsp lemon juice
15 ml/1 tbsp malt vinegar
30 ml/2 tbsp tomato purée (paste)
15 ml/1 tbsp Worcestershire sauce
30 ml/2 tbsp golden (light corn)
  syrup
1 packet savoury rice

Melt the fat in a large frying pan (skillet). Add the pork and fry (sauté) for 3 minutes on each side to brown. Blend together the remaining ingredients, except the rice. Spoon over the pork. Cook over a moderate heat for about 10 minutes, turning the meat occasionally, until the pork is coated in a sticky glaze. Meanwhile, cook the rice according to the packet directions. Serve the pork on a bed of savoury rice.

Spaghetti alla Carbonara

350 g/12 oz spaghetti
100 g/4 oz/³/₄ cup unsmoked streaky
*   bacon, finely diced*
75 g/3 oz/¹/₃ cup butter
5 eggs
30 ml/2 tbsp chopped parsley
Salt and freshly ground black pepper
50 g/2 oz/¹/₂ cup freshly grated
*   Parmesan cheese*

Cook the spaghetti according to the packet directions. Drain and return to the pan. Meanwhile, fry (sauté) the bacon in the butter until browned. Beat the eggs with the parsley, a little salt, lots of pepper and the cheese. Add the hot bacon in its fat to the spaghetti and toss over a gentle heat. Add the egg mixture and toss quickly until the spaghetti is coated but do not let it scramble. The mixture should be creamy and hot. Serve straight away.   •

Spaghetti alla Carbonara con Funghi

Prepare as for Spaghetti alla Carbonara but add 50 g/2 oz/1 cup sliced button mushrooms, 2 crushed garlic cloves and 30 ml/2 tbsp olive oil to the bacon and butter and fry (sauté) all together.

Spaghetti with Bacon, Eggs and Tomato

1 onion, finely chopped
2 garlic cloves, crushed
6 streaky bacon rashers (slices),
*   diced*
60 ml/4 tbsp olive oil
350 g/12 oz spaghetti
15 ml/1 tbsp chopped parsley
2 tomatoes, skinned, seeded and
*   chopped*
2 eggs
30 ml/2 tbsp milk or single (light)
*   cream*
Salt and freshly ground black pepper
Grated Parmesan cheese

Fry (sauté) the onion, garlic and bacon in the oil for 2 minutes, cover and cook gently for 5 minutes until the onion is soft. Meanwhile, cook the spaghetti according to the packet directions, drain and return to the pan. Stir in the bacon mixture, parsley and tomatoes. In a separate bowl, beat the eggs with the milk or cream, then add to the pan. Toss over a gentle heat until creamy but do not boil or the egg will scramble. Season and serve with grated Parmesan cheese.

Sweet and Sour Pork

Prepare as for Sweet and Sour Chicken (see page 112) but substitute 350 g/12 oz pork fillet for the chicken breasts and serve on a bed or cooked Chinese egg noodles.

Three-spice Pork

Prepare as for Three-spice Turkey (see page 119) but substitute 4 pork steaks for the turkey escalopes. Beat flat with a rolling pin or meat mallet before coating in flour and frying (sautéing).

Fillet of Pork with Vermouth

SERVES 4

Prepare as for Fillet of Turkey with Vermouth (see page 119) but substitute 2 slices of pork fillet for the turkey and use red vermouth instead of dry white vermouth.

Allspice Pork

SERVES 4

15 ml/1 tbsp sunflower oil
1 small onion, finely chopped
15 ml/1 tbsp clear honey
15 ml/1 tbsp allspice
5 ml/1 tsp ground cinnamon
2.5 ml/¹/₂ tsp dried thyme
Salt and freshly ground black pepper
4 pork chops
Treacly Apple Sauce (see page 249)

Mix together the oil, onion, honey, allspice, cinnamon, thyme, salt and pepper. Rub the mixture over the pork on all sides. Leave to marinate for 2 hours. Grill (broil) the pork for about 15 minutes on each side until thoroughly cooked through and crisp on the edges. Serve with Treacly Apple Sauce.

Gratin of Broccoli and Ham

SERVES 4

450 g/1 lb broccoli
4 ham slices, halved
25 g/1 oz/¹/₄ cup plain (all-purpose) flour
25 g/1 oz/2 tbsp butter or margarine
300 g/¹/₂ pt/1¹/₄ cups milk
100 g/4 oz/1 cup grated Cheddar cheese
Salt and freshly ground black pepper

Separate the broccoli into florets and cook in boiling, salted water for about 5 minutes until tender. Divide into 8 bundles and wrap a half-slice of ham around each. Lay side-by-side in a buttered ovenproof dish. Whisk the flour and fat into the milk in a pan. Bring to the boil and boil for 2 minutes, whisking all the time until thickened and smooth. Stir in 75 g/3 oz/³/₄ cup of the cheese and season to taste. Pour the sauce over the broccoli and ham. Sprinkle with the remaining cheese and grill (broil) for about 4 minutes until golden brown.

Pork Pockets

SERVES 4

4 pork escalopes
5 ml/1 tsp paprika
Salt and freshly ground black pepper
60 ml/4 tbsp tomato ketchup (catsup)
100 g/4 oz slices Emmental (Swiss) or strong hard cheese
30 ml/2 tbsp finely snipped chives
15 ml/1 tbsp sunflower oil

Beat the escalopes flat. Season with paprika, salt and pepper and brush with ketchup. Place a slice of cheese on one half of each escalope and sprinkle with chives. Fold over and secure with cocktail sticks (toothpicks). Brush with oil. Grill (broil) for about 8 minutes on each side, brushing with more oil if necessary. Serve straight away.

Deluxe Grill

SERVES 4

4 gammon steaks
200 g/7 oz/1 small can pineapple
 chunks
4 tomatoes, skinned and chopped
4 slices Havarti, Gruyère or
 Emmental (Swiss) cheese
Watercress

Snip the edges of the gammon with scissors to prevent curling. Drain and roughly chop the pineapple and mix with the tomatoes. Grill (broil) the gammon for 5 minutes on each side. Spread the fruit mixture over and top each with a slice of cheese. Return to the grill (broiler) until the cheese has melted and the fruit is hot. Garnish with watercress and serve.

Devilled Kidneys on Brown Rice

SERVES 4

175 g/6 oz/³/₄ cup brown rice
45 ml/3 tbsp chopped parsley
4 pigs' kidneys
4 rashers (slices) streaky bacon
50 g/2 oz/¹/₄ cup butter or margarine
5 ml/1 tsp mild curry powder
2.5 ml/¹/₂ tsp made English mustard
10 ml/2 tsp Worcestershire sauce
30 ml/2 tbsp tomato ketchup
 (catsup)
Salt and freshly ground black pepper

Cook the rice according to the packet directions. Stir in 30 ml/2 tbsp of the parsley. Meanwhile, cut the kidneys into bite-sized pieces, discarding the cores. Dice the bacon. Melt the fat in a frying pan (skillet) and fry (sauté) the kidneys and bacon over a moderate heat for 3 minutes, stirring. Add the remaining ingredients except the remaining parsley, mix well and cook, stirring for about 5–8 minutes until the kidneys are cooked but still tender, and bathed in sauce. Spoon on to the rice and garnish with the remaining parsley.

Quick Pork Burgers

SERVES 4

Prepare as for Quick Beefburgers (see page 62) but substitute minced (ground) pork for the beef and chopped sage for the mustard.

Greek-style Pork Kebabs

SERVES 4

Prepare as for Greek-Style Lamb Kebabs (see page 91) but substitute pork fillet for the lamb and use red (bell) pepper instead of green.

Crunchy Pork Escalopes

SERVES 4

Prepare as for Crunchy Turkey Escalopes (see page 107) but substitute 4 boneless pork steaks for the turkey fillets and use sage and onion stuffing mix instead of parsley and thyme. Garnish with apple slices fried (sautéed) in butter, if liked.

Pork Stroganoff

225 g/8 oz ribbon noodles
40 g/1¹/₂ oz/3 tbsp butter
350 g/12 oz pork fillet
1 onion, sliced
100 g/4 oz/2 cups button mushrooms,
  sliced
15 ml/1 tbsp brandy
150 ml/¹/₄ pt/²/₃ cup soured (dairy
  sour) cream
Salt and freshly ground black pepper
Chopped parsley

Cook the noodles according to the packet directions. Drain and toss in 15 g/¹/₂ oz/1 tbsp of the butter. Meanwhile, cut the pork into thin strips. Melt the remaining butter and fry (sauté) the onion and mushrooms for 3 minutes to soften. Add the pork strips and fry for 5–8 minutes until cooked through. Put the brandy in a soup ladle, set alight then pour into the pan. Cook until the flames subside. Stir in the cream and heat through, but do not boil. Season to taste. Spoon over the noodles and garnish with chopped parsley.

Oriental Pork Slices

8 belly pork slices
10 ml/2 tsp cornflour (cornstarch)
15 ml/1 tbsp vinegar
250 g/9 oz/1 small can crushed
  pineapple
30 ml/2 tbsp tomato ketchup
  (catsup)
15 ml/1 tbsp soy sauce
¹/₄ cucumber, diced

Discard any rind or bones in the pork, then fry (sauté) the slices over a moderate heat for about 15–20 minutes, turning once or twice until browned and cooked through. Meanwhile, blend the cornflour with the vinegar in a pan. Add the remaining ingredients. Bring to the boil, stirring, and simmer for 5 minutes, stirring occasionally. Spoon over the pork and serve.

Fegattini

350 g/12 oz pigs' liver
2 onions
1 slice bread
15 ml/1 tbsp chopped sage
1 egg, beaten
Salt and freshly ground black pepper
15 ml/1 tbsp olive oil
450 g/1 lb tomatoes, quartered
15 ml/1 tbsp tomato purée (paste)
60 ml/4 tbsp water
2.5 ml/¹/₂ tsp sugar
225 g/8 oz tagliatelle

Coarsely mince (grind) or process the liver, one onion and the bread. Add the sage, egg and seasoning and mix well. Heat the oil. Chop the remaining onion and soften in the oil for 2 minutes. Add the tomatoes, tomato purée and water, cover and cook for about 5 minutes, stirring occasionally until pulpy. Season and add the sugar. Meanwhile, bring a large pan of salted water to the boil. Drop in tablespoonfuls of the liver mixture and simmer for about 4 minutes until cooked through. Drain. Put the cooked balls of liver mixture in the sauce and heat through. Cook the tagliatelle according to the packet directions. Drain. Pile on to plates. Spoon the fegattini and sauce over and serve.

Sticky Orange Steaks

4 pork or bacon steaks
15 g/¹/₂ oz/1 tbsp butter
15 ml/1 tbsp orange jelly
marmalade
2.5 ml/¹/₂ tsp ground ginger
5 ml/1 tsp orange juice
Orange slices

Fry (sauté) the steaks on one side for 5 minutes in the butter. Mix together the marmalade, ginger and orange juice. Turn the steaks over and brush with this mixture. Fry for a further 5 minutes, basting occasionally with the juices. Place the pan under a hot grill (broiler) for 2 minutes until the glaze is sticky. Transfer the steaks to warmed serving plates, garnish with orange slices and serve.

Quick Cassoulet

4 bacon rashers (slices) or cooked
ham slices, diced
400 g/14 oz/1 large can hot dog
sausages, drained and cut into
pieces
425 g/15 oz/1 large can red kidney
beans, drained
425/15 oz/1 large can baked beans
in tomato sauce
275 g/10 oz/1 small can cut green
beans, drained

Dry-fry the bacon, if using, in a large saucepan. Stir in the remaining ingredients. Heat through, occasionally stirring gently, for about 5 minutes until piping hot. Serve in soup bowls.

Ham in Puff Pastry

450 g/1 lb frozen puff pastry (paste),
thawed
2 × 450 g/2 × 1 lb/2 large cans ham
215 g/7¹/₂ oz/ 1 small can creamed
mushrooms
10 ml/2 tsp dried marjoram or
oregano
Beaten egg, to glaze
45 ml/3 tbsp redcurrant jelly (clear
conserve)
45 ml/3 tbsp orange juice

Cut the pastry into 6 equal pieces and roll out each piece to a square about 18–20 cm/7–8 in. Trim the edges. Cut each can of ham into three slices, discarding the jelly. Divide the can of mushrooms between the centres of the pastry. Sprinkle with the herbs, then top each with a slice of ham. Brush the edges of the pastry with the beaten egg. Fold over the filling to form parcels. Place the parcels, folds down, on a dampened baking sheet. Make 'leaves' out of the pastry trimmings and place on the parcels. Brush with beaten egg to glaze. Bake in the oven at 220°C/425°F/ gas mark 7 for 12–15 minutes until golden brown. Meanwhile, heat the redcurrant jelly with the orange juice in a saucepan until it has dissolved. Transfer the ham parcels to warmed serving plates, spoon a little sauce to the side of each and serve hot.

Smoked Cheese and Frankfurter Flan

SERVES 4–6

225 g/8 oz shortcrust pastry (basic
 pie crust)
1 onion, chopped
15 ml/1 tbsp oil
225 g/8 oz/1 small can chopped
 tomatoes
2.5 ml/^{1}/$_2$ tsp ground cinnamon
15 ml/1 tbsp tomato purée (paste)
5 frankfurters (canned or
 vacuum-packed)
100 g/4 oz smoked cheese roll

Roll out the pastry and use to line a 23 cm/9 in flan dish (pie pan). Prick the base with a fork, line with crumpled foil and bake blind for 10 minutes. Remove the foil and return to the oven for 5 minutes to dry out. Meanwhile, fry (sauté) the onion in the oil for 3 minutes until soft but not brown. Add the tomatoes, cinnamon and tomato purée and simmer for 10 minutes. Chop the frankfurters, add to the sauce and turn into the flan case (pie shell). Slice the cheese and arrange around the top. Bake in the oven at 190°C/375°F/gas mark 5 for 15 minutes until the cheese is golden and the flan is heated through. Serve hot or cold.

Sauerkraut with Frankfurters

SERVES 4

450 g/1 lb potatoes, cut into even-
 sized pieces
500 g/1^1/$_4$ lb/1 large jar sauerkraut
15 ml/1 tbsp caraway seeds
12 frankfurters (canned or
 vacuum-packed)
German mustard

Cook the potatoes in boiling, salted water until tender but still holding their shape. Drain. Meanwhile, empty the sauerkraut into a saucepan. Add the caraway seeds and heat through. Drain. Heat the frankfurters according to the packet directions. Spoon the sauerkraut and frankfurters on to hot plates and surround with the potatoes. Serve with mustard.

Barbecued Bangers

SERVES 4

450 g/1 lb chipolata sausages
15 g/^{1}/$_2$ oz/1 tbsp butter or
 margarine
15 ml/1 tbsp lemon juice
15 ml/1 tbsp red wine vinegar
30 ml/2 tbsp tomato purée (paste)
15 ml/1 tbsp brown table sauce
30 ml/2 tbsp golden (light corn)
 syrup
1 packet savoury rice with
 mushrooms

Dry-fry the sausages in a large frying pan (skillet) for about 10 minutes until cooked through and brown all over. Heat the remaining ingredients except the rice together in a saucepan. Pour over the sausages and cook for a further 3 minutes until the sausages are coated in a sticky sauce. Meanwhile, cook the rice according to the packet directions. Spoon on to plates and top with the sausages.

Grilled Ham with Pineapple in a Hurry

450 g/1 lb/1 large can ham
225 g/8 oz/1 small can chopped
tomatoes, drained
75 g/3 oz/³/₄ cup grated Cheddar
cheese
225 g/8 oz/1 small can pineapple
slices

Cut the ham into four steaks, discarding the jelly. Place on a grill (broiler) rack and grill (broil) for 1 minute. Turn over and grill the other side for a further minute. Spoon the tomatoes over, top with the grated cheese and place a pineapple slice on each. Return to the grill and cook until bubbling, hot through and the top is turning golden. Serve hot.

Lime-glazed Ham Steaks

SERVES 4

450 g/1 lb/1 large can ham
15 g/¹/₂ oz/1 tbsp butter or
margarine
30 ml/2 tbsp fine-shred lime
marmalade
2.5 ml/¹/₂ tsp ground ginger
5 ml/1 tsp lime or lemon juice

Cut the ham into four steaks, discarding the jelly. Melt the butter or margarine in a frying pan (skillet) and fry (sauté) the ham for 2 minutes. Turn over. Mix the marmalade, ginger and juice together and spoon the mixture all over the steaks. Cook for about 3 minutes, basting with the glaze. Place the pan under a preheated grill (broiler) for 2 minutes until the meat is stickily glazed. Serve hot.

Mozzarella-topped Pasta Special

SERVES 4

350 g/12 oz/3 cups minced (ground)
pork
1 onion, finely chopped
2 garlic cloves, crushed
15 ml/1 tbsp olive oil
150 ml/¹/₄ pt/²/₃ cup white wine
400 g/14 oz/1 large can chopped
tomatoes
2.5 ml/¹/₂ tsp dried thyme
Salt and freshly ground black pepper
350 g/12 oz tagliatelle
60 ml/4 tbsp grated Mozzarella
cheese
30 ml/2 tbsp freshly grated
Parmesan cheese

Fry (sauté) the meat, onion and garlic in the oil, stirring until browned and all the grains of meat are separate. Add the wine, tomatoes, thyme and a little salt and pepper. Bring to the boil, reduce the heat, part-cover and simmer until nearly all the liquid has evaporated and the sauce is thick. Taste and re-season if necessary. Meanwhile, cook the pasta according to the packet directions. Drain and turn into a flameproof serving dish. Spoon the sauce over and sprinkle with the Mozzarella and Parmesan. Flash quickly under a hot grill (broiler) to melt the Mozzarella.

Parma Ham and Mushroom Ribbons

SERVES 4

30 ml/2 tbsp olive oil
100 g/4 oz/2 cups button
mushrooms, sliced
5 ml/1 tsp yeast extract
100 g/4 oz/1 cup Parma ham, cut into
thin strips
25 g/1 oz/2 tbsp butter
75 ml/5 tbsp crème fraîche
Salt and freshly ground black pepper
1.5 ml/¹/₄ tsp grated nutmeg
225 g/8 oz ribbon noodles
Freshly grated Parmesan or
Pecorino cheese

Heat the oil in a small saucepan and add the mushrooms. Cook gently for 2 minutes until softened. Stir in the yeast extract, ham strips and the butter in small flakes. Heat gently, stirring, until the butter melts. Stir in the crème fraîche, salt and pepper to taste and the nutmeg. Heat through for 2 minutes. Meanwhile, cook the pasta according to the packet directions. Drain and return to the saucepan. Add the sauce and toss well over a gentle heat before serving with grated Parmesan or Pecorino cheese.

Smoked Pork Sausage and Greens

SERVES 4

90 ml/6 tbsp olive oil
2 leeks, sliced
2 garlic cloves, crushed
350 g/12 oz spring greens (spring
cabbage), shredded
1 smoked pork ring, sliced
45 ml/3 tbsp water
8 stoned (pitted) black olives, sliced
15 g/¹/₂ oz/1 tbsp butter
Salt and freshly ground black pepper
225 g/8 oz/2 cups rigatoni
Freshly grated Parmesan cheese

Heat 60 ml/4 tbsp of the oil in a large saucepan. Add the leeks and garlic, cover and cook gently for 5 minutes until soft, but not brown. Add the greens and cook, stirring, for a few minutes until they begin to 'fall'. Add the sliced sausage and the water. Cover and cook gently for 5 minutes or until the greens are soft, stirring occasionally. Add the remaining oil and the olives and butter and season with a little salt and plenty of pepper. Meanwhile, cook the rigatoni according to the packet directions. Drain and return to the saucepan. Add the sausage mixture, toss over a gentle heat and serve with lots of freshly grated Parmesan cheese.

Sweet-cured Ham and Peas

SERVES 4

225 g/8 oz/2 cups cooked ham
pieces
2 onions, finely chopped
100 g/4 oz/¹/₂ cup butter
30 ml/2 tbsp olive oil
100 g/4 oz/1 cup frozen peas
75 g/3 oz/³/₄ cup freshly grated
Parmesan cheese
Salt and freshly ground black pepper
225 g/8 oz penne or other pasta
shapes

Cut the ham into very small dice, discarding any fat or gristle. Fry (sauté) the onions gently in half the butter and half the oil until soft, but not brown. Add the ham and peas, cover, reduce the heat and cook gently for 5 minutes, stirring occasionally. Add the remaining butter, two-thirds of the cheese, a very little salt and lots of pepper. Cook the pasta according to the packet directions. Drain and return to the saucepan. Add the sauce. Toss well, pile on to warm plates and drizzle with the remaining olive oil and serve with the remaining Parmesan cheese sprinkled over.

Neapolitan Bacon and Tomato Tumble

SERVES 4

1 onion, chopped
1 garlic clove, crushed
15 ml/1 tbsp olive oil
8 streaky bacon rashers (slices),
rinded and diced
400 g/14 oz/1 large can chopped
tomatoes
5 ml/1 tsp dried thyme
15 ml/1 tbsp tomato purée (paste)
1.5 ml/¹/₄ tsp caster (superfine)
sugar
Salt and freshly ground black pepper
225 g/8 oz fettuccine
Grated Mozzarella cheese

Fry (sauté) the onion and garlic in the oil until softened but not browned. Add the bacon and fry, stirring, for 2 minutes. Add the remaining ingredients, except the pasta and cheese, bring to the boil, reduce the heat and simmer for about 10 minutes until pulpy. Meanwhile, cook the pasta according to the packet directions. Drain and return to the saucepan. Add the sauce, toss well and serve with grated Mozzarella cheese sprinkled over.

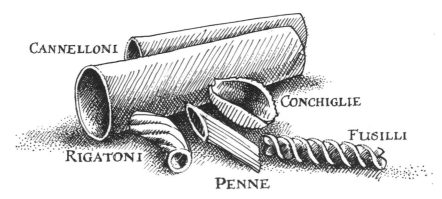

CANNELLONI

CONCHIGLIE

FUSILLI

RIGATONI

PENNE

Pork Paprikash

15 ml/1 tbsp oil
1 onion, chopped
350 g/12 oz pork fillet, diced
15 ml/1 tbsp paprika
190 g/6³/₄ oz/1 small can
   pimientos, drained and sliced
150 ml/¹/₄ pt/²/₃ cup chicken stock
Pinch of light brown sugar
Salt and white pepper
15 ml/1 tbsp plain (all-purpose)
   flour
15 ml/1 tbsp water
150 ml/¹/₄ pt/²/₃ cup soured (dairy-
   sour) cream
Buttered noodles
Crisp fried onion rings

Heat the oil in a saucepan and fry (sauté) the onion until soft but not brown. Add the meat and cook, stirring, for 4 minutes. Add the paprika and fry for 1 minute. Add the pimientos and stock. Season with the sugar and a little salt and pepper. Bring to the boil, reduce the heat, part-cover and simmer gently for 15 minutes. Blend the flour with the water and stir into the pan. Cook, stirring for 2 minutes. Stir in the cream and heat through. Taste and re-season if necessary. Spoon over the buttered noodles and garnish with crisp fried onion rings.

Chow Mein Supper

8 spring onions (scallions)
45 ml/3 tbsp sunflower oil
6 streaky bacon rashers (slices),
   rinded and cut into thin strips
2 celery sticks, cut into matchsticks
100 g/4 oz/2 cups button
   mushrooms, sliced
100 g/4 oz/¹/₂ small can bamboo
   shoots, cut into matchsticks
45 ml/3 tbsp soy sauce
150 ml/¹/₄ pt/²/₃ cup chicken stock
50 g/2 oz/¹/₂ cup peeled prawns
   (shrimp) (optional)
5 ml/1 tsp cornflour (cornstarch)
15 ml/1 tbsp dry sherry
225 g/8 oz chow mein noodles or
   spaghetti
A little butter
Prawn crackers

Trim the spring onions and cut into 2.5 cm/1 in lengths. Heat the oil in a large saucepan. Add the spring onions and bacon and fry (sauté), stirring, for 2 minutes. Add the celery and mushrooms and fry for a further 2 minutes, stirring. Add the bamboo shoots, soy sauce and chicken stock. Bring to the boil, part-cover and simmer gently for 5 minutes. Stir in the prawns, if using. Blend the cornflour with the sherry and stir into the sauce. Simmer, stirring, for 1 minute. Cook the noodles according to the packet directions. Drain and dry on kitchen paper. Fry the noodles in butter for 2–3 minutes, stirring. Add to the sauce and simmer for 3–5 minutes before serving with prawn crackers.

Cinnamon Pork

4 pork chops or cutlets
120 ml/4 fl oz/¹/₂ cup olive oil
45 ml/3 tbsp chopped mint
15 ml/1 tbsp lemon juice
5 ml/1 tsp ground cinnamon
1 lemon, sliced

Place the pork in a shallow dish. Mix together the oil, mint, lemon juice and cinnamon. Pour over the chops and leave to marinate for 2 hours. Lift the chops from the marinade. Grill (broil) for about 12 minutes each side, depending on thickness, brushing with marinade as they cook. Serve garnished with lemon slices.

Bratwurst with Tomato and Herb Sauce

450 ml/³/₄ pt/2 cups passata (sieved
tomatoes)
2 garlic cloves, crushed
5 ml/1 tsp dried oregano
5 ml/1 tsp dried rosemary
Salt and freshly ground black pepper
450 g/1 lb Bratwurst or good quality
English sausages

Mix together the passata, garlic, oregano, rosemary, salt and pepper. Brush over the sausages. Grill (broil) for about 15–20 minutes, turning regularly and brushing with more sauce. Meanwhile, heat the remaining sauce to serve with the sausages.

Gammon Steaks in Ale

4 gammon steaks
300 ml/¹/₂ pt/1¹/₄ cups light ale
4 onions, sliced
1 bay leaf
Salt and freshly ground black pepper
60 ml/4 tbsp black treacle (molasses)
15 ml/1 tbsp lemon juice
30 ml/2 tbsp olive oil

Place the gammon steaks in a shallow dish. Mix together the beer, onions, bay leaf, salt and pepper. Pour over the meat and leave to marinate for at least 2 hours. Lift the meat from the marinade, then strain the onions, retaining the liquid. Boil the marinade vigorously until reduced by half. Stir in the treacle and lemon juice. Heat the oil and fry (sauté) the onions until soft and golden brown. Brush the gammon with the reduced marinade and grill (broil) for about 20 minutes, turning and basting with the marinade during cooking. Cover with the onions and any remaining hot marinade and serve.

Pork Chops with Orange and Wine Sauce

SERVES 4

4 pork chops
15 ml/1 tbsp sunflower oil
2.5 ml/^{1}/$_2$ tsp salt
Pinch of black pepper
150 ml/^{1}/$_4$ pt/^{2}/$_3$ cup white wine
6.5 ml/1^1/$_4$ tsp cornflour (cornstarch)
1.5 ml/^{1}/$_4$ tsp ground cinnamon
250 ml/8 fl oz/1 cup orange juice
Grated rind and sliced flesh of 1
    orange
4 whole cloves

Fry (sauté) the chops in the oil for about 4 minutes each side. Add the salt, pepper and the wine, cover and simmer for about 20 minutes. Meanwhile, mix together the cornflour, cinnamon, half the orange juice, the orange rind and the orange slices. Remove the chops and keep warm. Add the remaining orange juice to the pan with the cloves and cook until the liquid is reduced by half, then remove the cloves and add the cornflour mixture. Boil for 2 minutes, stirring all the time. Pour over the chops and serve.

Spiced Pork with Cider

SERVES 4

450 g/1 lb pork fillet
Good pinch of ground ginger
Good pinch of mixed (apple pie)
    spice
Good pinch of cayenne
^{1}/$_2$ onion, thinly sliced
1 green (bell) pepper, seeded and
    thinly sliced
30 ml/2 tbsp sunflower oil
50 g/2 oz/^{1}/$_4$ cup unsalted (sweet)
    butter
175 g/6 oz/3 cups button
    mushrooms, quartered
150 ml/^{1}/$_4$ pt/^{2}/$_3$ cup cider
150 ml/^{1}/$_4$ pt/^{2}/$_3$ cup double (heavy)
    cream
Salt and freshly ground black pepper

Cut the pork fillet into 5 mm/^{1}/$_4$ in slices, then into thin strips and dust with the spices. Gently fry (sauté) the onion and pepper in the oil and butter until softened. Increase the heat and add the pork and mushrooms. Cook for 5 minutes, stirring, then pour in the cider and cook until reduced slightly. Lower the heat and blend in the cream. Reheat slowly for about 5–10 minutes until the sauce thickens. Season to taste. Serve hot.

Rolled Pork Slices

6 slices pork fillet
100 g/4 oz/1 cup raw cured ham
 (Westphalian, Parma, Serrano),
 chopped
25 g/1 oz/¹/₄ cup pine nuts, chopped
50 g/2 oz/¹/₃ cup sultanas (golden
 raisins), chopped
45 ml/3 tbsp fresh breadcrumbs
50 g/2 oz/¹/₂ cup capers, rinsed and
 dried
Salt and freshly ground black pepper
45 ml/3 tbsp olive oil
30 ml/2 tbsp white wine
45 ml/3 tbsp passata (sieved
 tomatoes)
1 green chilli, seeded and finely
 chopped

Beat the pork slices until they are very thin. Mix together the ham, nuts, sultanas, breadcrumbs and capers. Season the pork slices and spoon on the stuffing mixture. Roll the slices up and secure with cocktail sticks (toothpicks). Fry (sauté) the rolls in the olive oil until brown. Pour over the wine, add the passata and chilli. Cover and cook very gently for 1 hour.

Mediterranean Baked Pork

750 g/1¹/₂ lb pork fillet, trimmed
2 eggs, beaten
75 g/3 oz/³/₄ cup grated Parmesan
 cheese
50 g/2 oz/¹/₂ cup plain (all-purpose)
 flour
30 ml/2 tbsp olive oil
2 onions, chopped
1 garlic clove, crushed
4 bacon rashers (slices), rinded
400 g/14 oz/1 large can tomatoes
50 g/2 oz/¹/₄ cup tomato purée
 (paste)
Worcestershire sauce
5 ml/1 tsp dried mixed herbs
250 ml/8 fl oz/1 cup chicken stock
Salt and freshly ground black pepper
Cayenne
75 g/3 oz/³/₄ cup grated Cheddar
 cheese

Cut the pork fillet into chunks and dip into the egg. Mix half the Parmesan with the flour and use to coat the meat, then fry (sauté) the chunks in half of the oil. Meanwhile, make the tomato sauce by frying the onions, garlic and bacon in the remaining oil. Add the tomatoes, tomato purée, a good shake of Worcestershire sauce, herbs and stock. Season to taste with a little salt, pepper and cayenne. Cook for about 10 minutes. Layer the meat and sauce in a casserole dish (Dutch oven) and, before adding the last layer of sauce, sprinkle the Cheddar over. Cover with the last layer of sauce and then top with the remaining Parmesan. Bake for 1¹/₄ hours at 190°C/ 375°F/gas mark 5.

Nutty-topped Pork

SERVES 4

4 pork chops or steaks
10 ml/2 tsp mustard powder
20 ml/4 tsp light brown sugar
15 ml/1 tbsp salted peanuts,
  chopped
5 ml/1 tsp Worcestershire sauce
5 ml/1 tsp wine vinegar
2.5 ml/¹/₂ tsp salt
5 ml/1 tsp melted butter

Grill (broil) or fry (sauté) the pork until nearly cooked. Mix all the other ingredients together and spread over the chops. Grill until they are golden brown. Alternatively, you can bake them in the oven at 200°C/400°F/gas mark 6 for about 20 minutes until the topping is just golden brown.

Pork Tenderloin with Mushrooms

SERVES 6

750 g/1¹/₂ lb pork tenderloin
30 ml/2 tbsp oil
15 ml/1 tbsp lemon juice
Salt and freshly ground black pepper
1 garlic clove, crushed
50 g/2 oz/¹/₄ cup unsalted (sweet)
  butter
1 onion, finely sliced
175 g/6 oz/3 cups button mushrooms,
  finely sliced
30 ml/2 tbsp dry sherry
150 ml/¹/₄ pt/²/₃ cup double (heavy)
  cream
Chopped parsley

Cut the meat into 2 cm/³/₄ in slices. Lay the slices between clingfilm (plastic wrap) or greaseproof (waxed) paper and beat flat with a rolling pin. Arrange the slices in a shallow dish. Mix the oil and lemon juice, season with black pepper, add the garlic and spoon this marinade over the meat. Leave for a minimum of 30 minutes or preferably overnight, turning occasionally. Melt half the butter and fry (sauté) the onion until soft but not brown. Add the mushrooms and fry for 3 minutes. Remove from the pan and keep warm. Drain the pork from the marinade and fry gently in the remaining butter for 3–4 minutes, turning once. Transfer to a serving dish and keep warm. Add the sherry to the pan and heat until it reduces by half. Return the onions and mushrooms to the pan and season with salt and pepper to taste. Stir in the cream and heat gently. Remove from the heat and pour over the pork. Sprinkle with chopped parsley to garnish.

Easy Pork and Apricot Casserole

SERVES 4

1 onion, chopped
2 rashers (slices) bacon, chopped
25 g/1 oz/2 tbsp butter
750 g/1¹/₂ lb stewing pork, diced
25 g/1 oz/2 tbsp seasoned flour
30 ml/2 tbsp tomato purée (paste)
300 ml/¹/₂ pt/1¹/₄ cups white wine
1 chicken stock cube
50 g/2 oz dried apricots,
  chopped

Fry (sauté) the onion and bacon in the butter for 2–3 minutes. Toss the pork in the seasoned flour and brown in the pan. Add the tomato purée, wine, stock cube and apricots, stirring until thickened. Transfer to a casserole (Dutch oven) and cook in the oven at 160°C/325°F/gas mark 3 for 2–2¹/₂ hours or until really tender.

Herby Roast Pork with Cream Sauce

SERVES 6

5 ml/1 tsp mixed dried herbs
1.5 kg/3 lb pork loin, boned and
    rolled
A little sunflower oil
Salt and freshly ground black pepper
60 ml/4 tbsp sweet white vermouth
1 vegetable stock cube
150 ml/^{1}/$_4$ pt/^{2}/$_3$ cup single (light)
    cream

Sprinkle the herbs over the pork. Place on a trivet in a roasting tin (pan). Score the rind then rub oil and salt over it. Roast at 200°C/425°F/gas mark 7 for about 1^1/$_2$–2 hours until cooked through. Remove the meat from the tin and let it rest until ready to carve. To make the sauce, pour off and discard the fat from the tin, leaving any juices. Add the vermouth and stock cube. Bring to the boil, stirring constantly. Add the cream and continue to heat gently. If too thick, add a little water: if too thin add some cornflour (cornstarch) mixed with a little water. Season to taste. Carve the meat and serve with the sauce.

Spanish Pork Stew

SERVES 4

75 g/3 oz/^{1}/$_3$ cup butter
45 ml/3 tbsp olive oil
900 g/2 lb pork shoulder, cubed
1 Spanish onion, thinly sliced
2 garlic cloves, thinly sliced
1 green (bell) pepper, seeded and
    sliced
100 g/4 oz/2 cups button mushrooms,
    sliced
400 g/14 oz/1 large can tomatoes
225 ml/8 fl oz/1 cup dry white wine
10 ml/2 tsp dried oregano
5 ml/1 tsp dried rosemary
Finely grated rind of 1 lemon
Salt and freshly ground black pepper
450 g/1 lb courgettes (zucchini),
    sliced

Use a third of the butter and two thirds of the oil to fry (sauté) the pork until lightly browned. Set the meat aside. To the fat remaining in the pan, add half the remaining butter and the remaining olive oil. Add the onion, garlic and green pepper and fry for 8–9 minutes. Stir in the mushrooms and the can of tomatoes and cook for 3–4 minutes. Add the wine, oregano, rosemary and lemon rind and season with salt and pepper. Bring to the boil and stir to remove any sediment from the pan sides, then add the meat. Bring back to the boil, reduce the heat, cover and simmer for 2 hours (or cook in the oven for 2 hours at 160°C/325°F/gas mark 3). Meanwhile, fry the courgettes in the remaining butter until lightly coloured but not too soft. Add to the stew 5 minutes before serving. No extra vegetables are necessary.

Cidered Pork Fillet

750 g/1¹/₂ lb pork tenderloin
30 ml/2 tbsp olive oil
15 g/¹/₂ oz/1 tbsp butter
1 onion, chopped
1 red (bell) pepper, seeded and sliced into rings
15 ml/1 tbsp ground coriander (cilantro)
15 g/¹/₂ oz/2 tbsp plain (all-purpose) flour
300 ml/¹/₂ pt/1¹/₄ cups dry cider
150 ml/¹/₄ pt/²/₃ cup vegetable stock
Chopped coriander

Cut the pork into 1 cm/¹/₂ in slices and beat flat with a rolling pin between clingfilm (plastic wrap) or greaseproof (waxed) paper. Fry (sauté) in 15 ml/1 tbsp of the oil and the butter for 2 minutes on each side. Transfer to a casserole (Dutch oven). Fry the onion using the remaining oil and after 1 minute add the red pepper and cook for a further 3–4 minutes. Stir in the ground coriander and flour. Add the cider and stock. Bring to the boil and add to the casserole. Cook for 15 minutes in the oven at 180°C/350°F/gas mark 4, or until the pork is tender and cooked through.

Liver Hotpot

450 g/1 lb pigs' liver, cut into chunks
30 ml/2 tbsp milk
30 ml/2 tbsp sunflower oil
3 large onions, sliced
1 cooking (tart) apple, sliced
15 ml/1 tbsp plain (all-purpose) flour
1 beef stock cube
450 ml/³/₄ pt/2 cups boiling water
10 ml/2 tsp Worcestershire sauce
5 ml/1 tsp dried sage
Salt and freshly ground black pepper
450 g/1 lb potatoes, scrubbed and thinly sliced
15 ml/¹/₂ oz/1 tbsp butter

Soak the liver in the milk for 15 minutes. Drain, then dry on kitchen paper. Heat the oil in a flameproof casserole (Dutch oven) and fry (sauté) the onions, stirring, for 3 minutes until lightly golden. Add the liver and continue to fry quickly, stirring, until browned all over. Stir in the apple and the flour and cook, stirring, for 1 minute. Crumble the stock cube over, then stir in the water and Worcestershire sauce. Bring to the boil, stirring. Add the sage and a little salt and pepper. Lay the potatoes on top, overlapping the slices, and dot with butter. Cover with foil and bake in the oven at 190°C/375°F/gas mark 5 for 30 minutes. Remove the foil and cook for a further 30 minutes until the potatoes are golden and the liver is tender.

Sherried Pork with Spring Onions

SERVES 4

*450 g/1 lb pork fillet, cut into thin
strips*
*45 ml/3 tbsp plain (all-purpose)
flour*
Salt and freshly ground black pepper
40 g/1¹/₂ oz/3 tbsp butter
*1 bunch of spring onions (scallions),
cut into 2.5 cm/1 in diagonal
slices*
*50 g/2 oz/1 cup button mushrooms,
sliced*
30 ml/2 tbsp medium-dry sherry
*300 ml/¹/₂ pt/1¹/₄ cups pork or
chicken stock*
15 ml/1 tbsp tomato purée (paste)
Pinch of dried marjoram

Toss the pork in the flour, seasoned
with a little salt and pepper. Melt the
butter in a large frying pan (skillet), add
the onions and mushrooms and fry (sauté)
for 2 minutes, stirring. Remove from the
pan with a draining spoon. Add the pork
and fry quickly until browned on all sides.
Stir in the onion and mushroom mixture
and the remaining ingredients and simmer
gently for about 8 minutes until the pork
is cooked through and tender.

Sausage and Bacon Kebabs

SERVES 4

*8 rashers (slices) streaky bacon,
rinded and halved*
16 cocktail sausages
*1 courgette (zucchini), cut into 8
chunks*
*1 small red (bell) pepper, cut into
chunks*
Sunflower oil
5 ml/1 tsp dried oregano
*Ready-prepared chilli salsa from a
jar*

Stretch the halved bacon rashers with
the back of a knife. Wrap each half
tightly round a sausage. Thread on
skewers alternately with the courgette and
pepper. Lay on a grill (broiler) rack and
brush all over with oil. Sprinkle with
oregano and grill (broil) for about 10
minutes until golden brown and cooked
through, turning occasionally and
brushing with more oil if necessary. Serve
with chilli salsa.

Highland Stuffed Peppers

SERVES 4

4 large green (bell) peppers
175 g/6 oz/³/₄ cup meat dripping or
white vegetable fat (shortening)
2 large onions, finely chopped
8 rashers (slices) smoked streaky
bacon, rinded and finely diced
100 g/4 oz/1 cup medium oatmeal
5 ml/1 tsp yeast extract
100 g/4 oz/2 cups fresh breadcrumbs
Salt and freshly ground black pepper
15 ml/1 tbsp chopped parsley
100 g/4 oz/1 cup grated Cheddar
cheese

Cut the stalk ends off the peppers and remove and discard the seeds. Boil in water for 5 minutes. Drain, rinse with cold water and drain again. Melt the dripping in a saucepan. Add the onions and bacon and fry (sauté), stirring for 5 minutes. Sprinkle in the oatmeal and cook, stirring, over a gentle heat for 10 minutes. Add the remaining ingredients except the cheese and pack into the peppers. Place in a roasting tin (pan) containing enough boiling water to just cover the base of the tin. Cover with foil and bake at 180°C/350°F/gas mark 4 for 20 minutes. Remove the foil, sprinkle with the cheese and bake for a further 10 minutes or until the cheese has melted and the peppers are tender.

Bacon and Mushroom Soufflé

SERVES 4

4 rashers (slices) streaky bacon,
rinded and diced
100 g/4 oz/2 cups button
mushrooms, sliced
50 g/2 oz/¹/₄ cup butter
20 g/³/₄ oz/3 tbsp plain (all-purpose)
flour
150 ml/¹/₄ pt/²/₃ cup milk
2.5 ml/¹/₂ tsp mixed dried herbs
15 ml/1 tbsp chopped parsley
30 ml/2 tbsp grated Parmesan
cheese
Salt and freshly ground black pepper
3 eggs, separated

Fry (sauté) the bacon and mushrooms in the butter for 3 minutes, stirring. Add the flour and cook for 1 minute, stirring. Remove from the heat, blend in the milk, then bring to the boil, stirring until thick. Remove from the heat. Stir in the herbs, cheese and a little salt and pepper. Beat in the egg yolks. Whisk the egg whites until stiff. Add 15 ml/1 tbsp of the whites to the sauce and beat in well. Fold in the remaining whisked whites with a metal spoon. Turn into a greased 1.2 litre/2 pt/5 cup soufflé dish. Bake in the oven at 200°C/400°F/gas mark 6 for about 30 minutes until well risen and golden. Serve straight away.

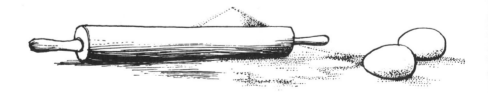

LAMB

One of the most versatile of meats, Lamb lends itself to dishes from all over the world.

Greek-style Lamb Kebabs

SERVES 4

350 g/12 oz lamb neck fillet
15 ml/1 tbsp olive oil
10 ml/2 tsp red wine vinegar
5 ml/1 tsp dried oregano
Salt and freshly ground black pepper
¹/₂ green (bell) pepper
8 button mushrooms
Buttered rice

Cut the meat into cubes. Put in a bowl. Drizzle with the oil, vinegar, herbs and seasoning. Toss and leave for at least 10 minutes (longer if possible). Cut the pepper into 8 pieces. Thread the meat on to 4 skewers, alternating with the mushrooms and pepper pieces. Grill (broil) for about 10 minutes until golden and cooked through, turning once or twice and brushing with any leftover marinade. Serve hot on a bed of buttered rice.

Rosie's Cutlets

SERVES 4

25 g/1 oz/2 tbsp butter
8 thin lamb cutlets
1 garlic clove, crushed
60 ml/4 tbsp water
Salt and freshly ground black pepper
Watercress

Melt the butter in a frying pan (skillet). Add the cutlets and brown on both sides. Add the remaining ingredients except the watercress, cover with foil or a lid and simmer for 10 minutes. Transfer to a warmed serving dish. Garnish with the watercress and serve.

Eastern Lamb

SERVES 4

1 onion, sliced
15 ml/1 tbsp oil
225 g/8 oz/2 cups cooked lamb, diced
1 garlic clove, crushed
2.5 ml/¹/₂ tsp ground ginger
2.5 ml/¹/₂ tsp ground cumin
2.5 ml/¹/₂ tsp ground coriander (cilantro)
7.5 ml/1¹/₂ tsp turmeric
150 ml/¹/₄ pt/²/₃ cup plain yoghurt
Salt and freshly ground black pepper
1 packet pilau rice
Desiccated (shredded) coconut
Currants

Fry (sauté) the onion in the oil for 3 minutes until turning golden. Add the lamb and the remaining ingredients, except the rice, coconut and currants. Simmer for about 20 minutes, stirring occasionally until almost dry (the mixture will curdle and look watery at first). Meanwhile, cook the rice according to the packet directions. Serve the lamb on a bed of pilau rice, with desiccated coconut and currants sprinkled over.

Lemon Glazed Cutlets

SERVES 4

4 lamb cutlets
15 g/1 tbsp seasoned plain (all-
purpose) flour
25 g/1 oz/2 tbsp butter
Grated rind and juice of 1 lemon
10 ml/2 tsp caster (superfine) sugar
Parsley sprigs

Coat the lamb cutlets in the seasoned flour, tapping off any excess. Fry (sauté) in the butter for about 10 minutes until browned and cooked through, turning once. Remove and keep warm. Drain off all but 15 ml/1 tbsp of the fat from the pan. Add the lemon rind and juice and the sugar and heat through until melted. Spoon over the cutlets, garnish with parsley and serve immediately.

Orange Glazed Cutlets

SERVES 4

Prepare as for Lemon Glazed Cutlets but substitute an orange for the lemon and add 5 ml/1 tsp chopped mint to the seasoned flour.

Liver with Bacon and Onion Sauce

SERVES 4

8 bacon rashers (slices)
15 ml/1 tbsp oil
4 or 8 slices lambs' liver
3 onions, roughly chopped
150 ml/¹/₄ pt/²/₃ cup water
20 g/³/₄ oz/3 tbsp plain (all-
purpose) flour
150 ml/¹/₄ pt/²/₃ cup milk
Salt and freshly ground black pepper
Chopped parsley

Dry-fry the bacon until browned on both sides in a frying pan (skillet). Transfer to a serving dish and keep warm. Heat the oil in the same pan and fry (sauté) the liver for about 4 minutes, turning once until browned and just cooked. Meanwhile, boil the onions in the water for 4 minutes in a covered pan. Blend the flour and milk, add to the pan and boil for 2 minutes, stirring. Season to taste. Garnish the liver and bacon with parsley and serve with the onion sauce.

Quick Moussaka

SERVES 4

1 onion, finely chopped
1 garlic clove, crushed
350 g/12 oz/3 cups minced (ground)
lamb
150 ml/¹/₄ pt/²/₃ cup lamb or chicken
stock
30 ml/2 tbsp tomato purée (paste)
5 ml/1 tsp ground cinnamon
5 ml/1 tsp dried oregano
Salt and freshly ground black pepper
1 aubergine (eggplant), sliced
150 ml/¹/₄ pt/²/₃ cup plain yoghurt
1 egg
75 g/3 oz/³/₄ cup grated Cheddar
cheese

Fry (sauté) the onion, garlic and mince together in a saucepan, stirring until the grains of meat are brown and separate. Add the stock and boil for about 5 minutes until nearly all the liquid has evaporated. Stir in the tomato purée, cinnamon, and oregano. Season to taste and simmer for 5 minutes. Meanwhile, boil the aubergine in salted water for about 5 minutes or until tender. Drain. Layer the meat mixture and aubergine in a 1.5 litre/2¹/₂ pt/6 cup flameproof dish, finishing with a layer of aubergine. Beat together the yoghurt, egg and cheese and spoon over. Place under a moderately hot grill (broiler) for about 5 minutes until the topping is set and golden.

Saucy Lamb with Capers

SERVES 4
---

75 g/3 oz/¹/₃ cup butter or margarine
3 slices bread, cubed
350 g/12 oz/3 cups marrow (squash), peeled and diced
100 g/4 oz/2 cups button mushrooms, quartered
175 g/6 oz/1¹/₂ cups cooked lamb, diced
15 ml/1 tbsp plain (all-purpose) flour
300 ml/¹/₂ pt/1¹/₄ cups chicken or lamb stock
15 ml/1 tbsp capers, chopped
15 ml/1 tbsp chopped parsley
1 egg, beaten
Salt and freshly ground black pepper

Melt 50 g/2 oz/¹/₄ cup of the butter or margarine in a pan. Toss the bread in it to coat, then remove from the pan and set aside. Melt the remaining fat in the pan. Add the marrow and mushrooms. Cover and cook gently for 5–10 minutes until the vegetables are tender, shaking the pan occasionally. Add the lamb and flour and cook, stirring, for 1 minute. Blend in the stock and add the capers. Bring to the boil and cook for 2 minutes, stirring. Blend in the parsley and egg and season to taste. Spoon into 4 fireproof individual dishes. Top with bread and place under a hot grill (broiler) until browned.

Saucy Lamb with Gherkins

SERVES 4

Prepare as for Saucy Lamb with Capers but substitute 1 large diced aubergine for the marrow and chopped gherkins (cornichons) for the capers. Omit the mushrooms if preferred.

Piquant Lambs' Liver

SERVES 4
---

2 onions, finely chopped
25 g/1 oz/2 tbsp butter
15 ml/1 tbsp olive oil
1 wineglass red vermouth
450 g/1 lb lambs' liver, trimmed and cut into strips
1 rosemary sprig
1 thyme sprig
Salt and freshly ground black pepper
450 g/1 lb/2 cups cooked mashed potato
Chopped parsley

Fry (sauté) the onions in the butter and oil until soft but not brown. Add the vermouth and simmer until reduced by half. Add the liver and herbs and cook quickly for about 2–3 minutes until brown but not dry. Season to taste. Discard the herbs. Meanwhile, spoon the potato into a nest on a flameproof serving plate. Place under a hot grill (broiler) until golden. Spoon the liver mixture into the centre. Sprinkle with parsley and serve.

Somerset Lamb

SERVES 4

1 onion, thinly sliced
1 cooking (tart) apple, sliced
15 ml/1 tbsp oil
4 lamb chump chops
20 g/³/₄ oz/3 tbsp plain (all- purpose)
flour
300 ml/¹/₂ pt/1¹/₄ cups cider or apple
juice
15 ml/1 tbsp chopped mint
Salt and freshly ground black pepper
Mint sprigs

Fry (sauté) the onion and apple in the oil for 3–4 minutes until softened. Remove from the pan. Trim any excess fat from the chops. Fry for abut 10–15 minutes, turning once, until just cooked through. Transfer the onion, apple and chops to a warmed serving dish, keep warm. Blend the flour with a little of the cider or apple juice. Stir in the remainder and pour into the pan. Add the mint, bring to the boil and cook for 2 minutes, stirring. Season to taste. Spoon the sauce over the lamb, garnish with mint sprigs and serve.

Tiddley Kidneys

SERVES 4

25 g/1 oz/2 tbsp butter or margarine
8 lambs' kidneys, cored and
quartered
100 g/4 oz/2 cups button mushrooms,
sliced
2 onions, sliced
45 ml/3 tbsp single (light) cream
15 ml/1 tbsp sherry
Salt and freshly ground black pepper
Buttered noodles
Chopped parsley

Melt the fat in a frying pan (skillet). Add the kidneys, mushrooms and onions. Cover with foil or a lid and cook, stirring occasionally, for 10 minutes. Add the cream, sherry and seasoning. Heat through. Spoon on to buttered noodles and sprinkle with chopped parsley.

Mediterranean Lamb Chops

SERVES 4

4 lamb chops
15 ml/1 tbsp oil
1 onion, chopped
Salt and freshly ground black pepper
298 g/10¹/₂ oz/1 small can
condensed tomato soup
5 ml/1 tsp dried basil
Black olives
Buttered noodles

Fry (sauté) the chops in the oil on each side to brown. Remove from the pan and fry the onions for 3 minutes until soft and turning golden. Drain off the fat from the pan. Return the chops, sprinkle with salt and pepper and spoon the soup over. Add the basil. Bring to the boil, reduce the heat, cover and simmer very gently for 45 minutes or until the chops are really tender. Stir gently, occasionally, and add a little water if necessary. Garnish with black olives and serve on buttered noodles.

Greek-style Lamb Lunch

SERVES 4

4 frozen minced (ground) lamb
*   steaks*
150 ml/¹/₄ pt/²/₃ cup plain yoghurt
1 garlic clove, crushed
5 ml/1 tsp dried mint
Salt and freshly ground black pepper
4 pitta breads
Shredded lettuce
Grated cucumber
Chopped tomato

Grill (broil), fry (sauté) or microwave the lamb steaks according to the packet directions. Meanwhile, mix the yoghurt with the garlic, mint and a little salt and pepper. Grill (broil) or microwave the pittas briefly to warm. Make a slit along one long edge of each and open up to form a pocket. Put a lamb steak in each pocket. Spoon in the yoghurt mixture and garnish each with shredded lettuce, grated cucumber and chopped tomato.

Lambs' Tongues in Caper Sauce

SERVES 4

350 g/12 oz/1 large can lambs'
*   tongues*
1 packet white sauce mix
300 ml/¹/₂ pt/1¹/₄ cups milk or water
*   (according to packet)*
15 ml/1 tbsp capers, chopped
450 g/1 lb/2 cups cooked mashed
*   potato*
15 ml/1 tbsp chopped parsley

Cut the lambs' tongues into neat slices. Make up the white sauce according to the packet directions. Stir in the capers. Add the meat to the sauce and heat through for about 5 minutes until piping hot. Meanwhile, spoon the mashed potato into 'nests' in 4 individual flameproof dishes. Brown under a hot grill (broiler). Spoon the meat and sauce into the centre of the nests, garnish with chopped parsley and serve.

Kidney and Mustard Sauce Boats

SERVES 4

1 French stick
50 g/2 oz/¹/₄ cup butter
4 lambs' kidneys
15 ml/1 tbsp olive oil
30 ml/2 tbsp brandy
15 ml/1 tbsp Dijon mustard
60 ml/4 tbsp double (heavy) cream
Salt and freshly ground black pepper
45 ml/3 tbsp snipped chives

Cut the French stick in half, then in half lengthways. Pull out most of the soft bread to form 'boats'. Spread the insides with 15 g/¹/₂ oz/1 tbsp of the butter. Place on a baking sheet and bake in the oven at 190°C /375°F /gas mark 5 for 10 minutes until crisp. Meanwhile, peel off any skin on the kidneys, then cut in halves. Snip out the cores with scissors, then snip the kidneys into small pieces. Heat the remaining butter and the oil in a frying pan (skillet). Add the kidneys and cook, stirring, for 2–3 minutes until browned and tender. Do not overcook. Add the brandy and ignite. When the flames die down, add the mustard and cream and heat through, stirring until well blended. Season to taste and stir in half the chives. Place the bread boats on warm serving plates, spoon in the kidneys in sauce and serve sprinkled with the remaining chives.

Lamb Goulash

1 onion, chopped
15 ml/1 tbsp oil
400 g/14 oz/1 large can chopped tomatoes
15 ml/1 tbsp tomato purée (paste)
2.5 ml/¹/₂ tsp caster (superfine) sugar
150 ml/¹/₄ pt/²/₃ cup chicken or beef stock
15 ml/1 tbsp paprika
225 g/8 oz/2 cups cooked lamb, diced
Salt and freshly ground black pepper
50 g/2 oz/¹/₂ cup frozen peas or cut green beans
350 g/12 oz flat, wide noodles (e.g. papardelle)
Soured (dairy sour) cream
Caraway seeds

Fry (sauté) the onion in the oil for 2 minutes until softened slightly but not browned. Add the tomatoes, tomato purée, sugar, stock, paprika, the lamb and a little salt and pepper. Bring to the boil, reduce the heat and simmer gently for about 30 minutes until pulpy and the meat is really tender. Add the peas or beans for the last 5 minutes cooking time. Taste and re-season if necessary. Meanwhile, cook the noodles according to the packet directions. Drain and pile on to warmed serving plates. Spoon over the goulash and add a swirl of soured cream and a sprinkling of caraway seeds before serving.

Lamb Armagnac

Grated rind and juice of 1 orange
15 ml/1 tbsp chopped basil
Pinch of dried oregano
Freshly ground black pepper
4 lamb chops
45 ml/3 tbsp Armagnac or brandy

Mix together the orange juice, basil, oregano and pepper. Pour over the chops and leave to marinate for 1 hour. Place on a grill (broiler) rack. Grill (broil) for 5–8 minutes each side until cooked to taste, basting with any remaining marinade. Place on a serving dish, spoon over the Armagnac or brandy and sprinkle with orange rind.

Crusted Lamb Cutlets

50 g/2 oz/1 cup fresh breadcrumbs
2.5 ml/¹/₂ tsp dried marjoram
2.5 ml/¹/₂ tsp dried rosemary
Salt and freshly ground black pepper
15 ml/1 tbsp dry sherry
30 ml/2 tbsp olive oil
4 lamb cutlets

Mix together the breadcrumbs, marjoram, rosemary, salt and pepper. Stir in the sherry and enough of the oil to moisten the mixture. Brush the cutlets with the remaining oil, then press on half the breadcrumb mixture. Grill (broil) for about 5–7 minutes. Turn over and press on the remaining breadcrumb mixture. Grill until golden and cooked to your liking.

Photograph opposite: **Italian lamb (page 97) with sautéed potatoes**

Rosé Lamb

SERVES 4

4 lamb steaks
2 rosemary sprigs
150 ml/¹/₄ pt/²/₃ cup rosé wine
150 ml/¹/₄ pt/²/₃ cup lemon juice
150 ml/¹/₄ pt/²/₃ cup sunflower oil
3 garlic cloves, crushed
Salt and freshly ground black pepper

Place the lamb in a shallow dish with the rosemary. Mix together the remaining ingredients and pour over the meat. Leave to marinate for 2 hours. Grill (broil) the lamb for about 10 minutes each side, depending on thickness, until cooked to your liking, basting frequently with the marinade during cooking.

Italian Lamb

SERVES 4

750 g/1¹/₂ lb lamb fillet, cut into medallions 5 mm/¹/₄ in thick
30 ml/2 tbsp seasoned flour
45 ml/3 tbsp olive oil
25 g/1 oz/2 tbsp butter
1 garlic clove, crushed
100 g/4 oz/2 cups button mushrooms, sliced
75 g/3 oz Parma ham, cut into thin strips
10 ml/2 tsp Pesto Sauce (see page 252) or from a jar
Grated Parmesan cheese

Flatten the lamb medallions slightly with a meat mallet or rolling pin and dust with the seasoned flour. Quickly fry (sauté) them in half the oil and butter, turning once. Remove the lamb and keep warm. Using the remaining oil and butter, fry the garlic and mushrooms for 3 minutes, then add the ham and pesto and cook for a further minute. Return the lamb to the pan and cook, stirring everything together, for a further 2 minutes. Sprinkle with the Parmesan and serve.

Rosemary Roasted Lamb Fillets

SERVES 6

3 × 275 g/3 × 10 oz lamb fillets
2 large rosemary sprigs
45 ml/3 tbsp olive oil
12 garlic cloves, peeled but not crushed
Extra rosemary sprigs

Cut any big pieces of fat off the lamb and reserve. Strip the leaves from the 2 rosemary sprigs and put them with the lamb, oil and garlic in a dish. Leave to marinate overnight. Put the reserved lamb fat in a frying pan (skillet) and heat gently to extract the oil. Use this to quickly fry (sauté) the garlic and seal the lamb fillets on all sides. Place the garlic and fillets in a roasting tin (pan) and pour the marinade over. Roast at 200°C/400°F/gas mark 6 for 15 minutes (rare) or 20 minutes (medium). Carve into thick slices, garnish with sprigs of rosemary and surround with the roasted garlic cloves.

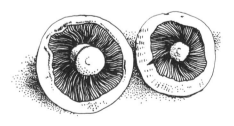

Photograph opposite: Chinese-style chicken with cashew nuts (page 107)

Mustard-Rosemary Lamb

SERVES 4

60 ml/4 tbsp chopped rosemary
1 garlic clove, crushed
5 ml/1 tsp mustard powder
5 ml/1 tsp dried oregano
Pinch of cayenne
Salt and freshly ground black pepper
4 or 8 lamb chops
30 ml/2 tbsp olive oil

Blend or grind together the rosemary, garlic, mustard, oregano, cayenne, and a little salt and pepper. Rub well into the lamb chops on all sides, then leave to stand for about 2 hours. Brush with oil and grill (broil) for about 10 minutes each side until cooked through.

Lamb with Curry Butter

SERVES 4

100 g/4 oz/¹/₂ cup unsalted (sweet)
butter, softened
4 spring onions (scallions) chopped
15 ml/1 tbsp curry powder
10 ml/2 tsp lemon juice
Salt and freshly ground black pepper
4 or 8 lamb cutlets or chops

Purée the butter, spring onions, curry powder and lemon juice in a blender or food processor until smooth. Season to taste with salt and pepper. Season the meat with salt and pepper and brush generously with the curry butter. Grill (broil) for about 8 minutes each side, brushing frequently with the flavoured butter.

Lamb Medallions with Cognac

SERVES 4

750 g/1¹/₂ lb lamb fillet, cut into
medallions 5 mm/¹/₄ in thick
30 ml/2 tbsp black peppercorns,
coarsely crushed
1.5 ml/¹/₄ tsp Salt
2 garlic cloves, crushed
50 g/2 oz/¹/₄ cup unsalted (sweet)
butter
60 ml/4 tbsp cognac

Flatten the lamb medallions slightly with a mallet or a rolling pin, coat with the crushed peppercorns and season with the salt. Quickly fry (sauté) them with the garlic in the butter. Add the Cognac to the pan and set alight. When the flames have died down, serve straight from the pan.

Roasted Soy Lamb Fillets

SERVES 4

2 × 350 g/2 × 12 oz lamb neck
fillets
Juice of 1 lime
30 ml/2 tbsp soy sauce
15 ml/1 tbsp olive oil
1 garlic clove, crushed

Trim the lamb of fat and sinews. Mix the remaining ingredients together and pour over the lamb. Leave to marinate for at least 12 hours. Remove the lamb from its marinade and roast on a rack in the oven at 230°C/450°F/gas mark 8 for 20 minutes (medium-rare) or 25 minutes (well done). Leave to rest for about 5 minutes before cutting into thin slices.

Lamb Chops in Port

SERVES 4

8 loin lamb chops or 4 chump
* chops*
100 g/4 oz/2 cups button mushrooms
15 ml/1 tbsp olive oil
1 onion, finely chopped
150 ml/¹/₄ pt/²/₃ cup port
150 ml/¹/₄ pt/²/₃ cup chicken stock
30 ml/2 tbsp redcurrant jelly (clear
* conserve)*
Salt and freshly ground black pepper

Fry (sauté) the chops and mushrooms in the oil until golden brown. Remove and set aside. Fry the onions gently in the same pan, stir in the port, stock, redcurrant jelly and seasoning. Boil for 2–3 minutes until the liquid begins to reduce slightly and thicken. Pour over the chops. Cook, covered, in the oven for 1¹/₄ hours at 180ºC/375ºF/gas mark 4 or gently on the hob for 45 minutes.

Highland Lamb

SERVES 4

225 g/8 oz lean lamb fillet
15 ml/1 tbsp whole black peppercorns
25 g/1 oz/2 tbsp butter
15 ml/1 tbsp sunflower oil
30 ml/2 tbsp Scotch whisky
5 ml/1 tsp French mustard
5 ml/1 tsp salt
45 ml/3 tbsp double (heavy) cream

Cut the lamb into 4 pieces and flatten to about 5 mm/¹/₄ in in thickness. Crush the peppercorns roughly and press well into the lamb on both sides. Heat the butter and oil and fry (sauté) the lamb pieces for about 6 minutes until cooked. Add the whisky to the pan and set alight.

When the flames have died down add the mustard, salt and cream and heat through. Do not boil. Serve straight away.

Tagine Barrogog Bis Basela

SERVES 4

550 g/1¹/₄ lb boned shoulder, leg or
* neck fillet of lamb, cut into large*
* pieces*
Salt
5 ml/1 tsp freshly ground black
* pepper*
1.5 ml/¹/₄ tsp saffron powder or
* turmeric*
2.5 ml/¹/₂ tsp ground ginger
1 garlic clove, crushed
1 small onion, grated
45 ml/3 tbsp finely chopped parsley
30 ml/2 tbsp oil
225 g/8 oz/1¹/₃ cups prunes, stoned
* (pitted) and chopped*
5 ml/1 tsp ground cinnamon
30 ml/2 tbsp clear honey
20 ml/4 tsp orange flower water
15 ml/1 tbsp chopped blanched
* almonds*

Put the lamb in a saucepan with a little salt, the pepper, saffron or tumeric, ginger, garlic, onion, parsley and 20 ml/4 tsp of the oil. Add enough water to cover and simmer, covered, for 1¹/₂ hours or until the meat is very tender. Add the prunes and cinnamon and cook for a further 15 minutes. Add the honey and the orange water and cook for a few more minutes until the sauce is quite thick. Just before serving, fry (sauté) the almonds in the remaining oil and sprinkle over the meat.

Braised Lamb with Herbes de Provence

SERVES 6

30 ml/2 tbsp olive oil
1.5 kg/3 lb boned shoulder of lamb
1 large onion, quartered
2 garlic cloves, halved
7.5 ml/1¹/₂ tsp herbes de Provence
600 ml/1 pt/2¹/₂ cups stock or water
60 ml/4 tbsp dry, red or white wine
2 large leeks, cut into short lengths
450 g/1 lb carrots, cut into short
  lengths
450 g/1 lb small potatoes, scrubbed

Heat the oil in a casserole (Dutch oven) and brown the meat on all sides. Add the onion and garlic with the herbs, stock or water and wine. Bring to the boil, cover and cook in the oven for 1 hour at 180°C/350°F/gas mark 4. Add the leeks and carrots to the casserole and cook for a further 30 minutes. Add the potatoes and cook for another 30 minutes. Skim the surface and serve immediately. No other vegetables are necessary.

Leg of Lamb in Red Wine

SERVES 6–8

2 kg/4¹/₂ lb leg of lamb
2 garlic cloves, cut into slivers
Small rosemary sprigs
15 ml/1 tbsp oil
Salt and freshly ground black pepper
10 ml/2 tsp ground ginger
50 g/2 oz/ ¹/₄ cup unsalted (sweet)
  butter
2 onions, sliced
2 carrots, chopped
4 thyme sprigs
300 ml/¹/₂ pt/1¹/₄ cups red wine
30 ml/2 tbsp redcurrant jelly (clear
  conserve)

Pierce the lamb with the point of a sharp knife and push garlic slivers and rosemary into these holes. Rub the skin with the oil, a little salt and pepper and the ginger. Melt the butter in a roasting tin (pan) and quickly brown the lamb all over. Remove from the tin and fry (sauté) the onions and carrots until golden brown. Put the thyme sprigs on top of the vegetables and the meat on top. Cover with foil. Roast at 220°C/425°F/gas mark 7 for 25 minutes. Pour the wine over, reduce the heat to 180°C/ 350°F/gas mark 4 and cook for a further 1¹/₄ hours, basting 2 or 3 times. Remove the joint, strain the cooking juices and add the redcurrant jelly. Boil until reduced by a third. Remove any fat from the juices and season if necessary. Pour into a sauce boat and serve with the lamb.

Moughal's Pilau

SERVES 4

175 g/6 oz/³/₄ cup basmati rice
30 ml/2 tbsp sunflower oil
1 large onion, thinly sliced
6 whole peppercorns
2.5 cm/1 in piece cinnamon stick
3 whole cloves
1 brown or green cardamom
225 g/8 oz/2 cups cooked lamb,
  diced
450 ml/³/₄ pt/2 cups water
2.5 ml/¹/₂ tsp salt

Wash and drain the rice. Heat the oil and fry (sauté) the onion with the peppercorns, cinnamon, cloves and cardamom until the onion is a dark reddish-brown. Add the meat and fry until the meat browns a little, stirring all the time. Add about 120 ml/4 fl oz/ ¹/₂ cup of the water and cook for 2 minutes to bring out the colour of the onion. Bring to the boil and stir until the liquid reduces by half. Add the rice, salt and the remaining water. Bring to the boil, reduce the heat and cook until the water has evaporated completely. Cover and leave to rest for about 5 minutes, then fluff up with a fork.

Quick Lamb Biryani

SERVES 4

30 ml/1 oz/2 tbsp butter
1 large onion, thinly sliced
5 ml/1 tsp curry paste
100 g/4 oz/1 cup cooked lamb, diced
5 ml/1 tsp ground coriander (cilantro)
5 ml/1 tsp ground cumin
1 tomato, finely chopped
5 ml/1 tsp salt
25 g/1 oz/¹⁄₆ cup sultanas (golden raisins)
225 g/8 oz/2 cups cooked basmati rice
45 ml/3 tbsp chopped coriander leaves
15 ml/1 tbsp toasted dessicated (shredded) coconut

Melt the butter and fry (sauté) the onion until golden brown. Mix the curry paste with 15 ml/1 tbsp of water and add to the onion along with the lamb, ground coriander, cumin, tomato and salt. Stir-fry for about 5 minutes. Add the sultanas, rice and coriander leaves and heat through. Sprinkle with toasted coconut before serving.

Lamb Kebabs with Spiced Apricots

SERVES 4

300 g/11 oz/scant 2 cups ready-to-eat dried apricots
450 g/1 lb lean lamb, cubed
75 ml/5 tbsp oil
Salt and freshly ground black pepper
1 onion, sliced
50 g/2 oz/¹⁄₃ cup sultanas (golden raisins)
50 g/2 oz/¹⁄₃ cup desiccated (shredded) coconut
60 ml/4 tbsp white wine vinegar
60 ml/4 tbsp apricot jam (conserve) or apple jelly (clear conserve)
45 ml/3 tbsp lemon juice
15 ml/1 tbsp cayenne

Halve 225 g/8 oz/1¹⁄₃ cups of the apricots. Thread on to soaked wooden skewers with the lamb. Brush with a little of the oil and season with salt and pepper. To make the sauce, heat 45 ml/3 tbsp of the oil and fry (sauté) the onion until soft but not brown. Chop the remaining apricots, add to the pan with the sultanas and coconut and stir over a low heat until well mixed. Add the vinegar, jam or jelly and simmer for 2 minutes, stirring. Add the lemon juice and cayenne and season to taste with salt and pepper. Grill (broil) the kebabs for about 6 minutes each side, turning regularly and brushing with more oil if necessary. Reheat the sauce and serve with the lamb.

Indian Lamb with Spinach

SERVES 4

Pinch of turmeric
Pinch of ground cinnamon
Pinch of ground ginger
5 ml/1 tsp garlic powder
Pinch of chilli powder
30 ml/2 tbsp sunflower oil
1 onion, halved and thinly sliced
75 ml/5 tbsp onion, grated or
    minced (ground)
60 ml/4 tbsp finely chopped
    coriander (cilantro)
1 large tomato, finely chopped
5 ml/1 tsp salt
5 ml/1 tsp sugar
100 g/4 oz/¹/₂ cup frozen chopped
    spinach
225 g/8 oz/2 cups cooked lamb, diced

Put the turmeric, cinnamon, ginger, garlic powder and chilli powder in a cup and add 30 ml/2 tbsp water. Heat the oil and fry (sauté) the sliced onion until golden brown. Add the grated or minced onion and stir-fry for 1 minute. Add the coriander and fry gently for 2 minutes. Add the spices from the cup and stir-fry for 1 minute. Add the tomato and stir-fry for 2 minutes. Add the salt, sugar, spinach and meat. Stir well to mix and cook for about 7 minutes until the meat is hot through.

Quick Lamb Burgers

SERVES 4

Prepare as for Quick Beef Burgers (see page 62) but substitute minced (ground) lamb for beef and dried mint for the mustard.

Lamb Chops Masala

SERVES 4

150 ml/¹/₄ pt/²/₃ cup plain yoghurt
15 ml/1 tbsp oil
5 ml/1 tsp ground ginger
5 ml/1 tsp garlic powder
5 ml/1 tsp chilli powder
5 ml/1 tsp ground cumin
5 ml/1 tsp salt
5 ml/1 tsp coarsely ground black
    pepper
4 large lamb chops

Mix together all the ingredients except the chops. Coat the chops in the yoghurt mixture, using your hands. Cover and chill overnight. Place the chops on foil on a grill (broiler) rack and grill (broil) for about 7 minutes each side, or place on a baking sheet and cook in the oven at 190°C/375°F/gas mark 5 for about 30 minutes, turning half-way through.

Lamb Paprikash

SERVES 4

Prepare as for Pork Paprikash (see page 82) but substitute well trimmed lamb neck fillet for the pork fillet.

Spicy Lamb Pizza

100 g/4 oz/1 cup minced (ground) lamb
15 ml/1 tbsp dried minced onion
¹/₂ red (bell) pepper, finely chopped
1 small red chilli, seeded and chopped or 2.5 ml/¹/₂ tsp chilli powder
15 ml/1 tbsp tomato purée (paste)
Salt and freshly ground black pepper
23 cm/9 in ready-to-bake Neapolitan-style cheese and tomato pizza
50 g/2 oz Mozzarella cheese, grated
Pinch of dried oregano
1 black olive

Fry (sauté) the lamb with the dried onion and chopped pepper until the grains of meat are brown and separate. Stir in the chilli, tomato purée and a little salt and pepper. Put the pizza on a baking sheet. Spread the meat mixture over and sprinkle with the Mozzarella and oregano. Top with the olive and bake in the oven at 220°C/425°F/gas mark 7 for about 15–20 minutes until the cheese is melted and bubbling and just turning golden.

Liver Diane

15 ml/1 tbsp plain (all-purpose) flour
30 ml/2 tbsp coarsely crushed black peppercorns
225 g/8 oz lambs' liver, very thinly sliced
25 g/1 oz/2 tbsp butter
30 ml/2 tbsp sunflower oil
15 ml/1 tbsp lemon juice
1 small onion, grated
15 ml/1 tbsp chopped parsley
45 ml/3 tbsp Worcestershire sauce

Mix the flour with the peppercorns and use to coat the liver slices. Melt the butter and oil in a large frying pan (skillet) and fry (sauté) the slices of liver on one side until the underside is browned. Turn over and cook only until the pink juices rise to the surface, no longer. Transfer to a warmed serving plate and keep warm. Add the remaining ingredients to the pan and cook, stirring for 1 minute. Spoon over the liver and serve straight away.

Greek-style Lamb and Potatoes

SERVES 4

1 kg/2¹/₄ lb fillet end half leg of
   lamb
12 potatoes, scrubbed and halved
1–2 garlic cloves, chopped
5 ml/1 tsp dried oregano
300 ml/¹/₂ pt/1¹/₄ cups chicken or
   lamb stock
Salt and freshly ground black pepper
Chopped parsley

Wipe the meat and put in a baking
tin (pan). Put the potatoes all around
and sprinkle the meat with the garlic and
oregano. Pour on the stock and season
well all over. Cover the pan with a lid (or
foil) and bake at 180°C/350°F/gas mark
4 for 2 hours until the potatoes and meat
are very tender. Cut the meat off the bones
and transfer to a serving dish with the
potatoes. Boil the juices rapidly until
reduced by half. Taste and re-season if
necessary. Spoon over the meat and
potatoes, and sprinkle with chopped
parsley.

Old English Liver and Bacon

SERVES 4

1 small swede (rutabaga), diced
4 large potatoes, diced
Salt and freshly ground black pepper
1 onion, finely chopped
50 g/2 oz/¹/₄ cup butter
4 rashers (slices) back bacon, rinded
8 slices lambs' liver
Seasoned flour
Gravy

Cook the swede and potatoes in
boiling, salted water until tender.
Drain, season with salt and pepper and
mash well. In a heavy-based frying pan
(skillet), fry (sauté) the onion in half the
butter for 3 minutes until softened but not
browned. Add the potato and swede
mixture and press down well. Cover with
a lid or a plate and fry gently for 15
minutes until crisp and golden
underneath. Meanwhile, dry-fry the bacon
in a separate pan. Remove and keep warm.
Toss the liver in a little seasoned flour.
Melt the remaining butter in the bacon pan
and fry the liver for about 4 minutes until
golden brown on both sides and just
cooked. Loosen the swede and potato cake
and carefully turn out on to a warmed
plate. Top with the liver and bacon and
serve hot with gravy.

Special Shepherd's Pie

2 large onions, chopped
50 g/2 oz/¹/₄ cup butter
225 g/8 oz lambs' liver, minced
   (ground) or finely chopped
225 g/8 oz/2 cups minced (ground)
   lamb
15 ml/1 tbsp tomato purée (paste)
300 ml/¹/₂ pt/1¹/₄ cups lamb or beef
   stock
2.5 ml/¹/₂ tsp mixed dried herbs
Salt and freshly ground black pepper
900 g/2 lb potatoes, cut into even-
   sized pieces
30 ml/2 tbsp milk
45 ml/3 tbsp plain (all-purpose)
   flour
60 ml/4 tbsp water
50 g/2 oz/¹/₂ cup grated Cheddar
   cheese

Fry (sauté) the onions in half the butter for 2 minutes until slightly softened. Stir in the minced meats and fry until brown and all the grains are separate. Stir in the tomato purée, stock, herbs and a little salt and pepper. Simmer gently for 10 minutes. Meanwhile, cook the potatoes in plenty of boiling, salted water until tender. Drain and mash with the remaining butter and the milk. Blend the flour with the water and stir into the meat mixture. Cook, stirring, for 2 minutes until thickened. Turn into an ovenproof dish. Top with the mashed potato and sprinkle with the cheese. Bake at 190°C/375°F/gas mark 5 for 30 minutes until golden and bubbling.

Lamb Lorenzo

1 onion, chopped
15 ml/1 tbsp olive oil
175 g/6 oz/1¹/₂ cups cooked lamb,
   chopped
397 g/14 oz/1 large can cream of
   tomato soup
5 ml/1 tsp dried basil
2 sun-dried tomatoes, chopped
   (optional)
Salt and freshly ground black pepper
350 g/12 oz tagliatelle
Grated Parmesan cheese

Fry (sauté) the onion in the oil for 3 minutes until softened and lightly golden. Add the remaining ingredients except the tagliatelle and cheese. Bring to the boil, half-cover, reduce the heat and simmer gently for 5–10 minutes or until the meat feels really tender. Meanwhile, cook the pasta according to the packet directions. Drain. Add to the tomato sauce, toss well and serve with grated Parmesan cheese.

POULTRY

Chicken and turkey are always excellent value for money and lend themselves to an infinite number of recipes. Duck is a more expensive proposition, but it has exquisite flavour, well worth treating yourself to.

Cheesy Chicken Topper

SERVES 4

4 chicken breast fillets
20 g/³/₄ oz/1¹/₂ tbsp butter, melted
4 lean ham slices
100 g/4 oz Gruyère (Swiss) or
** Cheddar cheese, grated**
Tomato wedges
Watercress

Place the chicken breasts one at a time in a plastic bag and beat with a rolling pin to flatten. Brush with melted butter and grill (broil) for 3 minutes on each side. Trim the ham to fit the chicken. Place on top and cover liberally with grated cheese. Grill until the cheese is melted and turning golden. Serve garnished with tomato wedges and watercress.

Chicken and Coconut Masala

SERVES 4

350 g/12 oz/3 cups boneless chicken
** meat, diced**
1 onion, chopped
1 small green (bell) pepper, sliced
15 ml/1 tbsp mild curry powder
30 ml/2 tbsp oil
450 ml/³/₄ pt/2 cups chicken stock
¹/₂ block creamed coconut
30 ml/2 tbsp ground almonds
15 ml/1 tbsp raisins
Salt and freshly ground black pepper
15 ml/1 tbsp chopped coriander
** (cilantro)**
1 packet pilau rice
Lemon wedges

Fry (sauté) the chicken, onion, pepper and curry powder in the oil for 4 minutes, stirring. Add the stock, coconut, ground almonds and raisins. Bring to the boil, reduce the heat and simmer for about 10 minutes until the chicken is cooked. If the sauce is still a little runny, remove the chicken with a draining spoon and boil the sauce rapidly, stirring, until reduced and thickened. Season to taste. Return the chicken to the sauce and stir in the chopped coriander. Meanwhile, cook the rice according to the packet directions. Serve the chicken on a bed of pilau rice, garnished with lemon wedges.

Chinese-style Chicken with Cashew Nuts

SERVES 4

225 g/8 oz boneless chicken thighs
1 bunch of spring onions (scallions)
30 ml/2 tbsp sunflower oil
1 carrot, grated
300 g/10 oz/2¹/₂ cups bean sprouts
25 g/1 oz/¹/₄ cup cashew nuts
300 ml/¹/₂ pt/1¹/₄ cups chicken stock
15 ml/1 tbsp cornflour (cornstarch)
15 ml/1 tbsp soy sauce
Plain boiled rice

Cut the meat into neat strips. Trim and chop the spring onions into 2.5 cm/1 in pieces. Heat the oil in a wok or large frying pan (skillet). Fry (sauté) the chicken, onions and carrot, stirring, for 5 minutes. Add the bean sprouts and cook, stirring, for 3 minutes. Add the cashew nuts and stock. Blend the cornflour with the soy sauce and stir into the pan. Bring to the boil and cook for 2 minutes. Serve on a bed of boiled rice.

Crunchy Turkey Escalopes

SERVES 4

4 small turkey breasts
1 egg, beaten
85 g/3¹/₂ oz/1 packet parsley and
thyme stuffing mix
Oil for shallow-frying
Lemon wedges
Watercress

Put a turkey breast in a plastic bag. Beat with a rolling pin to flatten. Repeat with remaining pieces. Dip the turkey breasts in beaten egg, then in stuffing mix to coat completely. Shallow-fry (sauté) in hot oil for about 3 minutes on each side until golden-brown and cooked through. Drain on kitchen paper. Transfer to warm serving plates. Garnish with lemon wedges and watercress and serve straight away.

Chicken in Filo Pastry

SERVES 4

4 boneless chicken breasts
25 g/1 oz/2 tbsp butter
4 filo pastry (paste) sheets
40 ml/8 tsp cranberry sauce
300 g/11 oz/1 small can asparagus
spears
30 ml/2 tbsp single (light) cream
1.5 ml/¹/₄ tsp grated nutmeg
Parsley sprigs

Fry (sauté) the chicken breasts in half the butter for 5 minutes until almost cooked, turning once. Melt the remaining butter. Brush a little on each pastry sheet and fold in half. Put 10 ml/ 2 tsp of cranberry sauce in the centre of each sheet. Top with the chicken. Fold the pastry over. Transfer, folded side down, to a buttered baking sheet and brush with any remaining butter. Bake in the oven at 200°C/400°F/gas mark 6 for about 15 minutes until golden brown. Meanwhile, drain the asparagus, reserving the liquid, and purée in a blender or food processor. Place in a small pan and add the cream. Thin with a little of the reserved liquid, if necessary. Add the nutmeg and heat through. Transfer the parcels to warmed serving plates. Spoon a little of the sauce to one side and garnish with parsley.

Duck Breasts with Orange

2 large duck breasts
Salt and freshly ground black pepper
25 g/1 oz/2 tbsp butter
15 ml/1 tbsp brandy
150 ml/¹/₄ pt/²/₃ cup chicken stock
5 ml/1 tsp light brown sugar
Grated rind and juice of 1 orange
15 ml/1 tbsp cornflour (cornstarch)
Watercress
Orange twists

Remove the skin from the duck. Season the fillets, then fry (sauté) in the butter, turning occasionally, for 15 minutes until just pink in the centre (or a little longer if you prefer it cooked well). Transfer to a warm dish and keep warm. Add the brandy to the pan and ignite. When the flames subside, add the stock and sugar. Blend the orange rind and juice with the cornflour. Stir into the pan, bring to the boil, stirring until thickened and clear. Season to taste. Cut the duck into neat slices. Arrange attractively on four warm serving plates. Spoon the sauce over and garnish with watercress and orange twists.

Fragrant Chicken Livers

2 onions, chopped
25 g/1 oz/2 tbsp butter
10 ml/2 tsp sunflower oil
1 wineglass medium-dry sherry
450 g/1 lb/4 cups chicken livers,
*   trimmed*
5 ml/1 tsp chopped sage
Salt and freshly ground black pepper
350 g/12 oz frozen leaf spinach

Fry (sauté) the onion in the butter and oil for about 3 minutes until soft and golden. Add the sherry and simmer, stirring, until the liquid has almost evaporated. Add the livers, sage and a little salt and pepper. Cook, stirring, over a moderate heat for about 5 minutes until the livers are cooked but still tender. Meanwhile, cook the spinach according to the packet directions. Drain. Spoon on to 4 warm serving plates. Spoon the livers to one side and serve.

Spaghetti with Turkey and Mushrooms

SERVES 4

60 ml/4 tbsp olive oil
175 g/6 oz/1¹/₂ cups boneless turkey, diced
1 carrot, finely chopped
1 celery stick, finely chopped
1 onion, finely chopped
1 garlic clove, crushed
100 g/4 oz/2 cups button mushrooms, sliced
4 tomatoes, chopped
50 g/2 oz/¹/₂ cup frozen peas
Salt and freshly ground black pepper
350 g/12 oz spaghetti
Grated Parmesan cheese

Heat the oil in a large pan. Fry (sauté) all the ingredients except the spaghetti and cheese for 3 minutes, stirring. Reduce the heat, cover and cook gently for about 10 minutes, stirring occasionally, until cooked through. Meanwhile, cook the spaghetti according to the packet directions. Drain. Add to the turkey mixture and toss well. Serve hot, sprinkled with Parmesan cheese.

Spanish Rice

SERVES 4

175 g/6 oz/1¹/₂ cups boneless chicken, diced
1 small green (bell) pepper, diced
1 small red (bell) pepper, diced
30 ml/2 tbsp olive oil
225 g/8 oz/1 cup long-grain rice
600 ml/1 pt/2¹/₂ cups chicken stock
100 g/4 oz/1 cup frozen peas with sweetcorn (corn)
100 g/4 oz/1 cup peeled prawns (shrimp)
Salt and freshly ground black pepper
Black olives
Chopped parsley

Fry (sauté) the chicken and peppers in the oil for 4 minutes, stirring. Add the rice and stir for 1 minute. Pour on the stock, bring to the boil, cover and simmer for 10 minutes. Add the peas and sweetcorn and prawns, re-cover and cook for a further 10 minutes until the rice is cooked and has absorbed nearly all the liquid. Season to taste. Serve garnished with olives and chopped parsley.

Chunky Chicken Parcels with Cranberry

SERVES 4

4 filo pastry (paste) sheets
25 g/1 oz/2 tbsp butter, melted
425 g/15 oz/1 large can chunky
  chicken
5 ml/1 tsp mixed dried herbs
60 ml/4 tbsp cranberry sauce
15 ml/1 tbsp port
Parsley sprigs

Lay a pastry sheet on the work surface. Brush lightly with a little of the melted butter and fold in half. Brush with butter again. Put a quarter of the chicken in the centre of the pastry and sprinkle with a quarter of the herbs. Draw the pastry up over the filling and brush with a little more melted butter. Repeat to make 3 more parcels. Bake in the oven at 200°C/400°F/gas mark 6 for 10–15 minutes until golden brown. Meanwhile, heat the cranberry sauce and port together in a saucepan, Transfer the chicken parcels to warmed serving plates. Spoon a little of the sauce around each and garnish with parsley before serving.

Spiced Chicken with Cider

SERVES 4

Prepare as for Spiced Pork with Cider (see page 84) but substitute 4 small chicken breasts for the pork fillet and leave whole instead of cutting into strips. Substitute crème fraîche for the double cream if you prefer.

Pan Casseroled Chicken

SERVES 4

4 chicken portions
30 ml/2 tbsp plain (all-purpose)
  flour
Salt and freshly ground black pepper
40 g/1¹/₂ oz/3 tbsp butter
5 ml/1 tsp curry powder or paste
298 g/10¹/₂ oz/1 small can
  condensed cream of mushroom
  soup

Wipe the chicken with kitchen paper. Mix the flour with a little salt and pepper and use to coat the chicken. Melt the butter in a flameproof casserole (Dutch oven) and fry (sauté) the chicken on all sides to brown. Take the chicken out of the casserole. Drain off all but 15 ml/1 tbsp of the fat. Stir in the curry powder or paste and fry for 1 minute. Blend in the soup. Return the chicken to the pan, bring to the boil, reduce the heat to as low as possible, cover and simmer for 45 minutes until the chicken is tender. Stir occasionally and add a little water if necessary to prevent sticking.

Chicken with Curry Butter

SERVES 4

Prepare as for Lamb with Curry Butter (see page 98) but substitute 4 chicken breasts for the lamb chops.

Maybe Chicken Chow Mein

250 g/9 oz/1 packet quick-cook
Chinese egg noodles
225 g/8 oz/2 cups cooked chicken,
cut into strips
425 g/15 oz/1 large can stir-fry
mixed vegetables, drained
1 garlic clove, crushed
30 ml/2 tbsp soy sauce
30 ml/2 tbsp sherry
5 ml/1 tsp ground ginger
15 ml/1 tbsp light brown sugar

Cook the noodles according to the packet directions. Drain. Put all the remaining ingredients in a large pan or wok and heat through, stirring occasionally, until piping hot. Stir in the noodles, reheat and serve.

Mock Peking Duck

1 bunch of spring onions (scallions)
¹/₄ cucumber
450 g/1 lb/4 cups turkey stir-fry
pieces
60 ml/4 tbsp soy sauce
7.5 ml/1¹/₂ tsp ground ginger
1 garlic clove, crushed
15 ml/1 tbsp red wine vinegar
Freshly ground black pepper
60 ml/4 tbsp plum jam (conserve)
5 ml/1 tsp lemon juice
12 tortillas
15 ml/1 tbsp oil

Trim the roots and tops off the spring onions, make several cuts lengthways through the white bulb to a depth of about 2.5 cm/1 in. Place in a bowl of cold water in the fridge. Cut the cucumber into thin strips. Place in a serving bowl and chill.

Put the turkey in a shallow dish. Mix together half the soy sauce, a third of the ginger, the garlic, vinegar and a good grinding of pepper and pour over. Leave to stand for at least 1 hour. Mix the plum jam with the remaining soy sauce and ginger and the lemon juice. Put in a small serving bowl. Warm the tortillas either on a covered plate over a pan of boiling water or in the microwave. Heat the oil in a large frying pan (skillet). Drain the turkey and stir-fry for about 5 minutes until cooked through. Turn into a serving dish. To serve, use a spring onion 'brush' to dip in the plum sauce and spread over the tortilla. Add a spoonful of meat and some cucumber. Roll up and eat with the fingers.

Oriental Chicken Loaf

350 g/12 oz/3 cups cooked chicken,
minced (ground)
75 g/3 oz onion, minced
440 g/15¹/₂ oz/1 large can crushed
pineapple
1 canned pimiento cap, chopped
15 ml/1 tbsp soy sauce
2 packets bread sauce mix
Salt and freshly ground black pepper
2 eggs, beaten

Mix all the ingredients together and place in a lightly greased loaf tin (pan). Cover with a double thickness of foil and steam for 1 hour. Leave to cool. Turn out on to a serving dish and serve cold, cut into slices.

Cheat Chicken Maryland

SERVES 4

450 g/1 lb crumb-coated chicken
nuggets
4–8 streaky bacon rashers (slices)
2 large bananas
Oil for shallow-frying
Corn Fritters (see page 36)

Grill (broil) or fry (sauté) the chicken nuggets according to the packet directions. Keep warm. Cut the bacon rashers in half, roll up and grill (broil) or fry until cooked through. Keep warm. Cut the bananas in half lengthways, then across to make 4 pieces. Fry in a little oil until just softening. Serve with the chicken, bacon and Corn Fritters.

Chicken and Vegetable Mornay

SERVES 4

1 packet cheese sauce mix
300 ml/^{1}/$_2$ pt/1^1/$_4$ cups milk or water
(according to the packet)
350 g/12 oz/3 cups cooked leftover
vegetables, chopped, or frozen
vegetables, cooked
175 g/6 oz/1^1/$_2$ cups cooked chicken,
roughly chopped
1.5 ml/^{1}/$_4$ tsp grated nutmeg
50 g/2 oz/^{1}/$_2$ cup grated Cheddar
cheese

Make up the cheese sauce according to the packet directions. Stir in the vegetables, chicken and nutmeg. Heat through for 3 minutes, stirring occasionally. Turn into a 1.2 litre/2 pt/5 cup flameproof dish. Sprinkle with the cheese and grill (broil) for 5 minutes until the cheese is melted and turning golden. Serve hot.

Sweet and Sour Chicken

SERVES 4

15 ml/1 tbsp sunflower oil
2 chicken breast fillets, cut into
small, thin strips
1 carrot, cut into matchsticks
^{1}/$_2$ small red (bell) pepper, cut into
thin strips
^{1}/$_4$ cucumber, diced
430 g/15^1/$_2$ oz/1 large can pineapple
pieces
30 ml/2 tbsp tomato purée (paste)
45 ml/3 tbsp soy sauce
2.5 ml/^{1}/$_2$ tsp ground ginger
60 ml/4 tbsp malt vinegar
10 ml/2 tsp cornflour (cornstarch)
15 ml/1 tbsp water
Plain boiled rice

Heat the oil in a large saucepan. Fry (sauté) the chicken in the oil for 4 minutes until cooked through. Remove from the pan. Add the remaining ingredients except the cornflour, water and rice. Bring to the boil and boil for 5 minutes. Blend the cornflour with the water and stir into the sauce. Cook, stirring, until thickened and clear. Return the chicken to the sauce and heat through. Spoon on to plain boiled rice and serve.

Turkey Veronica

300 ml/¹/₂ pt/1¹/₄ cups chicken stock
1 bay leaf
40 g/1¹/₂ oz/3 tbsp butter
225 g/8 oz/2 cups turkey stir-fry
  meat
25 g/1 oz/¹/₄ cup plain (all-purpose)
  flour
5 ml/1 tsp grated lemon rind
150 ml/¹/₄ pt/²/₃ cup single (light)
  cream
75 g/3 oz/¹/₂ cup seedless (pitless)
  white grapes, halved
Salt and white pepper
350 g/12 oz tagliatelle
Chopped parsley

Put the stock in a pan. Add the bay leaf. Bring to the boil and leave to infuse while preparing the rest of the sauce. Melt the butter in a separate pan. Add the turkey and cook, stirring, for 4–5 minutes until cooked through. Add the flour and cook, stirring for 1 minute. Discard the bay leaf, then gradually blend the stock into the turkey mixture, stirring all the time. Add the lemon rind. Bring to the boil and cook for 3 minutes, stirring. Stir in the cream, add the grapes and season to taste. Meanwhile, cook the tagliatelle according to the packet directions. Drain. Spoon on to warm plates, top with the turkey and garnish with parsley.

Chicken with Hot Olive Sauce

45 ml/3 tbsp olive oil
1 onion, finely chopped
2 garlic cloves, crushed
1 green (bell) pepper, chopped
400 g/14 oz/1 large can chopped
  tomatoes
175 g/3 oz/¹/₂ cup stoned (pitted)
  green olives, chopped
2.5 ml/¹/₂ tsp cayenne
Few drops of Worcestershire sauce
Salt and freshly ground black pepper
4 chicken portions

Make the sauce first. Heat 30 ml/ 2 tbsp of the oil and fry (sauté) the onion, garlic and pepper until soft, but not brown. Add the tomatoes, olives, cayenne, Worcestershire sauce and a little salt and pepper and simmer gently for 10 minutes. Brush the chicken generously with the remaining olive oil and grill (broil) for about 20 minutes, turning frequently and brushing with oil as needed. Reheat the sauce and serve with the chicken.

Chicken Fajitas

SERVES 4

1 onion, finely chopped
1 garlic clove, crushed
75 g/3 oz/¹/₃ cup light brown sugar
300 ml/¹/₂ pt/1¹/₄ cups lager
60 ml/4 tbsp red wine vinegar
15 ml/1 tbsp made mustard
4 chicken breasts, cut into strips
Sunflower oil
Salt and freshly ground black pepper
1 onion, sliced into rings
4 tortillas
15 ml/1 tbsp chopped parsley

Place the onion, garlic, sugar, lager, vinegar and mustard in a pan. Bring to the boil, then simmer for 5 minutes, stirring occasionally. Place the chicken in a shallow bowl, pour over the sauce and leave to marinate for 1 hour. Remove the chicken from the marinade. Heat a little oil in a frying pan (skillet) and fry (sauté) the chicken until cooked through. Season with salt and pepper. Meanwhile, fry the onion rings in a little oil in a separate pan for about 3 minutes on each side. Warm the tortillas. Sprinkle the chicken with parsley and serve with the onion rings and tortillas.

Herb-stuffed Chicken Rolls

SERVES 4

50 g/2 oz/1 cup fresh breadcrumbs
30 ml/2 tbsp chopped parsley
15 ml/1 tbsp chopped basil
2.5 ml/¹/₂ tsp dried oregano
Salt and freshly ground black pepper
1 egg, beaten
4 chicken breasts
Olive oil

Mix together the breadcrumbs, herbs, salt and pepper. Add just enough egg to hold the mixture together. Cut the chicken breasts in half lengthways so you have 8 thinner pieces of chicken. Place a spoonful of stuffing on each piece, roll up and secure with cocktail sticks (toothpicks). Brush generously with olive oil. Grill (broil) for about 8–10 minutes, turning and brushing with more oil as needed.

Thai Chicken and Coconut

SERVES 4

4 chicken breasts, cut into chunks
120 ml/4 fl oz/¹/₂ cup lime juice
250 ml/8 fl oz/1 cup canned
*   unsweetened coconut milk*
100 g/4 oz/¹/₂ cup peanut butter
50 g/2 oz/¹/₄ cup light brown sugar
45 ml/3 tbsp white wine vinegar
15 ml/1 tbsp cornflour (cornstarch)
5 ml/1 tsp curry powder
30 ml/2 tbsp oil
30 ml/2 tbsp desiccated (shredded)
*   coconut*

Marinate the chicken in the lime juice for 1 hour, turning occasionally. Blend together the coconut milk, peanut butter, sugar, vinegar, cornflour and curry powder. Bring gently to the boil, stirring, then simmer for 3 minutes. Drain the chicken and thread on to soaked wooden skewers. Brush with oil. Grill (broil) the kebabs for about 10 minutes, turning frequently. Reheat the sauce, pour over the kebabs and garnish with coconut.

Lemon Chicken with Herbs

4 chicken portions
75 ml/5 tbsp olive oil
Salt and freshly ground black pepper
50 g/2 oz/¹/₂ cup chopped mixed
*   herbs*
90 ml/6 tbsp lemon juice

Rub the chicken with a little oil, then season with salt and pepper. Grill (broil) the chicken for about 7–8 minutes each side until the skin is crispy and the flesh is almost cooked through. Whisk together the remaining oil, the herbs and lemon juice. Brush over the chicken and continue to grill for another 3–4 minutes until thoroughly cooked.

Spicy Chicken Wings

450 g/1 lb chicken wings
1 small onion, finely chopped
15 ml/1 tbsp light brown sugar
30 ml/2 tbsp Worcestershire sauce
15 ml/1 tbsp sunflower oil
5 ml/1 tsp cayenne
10 ml/2 tsp coarse sea salt
Freshly ground black pepper

Place the chicken wings in a bowl. Mix together the remaining ingredients and pour over the chicken wings, rubbing the mixture into the skin. Leave to marinate for 2 hours. Lift from the marinade and grill (broil) for about 15–20 minutes until cooked through and crispy.

Apple Chicken

4 chicken breasts or portions
¹/₂ small onion, finely chopped
1 garlic clove, crushed
15 ml/1 tbsp light brown sugar
15 ml/1 tbsp made mustard
15 ml/1 tbsp sunflower oil
250 ml/8 fl oz/1 cup apple juice
120 ml/4 fl oz/¹/₂ cup cider vinegar
15 ml/1 tbsp paprika
5 ml/1 tsp chilli powder
5 ml/1 tsp cayenne
Salt and freshly ground black pepper

Arrange the chicken in a shallow dish. Mix together all the remaining ingredients and pour over the chicken. Leave to marinate for 2 hours. Lift the chicken from the marinade. Boil the remaining marinade until reduced slightly. Grill (broil) the chicken for 20 minutes (chicken breasts will cook more quickly, larger portions will take longer), using the remaining marinade to brush the chicken as it cooks. Make sure the chicken is thoroughly cooked through before serving.

Spicy Turkey Legs

Prepare as for Spicy Chicken Wings, but use 4 small turkey legs and bake in the oven at 200°C/400°F/gas mark 6 for 1¹/₂ hours after marinating, then grill (broil) until crispy.

Chicken with Brandy and Orange Cream Sauce

SERVES 4
---

4 chicken breasts
30 ml/2 tbsp sunflower oil
Salt and freshly ground black pepper
100 g/4 oz/¹/₂ cup butter or
*   margarine, melted*
90 ml/6 tbsp double (heavy) or
*   whipping cream*
60 ml/4 tbsp brandy
30 ml/2 tbsp orange juice
1 egg

Brush the chicken breasts with oil and season with salt and pepper. Grill (broil) for about 10 minutes on each side until cooked through and crisp. Meanwhile, whisk together all the remaining ingredients and warm through gently, seasoning to taste with salt and pepper. Serve the sauce with the chicken.

Sweet and Spicy Duck

SERVES 4
---

4 duck breast portions
120 ml/4 fl oz/¹/₂ cup dry sherry
120 ml/4 fl oz/¹/₂ cup strong black
*   tea*
120 ml/4 fl oz/¹/₂ cup soy sauce
1 garlic clove, crushed
30 ml/2 tbsp sunflower oil
30 ml/2 tbsp clear honey
5 ml/1 tsp ground cloves
Salt and freshly ground black pepper

Arrange the duck in a shallow dish. Mix together the remaining ingredients. Pour over the duck and leave to marinate for 1 hour. Remove the duck from the marinade. Pour the marinade into a pan and boil until reduced by half. Grill (broil) the duck for about 12 minutes each side, depending on the size, brushing regularly with the remaining marinade.

Chicken with Piquant Caper Relish

SERVES 6
---

3 anchovy fillets, drained of their oil
2 garlic cloves, crushed
2.5 ml/¹/₂ tsp balsamic vinegar
15 ml/1 tbsp capers
60 ml/4 tbsp chopped parsley
150 ml/¹/₄ pt/²/₃ cup olive oil
Freshly ground black pepper
6 × 175 g/6 × 6 oz chicken breast
*   fillets*
25 g/1 oz/2 tbsp unsalted (sweet)
*   butter*
15 ml/1 tbsp sunflower oil

Purée the first five ingredients in a blender or food processor until well combined. Gradually add the olive oil, running the machine all the time, and season with pepper. Fry (sauté) the chicken breasts in the butter and sunflower oil for 5–6 minutes on each side until cooked through. Serve each with a spoonful of the salsa.

Chicken in Pesto Sauce

SERVES 4

4 chicken breast fillets
15 ml/1 tbsp plain (all-purpose)
*   flour*
30 ml/2 tbsp olive oil
1 onion, chopped
100 g/4 oz button mushrooms
5 tomatoes, skinned and chopped
300 ml/¹/₂ pt/1¹/₄ cups medium-dry
white wine
15 ml/1 tbsp tomato purée (paste)
30 ml/2 tbsp Pesto sauce (see page
252 or from a jar)
30 ml/2 tbsp chopped parsley
Salt and freshly ground black pepper

Coat the chicken in the flour and fry (sauté) in the oil until golden brown. Remove from the pan and keep warm. Fry the onion for 5 minutes and then add the mushrooms, tomatoes, wine and tomato purée. Bring to the boil, then simmer for 15 minutes. Return the chicken to the pan, add the pesto and parsley and season to taste. Cook for another 5 minutes.

Chicken with Tarragon Cream

SERVES 4

4 boneless chicken breasts
25 g/1 oz/2 tbsp unsalted (sweet)
*   butter*
10 ml/2 tsp plain (all-purpose) flour
2.5 ml/¹/₂ tsp salt
1.5 ml/¹/₄ tsp freshly ground black
pepper
2.5 ml/¹/₂ tsp dried tarragon
5 ml/1 tsp French mustard
120 ml/4 fl oz/¹/₂ cup white wine
120 ml/4 fl oz/¹/₂ cup double (heavy)
*   cream*

Fry (sauté) the chicken breasts in the butter for about 20 minutes until cooked through, then remove from the pan and keep warm. Add the flour, salt and pepper, tarragon and mustard to the pan. Gradually pour in the wine, stirring all the time. Bring to the boil and let it bubble until reduced by half. Add the cream, chicken breasts and any juices. Cook for a further 5–6 minutes over a gentle heat. Serve hot.

Fragrant Cardamom Chicken

SERVES 4

4 boneless chicken breasts
Salt and freshly ground black pepper
50 g/2 oz/¹/₄ cup butter
1 green (bell) pepper, seeded and
*   sliced*
8 green Cardamoms, crushed
150 ml/¹/₄ pt/²/₃ cup sweet white
*   vermouth*
5 ml/1 tsp yeast extract
300 ml/¹/₂ pt/1¹/₄ cups double
*   (heavy) cream*
Watercress

Season the chicken with the salt and pepper, then fry (sauté) in the butter for 20 minutes until cooked through. Remove from the pan and keep warm. Fry the sliced pepper and cardamom seeds in the chicken juices until the pepper is softening. Pour in the vermouth and stir to scrape up any sediment. Cook over a moderate heat for about 10 minutes until well reduced. Add the yeast extract and cream and cook until thickened (about 5 minutes). Serve the chicken pieces with the sauce poured over, garnished with the watercress.

Oriental Marinated Chicken

SERVES 6
---

45 ml/3 tbsp soy sauce
45 ml/3 tbsp clear honey
Juice of 2 oranges
1 garlic clove, crushed
15 ml/1 tbsp finely chopped fresh
*   root ginger*
10 ml/2 tsp light brown sugar
75 ml/5 tbsp sunflower oil
5 ml/1 tsp ground cumin
6 chicken breasts

Mix together the soy sauce, honey, orange juice, garlic, ginger, sugar, oil and cumin and pour over the meat. Leave to marinade overnight if possible, turning over occasionally to ensure the flavours are well absorbed by the meat. Bake in the oven at 180°C/350°F/gas mark 4 for 45 minutes.

Boozy Chicken

SERVES 4
---

4 chicken breasts, boneless and
*   skinned*
Salt and freshly ground black pepper
50 g/2 oz/¹/₄ cup butter
100 g/4 oz onions, sliced
1 garlic clove, chopped
200 g/8 oz/1 small can tomatoes,
*   chopped*
75 ml/5 tbsp port or sherry
10 ml/2 tsp dried basil
60 ml/4 tbsp chopped parsley
5 ml/1 tsp light brown sugar

Rub the chicken breasts with salt and pepper and fry (sauté) in half the butter for 20 minutes until cooked through. In a separate pan, cook the onion in the remaining butter for 5 minutes, adding the garlic after 2–3 minutes. Add the tomatoes and cook for 10 minutes.

Stir the port or sherry, the basil, parsley and sugar into the tomato mixture and bring to the boil. Add the chicken, reduce the heat, cover and simmer for 10 minutes.

Melting Moments Chicken Cordon Bleu

SERVES 4
---

4 chicken breasts, boneless and
*   skinned*
Butter and oil for shallow-frying
15 ml/1 tbsp chopped parsley
4 slices ham
8 mushrooms, sliced
150 ml/¹/₄ pt/²/₃ cup chicken stock
4 slices quick-melting cheese

Fry (sauté) the chicken in a little butter and oil on each side to brown. Top each with a little parsley, a slice of ham and sliced mushrooms. Add the chicken stock. Cover and simmer until cooked through. Top each breast with a slice of cheese. Cover again and cook until the cheese melts. Serve straight away.

Glazed Chicken Breasts

SERVES 4
---

4 chicken breasts, boneless and
*   skinned*
Butter and oil for shallow-frying
120 ml/4 fl oz/¹/₂ cup dry vermouth
Salt and freshly ground black pepper

Quickly fry (sauté) the chicken breasts on each side in a little butter and oil. Add the vermouth, cover and simmer for about 20 minutes until the chicken is cooked through. Add more vermouth if necessary to keep the pan from drying out and to form a fairly sticky sauce. Season lightly.

Turkey Escalopes in Ginger Wine

4 turkey escalopes
15 ml/1 tbsp olive oil
50 g/2 oz/¹/₄ cup unsalted (sweet)
butter
150 ml/¹/₄ pt/²/₃ cup ginger wine
10 ml/2 tsp lemon juice
5 ml/1 tsp chopped stem ginger
45 ml/3 tbsp double (heavy) cream
Salt and freshly ground black pepper

Gently fry (sauté) the escalopes in the oil and butter for 5–6 minutes on each side. Lift on to a serving dish and keep warm. Add the ginger wine to the pan and bring to the boil. Simmer for 5 minutes until the wine is syrupy. Stir in the lemon juice, stem ginger and cream. Simmer for 2–3 minutes until the sauce is a pale coffee colour. Season with salt and pepper. Pour the sauce over the meat and serve.

Three-spice Turkey

75 g/3 oz/¹/₃ cup unsalted (sweet)
butter
4 spring onions (scallions), finely
chopped
25 g/1 oz/¹/₄ cup plain (all-purpose)
flour
150 ml/¹/₄ pt/²/₃ cup white wine
300 ml/¹/₂ pt/1¹/₄ cups water
15 ml/1 tbsp ground cumin
15 ml/1 tbsp ground cardamom
30 ml/2 tbsp ground coriander
(cilantro)
1 garlic clove, crushed
Salt and freshly ground black pepper
4 turkey escalopes
Seasoned flour
150 ml/¹/₄ pt/²/₃ cup double (heavy)
cream

Melt half the butter in a pan and fry (sauté) the spring onions until softened, then stir in the flour and cook for a further minute. Add the wine, water, spices, garlic, salt and pepper and cook for a further 10–15 minutes until slightly thickened. Meanwhile, toss the turkey escalopes in seasoned flour and fry in a separate pan in the remaining butter. When browned on both sides (about 5–10 minutes), pour the other mixture over and continue to cook for 5 minutes. Add the cream and simmer for another 5 minutes. Serve hot.

Fillet of Turkey with Vermouth

2 turkey breasts
15–30 ml/1–2 tbsp plain (all-
purpose) flour
Salt and freshly ground black pepper
50 g/2 oz/¹/₄ cup butter
60 ml/4 tbsp chicken stock
60 ml/4 tbsp dry white vermouth
1 spring onion (scallion), chopped
1 parsley sprig, chopped
Pinch of chopped rosemary
¹/₄ small lemon, very thinly sliced

Slice the turkey into narrow strips. Season the flour with salt and pepper and dust the meat lightly with it. Quickly fry (sauté) the strips in the butter, then add the stock and vermouth. Boil rapidly until slightly thickened. Scatter the spring onion and parsley over the meat with the rosemary. Add the lemon slices and cook for a further 2–3 minutes.

Peppered Duck Breasts

SERVES 6

90 ml/6 tbsp cracked black
*   peppercorns*
6 small duck breasts, skinned
Salt
40 g/1¹/₂ oz/3 tbsp sunflower oil
45 ml/3 tbsp unsalted (sweet) butter
300 ml/¹/₂ pt/1¹/₄ cups cognac
300 ml/¹/₂ pt/1¹/₄ cups duck or
*   chicken stock*
300 ml/¹/₂ pt/1¹/₄ cups double
*   (heavy) cream*

Press the peppercorns into the breasts and season with a little salt. Fry (sauté) in the oil and butter for 4–5 minutes on each side. Remove from the pan and keep warm. Deglaze the pan with the cognac and stock. Stirring well, bring to the boil and continue boiling until the liquid is reduced by half. Add the cream and heat gently. Spoon over the duck and serve straight away.

Sautéed Duck with Port

SERVES 4

Salt
2 large duck breasts
90 ml/6 tbsp port
15 ml/1 tbsp redcurrant jelly (clear
*   conserve)*
Freshly ground black pepper
Watercress sprigs

Sprinkle a shallow frying pan (skillet) with salt, heat the pan and add the duck, skin-side down. Cook over a low heat for 5 minutes until the fat oozes from the skin. Turn the breasts over and cook on the other side for 5 minutes. Remove and keep warm in the oven, skin-side up. Pour the port into the pan and boil until reduced by half, then turn the heat down and add the redcurrant jelly. Stir to dissolve the jelly. Add pepper to taste. Cut the duck into chunky slices, put the slices into the pan with the sauce. If the slices are too rare for your taste, cook for another minute or so, otherwise check the flavour of the sauce. If it is too sweet or too thick, add a little more port. Garnish with watercress sprigs and serve.

Chicken Biryani

SERVES 4

25 g/1 oz/2 tbsp butter
1 large onion, thinly sliced
2 whole cloves
2.5 cm/1 in piece cinnamon stick
5 ml/1 tsp curry paste
100 g/4 oz/1 cup cooked chicken, in
*   bite-sized pieces*
225 g/8 oz/2 cups cooked basmati
*   rice*
15 ml/1 tbsp chopped coriander
*   (cilantro)*
25 g/1 oz/¹/₆ cup sultanas (golden
*   raisins)*
5 ml/1 tsp salt
15 ml/1 tbsp flaked almonds
15 ml/1 tbsp desiccated (shredded)
*   coconut*

Heat the butter and fry (sauté) the onion until golden brown, along with the cloves and cinnamon stick. Mix the curry paste with 15 ml/1 tbsp water and add to the onion. Stir-fry for 1 minute. Add the chicken and heat through for about 3 minutes. Add the rice, coriander, sultanas, salt and almonds. Stir and heat through thoroughly. Garnish with the desiccated coconut.

Chicken Tikka Biryani

Prepare as for Chicken Biryani, but substitute ready-cooked Chicken Tikka for the plain cooked chicken.

Chicken Stuffed with Lemon, Butter and Garlic

25 g/1 oz/2 tbsp butter
Finely grated rind of ¹/₂ lemon
5 ml/1 tsp garlic powder
2 × 150 g/2 × 5 oz chicken breasts

Mix together the butter, lemon rind and garlic powder. Divide into two portions and chill for about 30 minutes. Make a pocket along one side of each chicken breast with a sharp knife and stuff with a portion of garlic butter. Wrap the chicken in foil and bake in the oven at 190°C/375°F/gas mark 5 for 30 minutes. Open the foil for the last 10 minutes to allow the breasts to brown.

Old English Roast Stuffed Chicken Breasts

4 chicken breasts, skinned
100 g/4 oz/2 cups fresh breadcrumbs
1 onion, finely chopped
5 ml/1 tsp chopped thyme
5 ml/1 tsp salt
25 g/1 oz/2 tbsp butter
Freshly ground black pepper

Cut along the thicker side of each chicken breast to make a pocket. Put the breadcrumbs, onion, thyme and salt in a bowl and add the butter and a good grinding of pepper. Mix thoroughly with your hands until the mixture binds together. Divide the stuffing into 4 and stuff into each of the pockets. Wrap the breasts in foil and cook in the oven at 200°C/400°F/gas mark 6 for about 30 minutes until tender. Unwrap and serve.

Chicken Jalfrezi

225 g/8 oz chicken breast
5 ml/1 tsp garlic powder
5 ml/1 tsp ground ginger
5 ml/1 tsp chilli powder
30 ml/2 tbsp oil
1 large onion, thinly sliced
75 ml/5 tbsp grated or minced
*   (ground) onion*
10 ml/2 tsp curry paste
1 green (bell) pepper, diced
4 green chillies, seeded and
*   chopped*
45 ml/3 tbsp chopped coriander
*   (cilantro)*
5 ml/1 tsp salt
5 ml/1 tsp sugar
Plain boiled rice

Cut the chicken breast into about 8 pieces. Put the garlic powder, ginger and chilli powder in a cup and add 30 ml/ 2 tbsp water. Heat the oil and fry (sauté) the sliced onion until golden brown. Add the grated or minced onion and fry for 1 minute, stirring. Add the curry paste and spices from the cup and stir-fry for 1 minute. Add the chicken and green pepper and cook for about 7 minutes until the chicken is tender. Finally, add the chillies, coriander, salt and sugar and cook for 2 minutes. Serve with rice.

Chicken Omelette

SERVES 1 OR 2

Prepare as for Mushroom Omelette (see page 184) but substitute 100 g/4 oz/1 cup cooked chopped chicken for the mushrooms and fry (sauté) for 2 minutes only.

Turkey Pockets

SERVES 4

Prepare as for Pork Pockets (see page 75) but substitute turkey breast steaks, beaten flat, for the pork escalopes and chopped basil for snipped chives.

Chicken Honfleur

SERVES 4

75 g/3 oz/¹/₃ cup butter
75 g/3 oz/¹/₃ cup butter
2 onions, thinly sliced
4 chicken breasts
Salt and freshly ground black pepper
15 ml/1 tbsp plain (all-purpose)
* flour*
10 ml/2 tsp curry powder
60 ml/4 tbsp water
60 ml/4 tbsp calvados
300 ml/¹/₂ pt/1¹/₄ cups double
* (heavy) cream*
1 eating (dessert) apple, cored and
* cut into 4 rings*
Chopped parsley

Melt 50 g/2 oz/¹/₄ cup of the butter in a large heavy-based frying pan (skillet). Add the onions and chicken breasts. Season well. Cover and cook gently for 15 minutes until the chicken is just cooked through and the onions are tender. Transfer to a warmed dish and keep warm. Blend the flour, curry powder and water together. Stir into the pan juices, then quickly stir in the calvados and cream. Bring to the boil, stirring. Return the chicken and onion to the pan and simmer gently for 10 minutes. Meanwhile, fry the apple rings in the remaining butter until just cooked but still holding their shape. Transfer the chicken and sauce to 4 warmed serving plates. Top each with an apple ring and a sprinkling of parsley.

Pheasant with Tomato and Cheese Cream

SERVES 4

2 small pheasant, halved
15 ml/1 tbsp olive oil
15 g/¹/₂ oz/1 tbsp butter
15 ml/1 tbsp plain (all-purpose)
* flour*
150 ml/¹/₄ pt/²/₃ cup chicken stock
6 tomatoes, skinned, seeded and
* chopped*
2.5 ml/¹/₂ tsp caster (superfine)
* sugar*
150 ml/¹/₄ pt/²/₃ cup double (heavy)
* cream*
50 g/2 oz/¹/₂ cup grated Parmesan
* cheese*
Salt and freshly ground black pepper

Fry (sauté) the pheasant in the oil and butter until browned on all sides. Cover and continue to cook for about 20 minutes until tender. Remove with a draining spoon and keep warm. Drain off all but 15 ml/1 tbsp of the fat. Stir in the flour, blend in the stock and simmer, stirring for 2 minutes. Add the tomatoes and sugar and simmer for 2 minutes. Stir in the cream, cheese and a little salt and pepper and simmer for 2 minutes. Return the pheasant to the pan and simmer for 5 minutes.

Amazing Chicken

SERVES 4

225 g/8 oz pasta shapes
225 g/8 oz frozen asparagus
225 g/8 oz/2 cups cooked chicken,
cut into chunks
Salt and freshly ground black pepper
298 g/10¹/₂ oz/1 small can
*   condensed cream of chicken soup*
120 ml/4 fl oz/¹/₂ cup milk
150 ml/¹/₄ pt/²/₃ cup mayonnaise
50 g/2 oz/¹/₂ cup grated Cheddar
*   cheese*
50 g/2 oz/1 cup wholemeal
*   breadcrumbs*
15 g/¹/₂ oz/1 tbsp butter, melted

Cook the pasta according to the packet directions. Meanwhile, cook the asparagus according to the packet directions. Drain the pasta and place in a large ovenproof dish. Drain the asparagus and lay over the pasta. Arrange the chicken over. Season lightly. Blend the soup with the milk, mayonnaise and cheese. Spoon over. Mix the breadcrumbs with the butter and sprinkle over. Bake in the oven at 190°C/375°F/gas mark 5 for about 35 minutes until piping hot and the top is turning golden brown.

Glazzwill Turkey Fillets

SERVES 4

4 turkey fillet slices
150 ml/¹/₄ pt/²/₃ cup dry white wine
15 g/¹/₂ oz/1 tbsp butter
Salt and freshly ground black pepper
150 ml/¹/₄ pt/²/₃ cup passata (sieved
*   tomatoes)*
30 ml/2 tbsp tomato purée (paste)
5 ml/1 tsp caster (superfine) sugar
16 basil leaves
4 slices ham
75 g/3 oz Mozzarella cheese, grated

Place the turkey, wine and butter in a pan. Season lightly, bring to the boil, reduce the heat, cover and simmer gently for about 10 minutes or until the turkey is tender. Lift out the turkey and place on foil on the grill (broiler) rack. Boil the wine rapidly until reduced by half. Stir in the passata, tomato purée and sugar, bring to the boil and cook for about 4 minutes, stirring, until slightly thickened. Chop 8 of the basil leaves and stir in. Season to taste. Top each slice of turkey with a slice of ham. Cover each with grated cheese. Grill (broil) until the cheese has melted and is turning lightly golden. Spoon the sauce on to 4 warmed serving plates. Place a turkey slice on top and garnish with the remaining basil leaves.

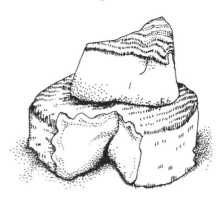

All-weather Barbecued Chicken Legs

65 g/2¹/₂ oz/good ¹/₄ cup butter
8 chicken legs
1 onion, finely chopped
150 ml/¹/₄ pt/²/₃ cup passata (sieved tomatoes)
30 ml/2 tbsp tomato ketchup (catsup)
15 ml/1 tbsp golden (light corn) syrup
60 ml/4 tbsp sweet brown table sauce
5 ml/1 tsp Worcestershire sauce
Salt and freshly ground black pepper

Melt half the butter in a roasting tin (pan). Add the chicken legs and roll in the butter. Roast in the oven at 200°C/ 400°F/gas mark 6 for 15 minutes. Meanwhile, melt the remaining butter in a saucepan. Add the onion and fry (sauté) for 3 minutes, stirring. Add the remaining ingredients and stir well. Bring to the boil and simmer for 5 minutes. Spoon over the chicken and cook for a further 20 minutes, turning once and basting occasionally with the sauce.

Turkey and Cranberry Burgers

SERVES 4

450 g/1 lb/4 cups minced (ground) turkey
1 small onion, finely chopped
15 ml/1 tbsp chopped parsley
15 ml/1 tbsp chopped thyme
1 garlic clove, crushed (optional)
45 ml/3 tbsp fresh breadcrumbs
Salt and freshly ground black pepper
1 egg, beaten
40 ml/8 tsp cranberry sauce

Mix the turkey with the onion, herbs, garlic, if using, breadcrumbs and a little salt and pepper. Add enough beaten egg to bind. Shape into 8 flat cakes. Divide the cranberry sauce between the centres of 4 of the patties. Top with the remaining patties and press the edges well together to seal. Grill (broil) for 5 minutes on each side until golden brown and cooked through.

Fragrant Parcelled Chicken

SERVES 4

15 g/¹/₂ oz/1 tbsp butter, for greasing
2 leeks, sliced into rings
1 courgette (zucchini), thinly sliced
2 carrots, thinly sliced
4 chicken breasts
Salt and freshly ground black pepper
4 rosemary sprigs
150 ml/¹/₄ pt/²/₃ cup medium-dry white wine
Small whole potatoes, scrubbed

Butter 4 large squares of foil. Divide the vegetables between the centres. Top each with a chicken breast and season lightly. Add a rosemary sprig to each and pour a quarter of the wine over each. Wrap loosely in the foil, twisting the edges to seal securely. Transfer to a baking sheet. Bake at 190°C/375°F/gas mark 5 for 35 minutes. Place the potatoes in the oven to bake at the same time. Carefully open the foil slightly to allow the chicken to brown and cook for a further 10 minutes. Transfer the foil parcels to serving plates and serve with the potatoes.

Chicken and Tarragon Lorenzo

SERVES 4

225 g/8 oz/2 cups chicken stir-fry
meat
1 small onion, chopped
1 garlic clove, crushed
15 ml/1 tbsp olive oil
397 g/14 oz/1 large can cream of
tomato soup
15 ml/1 tbsp chopped tarragon, or
5 ml/1 tsp dried
350 g/12 oz tagliatelle
Grated Pecorino cheese

Fry (sauté) the chicken, onion and garlic in the oil for 5 minutes, stirring, until golden and the chicken is cooked through. Add the soup and tarragon and simmer for 10 minutes. Meanwhile, cook the pasta according to the packet directions. Drain and add to the sauce. Toss well and serve with grated Pecorino cheese.

Pot-roasted Chicken with Orange and Walnuts

SERVES 4

1 bunch of spring onions (scallions),
chopped
2 carrots, diced
15 ml/1 tbsp olive oil
4 chicken portions
Grated rind and juice of 1 large
orange
300 ml/¹/₂ pt/1¹/₄ cups chicken stock
50 g/2 oz/¹/₂ cup walnut halves
1 bouquet garni sachet
Salt and freshly ground black pepper
10 ml/2 tsp cornflour (cornstarch)
15 ml/1 tbsp water

Fry (sauté) the spring onions and carrot in the oil in a flameproof casserole (Dutch oven) for 2 minutes. Top with the chicken portions. Blend the orange rind and juice with the stock and pour over. Add the walnuts and bouquet garni and season to taste. Cover and cook in the oven at 190°C/375°F/gas mark 5 for 1 hour. Discard the bouquet garni. Transfer the chicken to warmed plates. Blend the cornflour with the water and stir into the pan. Bring to the boil and simmer for 2 minutes, stirring. Taste and re-season if necessary. Pour over the chicken and serve.

SEAFOOD

Fish is by nature comparatively quick to cook, which makes it ideal for inclusion in this book. Many of the recipes in this section would also make good starters, served in smaller portions.

Baked Stuffed Plaice

SERVES 4

100 g/4 oz/2 cups button mushrooms,
  finely chopped
25 g/1 oz/2 tbsp butter
50 g/2 oz/1 cup fresh breadcrumbs
15 ml/1 tbsp chopped parsley
Salt and freshly ground black pepper
4 plaice fillets
150 ml/¹/₄ pt/²/₃ cup single (light)
  cream
Parsley sprigs

To make the stuffing, fry (sauté) the mushrooms in the butter for 2 minutes, stirring. Add the breadcrumbs, chopped parsley and a little salt and pepper. Remove any dark skin from the plaice fillets (do not worry about white skinned ones). Cut the fillets in half lengthways. Divide the stuffing among the fillets. Fold over into three to encase the filling. Transfer to 4 individual ovenproof dishes. Spoon the cream over. Cover with foil. Bake in the oven at 180°C/350°F/gas mark 4 for 20 minutes until cooked through. Garnish with parsley sprigs.

Buttery Mackerel

SERVES 4

4 whole mackerel, cleaned
Salt and freshly ground black pepper
65 g/2¹/₂ oz/5 tbsp butter
15 ml/1 tbsp oil
10 ml/2 tsp made English mustard
2.5 ml/¹/₂ tsp caster (superfine)
  sugar
5 ml/1 tsp lemon juice
Parsley sprigs

Cut the heads off the mackerel if you prefer. Wipe inside and out with kitchen paper. Slash the fish in several places along each side with a sharp knife and season with salt and pepper. Heat 15 g/¹/₂ oz/1 tbsp of the butter with the oil in a large frying pan (skillet). Add the fish and fry (sauté) for about 5 minutes on each side until browned and cooked through. Meanwhile, beat the remaining butter with the mustard, sugar, a little salt and pepper and the lemon juice. Shape into 4 neat pieces. Remove the fish from the pan, drain on kitchen paper and transfer to warm serving plates. Top each fish with a piece of the mustard butter and garnish with parsley.

Cod Provençale

SERVES 4

15 ml/1 tbsp olive oil
1 onion, chopped
1–2 garlic cloves, crushed
1 red (bell) pepper, sliced
400 g/14 oz/1 large can chopped
    tomatoes
15 ml/1 tbsp tomato purée (paste)
450 g/1 lb cod fillet, skinned and
    cubed
Salt and freshly ground black pepper
Plain boiled rice
Chopped parsley
Black olives

Put the oil in a pan with the onion
and garlic and cook, stirring, for 2
minutes until softened but not browned.
Add the pepper and fry (sauté) for one
minute. Stir in the tomatoes and purée,
bring to the boil and boil rapidly for 5
minutes, stirring occasionally. Add the
cod, reduce the heat and cook gently for
3–5 minutes until the fish is cooked but
not breaking up. Season to taste and serve
on a bed of boiled rice, garnished with
chopped parsley and black olives.

Fish Creole

SERVES 4

4 small white fish fillets, skinned
30 ml/2 tbsp plain (all-purpose)
    flour
Salt and freshly ground black pepper
2.5 ml/1/2 tsp chilli powder
25 g/1 oz/2 tbsp butter
30 ml/2 tbsp oil
2 bananas, halved
Lime or lemon wedges

Dust the fish with flour mixed with a
little salt and pepper and the chilli
powder. Melt half the butter and oil in a
frying pan (skillet) and fry (sauté) the fish
for 3 minutes on each side until lightly
golden and cooked through. Transfer to a
warmed serving dish and keep warm. Fry
the bananas in the remaining butter and
oil for about 2 minutes until softened.
Transfer to the serving dish. Garnish with
lime or lemon wedges and serve hot.

Fish and Potato Fry

SERVES 4

15 g/1/2 oz/1 tbsp butter or
    margarine
15 ml/1 tbsp oil
450 g/1 lb potatoes, grated
Salt and freshly ground black pepper
450 g/1 lb white fish fillet, skinned
    and cubed
300 ml/1/2 pt/1 1/4 cups passata
    (sieved tomatoes)
15 ml/1 tbsp tomato purée (paste)
2.5 ml/1/2 tsp granulated sugar

Melt the butter and oil in a medium-
sized frying pan (skillet). Add half
the potatoes and press down well. Season.
Add the fish in a layer, then top with the
remaining potatoes, press down and
season. Cover with a lid or foil and cook
gently for 30 minutes until cooked
through. Meanwhile, heat the passata in
a pan with the tomato purée, sugar and a
little pepper. Turn the fish and potato fry
out on to a warmed serving plate. Serve
cut into wedges with the tomato sauce.

Hearty Fish Stew

SERVES 4

1 onion, thinly sliced
1 carrot, thinly sliced
2 large potatoes, diced
1 large parsnip, diced
¹/₄ small cabbage, shredded
25 g/1 oz/2 tbsp butter or margarine
400 g/14 oz/1 large can chopped
  tomatoes
300 ml/¹/₂ pt/1¹/₄ cups water
5 ml/1 tsp anchovy essence (extract)
350 g/12 oz white fish, skinned and
  cubed
Salt and freshly ground black pepper
Chopped parsley

Place the prepared vegetables in a large pan with the butter or margarine. Fry (sauté) over a gentle heat, stirring occasionally, for 5 minutes. Add the tomatoes, water and anchovy essence. Bring to the boil, reduce the heat, cover and simmer for 15 minutes. Add the fish and simmer for a further 5 minutes or until cooked. Season to taste then spoon into warmed bowls and sprinkle with chopped parsley.

Quick Kedgeree

SERVES 4

225 g/8 oz/1 cup long-grain rice
5 ml/1 tsp turmeric
225 g/8 oz smoked fish fillet
  (haddock, cod, etc)
3 hard-boiled (hard-cooked) eggs,
roughly chopped
45 ml/3 tbsp chopped parsley
45 ml/3 tbsp single (light) cream or
  evaporated milk
Salt and freshly ground black pepper
Grated nutmeg

Cook the rice in lightly salted boiling water to which the turmeric has been added for 10 minutes or until just cooked. Drain and return to the saucepan. Meanwhile, skin the fish and poach in water for 5–10 minutes until it flakes easily with a fork. Drain. Break up the fish, discarding any bones. Mix in to the rice with the eggs, two-thirds of the parsley, the cream and seasonings. Garnish with the remaining parsley.

Trout in Soured Cream

SERVES 4

4 trout, cleaned
Salt and freshly ground black pepper
15 g/¹/₂ oz/1 tbsp butter
15 ml/1 tbsp olive oil
150 ml/¹/₄ pt/²/₃ cup soured (dairy
  sour) cream
15 ml/1 tbsp snipped chives
15 ml/1 tbsp chopped parsley
Toasted flaked almonds

Rinse the fish under running water. Pat dry on kitchen paper. Season and remove the heads if preferred. Heat the butter and oil in a large frying pan (skillet) and fry (sauté) the fish for 3 minutes on each side to brown. Add the soured cream, herbs and a little more seasoning, if liked. Cover with foil or a lid and simmer for 6–8 minutes until the fish is cooked through. Transfer the fish to warmed serving plates. Stir the juices and cream together well and spoon over. Sprinkle with toasted almonds and serve hot.

Photograph opposite: **Chicken biryani (page 120)**

Salmon Parcels

SERVES 4

4 small salmon steaks
4 filo pastry (paste) sheets
115 g/4¹/₂ oz/good ¹/₂ cup butter,
    melted
2 tomatoes, skinned and chopped
2 mushrooms, chopped
1.5 ml/¹/₄ tsp mixed dried herbs
2 eggs
30 ml/2 tbsp lemon juice
Pinch of cayenne
Cucumber slices

Remove any skin and bones from the fish. Brush the pastry sheets with a very little melted butter, fold in half and brush again. Put a salmon steak in the centre of each piece of pastry. Mix the tomato and mushrooms with the herbs and spoon on top. Draw the pastry up over the filling and squeeze together to form pouches. Transfer to a lightly buttered baking sheet and brush very lightly with butter. Bake in the oven at 200°C/400°F/ gas mark 6 for about 10–15 minutes until golden. Meanwhile, make the sauce: whisk the eggs in a small pan with the lemon juice and cayenne. Gradually whisk in the remaining butter then cook over a gentle heat, whisking all the time until the mixture thickens. Do not allow to boil. Taste and season if necessary. Serve on warmed plates, with little sauce to one side and garnish with cucumber.

Greek-style Trout

SERVES 4

Prepare as for Trout in Soured Cream but substitute thick Greek yoghurt for the soured cream and use chopped oregano instead of chives. Sprinkle with chopped pistachio nuts.

Tuna Gnocchi

SERVES 4

600 ml/1 pt/2¹/₂ cups milk
7.5 ml/1¹/₂ tsp salt
Freshly ground black pepper
1 bay leaf
1.5 ml/¹/₄ tsp grated nutmeg
150 g/5 oz/scant 1 cup semolina
    (cream of wheat)
2 eggs
100 g/4 oz/1 cup grated Cheddar
    cheese
185 g/6¹/₂ oz/1 small can tuna
295 g/10¹/₂ oz/1 small can condensed
    cream of mushroom soup
A little butter, melted
Chopped parsley

Put the milk, salt, a little pepper, the bay leaf, nutmeg and semolina in a saucepan. Bring to the boil and cook for 10 minutes, stirring until really thick. Discard the bay leaf. Beat in the eggs and 75 g/3 oz/³/₄ cup of the cheese. Turn into a well-greased baking tin (pan) and smooth out with a wet palette knife to a square about 2 cm/³/₄ in thick. Leave to cool, then chill for 1 hour. Meanwhile, drain the tuna and mix with the soup. Turn into a 1.2 litre/2 pt/5 cup ovenproof dish. Cut the gnocchi into 4 cm/1¹/₂ in squares and arrange round the top of the dish. Brush with a little melted butter and sprinkle with the remaining cheese. Bake in the oven at 200°C/400°F/gas mark 6 for 30 minutes until golden. Garnish with parsley before serving.

Photograph opposite: **Italian-style prawn and salami kebabs (page 143)**

129

Cheesy Prawn Supper

225 g/8 oz/2 cups peeled prawns
(shrimp)
295 g/10¹/₂ oz/1 small can condensed
cream of mushroom soup
15 ml/1 tbsp tomato ketchup
(catsup)
50 g/2 oz/1 cup fresh breadcrumbs
100 g/4 oz/1 cup grated Cheddar
cheese
Plain boiled rice
Toasted flaked almonds

Mix the prawns with the soup, ketchup and half the breadcrumbs and cheese. Turn into a fairly shallow ovenproof serving dish. Mix the remaining breadcrumbs with the cheese and spoon over. Bake in the oven at 200°C/400°F/ gas mark 6 for 20–25 minutes until golden and bubbling. Serve on a bed of rice garnished with toasted almonds.

Standby Smoked Mackerel Bake

4 frozen or canned smoked
mackerel fillets
300 g/11 oz/1 small can button
mushrooms
1 packet white sauce mix
300 ml/¹/₂ pt/1¹/₄ cups milk or water
(according to packet directions)
20 ml/4 tsp horseradish cream
50 g/2 oz cheese and onion
crisps (potato chips), crushed

Remove the skin from the fish fillets, break the mackerel into pieces and place in a fairly shallow ovenproof dish. Drain the mushrooms and scatter over. Make up the sauce according to the packet directions. Add the horseradish.

Pour the sauce over the fish and sprinkle with the crisps. Bake in the oven at 190°C/ 375°F/gas mark 5 for about 30 minutes or until bubbling and golden.

Saucy Smoked Mackerel

40 g/1¹/₂ oz/3 tbsp butter or
margarine
20 g/³/₄ oz/3 tbsp plain (all-purpose)
flour
300 ml/¹/₂ pt/1¹/₄ cups milk
Grated rind and juice of ¹/₂ lemon
15 ml/1 tbsp horseradish relish
Salt and freshly ground black pepper
4 smoked mackerel fillets
Lemon wedges
Parsley sprigs

To make the sauce, put half the butter or margarine in a saucepan with the flour and milk. Bring to the boil, whisking all the time until smooth. Stir in the lemon rind, horseradish and seasoning to taste. Cover with a circle of wet greaseproof (waxed) paper to prevent a skin forming. Put the mackerel fillets on the grill (broiler) rack. Dot with the remaining butter and drizzle with the lemon juice. Grill (broil) for 3–5 minutes on each side, basting occasionally with the pan juices, until cooked through. Transfer to a warmed serving dish and keep warm. Strain the juices and add to the sauce. Heat through. Spoon over the fish and garnish with lemon wedges and parsley sprigs.

Peasant-style Swordfish or Tuna Steaks

SERVES 4

4 swordfish or tuna steaks, skinned
15 ml/1 tbsp olive oil
15 g/¹/₂ oz/1 tbsp butter
1 garlic clove, chopped
15 ml/1 tbsp chopped parsley
Salt and freshly ground black pepper
Lemon wedges

Fry (sauté) the fish in the oil and butter for 5 minutes on one side until golden. Turn over. Sprinkle with garlic and parsley, a little salt and a good grinding of pepper. Cover with foil or a lid and continue cooking for 5 minutes or until cooked through. Garnish with lemon wedges.

Tandoori Fish

SERVES 4

450 g/1 lb white fish fillet
150 ml/¹/₄ pt/²/₃ cup plain yoghurt
15 ml/1 tbsp lemon juice
5 ml/1 tsp ground coriander (cilantro)
5 ml/1 tsp ground cumin
2.5 ml/¹/₂ tsp chilli powder
2.5 ml/¹/₂ tsp turmeric
Salt
175 g/6 oz/³/₄ cup long-grain rice
400 g/14 oz/1 large can chopped tomatoes
300 ml/¹/₂ pt/1¹/₄ cups water
15 ml/1 tbsp chopped coriander
Lemon wedges

Cut the fish into 4 equal pieces, discarding the skin and any bones. Lay in a shallow ovenproof dish just large enough to take the fish in a single layer.

Mix the yoghurt, lemon juice, ground coriander, spices and a good pinch of salt together. Spoon over the fish and turn the fish in the mixture to coat completely. If time, leave to marinate for up to 3 hours. If not, cook immediately in the oven at 180°C/350°F/gas mark 4 for 20 minutes, basting occasionally. Meanwhile, put the rice in a pan with the tomatoes and water. Bring to the boil, cover, reduce the heat and simmer for 20 minutes until cooked and the rice has absorbed the liquid. Add the chopped coriander and fork through. Serve the fish with the rice, garnished with lemon wedges.

Whiting with Cheese and Anchovies

SERVES 4

4 whiting fillets
15 g/¹/₂ oz/1 tbsp butter or margarine
10 ml/2 tsp sunflower oil
2 tomatoes, sliced
4 slices Gruyère or Emmental (Swiss) cheese
8 canned anchovy fillets, drained
Watercress sprigs

Skin the fillets and remove any bones. Heat the butter and oil in a large frying pan (skillet). Add the fish and fry (sauté) for 2 minutes. Top with the tomato slices, then the cheese, then the anchovy fillets in a cross on top of each fish fillet. Cover with a lid or foil and cook for 5–8 minutes until the fish is cooked and the cheese has melted. Transfer to warmed serving plates. Garnish with watercress and serve hot.

Salmon and Asparagus Gnocchi

Prepare as for Tuna Gnocchi (see page 129), but substitute a can of salmon (skinned and boned) for the tuna and asparagus soup for the mushroom soup. Add a drained small can of asparagus tips with the fish, if liked.

Quick Jansen's Temptation

2 × 275 g/2 × 10 oz/2 small cans
new potatoes
1 garlic clove, crushed
50 g/2 oz/1 small can anchovies
75 g/3 oz/¹/₃ cup butter, melted
150 ml/¹/₄ pt/²/₃ cup single (light)
cream
50 g/2 oz/1 cup breadcrumbs
50 g/2 oz/¹/₂ cup grated Cheddar
cheese

Drain and slice the potatoes. Mix with the garlic and the oil from the anchovies. Chop the fish and add. Grease an ovenproof serving dish with some of the butter. Tip in the potato mixture and level the surface. Pour the cream over. Mix the remaining butter with the breadcrumbs and cheese and sprinkle over the top. Bake at 200°C/400°F/gas mark 6 for about 35 minutes or until golden. Serve hot.

Salmon in Puff Pastry

425 g/15 oz/1 large can red salmon
375 g/13 oz ready-rolled puff pastry
(paste) sheet, thawed
215 g/7¹/₂ oz/1 small can creamed
mushrooms
Dried basil or dill (dill weed)
1 egg, beaten, to glaze
60–90 ml/4–6 tbsp passata (sieved
tomatoes)
Lemon wedges
Parsley sprigs

Drain the salmon and carefully remove the central backbone and any skin. Unroll the sheet of pastry on a board. Cut a thin strip off the end for decoration and cut the sheet into 4 or 6 rectangles. Place a spoonful of creamed mushrooms on the centre of each piece of pastry. Top each with a quarter or a sixth of the salmon (depending on how many you are making) and sprinkle with a good pinch of basil or dill. Brush the edges of the pastry with egg. Fold the pastry over the filling and press together to seal. Transfer to a dampened baking sheet, sealed sides down. Make 'leaves' out of the reserved pastry strip. Lay on top. Brush the parcels with a little more beaten egg and bake in the oven at 200°C/400°F/gas mark 6 for about 15 minutes until golden brown. Meanwhile, heat the passata. When ready to serve, put the parcels on warm serving plates. Put a spoonful of passata to one side of each parcel and garnish with lemon wedges and a parsley sprig.

Quick Party Paella

SERVES 4

1 packet savoury mushroom or
vegetable rice
450 ml/³/₄ pt/2 cups boiling water
100 g/4 oz/1 cup cooked chicken,
diced
250 g/9 oz/1 small can mussels,
drained
100 g/4 oz/1 cup peeled prawns
(shrimp)

Put the rice in a pan with the boiling water. Stir, cover and simmer for 12 minutes. Add the remaining ingredients, stir, cover and simmer gently for a further 8 minutes until all the liquid has been absorbed and the rice is tender.

Salmon Flan

SERVES 4

175 g/6 oz shortcrust pastry (basic
pie crust)
1 packet white sauce mix
300 ml/¹/₂ pt/1¹/₄ cups milk or water
(according to packet)
185 g/6¹/₂ oz/1 small can salmon
15 ml/1 tbsp tomato purée (paste)
1 canned pimiento cap, chopped
5 canned anchovy fillets
3 stuffed olives, halved

Roll out the pastry and use to line an 18 cm/7 in flan dish (pie pan). Prick the base with a fork, then line with crumpled foil and bake at 200°C/400°F/ gas mark 6 for 10 minutes. Remove the foil and bake for a further 5 minutes until golden brown. Meanwhile, make up the white sauce according to the packet directions. Flake the fish, discarding the bones and skin, and add to the sauce with the tomato purée and chopped pimiento.

If serving hot, reheat. Turn into the pastry case (shell), decorate with the anchovies and olives and serve hot. Alternatively, leave until cold before serving.

Smoked Haddock Florentine

SERVES 4

450 g/1 lb frozen chopped spinach
350 g/12 oz smoked haddock fillet
1 packet cheese sauce mix
300 ml/¹/₂ pt/1¹/₄ cups milk or water
(according to packet)
A little grated Cheddar cheese
4 poached eggs

Cook the spinach according to the packet directions. Drain and spread in the base of a 1.2 litre/2 pt/5 cup flameproof dish. Poach the fish in a little water for 5 minutes or until it flakes easily with a fork. Drain. Place on top of the spinach. Make up the sauce according to the packet directions. Spoon over and sprinkle with a little grated cheese. Place under a hot grill (broiler) until golden and bubbling. Serve with poached eggs on top.

White Fish and Tomato Florentine

SERVES 4

Prepare as for Smoked Haddock Florentine but substitute white fish (cod, haddock, whiting etc.) for the smoked haddock. Put a layer of a drained 200 g/7 oz/small can chopped tomatoes on top of the spinach before adding the poached fish.

Seaside Crumble

75 g/3 oz/³/₄ cup plain (all-purpose)
   flour
40 g/1¹/₂ oz/3 tbsp soft butter or
   margarine
50 g/2 oz/¹/₂ cup grated Cheddar
   cheese
450 g/1 lb white fish fillets
298 g/10¹/₂ oz/1 small can
   condensed celery soup
100 g/4 oz/1 cup frozen mixed
   vegetables
15 ml/1 tbsp chopped parsley

Put the flour in a bowl and work in the butter or margarine with a fork until crumbly. Stir in the cheese. Cut the fish into small dice, discarding any skin and bones. Place in an ovenproof serving dish and mix in the soup, vegetables and parsley. Spoon the crumble over and bake in the oven at 200°C/400°F/gas mark 6 for about 30 minutes until golden brown and cooked through.

Saucy Cod Puffs

350 g/12 oz frozen puff pastry
   (paste), just thawed
2 tomatoes, chopped (optional)
4 frozen cod steaks in parsley sauce
1 egg, beaten, to glaze

Cut the pastry into quarters. Roll out and trim each to about 18 cm/7 in square. If using the tomatoes, divide among the four pastry pieces. Carefully remove the fish and sauce from the bags and place on top of the tomato. Brush the edges of the pastry with beaten egg and fold over the fish to form parcels. Press the edges well together to seal. Transfer the parcels, sealed sides down, to a dampened baking sheet. Brush with beaten egg. Make 'leaves' out of any pastry trimmings, place on the parcels and brush with a little more egg. Bake at 220°C/4250F/gas mark 7 for 15–20 minutes until puffy, golden and cooked through.

Fish Mousse

425 g/15 oz/1 large can tuna or
   salmon
1 sachet powdered gelatine
30 ml/1 tbsp water
45 ml/3 tbsp mayonnaise
15 ml/1 tbsp tomato purée (paste)
10 ml/2 tsp anchovy essence
   (extract) (optional)
30 ml/2 tbsp lemon juice
Salt and freshly ground black pepper
300 ml/¹/₂ pt/1¹/₄ cups double
   (heavy) or whipping cream
Lettuce leaves

Drain the fish and mash well, discarding any skin and bones. Dissolve the gelatine in the water according to the packet directions. Add the mayonnaise, tomato purée, anchovy essence, if using, lemon juice and a little salt and pepper and beat well. Beat in the dissolved gelatine. Whip the cream until softly peaking and fold into the fish mixture with a metal spoon. Turn into an oiled fish or jelly mould (jello mold) or an attractive serving dish. Chill until set. Just before serving, turn out, if necessary, on to a bed of lettuce leaves.

Spaghetti with Clams

350 g/12 oz spaghetti
1 onion, chopped
1 garlic clove, crushed
15 ml/1 tbsp olive oil
300 ml/¹/₂ pt/1¹/₄ cups passata
(sieved tomatoes)
300 g/11 oz/1 small can baby clams,
drained
Salt and freshly ground black pepper
Chopped parsley

Cook the spaghetti in plenty of boiling, salted water for 10 minutes or until just tender, drain. Meanwhile, fry (sauté) the onion and garlic in the oil for 3 minutes, stirring, until soft but not brown. Add the passata, clams and a little salt and pepper and simmer for 5 minutes. Add to the spaghetti and toss well. Garnish with parsley and serve.

Smoky Jackets

4 large potatoes
25 g/1 oz/2 tbsp butter or margarine
225 g/8 oz/1 cup low-fat soft cheese
100 g/4 oz/1 small can smoked
mussels
15 ml/1 tbsp snipped chives
Lemon juice
Salt and freshly ground black pepper

Scrub the potatoes. Make a cut lengthways round the centre of each potato, ready to cut in half when cooked. Boil in water for about 20 minutes or until tender. (Alternatively, bake in a moderate oven for about 1 hour or microwave or pressure cook according to appliance instructions.) Cut the potatoes into halves and scoop out most of the flesh into a bowl, leaving a 'shell' of skin and potato. Mash the flesh with the butter or margarine and the cheese. Drain the mussels and roughly chop, or leave whole if preferred. Mix with the potato, add the chives, a little lemon juice and salt and pepper to taste. Pile back into the shells and place under a moderate grill (broiler) for about 5 minutes or until golden and heated through.

Peppered Trout

4 rainbow trout
15 ml/1 tbsp oil
15 ml/1 tbsp butter or margarine
80 g/3¹/₄ oz/scant ¹/₂ cup soft cheese
with black pepper
45 ml/3 tbsp milk
Chopped parsley

Rinse the fish, dry on kitchen paper and cut off the heads, if preferred. Heat the oil and butter or margarine in a large frying pan (skillet) and fry (sauté) the fish for 5 minutes on each side until cooked through. Transfer to a warmed serving plate and keep warm. Strain the cooking juices into a saucepan to avoid any bits of skin in the sauce. Add the cheese and 30 ml/2 tbsp of the milk. Heat through gently, stirring until the cheese melts. Add a little more milk until the sauce is a pouring consistency. Pour over the fish, sprinkle with chopped parsley and serve.

Hasty Crab Thermidor

SERVES 4

1 packet white sauce mix, plus milk
or water to make up, or 1
quantity Basic White Sauce (see
page 00)
15 ml/1 tbsp brandy
5 ml/1 tsp Dijon mustard
2.5 ml/¹/₂ tsp mixed dried herbs
2 × 170 g/2 × 6 oz/2 small cans
white crabmeat, drained
50 g/2 oz/1 cup breadcrumbs
25 g/1 oz/2 tbsp butter or
margarine, melted
50 g/2 oz/¹/₂ cup grated Cheddar
cheese
Small parsley sprigs

Make up the sauce, using slightly less than the recommended amount of liquid. Stir in the brandy, mustard and herbs. Spoon a layer of half the sauce into the base of 4 individual gratin or other shallow fireproof dishes. Top with the crabmeat, then cover with the rest of the sauce. Mix the breadcrumbs with the melted butter or margarine and the cheese. Sprinkle over. Place under a moderate grill (broiler) until golden brown and heated through, about 5–8 minutes. Garnish with small parsley sprigs.

Fisherman's Pizza

SERVES 2–4

23 cm/9 in ready-made pizza base
45 ml/3 tbsp tomato purée (paste)
2.5 ml/¹/₂ tsp dried oregano
1 packet cheese sauce mix
About 250 ml/8 fl oz/1 cup milk or
water (according to packet)
120 g/4¹/₂ oz/1 small can sild in oil
(or small sardines), drained
50 g/2 oz/¹/₂ cup grated Cheddar
cheese
Chopped parsley

Put the pizza base on a baking sheet. Spread with the tomato purée to within 1 cm/¹/₂ in of the edge. Sprinkle with the oregano. Make up the cheese sauce using less than the recommended amount of milk and water (to give a thicker consistency). Spread over the tomato purée. Arrange the sild in a starburst pattern on top and sprinkle with the cheese. Bake in the oven at 220°C/425°F/gas mark 7 for about 20 minutes or until golden and bubbling. Serve hot, garnished with parsley.

Quick Fish Pot

SERVES 4

350 g/12 oz white fish fillet
400 g/14 oz/1 large can chopped
*   tomatoes*
300 ml/¹/₂ pt/1¹/₄ cups vegetable or
fish stock
5 ml/1 tsp anchovy essence (extract)
275 g/10 oz/1 small can new
*   potatoes, drained and quartered*
275 g/10 oz/1 small can sliced
*   carrots, drained*
275 g/10 oz/1 small can garden
*   peas, drained*
Salt and freshly ground black pepper
Chopped parsley

Cut the fish into small chunks, discarding the skin and any bones. Place the tomatoes and stock in a large saucepan. Add the remaining ingredients except the parsley, adding the fish last. Bring to the boil, reduce the heat, cover and simmer for 5 minutes until the fish is tender. Stir gently and season to taste. Ladle into large, warmed soup bowls and garnish with parsley.

Madame Bovary's Omelette

SERVES 4

1 small onion, finely chopped
125 g/5 oz/²/₃ cup butter
2 × 100 g/2 × 4 oz/2 small cans soft
*   cod roes*
100 g/4 oz/1 small can tuna
8 eggs, beaten
Salt and freshly ground black pepper
15 g/1 tbsp chopped parsley
5 ml/1 tsp mixed dried herbs
Lemon juice

Fry (sauté) the onion in 50 g/2 oz/¹/₄ cup of the butter for about 3 minutes until soft but not brown. Drain the roes and tuna and mix with the onion. Stir into the beaten eggs and season. Melt 10 g/¹/₄ oz/¹/₂ tbsp of the remaining butter in an omelette pan. Add a quarter of the mixture and lift and stir the egg gently in the pan until just set and golden underneath. Fold twice to form a triangle and slide on to a warmed serving plate. Keep warm while you make three more omelettes. Melt the remaining butter and stir in the parsley, mixed herbs and a little lemon juice to taste. Pour a little around each omelette and serve.

Crab and Cheese Tart

SERVES 4

50 g/2 oz/¹/₄ cup butter, melted
8 filo pastry (paste) sheets
170 g/6 oz/1 small can crabmeat
175 g/6 oz Port Salut or St Paulin
*   cheese*
3 eggs
300 ml/¹/₂ pt/1¹/₄ cups crème fraîche
*   or single (light) cream*
Salt and freshly ground black pepper
2.5 ml/¹/₂ tsp dried thyme

Lightly butter a 20 cm/8 in flan dish (pie pan). Layer the sheets of pastry in the dish, brushing with butter between the layers, allowing the edges of the pastry to hang over the sides of the dish. Drain the crab and spread on the pastry base. Cut the orange rind off the cheese thinly and discard. Slice the cheese and lay over the crab. Beat the eggs with the crème fraîche, a little salt and pepper and the thyme. Pour over the filling, then gently fold the pastry flaps over the top. Brush the top lightly with the remaining butter. Bake in the oven at 180°C/350°F/gas mark 4 for about 30–35 minutes or until set and golden. Serve warm.

Spicy Cod with Beans

SERVES 4

25 g/1 oz/2 tbsp butter
4 cod steaks
200 g/7 oz/1 small can chopped
*   tomatoes*
15 ml/1 tbsp tomato purée (paste)
275 g/10 oz/1 small can green
*   beans, drained*
2.5 ml/¹/₂ tsp cayenne
5 ml/1 tsp caster (superfine) sugar
Salt and freshly ground black pepper
Plain boiled rice

Melt the butter in a large frying pan (skillet). Fry (sauté) the fish for 5 minutes on one side. Turn over. Add the remaining ingredients except the rice, cover with foil or a lid and simmer for 6 minutes. Serve on a bed of boiled rice.

Seafood and Fennel Farfalle

SERVES 4

1 fennel bulb
45 ml/3 tbsp olive oil
8 spring onions (scallions), chopped
30 ml/2 tbsp white wine
225 g/8 oz/2 cups frozen seafood
*   cocktail, thawed*
Salt and freshly ground black pepper
225 g/8 oz/2 cups farfalle (pasta
*   bows)*
Lemon twists

Finely chop the fennel, reserving the green fronds for garnish. Heat the oil in a saucepan. Add the chopped fennel and spring onions and cook, stirring, for 3 minutes. Cover with a lid and cook gently for 5 minutes until softened. Add the wine and the seafood. Bring to the boil, reduce the heat and cook gently, stirring, for about 3 minutes until heated through. Season to taste with salt and pepper. Meanwhile, cook the pasta according to the packet directions. Drain and return to the saucepan. Add the sauce and toss over a gentle heat. Garnish with lemon twists and the reserved fennel fronds before serving.

Tuscan Tuna and Bean Macaroni

SERVES 6

225 g/8 oz/2 cups short-cut
*   macaroni*
250 ml/8 fl oz/1 cup olive oil
100 ml/3¹/₂ fl oz/6¹/₂ tbsp lemon
*   juice*
2 garlic cloves, crushed
2 × 425 g/2 × 15 oz/2 large cans
*   cannellini beans, drained*
30 ml/2 tbsp chopped parsley
185 g/6¹/₂ oz/1 small can tuna,
*   drained*
Salt and freshly ground black pepper
A few stoned (pitted) black olives
Snipped chives

Cook the macaroni according to the packet directions. Drain. Meanwhile, mix together the oil, lemon juice, garlic, cannellini beans and parsley in a saucepan. Cook for 5 minutes, stirring occasionally until heated through. Gently fold in the tuna and a little salt and pepper and heat through, taking care not to break up the tuna chunks. Add to the macaroni and toss gently. Spoon on to warmed plates and garnish with a few black olives and some snipped chives before serving.

Cheesy Tuna and Sweetcorn

SERVES 4

175 g/6 oz/1¹/₂ cups rigatoni
20 g/³/₄ oz/3 tbsp plain (all-purpose) flour
20 g/³/₄ oz/1¹/₂ tbsp butter
300 ml/¹/₂ pt/1¹/₄ cups milk
50 g/2 oz/¹/₂ cup grated strong Cheddar cheese
Salt and freshly ground black pepper
185 g/6¹/₂ oz/1 small can tuna, drained
200 g/7 oz/1 small can sweetcorn (corn), drained
15 ml/1 tbsp chopped parsley
Garlic croûtons

Cook the pasta according to the packet directions. Drain. Whisk the flour, butter and milk together in a saucepan until the flour is well blended in. Bring to the boil, stirring all the time, until thickened and smooth. Simmer for 2 minutes. Add the pasta and the remaining ingredients except the croûtons, and heat through, stirring until piping hot. Pile on to warm plates and garnish with garlic croûtons.

Caviar-topped Prawn with Artichoke Nests

SERVES 4

45 ml/3 tbsp olive oil
1 onion, finely chopped
45 ml/3 tbsp dry white vermouth
425 g/15 oz/1 large can artichoke hearts, drained and chopped
100 g/4 oz/1 cup peeled prawns (shrimp)
6 stoned (pitted) green olives, halved
Freshly ground black pepper
15 ml/1 tbsp snipped chives
350 g/12 oz cappellini or other thin pasta strands
A little butter
50 g/2 oz/1 small jar Danish lumpfish roe

Heat the oil in a saucepan. Add the onion and fry (sauté) gently for 3 minutes until softened but not browned. Add the vermouth, bring to the boil and simmer for 1 minute. Add the artichokes, prawns, olives and a good grinding of pepper. Heat through, stirring gently, until piping hot. Add the chives. Meanwhile, cook the pasta according to the packet directions. Drain, add a few flakes of butter and toss gently. Divide between serving plates and coil round to form 'nests'. Spoon the sauce in the centre and top each with a spoonful of lumpfish roe.

Cod Ragu

SERVES 4–6

1 onion, chopped
1 garlic clove, crushed
15 ml/1 tbsp olive oil
100 g/4 oz/2 cups button mushrooms,
  sliced
400 g/14 oz/1 large can chopped
  tomatoes
15 ml/1 tbsp tomato purée (paste)
50 g/2 oz/¹/₂ cup shelled peas
15 ml/1 tbsp chopped basil leaves
Salt and freshly ground black pepper
450 g/1 lb cod fillet, skinned and
  diced
Boiled brown rice
Grated Cheddar cheese

Fry (sauté) the onion and garlic in the oil for 2 minutes until softened but not browned. Add the remaining ingredients except the cod, rice and cheese. Bring to the boil, reduce the heat and simmer for 10 minutes until pulpy. Add the fish and cook for a further 5 minutes, stirring gently occasionally until the fish is cooked. Spoon on to a bed of brown rice and sprinkle with grated cheese.

Welsh Scallop and Bacon Pie

SERVES 4

2 small leeks, sliced
25 g/1 oz/2 tbsp butter
90 ml/6 tbsp fish stock
3 streaky bacon rashers (slices)
175 g/6 oz/1¹/₂ cups baby scallops
50 g/2 oz/¹/₄ cup fromage frais
Salt and freshly ground black pepper
450 g/1 lb/2 cups cooked mashed
  potato
15 ml/1 tbsp chopped parsley

Fry (sauté) the leeks in half the butter for 2 minutes until softened but not browned. Add the stock, cover and simmer gently for 5 minutes until tender. Purée in a blender or food processor, then return to the saucepan. Meanwhile, dry-fry the bacon until the fat runs. Add the scallops and cook quickly, tossing for 2 minutes until cooked through. Stir the fromage frais into the leek purée. Add the bacon and scallops and stir in gently. Season to taste and heat through until piping hot. Make the mashed potato into a nest on a flameproof dish and dot with the remaining butter. Place under a hot grill (broiler) to brown. Spoon the scallop mixture in the centre and sprinkle with the parsley.

Tagliatelle Alla Rustica

SERVES 4

350 g/12 oz tagliatelle (preferably
  fresh)
2 garlic cloves, crushed
90 ml/6 tbsp olive oil
50 g/2 oz/1 small can anchovy
  fillets, chopped, reserving the oil
5 ml/1 tsp dried oregano
Salt and freshly ground black pepper
45 ml/3 tbsp roughly chopped
  parsley
Fresh Parmesan cheese

Cook the pasta according to the packet directions. Drain and return to the saucepan. Meanwhile, fry (sauté) the garlic in the oil until golden brown. Remove from the heat and add the anchovies in their oil. Return to the heat and cook gently, stirring, until the anchovies form a paste. Stir in the oregano, a very little salt and lots of black pepper. Add to the tagliatelle and toss well. Spoon on to plates and sprinkle with the parsley and Parmesan cheese thinly shaved from the block with a potato peeler.

Smoked Salmon, Egg and Broccoli Grill

SERVES 6

225 g/8 oz tagliatelle al pomodoro (red pasta)
225 g/8 oz broccoli, cut into tiny florets
100 g/4 oz/1 cup smoked salmon pieces
300 ml/¹/₂ pt/1¹/₄ cups crème fraîche
15 ml/1 tbsp chopped dill (dill weed)
2 hard-boiled (hard-cooked) eggs, roughly chopped
Salt and freshly ground black pepper
A little butter
50 g/2 oz/¹/₂ cup Mozzarella cheese, grated
Small dill (dill weed) sprigs

Cook the pasta according to the packet directions. Drain and return to the saucepan. Steam the broccoli or boil in a little salted water until just tender. Drain and return to the pan. Add the remaining ingredients except the butter, cheese and dill sprigs. Heat through gently, stirring lightly until piping hot. Add the pasta, toss gently and turn into a flameproof dish. Dot with butter and sprinkle with cheese. Place under a hot grill (broiler) until the cheese melts. Garnish with dill before serving.

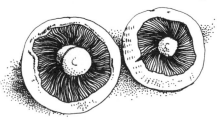

Scottish Smoked Haddock

SERVES 4

225 g/8 oz/2 cups elbow macaroni
225 g/8 oz smoked haddock fillet
450 ml/³/₄ pt/2 cups milk
1 bay leaf
25 g/1 oz/2 tbsp butter
100 g/4 oz/2 cups button mushrooms, sliced
25 g/1 oz/¹/₄ cup plain (all-purpose) flour
75 g/3 oz/³/₄ cup grated Cheddar cheese
Salt and white pepper
300 ml/¹/₂ pt/1¹/₄ cups warmed passata (sieved tomatoes)

Cook the pasta according to the packet directions. Drain. Meanwhile, poach the fish in the milk with the bay leaf for 5 minutes or until it flakes easily with a fork. Reserve the milk. Discard the skin and any bones from the fish and break into bite-sized pieces. Melt the butter in the saucepan, add the mushrooms and cook gently, stirring, for 1 minute. Add the flour and cook for a further minute. Remove from the heat and gradually blend in the reserved milk, discarding the bay leaf. Return to the heat, bring to the boil and cook for 2 minutes, stirring. Stir in the cheese and season to taste. Gently fold in the fish and reheat until piping hot. Add the cooked macaroni and toss well. If liked, sprinkle with a little more grated cheese and flash under a hot grill (broiler) to brown the top. Serve with the warmed passata handed separately.

Cidered Prawns with Courgettes

50 g/2 oz/¹/₄ cup butter
1 bunch of spring onions (scallions),
chopped
2 courgettes (zucchini), sliced
450 ml/³/₄ pt/2 cups fish stock
150 ml/¹/₄ pt/²/₃ cup dry cider
30 ml/2 tbsp cornflour (cornstarch)
175 g/6 oz/1¹/₂ cups peeled prawns
(shrimp)
15 ml/1 tbsp chopped parsley
Salt and white pepper
150 ml/¹/₄ pt/²/₃ cup single (light)
cream
Buttered rice

Melt the butter in a saucepan. Add the spring onions and courgettes and fry (sauté) gently for 2 minutes. Cover and cook for 5 minutes until softened but not browned, stirring occasionally. Add the stock and bring to the boil. Simmer for 2 minutes. Blend the cider with the cornflour and stir into the mixture. Bring to the boil and simmer for 1 minute, stirring all the time. Stir in the prawns, parsley, a little salt and pepper and the cream. Heat through gently until piping hot. Spoon on to buttered rice and serve hot.

Cidered Crab with Cucumber

Prepare as for Cidered Prawns with Courgettes but substitute diced crabsticks for the prawns (shrimp) and ¹/₄ cucumber, diced, for the courgettes (zucchini).

Olympian Tuna and Tomato Supper

1 garlic clove, crushed
150 ml/¹/₄ pt/²/₃ cup chicken stock
200 g/7 oz/1 small can chopped
tomatoes
15 ml/1 tbsp tomato purée (paste)
30 ml/2 tbsp snipped chives
45 ml/3 tbsp dry vermouth
185 g/6¹/₂ oz/1 small can tuna,
drained
10 ml/2 tsp cornflour (cornstarch)
15 ml/1 tbsp water
Salt and freshly ground black pepper
15 ml/1 tbsp olive oil
350 g/12 oz tagliatelle
30 ml/2 tbsp single (light) cream

Place the garlic, stock, tomatoes, tomato purée, chives and vermouth in a saucepan. Bring to the boil, reduce the heat and simmer for 5 minutes or until reduced by half. Add the tuna and heat through, stirring. Blend the cornflour with the water. Add to the sauce, bring to the boil and simmer for 1 minute stirring. Season to taste and stir in the olive oil. Meanwhile, cook the pasta according to the packet directions. Drain. Toss in the cream and heat through gently. Sprinkle well with black pepper. Pile on to plates and spoon the sauce on top.

Sharp Cumin Prawn Kebabs

SERVES 4

15 ml/1 tbsp cumin seeds
15 ml/1 tbsp grated lemon rind
1 spring onion (scallion), finely
*   chopped*
30 ml/2 tbsp chopped parsley
5 ml/1 tsp sugar
60 ml/4 tbsp oil
45 ml/3 tbsp lemon juice
Salt and freshly ground black pepper
450 g/1 lb large raw prawns
*   (shrimp)*

Lightly brown the cumin seeds in a dry frying pan (skillet). Crush the seeds and mix with the lemon rind, spring onion, parsley, sugar, oil and lemon juice. Season with salt and pepper. Rub over the prawns and leave to stand for about 2 hours. Thread the prawns on to soaked wooden skewers and grill (broil) for about 10 minutes, turning regularly.

Italian-style Prawn and Salami Kebabs

SERVES 4

450 g/1 lb raw king prawns (shrimp)
225 g/8 oz salami
Salt and freshly ground black pepper
60 ml/4 tbsp extra virgin olive oil
225 g/8 oz Mozzarella cheese, diced
4 ripe tomatoes, sliced
15 ml/1 tbsp balsamic vinegar
30 ml/2 tbsp chopped basil

Peel the prawns if you wish and remove or leave the tails, as you prefer. Cut the salami into small chunks. Thread the prawns and salami alternately on to soaked wooden skewers and season with salt and pepper. Brush with a little oil. Grill (broil) the kebabs for about 5 minutes, turning frequently. Arrange the cheese and tomato slices in overlapping rows in a flat serving dish and sprinkle with the remaining oil, the vinegar and basil. Season generously with pepper and a little salt. Place the kebabs on top of the cheese to serve.

Scallop and Courgette Kebabs

SERVES 4

50 g/2 oz/¹/₄ cup butter or
*   margarine, melted*
225 g/8 oz/2 cups shallots or onions,
*   chopped*
400 g/14 oz/1 large can chopped
*   tomatoes*
30 ml/2 tbsp chopped fresh basil
Salt and freshly ground black pepper
350 g/12 oz/3 cups shelled scallops
2 courgettes (zucchini), cut into
*   chunks*
15 ml/1 tbsp oil

Heat the butter or margarine and fry (sauté) the onions until soft, but not brown. Add the tomatoes and simmer gently for about 5 minutes. Stir in the basil and season with salt and pepper. Thread the scallops and courgette chunks alternately on to soaked wooden skewers. Season with salt and pepper and brush with a little oil. Grill (broil) the kebabs for about 10 minutes, turning and brushing with more oil if necessary. Meanwhile, reheat the sauce to serve with the kebabs.

Spiced Scallop and Mangetout Kebabs

SERVES 4

30 ml/2 tbsp oil
1 onion, finely chopped
2 garlic cloves, crushed
60 ml/4 tbsp soy sauce
45 ml/3 tbsp tomato purée (paste)
45 ml/3 tbsp red wine vinegar
30 ml/2 tbsp light brown sugar
2.5 ml/¹/₂ tsp ground ginger
2.5 ml/¹/₂ tsp chilli powder
350 g/12 oz/3 cups shelled scallops
225 g/8 oz mangetout (snow peas)

Heat the oil and fry (sauté) the onion and garlic until soft, but not brown. Add the soy sauce, tomato purée, vinegar, sugar, ginger and chilli, bring to the boil, then simmer for 3 minutes, stirring. Thread the scallops and mangetout alternately on to soaked wooden skewers. Brush with the sauce. Grill (broil) the kebabs for about 10 minutes, turning frequently and brushing with more sauce. Serve with any remaining sauce.

Baked Florida Haddock Parcels

SERVES 4

25 g/1 oz/2 tbsp butter or margarine
10 ml/2 tsp finely grated orange rind
10 ml/2 tsp finely grated grapefruit rind
Freshly grated nutmeg
4 haddock or other white fish fillets
Salt and freshly ground black pepper

Grease 4 squares of foil with half the butter or margarine and sprinkle with half the grated rinds and a little nutmeg. Season the fish on both sides with salt and pepper and lay the fish on the foil.

Sprinkle with the remaining rind and a little more nutmeg. Dot with the remaining butter. Close the foil parcels and place on a baking sheet. Bake in the oven at 180°C/350°F/gas mark 4 for about 25 minutes until the fish is cooked. Transfer the parcels to serving plates and open them at the table.

Herring with Chick Peas

SERVES 4

4 herring, cleaned
30 ml/2 tbsp oil
Salt and freshly ground black pepper
400 g/14 oz/1 large can chick peas (garbanzos)
60 ml/4 tbsp passata (sieved tomatoes
15 ml/1 tbsp chopped coriander (cilantro) or parsley

Slash the herring diagonally 2 or 3 times on each side. Brush with oil and season with salt and pepper. Grill (broil) the herring for about 8 minutes on each side, depending on the size, until cooked through and crisp. Meanwhile, warm the chick peas in a pan. Drain, then mix in the passata and warm through gently, stirring. Season with salt and pepper. Arrange the chick pea mixture in a serving dish, lay the grilled fish on top and sprinkle with coriander or parsley.

Mackerel with Fresh Mango Chutney

SERVES 4

4 mackerel, cleaned
90 ml/6 tbsp lime juice
15 ml/1 tbsp lemon juice
Salt and freshly ground black pepper
Oil
1 mango, chopped
1 red onion, chopped
15 ml/1 tbsp chopped fresh chilli
15 ml/1 tbsp chopped
coriander (cilantro)
Few drops of Tabasco sauce

Slash the mackerel diagonally through the skin 3 or 4 times on each side. Place in a shallow dish, pour over half the lime juice and the lemon juice and season with salt and pepper. Leave to marinate for at least 1 hour, preferably 3 hours. Mix together the remaining ingredients and turn into a small serving dish. Brush the fish with oil and grill (broil) for about 6–8 minutes on each side, depending on the size. Serve with the chutney.

Marmalade Mackerel

SERVES 4

100 g/4 oz/¹/₃ cup marmalade
4 mackerel, cleaned
50 g/2 oz/¹/₄ cup butter or
margarine, melted
Salt and freshly ground black pepper
45 ml/3 tbsp fine oatmeal
15 ml/1 tbsp chopped parsley
Lemon slices

Spoon the marmalade inside the cavity of each fish and secure with cocktail sticks (toothpicks). Brush the fish generously with butter or margarine. Season with salt and pepper and dust with oatmeal. Grill (broil) for about 8 minutes on each side until cooked through and crisp. Sprinkle with parsley and serve with lemon slices.

Roughy with Hot Sauce

SERVES 4

1.5 ml/¹/₄ tsp chilli powder
Pinch of dried thyme
45 ml/3 tbsp butter or margarine,
softened
550 g/1¹/₄ lb roughy (or other firm
white fish) fillets
Salt and freshly ground black pepper
15 ml/1 tbsp Tabasco sauce
3 spring onions (scallions), finely
chopped
375 ml/13 fl oz/1¹/₂ cups plain
yoghurt

Blend the chilli powder and thyme into the butter or margarine and spread half the butter over one side of the fish. Season with salt and pepper. Place on foil on a grill (broiler) rack. Grill (broil) for about 5 minutes on one side, then turn and spread the other side with the remaining butter. Season with salt and pepper and grill for a further 3 minutes until just cooked. Meanwhile, stir the Tabasco sauce and spring onions into the yoghurt. Serve with the cooked fillets.

Salmon with Sesame Seeds

SERVES 4

75 ml/5 tbsp sesame seeds
4 salmon steaks
45 ml/3 tbsp oil
Salt and freshly ground black pepper
1 bunch of watercress
8 salad leaves, cut into chunks
6 spring onions (scallions), sliced
60 ml/4 tbsp olive oil
30 ml/2 tbsp sesame oil
45 ml/3 tbsp red wine vinegar
30 ml/2 tbsp soy sauce
15 ml/1 tbsp grated fresh root ginger
5 ml/1 tsp sugar

Toast the sesame seeds in a dry pan until golden, shaking the pan regularly. Brush the salmon with oil and season with salt and pepper. Grill (broil) for about 5 minutes on each side. Mix together the watercress, salad leaves and spring onions in a shallow serving bowl. Whisk together the remaining ingredients, pour over the salad and toss well. Arrange the salmon on the salad and serve garnished with the sesame seeds.

Salmon with Pesto

SERVES 4

4 salmon steaks
200 g/7 oz/scant 1 cup Pesto Sauce
   (see page 252) or from a jar
150 ml/¼ pt/⅔ cup dry white wine

Place the salmon in a shallow bowl. Mix together the Pesto Sauce and wine and spoon over the fish, coating it well. Leave to marinate for 1 hour. Place on foil on a grill (broiler) rack. Grill (broil) the salmon for about 8 minutes on each side, basting with more sauce as it cooks. Serve with any remaining sauce on the side.

Dill Salmon

SERVES 4

50 g/2 oz/¼ cup chopped dill
   (dill weed)
50 g/2 oz/¼ cup light brown sugar
Salt and freshly ground black pepper
4 salmon steaks
75 ml/5 tbsp oil
120 ml/4 fl oz/½ cup white wine
   vinegar
Dill sprigs

Mix together the dill, sugar, salt and pepper and rub over the steaks; you should use about ¾ of the mixture. Leave to marinate for 2 hours. Mix the remaining herb mixture with the oil and vinegar and brush over the steaks on both sides. Grill (broil) for about 5–6 minutes on each side until cooked through and browned, brushing frequently with the oil and vinegar mixture. Transfer to warmed plates and spoon any juices over. Garnish with dill sprigs.

Mediterranean Sardines

SERVES 4

90 ml/6 tbsp olive oil
15 ml/1 tbsp white wine vinegar
2 garlic cloves, crushed
1 shallot, finely chopped
30 ml/2 tbsp chopped basil
15 ml/1 tbsp chopped parsley
Juice and grated rind of 1 lemon
2.5 ml/½ tsp Dijon mustard
45 ml/3 tbsp plain (all-purpose)
   flour
Salt and freshly ground black pepper
450 g/1 lb sardines

Make the sauce in advance to allow the flavours to develop: purée half the oil with the vinegar, garlic, shallot, herbs, lemon juice and rind and the mustard. Pour into a small bowl. Season the flour with salt and pepper. Dip the sardines in the flour, then shake off any excess. Fry (sauté) in the remaining oil for about 3 minutes on each side. Drain on kitchen paper. Serve with the sauce.

Drunken Swordfish

SERVES 4

175 ml/6 fl oz/³/4 cup bourbon or
  whisky
175 ml/6 fl oz/³/4 cup fish or chicken
  stock
75 ml/5 tbsp groundnut (peanut) oil
2 garlic cloves, crushed
Salt and freshly ground black pepper
4 swordfish steaks

Mix together the bourbon or whisky, stock, oil and garlic and season very generously with salt and pepper. Place the steaks in a glass or ceramic bowl, pour over the marinade, cover and leave to marinate for at least 1¹/2 hours. Drain the fish, season generously on both sides with salt and pepper and leave to stand until you are ready to cook. Boil the marinade vigorously until it is reduced by half. Keep warm. Grill (broil) the fish for about 10–15 minutes on each side depending on the thickness, drizzling occasionally with the marinade. Serve with the remaining marinade spooned over.

Mustard-rosemary Swordfish

SERVES 4

Prepare as for Mustard-Rosemary Lamb (see page 98), but substitute 4 skinned swordfish steaks for the lamb chops.

Lemon and Mint Trout

SERVES 4

4 trout, cleaned
15 ml/1 tbsp groundnut (peanut) oil
Salt and freshly ground black pepper
1 lemon, sliced
90 ml/6 tbsp chopped mint
50 g/2 oz/¹/4 cup sugar

Brush the fish inside and out with the oil, then season generously inside and out. Lay out 4 squares of foil. Arrange half the lemon slices in a line on the squares of foil, then sprinkle with half the mint and sugar. Lay the fish on top then sprinkle with the remaining mint and sugar, and place the remaining lemon slices across the top. Close the parcels. Place on a baking sheet and bake in the oven at 190°C/375°F/gas mark 5 for 25–30 minutes until the fish is cooked through. Transfer the parcels to serving plates and serve straight away.

Thai Grilled Fish

SERVES 4

8 plaice fillets, skinned
5 ml/1 tsp salt
Juice of 3 limes
90 ml/6 tbsp light brown sugar
Lime wedges

Sprinkle the fillets with the salt and lime juice and leave to marinate for 20–25 minutes. Sprinkle the sugar over and grill (broil) for about 5 minutes until the fillets are cooked and the sugar has caramelized. Serve garnished with lime wedges.

Sweet and Sour Monkfish Kebabs

SERVES 4

750 g/1¹/₂ lb monkfish or other firm-
fleshed fish
2 onions, sliced into rings
3 courgettes (zucchini), sliced
1 lemon, thinly sliced
60 ml/4 tbsp clear honey
30 ml/2 tbsp lemon juice
15 ml/1 tbsp soy sauce
Pinch of chilli powder

Cut the fish into large chunks. Thread the fish, onions, courgettes and lemon alternately on to soaked wooden skewers. Lay the kebabs in a shallow dish. Mix together the remaining ingredients and pour over the kebabs. Leave to marinate for 30 minutes. Grill (broil) the kebabs for about 15 minutes, turning frequently and basting with the remaining marinade.

Lemon-Tabasco Fish

SERVES 4

4 cod or other white fish fillets
120 ml/4 fl oz/¹/₂ cup oil
45 ml/3 tbsp lemon juice
5 ml/1 tsp Tabasco sauce
8 spring onions (scallions), trimmed

Place the fish in a shallow dish. Mix together the oil, lemon juice and Tabasco sauce and pour over the fish. Leave to marinate for 1 hour. Lay the fish on foil on a grill (broiler) rack. Grill (broil) for about 5 minutes each side, depending on the thickness, basting with more marinade while they cook. Add the spring onions to the grill for the last few minutes of cooking and serve with the fish.

Pascada à la Marina

SERVES 6

750 g/1¹/₂ lb haddock or cod fillets,
cut into strips
2 bay leaves
60 ml/4 tbsp olive oil
30 ml/2 tbsp lemon juice
1 small onion, finely chopped
1 garlic clove, crushed
5 ml/1 tsp salt
Freshly ground black pepper
Grated nutmeg
1 egg, lightly beaten
100 g/4 oz/2 cups fresh white
breadcrumbs
Oil for shallow-frying

Put the fish into a shallow dish with the bay leaves on top. Blend the oil, lemon juice, onion, garlic and seasoning and pour over. Leave to marinate for at least 1 hour, turning from time to time. Dry the fish on kitchen paper, dip in the egg then the breadcrumbs. Leave the coating to harden before frying. Fry (sauté) the fish on both sides in hot oil and drain on kitchen paper. Serve hot or cold.

Trout in Lemon Butter Sauce

SERVES 4

4 large trout fillets
2.5 ml/¹/₂ tsp dried rosemary
2.5 ml/¹/₂ tsp salt
1.5 ml/¹/₄ tsp freshly ground black
pepper
25 g/1 oz/¹/₄ cup plain (all-purpose)
flour
120 ml/4 fl oz/¹/₂ cup sunflower oil
50 g/2 oz/¹/₄ cup butter
Juice of 1 lemon
30 ml/2 tbsp finely chopped parsley

Sprinkle the fish with the rosemary, salt and pepper and coat with flour. Fry (sauté) the fish in the oil until just cooked (4–5 minutes). Transfer to warmed serving plates. Pour off the oil, add the butter, lemon juice and parsley and cook for about 1 minute, scraping any residue from the bottom of the pan. Pour the sauce over the fish and serve.

Trout in Pernod Sauce

SERVES 4

4 large trout fillets
Seasoned flour
100 g/4 oz/¹/₂ cup unsalted (sweet) butter
225 g/8 oz/4 cups button mushrooms, thinly sliced
1 garlic clove, crushed
45 ml/3 tbsp Pernod or Pastis
150 ml/¹/₄ pt/²/₃ cup double (heavy) cream
Salt and freshly ground black pepper

Coat the trout fillets in seasoned flour and fry (sauté) in the butter for 4–5 minutes. Tranfer the trout to a serving dish and keep warm. Fry the mushrooms and garlic in the trout juices over a gentle heat for 3–4 minutes. Stir in the Pernod or Pastis and simmer for 3–4 minutes until reduced slightly. Add the cream and seasoning and heat gently. Pour the sauce over the trout and serve.

Salmon Casserole

SERVES 4

25 g/1 oz/2 tbsp unsalted (sweet) butter
25 g/1 oz/¹/₄ cup plain (all-purpose) flour
300 ml/¹/₂ pt/1¹/₄ cups fish stock
300 ml/¹/₂ pt/1¹/₄ cups white wine
300 ml/¹/₂ pt/1¹/₄ cups single (light) cream
750 g/1¹/₂ lb new potatoes, boiled
400 g/14 oz/1 large can pink salmon, drained
Salt and freshly ground black pepper
1 bunch of watercress

Melt the butter, then add the flour and cook for 1 minute, stirring all the time. Remove from the heat and gradually stir in the fish stock, then the wine and return to the heat. Bring to the boil and cook, stirring until thickened. Reduce the heat and stir in the cream. Add the potatoes and salmon, discarding any skin and bone. Season well. Cook for about 3 minutes to heat all the ingredients. Reserve a few watercress sprigs for garnish, chop the rest and fold into the fish mixture, being careful not to break up the salmon too much. Garnish with the reserved watercress sprigs.

Heavenly Fish Dish

SERVES 6

6 × 100 g/6 × 4 oz cod steaks
450 ml/³/₄ pt/2 cups milk
6 peppercorns
2 bay leaves
2 leeks, thinly sliced
50 g/2 oz/¹/₄ cup unsalted (sweet)
butter
25 g/1 oz/¹/₄ cup plain (all-purpose)
flour
250 ml/8 fl oz/1 cup white wine
10 ml/2 tsp dried dill (dill weed)
5 ml/1 tsp dill seed
30 ml/2 tbsp lemon juice
Salt and freshly ground black pepper
450 g/1 lb/4 cups peeled prawns
(shrimp)
4 tomatoes, chopped
750 g/1¹/₂ lb potatoes, cooked and
thinly sliced
30 ml/2 tbsp olive oil
30 ml/2 tbsp grated Parmesan
cheese

Bring the cod, milk, peppercorns and bay leaves to the boil in a saucepan, then simmer for 6–7 minutes. Remove the fish, break into biggish flakes and put into an ovenproof dish. Strain the milk and set aside. Fry (sauté) the leeks gently in the butter for 5 minutes. Stir in the flour and cook for a minute. Gradually stir in the reserved milk and the wine and cook, stirring all the time, until thickened and smooth. Remove from the heat and add the dill and dill seed, lemon juice and salt and pepper. Arrange the prawns and tomatoes on top of the cod and pour the sauce over. Top with the sliced potatoes, brush with olive oil and sprinkle with the Parmesan. Cook in the oven at 190°C/375°F/gas mark 5 for about 30 minutes until the topping is golden brown. Serve hot.

Seafood Surprises

SERVES 4

4 leeks, thinly sliced
4 × 100 g/4 × 4 oz cod fillets
100 g/4 oz/1 cup peeled prawns
(shrimp)
30 ml/2 tbsp dill (dill weed), roughly
chopped
Salt and freshly ground black pepper
Juice of 1 lemon
25 g/1 oz/2 tbsp unsalted (sweet)
butter, melted
Lemon slices

Cut 4 circles of baking parchment, about 30 cm/12 in diameter. Fold in half, then open out again. Scatter the leeks over half of each circle and top with the cod. Divide the prawns equally between the parcels, sprinkle over the dill and seasoning and pour on the lemon juice and melted butter. Fold over the empty half of each parcel and roll the edges tightly together. Place on a baking sheet and cook in the oven at 200°C/400°F/gas mark 6 for 10–15 minutes. Put each parcel on a dinner plate and garnish with the lemon. Serve at once, opening at the table.

Sole Knots

SERVES 6

900 g/2 lb sole fillets, skinned and
cut into 6 long strips
1 onion, finely chopped
50 g/2 oz/¹/₄ cup butter
6 tomatoes, skinned, seeded and
chopped
6 anchovy fillets, chopped
175 g/6 oz/3 cups button
mushrooms, sliced
Salt and freshly ground black pepper
Croûtons (see page 17)

Tie the strips of fish into knots and put into an ovenproof dish. Fry (sauté) the onion in the butter and when golden add the tomatoes and cook together for 2–3 minutes. Add the anchovy fillets, mushrooms, salt and pepper and cook for a further 2 minutes. Spoon this mixture over the sole knots. Cover and bake in the oven at 190°C/375°F/gas mark 5 for 25 minutes. Garnish with croûtons and serve hot.

Marinated Salmon Steaks

SERVES 6

100 ml/4 fl oz/¹/₂ cup vegetable oil
Grated rind and juice of 2 limes
45 ml/3 tbsp orange juice
5 ml/1 tsp clear honey
2 green cardamoms, crushed
6 × 175 g/6 × 6 oz salmon steaks

Mix together 75 ml/5 tbsp of the oil with the lime rind and juices, honey and the green cardamoms. Pour this marinade over the fish and leave for 12 hours if possible. Drain, reserving the marinade. Grill (broil) the salmon for about 4 minutes on each side. Meanwhile, bring the marinade to the boil and keep warm. Serve the steaks with the sauce poured over.

Fish Parcels

SERVES 4

24 rashers (slices) streaky bacon, rinded
4 × 100 g/4 × 4 oz cod fillets
1 onion, finely chopped
50 g/2 oz/¹/₄ cup unsalted (sweet) butter
150 ml/¹/₄ pt/²/₃ cup white wine
2.5 ml/¹/₂ tsp dried tarragon
60 ml/4 tbsp double (heavy) cream

Stretch the bacon rashers with the back of a knife. Weave 6 of them into a square and put one of the fish portions into the centre. Fold the overlapping bacon around the fish to enclose it. Repeat with the remaining bacon and fish to make another 3 parcels. Fry (sauté) the onion in the butter until soft, then add the fish parcels and fry for 3 minutes until slightly brown. Add the wine and tarragon to the pan, bring to the boil, cover and simmer for 10 minutes. Add the cream and seasoning to taste. Heat through and serve straight away.

Prawn Pilau

SERVES 4

30 ml/2 tbsp oil
25 g/1 oz/¹/₄ cup flaked almonds
2 onions, finely chopped
1 large tomato, chopped
50 g/2 oz/¹/₃ cup sultanas (golden raisins)
225 g/8 oz/2 cups peeled prawns (shrimp)
Good pinch of turmeric
225 g/8 oz/2 cups plain boiled rice
5 ml/1 tsp sugar
5 ml/1 tsp salt

Heat the oil and fry (sauté) the almonds until golden, then remove and keep to one side. Add the onions to the oil and fry until golden brown. Add the tomato and sultanas and fry for about 3 minutes. Add the prawns and cook for 3 minutes. Add the turmeric, rice, sugar and salt. Stir until thoroughly mixed and heated through. The rice can be kept covered in the oven at 140°C/275°F/gas mark 1 for up to an hour before serving.

151

Fish Balls with Yoghurt and Mustard Sauce

SERVES 4

Pinch of turmeric
Pinch of garlic Powder
Pinch of ground coriander
Pinch of ground cumin
Pinch of chilli powder
30 ml/2 tbsp oil
50 g/2 oz/¹/₂ cup finely chopped
*   onion*
225 g/8 oz white fish fillet, cooked
225 g/8 oz/1 cup cooked mashed
*   potato*
15 ml/1 tbsp finely chopped
*   coriander leaves*
5 ml/1 tsp salt
1 egg, beaten
50 g/2 oz/1 cup fresh breadcrumbs
Yoghurt and Mustard Sauce (see
*   page 247)*

Place all the ground spices in a cup with 10 ml/2 tsp water. Heat the oil and fry (sauté) the onion until golden brown. Add the spice mix from the cup and cook gently for about 1 minute. Mash the cooked fish, add to the pan and fry for about 2 minutes. Finally, mix in the mashed potato, coriander leaves and salt. Allow to cool. Shape into about 16 balls. Dip in the egg and then in the breadcrumbs. Deep-fry in batches for about 2 minutes until golden or bake in the oven at 190°C/375°F/gas mark 5 for about 25 minutes. Serve the balls with Yoghurt and Mustard Sauce.

Prawns with Garlic, Spices and Herbs

SERVES 4

Pinch of ground coriander (cilantro)
Pinch of chilli powder
Pinch of ground cumin
5 ml/1 tsp garlic powder
30 ml/2 tbsp oil
100 g/4 oz/1 cup onion, finely
*   chopped*
25 g/1 oz/¹/₄ cup fresh root ginger,
finely chopped
225 g/8 oz/2 cups peeled prawns
*   (shrimp)*
1 large tomato, finely chopped
8 spring onions (scallions), finely
*   chopped*
45 ml/3 tbsp finely chopped
*   coriander*
Pinch of salt
5 ml/1 tsp sugar

Put all the ground spices and garlic powder in a cup and add 15 ml/1 tbsp water. Heat the oil and fry (sauté) the onion until golden brown. Add the ginger and cook for 1 minute, then add the spices from the cup and cook for a further minute. Add the prawns and tomato and stir-fry for about 4 minutes. Add the spring onions, coriander leaves, salt and sugar and cook for about 2 minutes. Serve hot.

Pissaladière

175 g/6 oz/1¹/₂ cups plain (all-purpose) flour
5 ml/1 tsp ground cinnamon
75 g/3 oz/¹/₃ cup butter
30 ml/2 tbsp olive oil
3 onions, chopped
1 garlic clove, crushed
450 g/1 lb/ tomatoes, roughly chopped
15 ml/1 tbsp tomato purée (paste)
2.5 ml/¹/₂ tsp caster (superfine) sugar
Salt and freshly ground black pepper
50 g/2 oz/1 small can anchovy fillets, drained
6 black olives
Chopped parsley

Mix the flour and cinnamon together. Rub in the butter and mix with enough cold water to form a firm dough. Roll out and use to line a 20 cm/8 in flan dish (pie pan). Prick the base with a fork, add some crumpled foil and bake 'blind' for 8 minutes in the oven at 200°C/400°F/gas mark 6. Remove the foil and cook for a further 4 minutes. Meanwhile, heat the oil and soften the onion and garlic for 2 minutes in a large pan. Add the tomatoes, stir, cover and cook for 8 minutes until pulpy. Stir in the tomato purée, sugar and a little salt and pepper. Turn into the pastry case. Spread out and decorate with the anchovies and the olives in a criss-cross pattern. Return to the hot oven for 10 minutes. Garnish with chopped parsley.

Country Cod and Vegetable Fettuccine

300 ml/¹/₂ pt/1¹/₄ cups fish or vegetable stock
60 ml/4 tbsp tomato ketchup (catsup)
30 ml/2 tbsp mayonnaise (not salad cream)
350 g/12 oz/3 cups frozen mixed country vegetables
Salt and freshly ground black pepper
450 g/1 lb cod fillet, skinned and cubed
2.5 ml/¹/₂ tsp mixed dried herbs
350 g/12 oz fettuccine
50 g/2 oz/¹/₂ cup grated Cheddar cheese

Mix together the stock, ketchup and mayonnaise in a saucepan. Add the vegetables and a little seasoning. Cover and simmer for 10 minutes or until tender. Add the fish and herbs and simmer for 5 minutes. Meanwhile, cook the fettuccine according to the packet directions. Drain and pile on to plates. Spoon the sauce over and serve with a little grated cheese sprinkled on top.

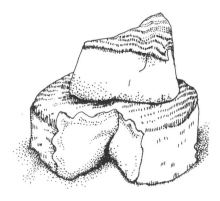

Fruity Curried Haddock

350 g/12 oz haddock fillet, skinned
300 ml/¹/₂ pt/1¹/₄ cups water
30 ml/2 tbsp dried milk powder
  (non-fat dry milk)
25 g/1 oz/2 tbsp butter
2 onions, thinly sliced
30 ml/2 tbsp mild curry powder
25 g/1 oz/¹/₄ cup plain (all-purpose)
  flour
300 ml/¹/₂ pt/1¹/₄ cups apple juice
150 ml/¹/₄ pt/²/₃ cup fish or chicken
  stock
1 eating (dessert) apple, sliced
50 g/2 oz/¹/₃ cup dried apricots,
  chopped
25 g/1 oz/¹/₆ cup sultanas (golden
  raisins)
5 ml/1 tsp caster (superfine) sugar
100 g/4 oz/1 cup peeled prawns
  (shrimp)
Salt and freshly ground black pepper
Plain boiled rice
30 ml/2 tbsp desiccated (shredded)
  coconut

Poach the haddock in the water with the milk powder added for about 8 minutes until it flakes easily with a fork. Drain and roughly break up. Meanwhile, melt the butter in a saucepan. Add the onion and fry (sauté) for 3 minutes until softened and lightly golden. Stir in the curry powder and fry for 1 minute. Remove from the heat, blend in the flour, then the juice and stock. Return to the heat, bring to the boil and cook for 2 minutes, stirring. Add the remaining ingredients except the rice and cocnut and simmer gently for 10 minutes, stirring occasionally. Taste and re-season if necessary. Spoon on to boiled rice and sprinkle with the coconut.

Hake Dolcelatte

75 g/3 oz/¹/₃ cup butter
4 hake fillets, skinned
10 ml/2 tsp lemon juice
225 g/8 oz Dolcelatte cheese
60 ml/4 tbsp single (light) cream
15 ml/1 tbsp chopped parsley
Salt and freshly ground black pepper

Use a little of the butter to grease a large piece of foil on the grill (broiler) rack. Lay the hake, skinned sides up, on the foil. Dot with a third of the remaining butter and sprinkle with lemon juice. Grill (broil) for 5 minutes until almost cooked. Carefully turn over. Meanwhile, mash the remaining butter with the Dolcelatte, cream and parsley. Season with a little salt and lots of pepper. Spread this mixture over the fish and grill for a further 5–8 minutes or until the cheese has melted and is turning golden brown.

Cod Baked with Peppers and Mushrooms

25 g/1 oz/2 tbsp butter
350 g/12 oz/6 cups button
  mushrooms, sliced
Salt and freshly ground black pepper
4 cod steaks
400 g/14 oz/1 large can chopped
  tomatoes
10 ml/2 tsp cornflour (cornstarch)
15 ml/1 tbsp water
15 ml/1 tbsp tomato purée (paste)
1 green (bell) pepper, thinly sliced
  into rings
5 ml/1 tsp dried oregano

Butter a shallow ovenproof dish. Lay the mushrooms in the base and season lightly. Top with the fish. Empty the tomatoes into a saucepan. Blend the cornflour with the water and tomato purée and stir into the pan. Bring to the boil, stirring until thickened. Pour over the fish. Top with the pepper rings and sprinkle with oregano and a little more salt and pepper. Bake in the oven at 180°C/350°F/gas mark 4 for 30 minutes until the fish and mushrooms are cooked through.

Monkfish and Bacon Kebabs

SERVES 4

450 g/1 lb monkfish tail, cubed
30 ml/1 tbsp lemon juice
60 ml/4 tbsp olive oil
Salt and freshly ground black pepper
1 garlic clove, chopped
15 ml/1 tbsp chopped parsley
15 ml/1 tbsp snipped chives
4 rashers (slices) streaky bacon,
*   rinded and cut into squares*
8 cherry tomatoes

Place the fish in a shallow dish. Pour over the lemon juice and oil and add a little salt and pepper, the garlic and herbs. Toss well and leave to marinate for 2 hours. Thread the fish on to skewers with the bacon and tomatoes. Place on a piece of foil on the grill (broiler) rack and brush with the marinade. Grill (broil) for 8–10 minutes until cooked through, turning and basting with the marinade from time to time.

Nutty Garlic and Herb Stuffed Mackerel

SERVES 4

4 mackerel, cleaned
80 g/3¹/₂ oz/1 small packet soft
*   cheese with garlic and herbs*
100 g/4 oz/2 cups wholemeal
*   breadcrumbs*
Grated rind and juice of 1 lime
25 g/1 oz/¹/₄ cup chopped mixed
*   nuts*
1 size 1 egg, beaten
Salt and freshly ground black pepper
Butter for greasing
Lime wedges

To bone the mackerel, cut off the head and tail, slit right along the stomach and carefully open out skin-side up on a board. Run your thumb firmly down the backbone two or three times to loosen it. Turn over, remove the backbone, any loose bones and the fins. Mash the cheese with the breadcrumbs, lime rind and juice, nuts and egg. Season with a little salt and lots of pepper. Spread along one side of the flesh and fold over the other side. Wrap each in buttered foil. Place on a baking sheet and bake in the oven at 190°C/375°F/gas mark 5 for 30 minutes or until the fish are cooked through. Unwrap and serve garnished with lime wedges.

Crunchy-topped Salmon and Flageolet Casserole

SERVES 4

200 g/7 oz/1 small can pink or red
salmon, drained
425 g/15 oz/1 large can flageolet
beans, drained
298 g/10¹/₂ oz/1 small can condensed
celery soup
60 ml/4 tbsp milk
75 g/3 oz/³/₄ cup grated Cheddar
cheese
3 tomatoes, sliced
2 × 25 g/2 × 1 oz/2 small packets
cheese and onion or plain potato
crisps (chips), crushed

Discard the bones and any skin from the fish and roughly flake in an ovenproof dish. Spoon the beans over. Blend the soup with the milk and cheese and pour over. Top with tomato slices, then sprinkle the crushed crisps over the surface. Bake in the oven at 180°C/350°F/gas mark 4 for about 25 minutes or until piping hot and the top is well browned.

Tuna and Corn Casserole

SERVES 4

Prepare as for Crunchy-topped Salmon and Flageolet Casserole, but substitute tuna for the salmon and a 350 g/12 oz/1 large can sweetcorn (corn) for the flageolet beans. Use bacon-flavoured crisps for the topping.

Mackerel in Oatmeal with Horseradish Mayonnaise

SERVES 4

4 mackerel, cleaned
Salt and freshly ground black pepper
100 g/4 oz/1 cup medium oatmeal
50 g/2 oz/¹/₄ cup butter
30 ml/2 tbsp olive oil
60 ml/4 tbsp mayonnaise
10 ml/2 tsp horseradish cream
Lemon wedges

Bone the mackerel (see Nutty Garlic and Herb Stuffed Mackerel, page 155). Season with salt and pepper and coat thoroughly in the oatmeal. Heat the butter and oil in a large frying pan (skillet) and fry (sauté) the fish for 5 minutes on each side until crisp, golden and cooked through. Drain on kitchen paper and transfer to warmed serving plates. Mix the mayonnaise with the horseradish and season to taste. Put a spoonful to the side of each mackerel and garnish the plates with lemon wedges.

Seafood Speciality Pizza

SERVES 4

225 g/8 oz/2 cups self-raising (self-rising) flour
5 ml/1 tsp baking powder
2.5 ml/¹/₂ tsp salt
30 ml/2 tbsp olive oil
45 ml/3 tbsp passata (sieved tomatoes)
30 ml/2 tbsp tomato purée (paste)
100 g/4 oz Mozzarella cheese, grated
185 g/6¹/₂ oz/1 small can tuna, drained and flaked
50 g/2 oz/¹/₂ cup peeled prawns (shrimp)
50 g/2 oz/1 small can anchovies, drained
5 ml/1 tsp dried oregano
A few black olives

Sift the flour, baking powder and salt into a bowl. Stir in the oil. Add enough water to form a soft but not sticky dough. Knead gently on a lightly floured surface. Roll out fairly thinly to a round about 20–23 cm/8–9 in diameter. Transfer to a lightly greased baking sheet. Blend the passata with the tomato purée and spread over the surface to within 1 cm/¹/₂ in of the edge. Sprinkle half the cheese over. Scatter the tuna and prawns over, then sprinkle with the remaining cheese. Arrange the anchovies attractively on top, sprinkle with oregano and decorate with the olives. Bake in the oven at 200°C/400°F/gas mark 6 for about 20 minutes or until the edge is golden and crisp and the topping bubbling and just beginning to brown.

Portuguese Fish Cakes

SERVES 4

2 × 120 g/2 × 4¹/₂ oz/2 small cans sardines in oil, drained, boned and mashed
225 g/8 oz/1 cup cooked mashed potato
2 spring onions (scallions), very finely chopped
15 ml/1 tbsp chopped parsley
10 ml/2 tsp lemon juice
Salt and freshly ground black pepper
1.5 ml/¹/₄ tsp cayenne
1 egg, beaten
75 g/3 oz/³/₄ cup dried breadcrumbs
Oil for shallow-frying

Mix the fish with the potato, onions, parsley, lemon juice, a little salt and pepper and the cayenne. Shape into 8 flat cakes. Dip in the beaten egg then the breadcrumbs. Shallow-fry in hot oil until crisp and golden brown on each side. Drain on kitchen paper and serve hot.

VEGETARIAN MAIN MEALS

None of the following recipes contains meat or fish. If, however, you are cooking for serious vegetarians, make sure that any cheese or condiments you buy are suitable – check the labels before you buy (even Worcestershire sauce has anchovies in it!). And don't be afraid to 'go meatless' for a change – all the dishes in this chapter would tempt even the most hardened carnivore!

Spinach and Cheese Patties

SERVES 4

450 g/1 lb/2¹/₂ cups frozen, chopped spinach, thawed
225 g/8 oz/2 cups strong cheese, grated
Salt and freshly ground black pepper
Pinch of grated nutmeg
2 egg yolks, beaten
15 ml/1 tbsp melted butter or margarine
1 whole egg, beaten
100 g/4 oz/1 cup dried breadcrumbs
Oil for shallow-frying

Place the spinach in a colander and press it down to drain it thoroughly. Transfer to a bowl. Beat in the cheese, salt, pepper and nutmeg. Beat the egg yolks with the butter or margarine and stir into the mixture to bind it together. Shape into patties. Brush the patties with beaten egg and roll in breadcrumbs until covered, pressing them on firmly. Chill well. Heat a little oil in a large frying pan (skillet) and fry (sauté) the patties on each side until golden brown and piping hot. Drain on kitchen paper.

Asparagus, Quorn and Lemon Kebabs

SERVES 4

450 g/1 lb/4 cups quorn or smoked tofu cubes
225 g/8 oz asparagus spears, cut into chunks
1 lemon, thinly sliced
10 ml/2 tsp lemon juice
25 g/1 oz/2 tbsp butter or margarine, melted
Salt and freshly ground black pepper

Thread the Quorn or tofu, asparagus and lemon slices alternately on to soaked wooden skewers. Sprinkle with lemon juice, brush with melted butter or margarine and season with salt and pepper. Grill (broil) for about 10 minutes until cooked through and golden.

Nutty Burgers

SERVES 4

175 g/6 oz/1 cup bulgar
1 litre/1³/₄ pts/4¹/₂ cups water
Salt and freshly ground black pepper
100 g/4 oz/1 cup cornmeal
15 ml/1 tbsp peanut butter
75 g/3 oz/³/₄ cup salted peanuts,
*   finely chopped*
45 ml/3 tbsp oil

Place the bulgar in a heavy pan and heat gently for a few minutes until it is lightly browned, shaking the pan as it heats. Pour in 450 ml/³/₄ pt/2 cups of the water, stir well and bring to the boil. Cover and simmer for 20 minutes, stirring occasionally to prevent it sticking. Season with salt and pepper. Bring the remaining water to the boil in a large pan, stir in the cornmeal, peanut butter, peanuts, salt and pepper, cover and simmer very gently for 30 minutes, stirring frequently, until the mixture is firm and comes away from the sides of the pan. Leave to cool. Mix together the cornmeal mixture with the bulgar and shape into patties. Chill well. Brush with oil and grill (broil) or shallow-fry in a little hot oil, turning once, until golden brown on both sides.

Stuffed Pizzas

SERVES 4

2 pizza base mixes
215 g/7¹/₂ oz/1 small can creamed
mushrooms
225 g/8 oz/1 small can chopped
*   tomatoes, drained*
1 canned pimiento cap, chopped
*   (optional)*
5 ml/1 tsp capers
15 ml/1 tbsp cooked peas or green
beans
75 g/3 oz/³/₄ cup grated Mozzarella
*   or Cheddar cheese*
Passata (sieved tomatoes)
Grated Parmesan cheese

Make up the pizza mixes together according to the packet directions. Knead gently and cut into quarters. Roll out each piece, or flatten between the hands to rounds about 20 cm/8 in in diameter. Divide all the remaining ingredients except the passata and Parmesan between the centres of each round of dough. Brush the edges with water and draw up over the filling to seal. Place on a lightly greased baking sheet, sealed sides down. Bake in the oven at 200°C/400°F/gas mark 6 for about 20 minutes or until golden brown. Transfer to warm serving plates. Spoon a little hot passata over, sprinkle with Parmesan cheese and serve.

Broccoli and Cider Cheese

SERVES 4

350 g/12 oz broccoli florets
1 packet cheese sauce mix
300 ml/¹/₂ pt/1¹/₄ cups cider
50 g/2 oz/¹/₂ cup grated Cheddar
*   cheese*
Grilled (broiled) tomatoes
Crusty bread

Cook the broccoli in boiling, salted water until just tender. Drain and arrange in a fairly shallow flameproof dish. Make up the cheese sauce using cider instead of milk. Pour over the broccoli and top with the grated cheese. Place under a hot grill (broiler) until golden brown and bubbling (about 5 minutes). Serve with grilled tomatoes and crusty bread.

Savoury Golden Cheese and Onion Flan

SERVES 6

225 g/8 oz shortcrust pastry (basic pie crust)
2 onions, chopped
25 g/1 oz/2 tbsp butter
5 ml/1 tsp French mustard
20 ml/4 tsp plain (all-purpose) flour
300 ml/¹/₂ pt/1¹/₄ cups single (light)
*   cream*
50 g/2 oz/¹/₂ cup grated Cheddar
*   cheese*
100 g/4 oz/1 cup sweetcorn (corn)
1 egg, lightly beaten
Salt and freshly ground black pepper
1 yellow (bell) pepper, sliced into
*   rings*
Coriander (cilantro) sprig

Roll out the pastry and use to line a flan (pie) ring. Place on a baking sheet and chill while making the filling. Cook the onions in the butter for 5–10 minutes until golden and soft. Stir in the mustard and flour, then gradually pour in the cream and bring to the boil, stirring all the time. Reduce the heat and simmer for 2–3 minutes until thickened. Add the cheese, remove from the heat, and cool for 2–3 minutes before adding the sweetcorn, egg and seasoning. Pour into the flan ring and arrange the pepper rings attractively over. Bake for 35–40 minutes at 200°C/400°F/gas mark 6 until the filling is set and golden. Garnish with a sprig of coriander and serve.

Pizza Puffs

SERVES 6

3 × 20 cm/3 × 8 in sheets ready-
*   rolled puff pastry (paste)*
3 spring onions (scallions), chopped
25 g/1 oz/2 tbsp butter, melted
Grated rind and juice of 1 lemon
Salt and freshly ground black pepper
30 ml/2 tbsp Pesto Sauce (see page
*   252) or use a jar*
350 g/12 oz/3 cups tomatoes, sliced
225 g/8 oz/2 cups courgettes
*   (zucchini), cut into thin slices*
Grated Parmesan cheese

From the pastry, cut out 6 rounds, 1 cm/4 in diameter. Place on a baking sheet. Prick the circles with a fork and bake at 230°C/450°F/gas mark 8 for about 8 minutes until risen and golden. Meanwhile, stir the onions into the melted butter with the lemon rind and 15 ml/1 tbsp of the lemon juice and season well. Spread each cooked pastry circle with pesto and arrange the tomato and courgettes alternately on top. Brush with the melted butter mixture. Return to the oven and cook for 12–14 minutes or until the courgettes are softened and the edges of the pastry are puffed and golden. Sprinkle with Parmesan and serve hot.

Sensational Onion Tart

SERVES 6

*225 g/8 oz shortcrust pastry (basic
pie crust)*
3 large onions, finely sliced
25 g/1 oz/2 tbsp butter
1 whole egg
1 egg yolk
*150 ml/¹/₄ pt/²/₃ cup double (heavy)
cream*
Salt and freshly ground black pepper
2.5 ml/¹/₂ tsp grated nutmeg

Roll out the pastry and use to line a
flan (pie) ring. Place on a baking sheet
and chill while preparing the filling. Fry
(sauté) the onions in the butter until soft.
Beat the egg, egg yolk and cream together
and stir into the onions. Season with salt,
pepper and nutmeg. Pour into the flan ring
and bake at 200°C/400°F/gas mark 6 for
30 minutes until golden and bubbling.

Broccoli and Roquefort
Tagliatelle

SERVES 4

*150 ml/¹/₄ pt/²/₃ cup double (heavy)
cream*
*100 g/4 oz Roquefort cheese,
crumbled*
*225 g/8 oz broccoli florets, cooked
until just tender*
Salt and freshly ground black pepper
225 g/8 oz tagliatelle, cooked
Chopped parsley
Toasted flaked almonds

Put the cream into a saucepan and
add the cheese. Heat gently, stirring
all the time, until the cheese melts. Stir in
the broccoli and seasoning. Fold the
tagliatelle through the sauce, heat through
gently, and garnish with chopped parsley
and a few toasted, flaked almonds.

Red and White Aubergines

SERVES 4

Salt
*2 large aubergines (eggplants),
halved lengthways*
45 ml/3 tbsp olive oil
*1 red (bell) pepper, seeded and
chopped*
3 shallots, chopped
Freshly ground black pepper
*175 g/6 oz/1¹/₂ cups cherry
tomatoes, halved*
*175 g/6 oz/1¹/₂ cups firm goat's
cheese, sliced*
10 ml/2 tsp chopped thyme

Sprinkle salt on the cut surfaces of the
aubergines and leave for 30 minutes.
Drain and pat dry with kitchen paper. Place
in a roasting tin (pan), brush with a little
of the oil and bake at 200°C/400°F/gas
mark 6 for 35–40 minutes. Scoop out the
flesh to within 1 cm/¹/₂ in of the skin. Chop
the flesh. Fry (sauté) the pepper and
shallots in 15 ml/1 tbsp of the remaining
oil until soft. Add the aubergine flesh and
seasoning and mix well. Pile this mixture
into the shells and arrange the tomatoes
and goat's cheese in alternate rows along
the top. Drizzle with oil and sprinkle with
the thyme. Return to the oven for 20–25
minutes. Serve hot.

Roast Vegetable Casserole

SERVES 6

1 large aubergine (eggplant), cut
into chunks
Salt
1.1 kg/2¹/₂ lb potatoes
2 large onions, roughly chopped
2 red and 2 green (bell) peppers,
thickly sliced
3 garlic cloves, crushed
450 g/1 lb courgettes (zucchini), cut
into chunks
5 ml/1 tsp dried oregano
90 ml/6 tbsp olive oil
400 g/14 oz/1 large can chopped
tomatoes
400 g/14 oz/1 large jar tomato sauce
for pasta
Few drops of Tabasco sauce
15 ml/1 tbsp French mustard
Freshly ground black pepper
450 g/1 lb/8 cups button mushrooms,
chopped
400 g/14 oz/1 large can sweetcorn
(corn) or baby corn cobs
Watercress

Sprinkle the aubergines with salt and leave to stand for 30 minutes. Cut the potatoes into chunks and boil for 10 minutes. Drain the aubergines, pat dry with kitchen paper and put them in a roasting tin (pan) with the onions, peppers, garlic and courgettes. Sprinkle with the oregano and most of the oil, tossing to ensure they are well coated. In another dish, mix the potatoes with the tomatoes, remaining oil, tomato sauce, Tabasco, mustard and salt and pepper. Cook both dishes in the oven at 190°C/ 375°F/gas mark 5 for 1 hour. Add the mushrooms and corn to the mixed vegetables and cook for a further 30 minutes. Transfer the mixed vegetables to a warmed serving dish and arrange the potato and tomato mixture around the outside. Garnish with watercress sprigs and serve hot.

Cauliflower with Feta and Tomato Sauce

SERVES 4

1 large cauliflower
3 garlic cloves, crushed
1 large onion, finely chopped
60 ml/4 tbsp olive oil
2 × 400 g/2 × 14 oz/2 large cans
chopped tomatoes
1 bay leaf
10 ml/2 tsp dried oregano
1 cinnamon stick
Salt and freshly ground black pepper
15 ml/1 tbsp lemon juice
100 g/4 oz Feta cheese, crumbled
100 g/4 oz Emmental (Swiss) cheese,
grated

Cut the cauliflower into florets and boil until just tender. Cook the garlic and onions in half the oil until soft, then add the tomatoes, herbs, cinnamon stick and seasoning. Bring to the boil and simmer for 5 minutes. Put the cauliflower into a shallow ovenproof dish and cover with the tomato sauce, discarding the cinnamon stick and bay leaf. Sprinkle with the lemon juice and remaining oil and cover with the cheeses. Bake in the oven at 190°C/375°F/ gas mark 5 for 25 minutes. Serve immediately.

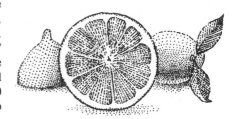

Risotto Bake

450 g/1 lb leeks, thinly sliced
15 ml/1 tbsp olive oil
50 g/2 oz/¹/₄ cup butter
1 onion, finely chopped
1 garlic clove, crushed
225 g/8 oz/1 cup risotto rice
150 ml/¹/₄ pt/²/₃ cup white wine
450 ml/³/₄ pt/2 cups vegetable stock
   stock
2 eggs, lightly beaten
100 g/4 oz/¹/₂ cup crème fraîche
30 ml/2 tbsp chopped parsley
15 ml/1 tbsp chopped sage
1.5 ml/¹/₄ tsp grated nutmeg
50 g/2 oz/¹/₂ cup grated Parmesan
   cheese
Salt and freshly ground black pepper
Extra grated Parmesan cheese

Fry (sauté) the leeks in the oil for 10 minutes and set aside. Using most of the butter, fry the onion and garlic for 3 minutes. Stir in the rice and cook for 1 minute. When the rice is transparent, stir in the wine and simmer until it is absorbed. Add the stock, little by little, and cook until this is absorbed (about 20–25 minutes). Add the rice to the leeks. Mix together the eggs, half the crème fraîche, the parsley, sage, nutmeg and most of the Parmesan. Stir this into the rice. Add seasoning and turn into a greased flan dish (pie pan). Sprinkle with the remaining measured cheese and dot the remaining butter over the surface. Bake in the oven at 200°C/400°F/gas mark 6 for 25 minutes until set and golden brown. Cut into wedges and top each with a little of the remaining crème fraîche and sprinkle with extra Parmesan.

Potato Pesto Pie

750 g/1¹/₂ lb potatoes
1 onion, sliced
75 g/3 oz/¹/₃ cup butter
2 garlic cloves, crushed
30 ml/2 tbsp Pesto Sauce (see page
   252) or use a jar
75 g/3 oz/³/₄ cup grated Parmesan
   cheese
Salt and freshly ground black pepper
120 ml/4 fl oz/¹/₂ cup double (heavy)
   cream
1 size 1 egg, beaten
175 g/6 oz puff pastry (paste)
Extra beaten egg, to glaze

Slice the potatoes thinly and boil for 5 minutes. Fry (sauté) the onion in the butter for 5 minutes then add the garlic and pesto and cook for a further minute. In a flan dish (pie pan) layer the onion mixture and sliced potatoes with the Parmesan and seasoning. Mix the cream and egg together and pour over the layers. Top with the pastry and glaze with the extra egg. Cut two slits in the pastry to let the steam escape. Bake in the oven at 200°C/400°F/gas mark 6 for 1 hour.

Turkish Aubergines and Tomatoes

SERVES 4

800 g/1³/₄ lb aubergines (eggplants),
*   chopped*
Salt
60 ml/4 tbsp olive oil
1 large onion, chopped
6 large tomatoes, skinned and
*   chopped*
2 garlic cloves, crushed
30 ml/2 tbsp chopped parsley
1.5 ml/¹/₄ tsp ground allspice
1.5 ml/¹/₄ tsp ground cinnamon
1.5 ml/¹/₄ tsp caster (superfine)
*   sugar*
Freshly ground black pepper
25 g/1 oz/2 tbsp butter
45 ml/3 tbsp fresh breadcrumbs
30 ml/2 tbsp crumbled Feta cheese

Sprinkle the aubergines with salt and leave to stand for 30 minutes. Drain and dry on kitchen paper. Fry them in the oil until they start to go pale golden brown, then add the onion. When soft, add the tomatoes, garlic, parsley, spices, sugar and seasoning. Simmer for 5 minutes, stirring occasionally. Grease an ovenproof dish with half the butter. Transfer the mixture to the dish. Top with the breadcrumbs and cheese and dot with the remaining butter. Bake in the oven at 190°C/375°F/gas mark 5 for 30 minutes.

Leek and Goat's Cheese Pie

SERVES 8

225 g/8 oz shortcrust pastry (basic
pie crust)
900 g/2 lb leeks, sliced
50 g/2 oz/¹/₄ cup butter
15 ml/1 tbsp oil
100 g/4 oz goat's cheese, crumbled
300 ml/¹/₂ pt/1¹/₄ cups double
*   (heavy) cream*
2 size 1 eggs, lightly beaten
Salt and freshly ground black pepper
225 g/8 oz puff pastry (paste)
Beaten egg, to glaze

Roll out the shortcrust pastry to line the base of a 23 cm/9 in pie dish. Fry (sauté) the leeks in the butter and oil for 5 minutes, cool slightly then spoon into the pie dish. Sprinkle the cheese over the leeks. Beat the cream and eggs together, pour this mixture into the pie dish and season with salt and pepper. Roll out the puff pastry and top the pie with it. Glaze with a little beaten egg then bake in the oven at 200°C/400°F/gas mark 6 for 40 minutes until the pie is golden.

Rich Tomato and Aubergine Casserole

1 onion, chopped
5 ml/1 tsp cumin seeds
15 ml/1 tbsp ground ginger
45 ml/3 tbsp olive oil
2 large aubergines (eggplants),
 finely diced
300 ml/¹/₂ pt/1¹/₄ cups red wine
400 g/14 oz/1 large can chopped
 tomatoes
45 ml/3 tbsp sun-dried tomatoes
 in oil, chopped
30 ml/2 tbsp tomato purée (paste)
10 ml/2 tsp caster (superfine) sugar
Buttered flageolet beans

Fry (sauté) the onion, cumin seeds and ginger in the oil until the onion has softened. Add the aubergines and cook for a further 5 minutes, stirring frequently. Pour in the wine, then the tomatoes, sun-dried tomatoes, tomato purée and sugar. Simmer for 30 minutes until the aubergines are tender. Turn into a serving dish and serve with lots of flageolet beans, tossed in butter.

Chilli Non Carne

1 onion, chopped
45 ml/3 tbsp olive oil
1 large green (bell) pepper, chopped
2 carrots, sliced
1 garlic clove, crushed
5 ml/1 tsp cumin seeds, crushed
5–10 ml/1–2 tsp chilli powder
 (depending on strength)
2 celery sticks, sliced
4 courgettes (zucchini), sliced
400 g/14 oz/1 large can tomatoes
15 ml/1 tbsp tomato purée (paste)
150 ml/¹/₄ pt/²/₃ cup vegetable stock
5 ml/1 tsp dried oregano
Salt and freshly ground black pepper
425 g/15 oz/1 large can red kidney
 beans, drained
Plain boiled rice
Grated Cheddar cheese

Fry (sauté) the onion in the oil for 3–4 minutes. Add the green pepper, carrots and garlic and continue cooking until the onions are soft but not brown. Stir in the cumin seeds and chilli to taste (more can be added later so be careful at this stage). Add the remaining ingredients except the beans, rice and cheese, bring to the boil, cover and cook for 30 minutes. Add the beans and adjust the seasoning. Cook for a further 15 minutes. Spoon over plain boiled rice and serve with grated cheese to sprinkle over.

Vegetarian Hotpot

SERVES 4

2 large carrots, sliced
1 small turnip, diced
2 celery sticks, sliced
50 g/2 oz/¼ cup butter
12 small leeks
25 g/ 1 oz/¼ cup plain (all-purpose)
* flour*
450 ml/³/₄ pt/2 cups vegetable stock
Salt and freshly ground black pepper
5 ml/1 tsp Worcestershire sauce
45 ml/3 tbsp chopped parsley
450 g/1 lb potatoes, thinly sliced
50 g/2 oz/¹/₂ cup grated Cheddar
* cheese*

Fry (sauté) the carrots, turnip and celery gently in the butter for 7–8 minutes and put into a flameproof casserole (Dutch oven) using a draining spoon. Fry the leeks for 2–3 minutes and put into the casserole. Stir the flour into the pan and gradually add the stock. Bring to the boil, stirring. Season with salt and pepper and Worcestershire sauce. Simmer for 3 minutes and mix in 30 ml/2 tbsp of the parsley. Pour over the vegetables in the casserole and turn them so they are thoroughly mixed. Arrange the sliced potatoes in overlapping circles on top of the vegetables. Cover the casserole with a lid or foil and bake in the oven for 1¹/₂ hours at 180ºC/350ºF/gas mark 4 until the potatoes are tender. Sprinkle the cheese over the potato topping and grill (broil) until browned. Serve garnished with the remaining parsley.

Chakchouka

SERVES 4

1 large onion, chopped
45–60 ml/3–4 tbsp olive oil
2 garlic cloves, crushed
1 cauliflower, cut into florets
1 small green and 1 small red (bell)
* pepper, each cut into small*
* pieces*
450 g/1 lb tomatoes, skinned and
* chopped*
Salt and freshly ground black pepper
10 ml/2 tsp paprika
Good pinch of cayenne or chilli
* powder*
4 eggs
Chopped parsley

Cook the onion in the oil for 5 minutes until soft. Add the garlic and cook for 1 minute. Add the cauliflower, peppers and tomatoes. Season with salt and pepper, paprika and cayenne or chilli. Add a little water if necessary. Cook over a low heat for about 20 minutes until the vegetables are tender, adding a little water if the mixture becomes dry. Carefully break the eggs into the vegetable mixture, cover and cook until they are set, stirring with a fork from time to time if liked or leave whole. Sprinkle with parsley and serve.

Swiss Tomato Casserole

SERVES 4

40 g/1¹/₂ oz/3 tbsp butter
*40 g/1¹/₂ oz/¹/₃ cup plain (all-
purpose) flour*
450 ml/³/₄ pt/2 cups milk
Salt and freshly ground black pepper
*100 g/4 oz Gruyère (Swiss) cheese,
grated*
60 ml/4 tbsp single (light) cream
750 g/1¹/₂ lb firm tomatoes, sliced
5 ml/1 tsp chopped basil
10 ml/2 tsp caster (superfine) sugar
*25 g/1 oz/¹/₄ cup grated Parmesan
cheese*
Basil leaves

Blend the butter, flour and milk and
cook gently, stirring, until thick. Add
the salt, pepper, cheese and cream.
Arrange a layer of tomatoes in a small
casserole dish (Dutch oven), sprinkle with
salt and pepper and the basil and sugar.
Cover with a little sauce. Continue
layering, finishing with a layer of sauce.
Sprinkle with the Parmesan, cover and
cook in the oven at 190°C/375°F/gas mark
5 for 30 minutes. Garnish with a few fresh
basil leaves.

Stuffed Courgettes

SERVES 4

*175 g/6 oz/1¹/₂ cups sweetcorn
(corn)*
100 g/4 oz/¹/₂ cup cottage cheese
Salt and freshly ground black pepper
2 shallots, finely chopped
*4 courgettes (zucchini), halved and
seeds removed*
*45 ml/3 tbsp grated Parmesan
cheese (fresh if possible)*

Mix together the sweetcorn, cottage
cheese, salt, pepper and shallots.
Spoon the mixture into the courgette
halves, mounding it up a little. Top with
the Parmesan cheese. Put the courgettes
into a greased, shallow baking dish and
bake in the oven for 15 minutes at 200°C/
400°F/gas mark 6 until tender and the
topping melts.

Vegetable Curry

SERVES 4

30 ml/2 tbsp sunflower oil
*10 ml/2 tsp ground coriander
(cilantro)*
5 ml/1 tsp ground cumin
2.5–5 ml/¹/₂–1 tsp chilli powder
2.5 ml/¹/₂ tsp turmeric
2 garlic cloves, crushed
1 onion, chopped
1 small cauliflower, cut into florets
2 potatoes, chopped
2 carrots, chopped
*1 small green and 1 small red (bell)
pepper, chopped*
225 g/8 oz tomatoes, chopped
5 ml/1 tsp garam masala
150 ml/¹/₄ pt/²/₃ cup plain yoghurt
Salt and freshly ground black pepper
Plain boiled rice

Heat the oil, add the coriander,
cumin, chilli, turmeric, garlic and
onion and fry (sauté) for 2–3 minutes. Add
the cauliflower, potatoes, carrots and
peppers and stir to coat in the spices. Stir
in the tomatoes and add 150 ml/¹/₄ pt/²/₃
cup water. Bring to the boil, cover and
simmer for 30 minutes. Add the garam
masala. Remove from the heat and stir in
the yoghurt. Season to taste. Serve with
plain boiled rice and all the usual curry
accompaniments.

Scalloped Aubergines

2 aubergines (eggplants), diced
1 onion, chopped
2 garlic cloves, finely chopped
15 ml/1 tbsp olive oil
5 ml/1 tsp dried oregano
5 ml/1 tsp dried rosemary
2.5 ml/¹/₂ tsp salt
1.5 ml/¹/₄ tsp freshly ground black
pepper
4 tomatoes, skinned and chopped
(or a small can)
100 g/4 oz Gruyère (Swiss) cheese,
grated

Put the aubergines into lightly salted boiling water and bring to the boil for 1 minute. Drain and set aside. Fry (sauté) the onion and garlic in the oil gently for 5 minutes. Put the aubergines in a buttered dish, top with the onions, garlic, oregano, rosemary, salt, pepper and tomatoes. Bake for 25 minutes at 190°C/375°F/gas mark 5. Sprinkle with the cheese and bake for a further 5 minutes until the cheese melts.

Extra Rich Scalloped Aubergines

SERVES 4

Prepare as for Scalloped Aubergines but pour an egg, beaten with 120 ml/ 4 fl oz/¹/₂ cup single (light) cream, over the aubergines before baking.

Vegetarian Goulash

SERVES 4

1 onion, finely chopped
30 ml/2 tbsp olive oil
1 courgette (zucchini), diced
225 g/8 oz carrots, diced
225 g/8 oz parsnips, diced
2 celery sticks, sliced
5 ml/1 tsp paprika
2.5 ml/¹/₂ tsp dried basil
2.5 ml/¹/₂ tsp caraway seeds
15 ml/1 tbsp chopped parsley
5 ml/1 tsp yeast extract
600 ml/1 pt/2/¹/₂ cups passata (sieved
tomatoes)
450 ml/³/₄ pt/2 cups vegetable stock
12 small potatoes
Salt and freshly ground black pepper
150 ml/¹/₄ pt/²/₃ cup plain yoghurt
Chopped parsley

Fry (sauté) the onion in the oil until soft but not brown. Add all the vegetables except the potatoes. Cover and cook for 10 minutes over a gentle heat. Stir in the spices and herbs, add the yeast extract, passata, stock and potatoes. Bring to the boil, then simmer for 20–30 minutes until the vegetables are tender. Add the seasoning to taste and stir in the yoghurt. Garnish with parsley.

Mushroom and Cashew Nut Pilaff

SERVES 4

100 g/4 oz/¹/₂ cup brown rice
1 onion, sliced
Sunflower oil
1 garlic clove, crushed
2 celery sticks, sliced
225 g/8 oz/4 cups button
mushrooms, sliced
1 red (bell) pepper, sliced
1 green (bell) pepper, sliced
100 g/4 oz/1 cup cashew nuts
Soy sauce

Cook the rice according to the packet directions. Drain. Meanwhile, fry (sauté) the onion in the oil for 5 minutes. Add the garlic, celery, mushrooms, peppers and nuts. Mix together and fry for 2 minutes. Add soy sauce to taste, remembering that it is very salty. Fry for 5 minutes. Add the cooked rice, mix together and heat through.

Fluffy Cheese Pudding

SERVES 4

25 g/1 oz/2 tbsp butter
2 eggs, separated
300 ml/¹/₂ pt/1¹/₄ cups milk
75 g/3 oz/1¹/₂ cups fresh
breadcrumbs
100 g/4 oz/1 cup grated Cheddar
cheese
Salt and freshly ground black pepper

Grease a 1.2 litre/2 pt/5 cup ovenproof dish well with the butter. Beat the egg yolks with the milk and stir in the breadcrumbs, cheese and a little salt and pepper. Leave to stand for 15 minutes. Whisk the egg whites until stiff and fold into the mixture with a metal spoon. Turn into the prepared dish. Cook in the oven

at 200°C/400°F/gas mark 6 for 35 minutes until risen and golden. Serve immediately.

Oven Omelette

SERVES 4

4 eggs, beaten
225 g/8 oz/1 cup cottage cheese
150 ml/¹/₄ pt/²/₃ cup milk
Salt and freshly ground black pepper
100 g/4 oz/2 cups button mushrooms,
sliced
1 onion, chopped
Pinch of mixed dried herbs

Mix all the ingredients in a bowl. Pour into a well-greased ovenproof dish. Bake in the oven at 200°C/400°F/gas mark 6 for 20 minutes until brown and firm. Serve cut into wedges.

French Omelette

SERVES 1

2 eggs
1.5 ml/¹/₄ tsp dried marjoram
15 ml/1 tbsp milk
Salt and freshly ground black pepper
Olive oil
1 small onion, chopped
50 g/2 oz Brie or Camembert, sliced

Beat together the eggs, herbs, milk and seasoning. Heat a little oil in a frying pan (skillet) and lightly fry the onion for 2 minutes. Remove the onion, then pour the egg mixture into the pan and cook gently until almost set and firm underneath. Sprinkle the onion and cheese over one half of the omelette, fold in half and press lightly. Cook for a further 1–2 minutes. Serve straight away.

Spanish-style Omelette

SERVES 4

15 ml/1 tbsp olive oil
225 g/8 oz cooked potatoes, diced
175 g/6 oz/1¹/₂ cups frozen peas,
* thawed*
1 small red (bell) pepper, diced
225 g/8 oz/4 cups button mushrooms,
* sliced*
25 g/1 oz/2 tbsp butter
6 eggs
30 ml/2 tbsp water
5 ml/1 tsp mixed dried herbs
Salt and freshly ground black pepper
175 g/6 oz/1¹/₂ cups grated Cheddar
* cheese*

Heat the oil and fry (sauté) the vegetables for a few minutes until soft. Add the butter. Whisk together the eggs, water and herbs and season with salt and pepper. Add to the pan and keep stirring with a fork to prevent sticking, especially in the middle. When almost set, level the top and sprinkle with cheese. Brown under a hot grill (broiler) for a few minutes.

Curried Eggs

SERVES 4

25 g/1 oz/2 tbsp margarine
1 onion, chopped
15 ml/1 tbsp plain (all-purpose)
* flour*
15 ml/1 tbsp curry powder
600 ml/1 pt/2¹/₂ cups vegetable stock
5 ml/1 tsp sweet pickle
25 g/1 oz/¹/₄ cup creamed coconut
4 hard-boiled (hard-cooked) eggs,
* halved*
Dash of lemon juice
Salt and freshly ground black pepper
Plain boiled rice

Melt the margarine and fry (sauté) the onion for a few minutes until soft. Add the flour and curry powder and cook, stirring, for 1–2 minutes. Add the stock and stir until smooth. Simmer for 20 minutes. Add the remaining ingredients except the rice and simmer for a further 3–4 minutes. Serve on a bed of plain boiled rice.

Spinach and Mushroom Roll

SERVES 4

300 g/11 oz frozen spinach, thawed
Pinch of grated nutmeg
4 eggs, separated
Salt and freshly ground black pepper
215 g/7¹/₂ oz/1 small can creamed
mushrooms
Hot passata (sieved tomatoes)

Grease and line an 18 × 28 cm/7 × 11 in Swiss roll tin (jelly roll pan) and line with baking parchment. Cook the spinach according to the packet directions, drain well. Add the nutmeg and egg yolks and beat well. Season with a little salt and pepper. Whisk the egg whites until stiff. Fold into the spinach with a metal spoon. Turn into the prepared tin. Bake in the oven at 200°C/400°F/gas mark 6 for 20 minutes or until just firm to the touch. Heat the creamed mushrooms. Turn the spinach mixture out on to a clean sheet of baking parchment. Quickly spread with the creamed mushrooms and roll up using the baking parchment to help. Transfer to a serving plate and serve sliced with hot passata spooned over.

The Fastest Mushroom Soufflé in the West

Butter for greasing
300 g/11 oz/1 small can sliced
mushrooms, drained
295 g/10¹/₂ oz/1 small can condensed
cream of mushroom soup
75 g/3 oz/³/₄ cup grated Cheddar or
Parmesan (or half and half)
cheese
4 eggs, separated
Freshly ground black pepper

Grease an 18 cm/7 in soufflé dish with the butter. Put the mushrooms in the base of the dish. Empty the soup into a bowl. Whisk in the cheese and egg yolks. Season with pepper. Whisk the egg whites until stiff. Fold into the mixture with a metal spoon. Turn into the prepared dish and bake in the oven at 200°C/400°F/gas mark 6 for 25–30 minutes until risen, golden and just set. Serve immediately.

Ratatouille Soufflé

SERVES 4

Prepare as for The Fastest Mushroom Soufflé in the West but substitute ¹/₂ can ratatouille for the sliced mushrooms and tomato soup for the mushroom soup.

Asparagus Soufflé

SERVES 4

Prepare as for The Fastest Mushroom Soufflé in the West but substitute drained canned asparagus tips and asparagus soup for the mushrooms and mushroom soup.

Celery Soufflé

SERVES 4

Prepare as for The Fastest Mushroom Soufflé in the West but substitute drained canned cut celery and celery soup for the mushrooms and mushroom soup.

Waldorf Grill

SERVES 4

515 g/18¹/₂ oz/1 large can celery
hearts
1 eating (dessert) apple, thinly
sliced
1 packet cheese sauce mix
30 ml/¹/₂ pt/1¹/₄ cups milk or water
(according to packet)
50 g/2 oz/¹/₂ cup walnut pieces,
chopped
50 g/2 oz/¹/₂ cup grated Cheddar
cheese

Empty the celery into a flameproof casserole (Dutch oven). Add the apple slices. Bring to the boil, simmer for 2 minutes, then drain off the liquid. Meanwhile, make up the cheese sauce according to the packet directions. Stir in the walnuts. Pour the sauce over the celery and apple and cover with the grated cheese. Place under a hot grill (broiler) for about 5 minutes until golden and bubbling. Serve hot.

Bean Stew with Dumplings

SERVES 4–6

425 g/15 oz/1 large can butter
beans, drained
425 g/15 oz/1 large can black-eyed
beans, drained
400 g/14 oz/1 large can chopped
tomatoes
1 garlic clove, crushed
15 ml/1 tbsp tomato purée (paste)
200 g/7 oz/1 small can Mexican
sweetcorn (corn with bell
peppers)
275 g/10 oz/1 small can cut green
beans
300 ml/¹/₂ pt/1¹/₄ cups vegetable
stock
1 bay leaf
Salt and freshly ground black pepper
1 packet dumpling mix
50 g/2 oz/¹/₂ cup grated Cheddar
cheese
2.5 ml/¹/₂ tsp mixed dried herbs

Empty the butter and black-eyed beans into a saucepan with the tomatoes, garlic, tomato purée, the contents of the cans of sweetcorn and green beans (not drained), the stock, bay leaf and a little salt and pepper. Bring to the boil, reduce the heat, cover and simmer for 5 minutes. Meanwhile, empty the dumpling mix into a bowl with the cheese and herbs. Add enough cold water to form a soft but not sticky dough. Shape into 8 balls. Discard the bay leaf. Arrange the dumplings around the top of the stew, cover and simmer for 15–20 minutes until the dumplings are fluffy. Serve hot.

Mixed Vegetable Fritters with Garlic Mayonnaise

SERVES 4

3 garlic cloves, crushed
150 ml/¹/₄ pt/¹/₃ cup Basic
Mayonnaise (see page 229 or use
bought)
Salt and freshly ground black pepper
75 g/3 oz/³/₄ cup plain (all-purpose)
flour
120 ml/4 fl oz/¹/₂ cup tepid water
15 ml/1 tbsp sunflower oil
275 g/10 oz/1 small can mixed
vegetables, thoughly drained
1 egg white
Oil for deep-frying

Mix the garlic with the mayonnaise and a little seasoning. Cover well and chill until ready to serve. To make the fritters, mix the flour with the water and oil until smooth. Stir in the vegetables. Whisk the egg white until stiff and fold into the batter with a metal spoon. Heat the oil until a cube of day-old bread browns in 30 seconds. Deep-fry spoonfuls of the mixture, a few at a time, until crisp and golden. Drain on kitchen paper and serve hot with the chilled garlic mayonnaise.

Stuffed Cabbage Leaves

SERVES 4

8 large cabbage leaves
425 g/15 oz/1 large can ratatouille
60 ml/4 tbsp cooked long-grain rice
300 ml/¹/₂ pt/1¹/₄ cups vegetable stock
45 ml/3 tbsp passata
(sieved tomatoes)
Salt and freshly ground black pepper
Grated Cheddar cheese

Cut out the thick central base stalk from the cabbage leaves. Put the leaves in a pan of boiling water and cook for 3–4 minutes to soften. Drain, rinse with cold water and drain again. Mix the ratatouille with the rice. Dry the leaves with kitchen paper. Lay upside-down on a board. Overlap the two points where the stalk was. Put a good spoonful of filling on top. Fold in the sides, then roll up. Pack into the base of a lightly greased heavy flameproof casserole (Dutch oven). Mix the stock with the passata and pour over. Sprinkle with a little salt and pepper. Bring to the boil, reduce the heat, cover and simmer for 20 minutes or until the cabbage is tender. Serve hot with grated cheese sprinkled over.

Egg and Vegetable Platter

SERVES 4

*350 g/12 oz cooked leftover
vegetables, including potatoes (or
cooked frozen vegetables and a
little prepared instant mash)
Freshly ground black pepper
15 g/¹/₂ oz/1 tbsp butter
15 ml/1 tbsp brown table sauce
4 eggs
Sunflower oil*

Chop the vegetables. Season lightly with pepper. Melt the butter in a large frying pan (skillet) and add half the vegetables. Press down flat. Spread the brown sauce over the top with the rest of the vegetables, again pressing down well. Cover with a plate and cook gently for about 15 minutes. Then loosen the base and turn out on to a plate. Cut into quarters. Meanwhile, fry (sauté) the eggs in a little oil (or poach in water). Slide one egg on top of each wedge and serve hot.

Cheesy Grilled Polenta

SERVES 4

*900 ml/1¹/₂ pts/3³/₄ cups water
10 ml/2 tsp salt
225 g/8 oz/2 cups polenta
75 g/3 oz/¹/₃ cup butter or margarine
50 g/2 oz/¹/₂ cup grated Parmesan or
    other strong cheese
60 ml/4 tbsp olive oil
Extra grated cheese
Basil sprigs*

Bring the water and salt to the boil, gradually add the polenta and stir until the mixture begins to thicken. Simmer very gently, stirring occasionally, for about 20 minutes until thick. Stir in the butter or margarine and the cheese. Spoon into a flat-based tin (pan) so that the polenta is about 2.5 cm/1 in thick. Leave to cool, then chill. When ready to cook, cut the polenta into 5 cm/2 in squares and brush with oil. Grill (broil) for about 5 minutes each side until golden brown. Serve sprinkled with more cheese and basil springs.

Potato and Coriander Burgers

SERVES 4

750 g/1¹/₂ lb potatoes
50 g/2 oz/¹/₃ cup Split red lentils
30 ml/2 tbsp sunflower oil
2.5 ml/¹/₂ tsp cumin seeds
30 ml/2 tbsp finely chopped onion
45 ml/3 tbsp chopped coriander
*   (cilantro)*
1.5 ml/¹/₄ tsp ground coriander
Pinch of ground cumin
Pinch of cayenne
Salt and freshly ground black pepper
Flour for dusting
Sunflower oil for cooking

Boil the potatoes in their skins, leave to cool slightly, then peel and mash. Boil the lentils in water to cover until soft, then drain thoroughly. Heat the oil and fry (sauté) the cumin seeds for a few seconds. Add the onion, coriander and spices and fry for 2 minutes. Stir in the lentils, salt and pepper and simmer, stirring frequently, until the mixture is dry. Leave to cool. Divide each mixture into 8 pieces and shape into rounds. Push a ball of lentil filling into each ball of potato and press gently into patty shapes. Dust with flour and chill until firm. Brush the patties with oil and grill (broil) or fry (sauté) in a little oil until golden brown on both sides.

Creamy Stroganoff

SERVES 4

25 g/1 oz/2 tbsp butter
2 onions, chopped
4 garlic cloves, crushed
5 ml/1 tsp mixed dried herbs
225 g/8 oz/2 cups tofu, cubed
100 g/4 oz/2 cups button mushrooms,
*   sliced*
120 ml/4 fl oz/¹/₂ cup red wine
15 ml/1 tbsp plain (all-purpose)
*   flour*
150 ml/¹/₄ pt/²/₃ cup milk
150 ml/¹/₄ pt/²/₃ cup single (light)
*   cream*
5 ml/1 tsp dried tarragon
Salt and freshly ground black pepper
Pasta or rice

Melt the margarine and fry the onions, garlic and herbs for 3 minutes. Add the tofu, mushrooms and wine and simmer for 5 minutes. Blend the flour with a little of the milk. Stir in the remaining milk, then add to the pan and bring to the boil, stirring. Add the cream, tarragon and salt and pepper. Simmer for 20 minutes. Serve with pasta or rice.

Quorn Mattar

SERVES 4

15 ml/1 tbsp sunflower oil
2 onions, chopped
3 garlic cloves, crushed
350 g/12 oz/3 cups frozen peas
5 ml/1 tsp ground ginger
5 ml/1 tsp chilli powder
10 ml/2 tsp ground cumin
15 ml/1 tbsp ground coriander
  (cilantro)
30 ml/2 tbsp chopped mint
2.5 ml/¹/₂ tsp salt
225 g/8 oz/2 cups minced (ground)
  quorn
10 ml/2 tsp yeast extract
150 ml/¹/₄ pt/²/₃ cup water
150 ml/¹/₄ pt/²/₃ cup plain yoghurt
45 ml/3 tbsp lemon juice
Chapattis (see page 294)

Heat the oil and fry (sauté) the vegetables, spices, mint and salt for a few minutes until softened. Add the quorn, yeast extract and water, bring to the boil, cover, reduce the heat and simmer for 30 minutes. Stir in the yoghurt and lemon juice and stir until absorbed and heated through. Serve hot with Chapattis.

Cheesy Quorn Mattar

SERVES 4

Prepare as for Quorn Mattar but substitute cream cheese for the yoghurt and sprinkle with a fresh chopped green or red chilli before serving.

Spaghetti Volognese

SERVES 4

15 ml/1 tbsp olive oil
1 onion, chopped
1 garlic clove, crushed
225 g/8 oz/2 cups minced (ground)
  quorn
100 g/4 oz/2 cups button mushrooms,
  sliced
400 g/14 oz/1 large can chopped
  tomatoes
30 ml/2 tbsp tomato purée (paste)
120 ml/4 fl oz/¹/₂ cup red wine
15 ml/1 tbsp yeast extract
2.5 ml/¹/₂ tsp red wine vinegar
2.5 ml/¹/₂ tsp caster (superfine)
  sugar
5 ml/1 tsp dried oregano
Salt and freshly ground black pepper
350 g/12 oz spaghetti
Grated Parmesan cheese

Heat the oil and fry (sauté) the onion and garlic until soft. Add the remaining ingredients except the spaghetti and cheese and simmer for 30 minutes. Meanwhile, cook the spaghetti in boiling salted water until just tender. Drain. Spoon the spaghetti on to a serving dish and pour the sauce over the top. Serve with grated Parmesan cheese.

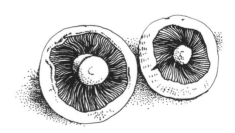

Cottage Pie

10 ml/2 tsp sunflower oil
1 small onion, chopped
225 g/8 oz/2 cups minced (ground)
  quorn
15 ml/1 tbsp plain (all-purpose)
  flour
150 ml/¹/₄ pt/²/₃ cup vegetable stock
15 ml/1 tbsp tomato purée (paste)
225 g/8 oz/2 cups chopped cooked
  vegetables
15 ml/1 tbsp yeast extract
450 g/1 lb/2 cups cooked mashed
  potato
15 g/¹/₂ oz/1 tbsp butter

Heat the oil and fry (sauté) the onion for a few minutes until soft. Stir in the remaining ingredients except the potato and butter and simmer, stirring, for 3 minutes. Spoon into an ovenproof dish. Spread the mashed potato on the top. Dot with the butter. Bake in the oven at 200°C/ 400°F/gas mark 6 for 30 minutes until crisp and browned.

Scone Pizza

SERVES 2–4

225 g/8 oz/2 cups plain (all-purpose)
  flour
50 g/2 oz/¹/₄ cup margarine
90 ml/6 tbsp water
400 g/14 oz/1 large can tomatoes
1 small onion, chopped
30 ml/2 tbsp tomato purée (paste)
Freshly ground black pepper
100 g/4 oz/1 cup grated Cheddar
  cheese
5 ml/1 tsp mixed dried herbs, or
  oregano or marjoram

Rub the flour and margarine together until the mixture looks like breadcrumbs. Add a little water at a time until the mixture makes a soft dough; you may not need all the water. Knead until smooth. Roll out to a 20 cm/8 in (or a little larger if you prefer a thinner dough) circle on a lightly floured surface until it is as thick or thin as you prefer. Place on an oiled baking sheet. Boil together the remaining ingredients except the cheese and herbs for about 10 minutes until most of the liquid has evaporated and the mixture is quite thick. Spread the topping over the pizza base and sprinkle with the cheese. Sprinkle with the herbs. Bake in the oven at 200°C/400°F/gas mark 6 for 20 minutes until browned and bubbling.

Mushroom and Pepper Pizza

SERVES 2–4

Prepare as for Scone Pizza but add 50 g/2 oz/1 cup sliced mushrooms when cooking the tomato mixture and decorate with thinly sliced (bell) pepper on top of the cheese.

Olive and Sweetcorn Pizza

SERVES 2–4

Prepare as for Scone Pizza but sprinkle 200 g/7 oz/1 small can drained sweetcorn (corn) over the tomato mixture on the pizza base and decorate with stoned (pitted) black olives over the cheese.

Vegetable and Chick Pea Curry

<u>SERVES 4</u>

30 ml/2 tbsp oil
2 bay leaves
2.5 cm/1 in piece of cinnamon stick
10 cardamom pods, split
5 whole cloves
15 ml/1 tbsp ground coriander
(cilantro)
15 ml/1 tbsp ground cumin
Pinch of chilli powder
10 ml/2 tsp sweet pickle
15 ml/1 tbsp tomato purée (paste)
2 garlic cloves
1 onion, chopped
450 g/1 lb potatoes, diced
100 g/4 oz/1 cup frozen peas
150 ml/¹/₄ pt/²/₃ cup vegetable stock
Salt and freshly ground black pepper
425 g/15 oz/1 large can chick peas
(garbanzos)
50–75 g/2–3 oz/¹/₂–³/₄ cup creamed
coconut
15 ml/1 tbsp garam masala
Plain boiled rice

Heat the oil and fry (sauté) the bay leaves, spices, pickle and tomato purée for 1 minute. Add the garlic and onion and fry for 3 minutes. Add the vegetables and stock. Season lightly, bring to the boil, then simmer for at least 1 hour, adding more water if the mixture becomes too dry. Add the chick peas half-way through cooking. Stir in the coconut and garam masala just before serving and heat through. Serve on a bed of plain boiled rice.

Sweet and Sour Stir-fry

<u>SERVES 4</u>

15 ml/1 tbsp sunflower oil
1 onion, sliced
1 red or green (bell) pepper, sliced
175 g/6 oz/3 cups button mushrooms,
sliced
425 g/15 oz/1 large can pineapple
chunks in juice
30 ml/2 tbsp tomato ketchup
(catsup)
30 ml/2 tbsp soy sauce
30 ml/2 tbsp vinegar
15 ml/1 tbsp clear honey
60 ml/4 tbsp vegetable stock
15 ml/1 tbsp cornflour (cornstarch)
Freshly ground black pepper
225 g/6 oz/1¹/₂ cups bean sprouts
Chinese egg noodles, cooked

Heat the oil in a wok or large frying pan (skillet) until almost smoking. Add the onion, pepper and mushrooms and stir-fry for 3–4 minutes. Meanwhile, mix together all the remaining ingredients except the bean sprouts and noodles. Add to the pan and heat through, stirring. Add the bean sprouts and stir-fry for 2 minutes until hot. Serve at once with Chinese noodles.

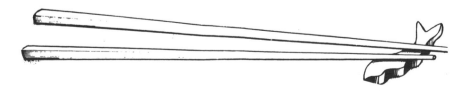

Squashed Kidney Beans

SERVES 4

30 ml/2 tbsp oil
1 onion, chopped
2 garlic cloves, crushed
5 ml/1 tsp chilli powder
5 ml/1 tsp salt
60 ml/4 tbsp tomato ketchup
*   (catsup)*
2 × 425 g/2 × 15 oz/2 large cans red
*   kidney beans, drained*
175 g/6 oz/1¹/₂ cups grated Cheddar
*   cheese*
Plain boiled rice

Heat the oil in a large frying pan (skillet) or wok and fry (sauté) the onion and garlic for about 4 minutes until soft. Stir in the chilli powder, salt and ketchup. Mash the beans with a fork or potato masher. Add them to the pan with a little water until the mixture is thick and moist but not too runny. Stir until heated through. Stir in the cheese until melted. Serve with rice.

Mushroom Stroganoff

SERVES 4

75 g/3 oz/¹/₂ cup butter or margarine
1 onion, chopped
2 garlic cloves, crushed
1.5 kg/3 lb mushrooms, sliced
150 ml/¹/₄ pt/²/₃ cup white wine
15 ml/1 tbsp cornflour (cornstarch)
300 ml/¹/₂ pt/1¹/₄ cups single (light)
*   cream*
15 ml/1 tbsp lemon juice
Salt and freshly ground black pepper
Buttered noodles

Melt the butter or margarine and fry (sauté) the onion and garlic for a few minutes until softened. Add the mushrooms and simmer for up to 30 minutes until the liquid has evaporated. Add the wine and simmer for 5 minutes. Mix the cornflour with a little water, then stir into the pan with the cream. Bring to the boil, then simmer for 5 minutes until thickened, stirring continuously. Add the lemon juice and seasoning. Serve hot with buttered noodles.

Cashew Paella

SERVES 4

15 ml/1 tbsp oil
1 leek, chopped
1 red (bell) pepper, chopped
1 green (bell) pepper, chopped
100 g/4 oz/2 cups button mushrooms,
*   sliced*
225 g/8 oz/1 cup long-grain rice
100 g/4 oz/1 cup cashew nuts
600 ml/1 pt/2¹/₂ cups vegetable stock
Freshly ground black pepper
Pinch of mixed dried herbs

Heat the oil and fry (sauté) the vegetables gently for 5 minutes until soft. Add the rice and fry for a further 3 minutes, stirring. Add the nuts, stock, seasoning and herbs, bring to the boil and simmer for about 20 minutes, stirring occasionally, until the rice is cooked and most of the water has been absorbed.

Sue's Stew

15 ml/1 tbsp sunflower oil
1 large onion, chopped
1 red (bell) pepper, sliced
1 garlic clove, crushed
5 ml/1 tsp ground cumin
5 ml/1 tsp ground coriander
(cilantro)
1.5 ml/^{1}/$_4$ tsp ground cinnamon
1.5 ml/^{1}/$_4$ tsp ground cloves
Pinch of chilli powder
15 ml/1 tbsp tomato purée (paste)
300 ml/^{1}/$_2$ pt/ 1^1/$_4$ cups vegetable
stock
430 g/15^1/$_2$ oz/1 large can chick peas
(garbanzos), drained
430 g/15^1/$_2$ oz/1 large can haricot
(navy) or pinto beans, drained
430 g/15^1/$_2$ oz/1 large can black-eyed
or kidney beans, drained
5 ml/1 tsp mixed dried herbs
Pitta bread

Heat the oil and fry (sauté) the onion, pepper, garlic and spices for 5 minutes, stirring. Add the tomato purée, stock, beans and herbs, bring to the boil, then cover and simmer for about 30 minutes until richly bathed in sauce. Check occasionally and add a little water if the mixture becomes too dry. Serve with pitta bread.

Tasty Chillied Quorn

15 ml/1 tbsp oil
2 garlic cloves, crushed
1 onion, chopped
5 ml/1 tsp chilli powder
225 g/8 oz/2 cups minced (ground)
quorn
400 g/14 oz/1 large can tomatoes
30 ml/2 tbsp tomato purée (paste)
100 g/4 oz/2 cups button mushrooms,
sliced
425 g/15 oz/1 large can kidney
beans, drained
1 vegetable stock cube
15 ml/1 tbsp yeast extract
Salt and freshly ground black pepper
Plain boiled rice

Heat the oil and fry (sauté) the garlic, onion and chilli powder for 3 minutes until soft. Add the remaining ingredients except the rice. Bring to the boil and simmer for at least 30 minutes, adding a little water if the mixture becomes too dry. Adjust the seasoning to taste. Serve with rice.

Chilli Cottage Pie

Prepare as for Tasty Chillied Quorn but turn the cooked mixture into an ovenproof dish, top with mashed potato, dot with butter and place under a hot grill (broiler) until golden brown.

179

Watercress Roulade

1 onion, chopped
15 ml/1 tbsp olive oil
4 tomatoes, chopped
15 ml/1 tbsp tomato purée (paste)
5 ml/1 tsp caster (superfine) sugar
Salt and freshly ground black pepper
1 bunch of watercress, chopped
15 ml/1 tbsp snipped chives
45 ml/3 tbsp grated Parmesan
*   cheese*
4 eggs, separated

Fry (sauté) the onion in the oil for 2 minutes to soften. Add the tomatoes, cover and cook gently for about 5 minutes or until pulpy. Add the purée and sugar and season to taste. Keep warm. Meanwhile, make the roulade: grease an 18 × 28 cm/7 × 11 in Swiss roll tin (jelly roll pan). Line with baking parchment. Mix the watercress with the chives, 30 ml/2 tbsp of the Parmesan and a little seasoning. Beat in the egg yolks. Whisk the egg whites until stiff and fold into the watercress mixture with a metal spoon. Turn the mixture into the prepared tin, smooth the surface and cook towards the top of the oven at 200°C/400°F/gas mark 6 for about 10 minutes until golden and firm to the touch. Dust a sheet of baking parchment with the remaining Parmesan. Turn the roulade out on to this and remove the lining paper, easing it away with a palette knife. Spread with the tomato mixture and roll up, starting with a short end. Transfer the roulade to a warm serving dish and serve sliced.

Couscous

175 g/6 oz/1 cup couscous
15 ml/1 tbsp oil
1 red or green (bell) pepper, diced
1 onion, chopped
50 g/2 oz/^{1}/$_3$ cup sultanas (golden
*   raisins)*
5 ml/1 tsp lemon juice
Pinch of ground ginger
Dash of soy sauce
Salt and freshly ground black pepper

Put the couscous into a sieve (strainer) and place over a pan of water, making sure the couscous does not touch the water. Bring the water to the boil, then cover and simmer for 20 minutes to steam the couscous until tender. Heat the oil and fry (sauté) the pepper and onion until tender. Add the remaining ingredients and simmer, stirring, for 2 minutes to blend the flavours.

Pizza Parcels

4 filo pastry (paste) sheets
15 g/^{1}/$_2$ oz/1 tbsp butter, melted
1 canned pimiento, chopped
4 mushrooms, sliced
2 tomatoes, sliced
8 basil leaves, torn
Freshly ground black pepper
100 g/4 oz Mozzarella cheese, grated
Black olives

Brush the filo pastry sheets with a very little butter. Fold in half and brush again. Divide the pimiento, mushrooms and tomatoes between the 4 pieces of pastry. Top with the torn basil leaves, some pepper and the cheese. Draw the pastry up over the filling to form parcels, squeezing between the finger and thumb to secure. Transfer to a buttered baking sheet. Brush with any remaining butter. Bake in the oven at 200°C/400°F/ gas mark 6 for about 12–15 minutes until golden. Transfer to warm plates. Garnish with olives and serve straight away.

Vegetable Fajitas

SERVES 4

450 g/1 lb ripe tomatoes, diced
1 onion, finely chopped
4 fresh green chillies, finely
*   chopped*
60 ml/4 tbsp chopped coriander
*   (cilantro)*
1 garlic clove, crushed
30 ml/2 tbsp lime juice
Salt and freshly ground black pepper
1 aubergine (eggplant)
1 green (bell) pepper
1 red onion
225 g/8 oz/2 cups cherry tomatoes
225 g/8 oz/2 cups button mushrooms
90 ml/6 tbsp oil
12 tortillas

Make the sauce up to 2 days in advance. Mix together the tomatoes, finely chopped onion, chillies, coriander, garlic and lime juice. Season to taste with salt and pepper. Cover and chill until ready to use. Cut the aubergine, pepper and onion into 2 cm/³/₄ in cubes. Thread alternately on to soaked wooden skewers with the tomatoes and mushrooms. Season the oil with salt and pepper and brush over the vegetables. Grill (broil) for about 8 minutes, turning frequently and brushing with seasoned oil as they cook. Meanwhile, warm the tortillas on a plate over a pan of hot water or in the microwave. To serve, push the vegetables on to the hot tortillas and top with the tomato sauce. Roll up.

Chanterelle Cream Ragu

SERVES 4

100 g/4 oz leeks, sliced
25 g/1 oz/2 tbsp butter
2 large onions, halved and sliced
450 g/1 lb chanterelles, halved
150 ml/¹/₄ pt/²/₃ cup white wine
150 ml/¹/₄ pt/²/₃ cup vegetable stock
30 ml/2 tbsp soy sauce
Freshly ground black pepper
15 ml/1 tbsp cornflour (cornstarch)
120 ml/4 fl oz/¹/₂ cup single (light)
cream
Plain boiled rice
30 ml/2 tbsp chopped coriander
*   (cilantro) or parsley*

Fry (sauté) the leeks in the butter for 2 minutes, stirring. Add the onion and cook, stirring for 2 minutes until softened. Add the chanterelles, wine, stock, soy sauce and a good grinding of pepper. Stir well, then bring to the boil. Reduce the heat and simmer for 10 minutes. Blend the cornflour with the cream. Stir into the mixture, bring to the boil and cook, stirring, for 2 minutes. Spoon on to a bed of boiled rice and sprinkle with chopped coriander or parsley before serving.

Cucumber and Potato Gourmet

450 g/1 lb potatoes, diced
2 cucumbers, cut in bite-sized
chunks
150 ml/¹/₄ pt/²/₃ cup white wine
300 ml/¹/₂ pt/1¹/₄ cups milk
25 g/1 oz/2 tbsp butter or margarine
25 g/1 oz/¹/₄ cup plain (all-purpose)
flour
175 g/6 oz/1¹/₂ cups grated Cheddar
cheese
Salt and freshly ground black pepper
5 ml/1 tsp Dijon mustard

Cook the potatoes in boiling water for about 4–5 minutes until just tender. Drain. Put the cucumber in a pan with the wine. Cover and cook for about 8–10 minutes until tender. Remove the cucumber from the wine, with a draining spoon. Add the milk to the wine, then whisk in the butter and flour. Bring to the boil and cook for 2 minutes, whisking all the time. Stir in half the cheese and season to taste with salt, pepper and the mustard. Fold in the cooked potatoes and cucumber and heat through. Turn into a lightly buttered flameproof dish and sprinkle with the remaining cheese. Grill (broil) until golden and bubbling. Serve hot.

Sweet Potato and Cucumber Cheese

Prepare as for Cucumber and Potato Gourmet but substitute 1 large sweet potato for the ordinary potato and use half Gruyère (Swiss) and half Cheddar cheese.

Chick Pea Goulash

2 onions, chopped
2 garlic cloves, crushed
2 carrots, finely diced
60 ml/4 tbsp olive oil
30 ml/2 tbsp paprika
2 × 430 g/2 × 15¹/₂ oz/2 large cans
chick peas (garbanzos)
120 ml/4 fl oz/¹/₂ cup passata (sieved
tomatoes)
30 ml/2 tbsp tomato purée (paste)
5 ml/1 tsp mixed dried herbs
Salt and freshly ground black pepper
100 g/4 oz/1 cup frozen peas
Soured (dairy sour) cream
Caraway seeds

Fry (sauté) the onions, garlic and carrots in the oil for 2 minutes until softened but not browned. Add the paprika and fry for 1 minute, stirring. Add the contents of the cans of chick peas (including the liquid) and the remaining ingredients, except the cream and caraway seeds. Bring to the boil, reduce the heat and simmer gently for about 10 minutes until thickened. Spoon into warmed bowls and top each with a spoonful of soured cream and a sprinkling of caraway seeds.

Rustic Aubergine and Red Kidney Beans

SERVES 4

1 small aubergine (eggplant), diced
Salt
45 ml/3 tbsp olive oil
1 garlic clove, crushed
425 g/15 oz/1 large can red
*   kidney beans, drained*
30 ml/2 tbsp tomato purée (paste)
1 sun-dried tomato, chopped
150 ml/¹/₄ pt/²/₃ cup vegetable stock
Freshly ground black pepper
15 ml/1 tbsp chopped basil
Cooked brown rice
30 ml/2 tbsp Mascarpone cheese

Sprinkle the aubergine with salt in a colander and leave to stand for 30 minutes. Rinse thoroughly in cold water and pat dry with kitchen paper. Heat the oil in a saucepan, add the garlic and aubergine and fry (sauté), stirring, for 5 minutes. Add the remaining ingredients, except the basil, cheese and rice, bring to the boil, reduce the heat and simmer gently for 15 minutes until the sauce is reduced and slightly thickened. Stir in the chopped basil. Spoon over a bed of cooked brown rice and top with the mascarpone cheese.

Omelette Curry

SERVES 4

5 ml/1 tsp garlic powder
Pinch of chilli powder
Pinch of turmeric
4 eggs
10 ml/2 tsp salt
15 ml/1 tbsp butter
30 ml/2 tbsp oil
100 g/4 oz potato, cooked and diced
75 ml/5 tbsp grated onion
5 ml/1 tsp tomato purée (paste)
5 ml/1 tsp caster (superfine) sugar
5 ml/1 tsp finely chopped coriander
*   (cilantro)*

Put all the ground spices in a cup with 30 ml/2 tbsp water. Whisk together the eggs, 5 ml/1tsp of the salt and 15 ml/1 tbsp water. Heat the butter in a pan and add the whisked egg. Make a flat omelette in the usual way. Remove from the pan and cut into four triangles. Heat the oil and stir-fry the diced potato until golden. Remove. Add the grated onion to the pan along with the tomato purée, the remaining salt, sugar and spices from the cup. Cook for 3 minutes. Return the potato and the quartered omelette to the pan and heat through for about 3 minutes. Sprinkle with the coriander before serving.

Indian Omelette

SERVES 2

Pinch of chilli powder
5 ml/1 tsp ground coriander
   (cilantro)
5 ml/1 tsp garlic powder
5 ml/1 tsp ground cumin
5 ml/1 tsp paprika
Good pinch of turmeric
30 ml/2 tbsp sunflower oil
1 onion, finely chopped
1 whole green chilli, seeded and
   chopped
1 red (bell) pepper, diced
2 potatoes, cooked and diced
10 ml/2 tsp salt
5 ml/1 tsp caster (superfine) sugar
4 eggs
15 ml/1 tbsp water
15 ml/¹/₂ oz/1 tbsp butter
5 ml/1 tsp chopped coriander
   (cilantro)
1 tomato, sliced

Put all the ground spices in a cup with 45 ml/3 tbsp water. To make the filling, heat the oil and fry (sauté) the onion until golden brown, then add the green chilli. Add the spices from the cup and cook for about 3 minutes. Add the diced pepper, potato, salt and sugar and cook for about 5 minutes. Keep to one side. Beat the eggs with the water and remaining salt. Heat the butter in an omelette pan and fry the mixture, lifting and stirring until just set. Spread the filling on to one half of the omelette and fold the other half on top. Garnish the top of the omelette with the chopped coriander and tomato.

Mushroom Omelette

SERVES 2

25 g/1 oz/2 tbsp butter
175 g/6 oz/3 cups button mushrooms
4 eggs
15 ml/1 tbsp water
Salt and freshly ground black pepper
Parsley sprigs

Heat half the butter in an omelette pan and fry (sauté) the mushrooms for about 5 minutes. Remove from the pan. Beat the eggs with the water and a little salt and pepper. Melt half the remaining butter in the pan and make an omelette in the usual way using half the egg mixture. Top half the omelette with half the mushrooms. Fold over and transfer to a warmed plate. Repeat with the remaining ingredients. Garnish with parsley.

Spinach Omelette

SERVES 2

Prepare as for Mushroom Omelette but substitute 100 g/4 oz/¹/₂ cup thawed frozen, chopped spinach for the mushrooms.

Chick Pea Curry

5 ml/1 tsp ground ginger
10 ml/2 tsp garlic powder
5 ml/1 tsp ground coriander
(cilantro)
Pinch of chilli powder
Pinch of ground turmeric
30 ml/2 tbsp sunflower oil
10 ml/2 tsp curry paste
1 large tomato, finely chopped
1 × 430g/1 × 15¹/₂ oz/1 large can
chick peas (garbanzos), drained
15 ml/1 tbsp chopped coriander
Simple Pilau (see page 211)

Put the ginger, garlic powder, ground coriander, chilli powder and turmeric in a cup and mix together with 15 ml/1 tbsp water. Heat the oil and add the spices from the cup and the curry paste and stir-fry gently for 1 minute. Add the tomato and 30 ml/2 tbsp water and cook until soft. Stir in the chick peas and coriander and simmer gently for 5 minutes. Serve with Simple Pilau rice.

Pasta Surprise

225 g/8 oz/2 cups pasta shapes
300 ml/¹/₂ pt/1¹/₄ cups passata
(sieved tomatoes)
200 g/7 oz/1 small can sweetcorn
(corn)
2.5 ml/¹/₂ tsp dried oregano
Salt and freshly ground black pepper
225 g/8 oz frozen chopped spinach
1 packet cheese sauce mix
300 ml/¹/₂ pt/1¹/₄ cups milk or water
(according to packet)
Grated Parmesan cheese

Cook the pasta according to the packet directions. Drain, stir in the passata, sweetcorn, oregano and seasoning and heat through. Cook the spinach according to the packet directions, drain if necessary. Make up the cheese sauce according to the packet directions. Put half the pasta mixture into the base of a 1.5 litre/2¹/₂ pt/6 cup fireproof dish. Top with the spinach, then the rest of the pasta. Spoon the sauce over, sprinkle well with grated Parmesan and brown under a hot grill (broiler) for about 5 minutes. Serve hot.

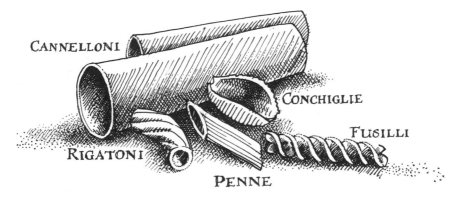

CANNELLONI

CONCHIGLIE

FUSILLI

RIGATONI

PENNE

Spaghetti with Green Herbs and Mushrooms

SERVES 4

50 g/2 oz/¹/₄ cup butter
100 g/4 oz/2 cups button mushrooms,
  sliced
1 garlic clove, crushed
50 g/2 oz/¹/₂ cup ground almonds
30 ml/2 tbsp grated Parmesan
  cheese
30 ml/2 tbsp olive oil
30 ml/2 tbsp chopped parsley
10 ml/2 tsp chopped sage
15 ml/1 tbsp chopped oregano
Salt and freshly ground black pepper
350 g/12 oz spaghetti

Melt half the butter in a pan and fry (sauté) the mushrooms gently for 3 minutes. Put to one side. Mash the remaining butter with the garlic, almonds and cheese. Gradually work in the oil, herbs and seasoning. Cook the spaghetti according to the packet directions. Drain, return to the saucepan and add the mushrooms and herb mixture. Stir over a gentle heat until the spaghetti is well coated in the sauce. Serve hot.

Spaghetti with Basil and Mushrooms

SERVES 4

Prepare as for Spaghetti with Green Herbs and Mushrooms but omit the parsley, sage and oregano and add 60 ml/ 4 tbsp chopped basil instead.

Courgette Pasta

SERVES 4

50 g/2 oz/¹/₄ cup butter or margarine
450 g/1 lb courgettes (zucchini),
  sliced
1 onion, chopped
Pinch of dried tarragon
25 g/1 oz/¹/₄ cup plain (all-purpose)
  flour
300 ml/¹/₂ pt/1¹/₄ cups milk
Salt and freshly ground black pepper
225 g/8 oz tagliatelle

Melt half the butter or margarine in a saucepan and fry (sauté) the courgettes, onions and tarragon gently until soft. Remove from the pan with a draining spoon and keep warm. Add the remaining butter to the pan and whisk in the flour and milk. Bring to the boil, whisking all the time. Season with salt and pepper. Meanwhile, cook the tagliatelle in boiling salted water until just soft. Drain and turn into a serving dish. Spoon the vegetables over the pasta. Pour the white sauce over and glaze under a hot grill (broiler).

Cheese and Chive Spaghetti

SERVES 4

225 g/8 oz spaghetti
100 g/4 oz/1 cup grated Parmesan
  cheese
50 g/2 oz/¹/₄ cup butter or margarine
Salt and freshly ground black pepper
Snipped chives

Cook the spaghetti according to the packet directions. Drain, then return to the hot saucepan. Add the cheese and butter or margarine and season with salt and pepper. Toss well, add the chives and toss again. Serve straight away.

Neapolitan Pasta

225 g/8 oz/2 cups pasta shapes
15 ml/1 tbsp olive oil
2 garlic cloves, crushed
1 onion, chopped
4 tomatoes, skinned and chopped
15 ml/1 tbsp tomato purée (paste)
2.5 ml/¹/₂ tsp dried oregano
2.5 ml/¹/₂ tsp dried marjoram
Salt and freshly ground black pepper
Black olives

Cook the pasta in boiling salted water until just tender. Drain. Meanwhile, heat the oil and fry (sauté) the garlic and onion for 5 minutes. Stir in the tomatoes, tomato purée and herbs. Add the drained pasta and toss over a gentle heat. Season with salt and pepper. Garnish with black olives before serving.

Tempting Tagliatelle

225 g/8 oz tagliatelle
15 g/¹/₂ oz/1 tbsp butter
1 onion, chopped
1 garlic clove, crushed
100 g/4 oz/2 cups button mushrooms, sliced
200 g/7 oz/1 small can sweetcorn (corn)
150 ml/¹/₄ pt/²/₃ cup single (light) cream
Salt and freshly ground black pepper
Pinch of mixed dried herbs

Cook the pasta according to the packet directions. Drain. Melt the butter and fry (sauté) the onion, garlic and mushrooms for 5 minutes until soft. Stir in the pasta, sweetcorn and cream and heat through. Season to taste with salt, pepper and herbs.

Creamy Tarragon Pasta

225 g/8 oz/2 cups conchiglie (pasta shells)
300 ml/¹/₂ pt/1¹/₄ cups single (light) cream
100 g/4 oz/¹/₂ cup soft cheese
15 ml/1 tbsp chopped tarragon
Salt and freshly ground black pepper

Cook the pasta according to the packet directions. Drain. Heat the cream, cheese, tarragon and a little salt and pepper, stirring until smooth, then stir in the pasta. Serve straight away.

Nutty Rigatoni

25 g/1 oz/2 tbsp butter or margarine
1 onion, thinly sliced
225 g/8 oz/4 cups button mushrooms, sliced
75 g/3 oz/³/₄ cup walnuts, chopped
300 ml/¹/₂ pt/1¹/₄ cups soured (dairy sour) cream
Pinch of dried tarragon
Salt and freshly ground black pepper
175 g/6 oz/1¹/₂ cups rigatoni
Chopped parsley

Melt the butter or margarine and fry (sauté) the onion and mushrooms for 4 minutes until soft. Add the walnuts, cream and seasonings and heat through, stirring. Meanwhile, cook the rigatoni according to the packet directions. Drain well. Spoon the pasta on to serving plates and pour over the sauce. Sprinkle with chopped parsley.

Spicy Pinto Stew

SERVES 4

15 ml/1 tbsp oil
1 garlic clove, crushed
2.5 ml/¹/₂ tsp ground ginger
2 × 425 g/2 × 15 oz/2 large cans
*   pinto beans, drained*
200 g/7 oz/1 small can chopped
*   tomatoes*
1 onion, chopped
30 ml/2 tbsp soy sauce
5 ml/1 tsp five-spice powder
150 ml/¹/₄ pt/²/₃ cup vegetable stock
1 red (bell) pepper, chopped
225 g/8 oz/4 cups button mushrooms,
*   sliced*
4 courgettes (zucchini), sliced
Salt and freshly ground black pepper

Heat the oil and fry (sauté) the garlic and ginger very gently for 2 minutes. Add the remaining ingredients, bring to the boil, cover and simmer for 20 minutes. Season to taste, then serve hot.

Egg and Mushroom Pie

SERVES 4

900 g/2 lb potatoes
15 g/¹/₂ oz/1 tbsp butter or margarine
30 ml/2 tbsp milk
295 g/10¹/₂ oz/1 small can condensed
*   mushroom soup*
6 hard-boiled (hard-cooked) eggs,
sliced
100 g/4 oz/2 cups button mushrooms,
*   sliced*
15 ml/1 tbsp chopped parsley
50 g/2 oz/¹/₂ cup grated Cheddar
*   cheese*

Boil the potatoes until tender, then drain and mash with the butter or margarine and milk. Heat the soup without allowing it to boil. Stir in the eggs, mushrooms and parsley and pour into a casserole (Dutch oven). Cover with the mashed potatoes and sprinkle over the grated cheese. Bake in the oven at 200°C/400°F/gas mark 6 for about 15 minutes until piping hot and the cheese is browned.

Quick Bean Bake

SERVES 4

425 g/15 oz/1 large can ratatouille
425 g/15 oz/1 large can red kidney
*   beans, drained*
2.5 ml/¹/₂ tsp dried tarragon
Freshly ground black pepper
50 g/2 oz/¹/₂ cup toasted
*   breadcrumbs*
50 g/2 oz/¹/₂ cup grated Cheddar
*   cheese*

Heat together the ratatouille, kidney beans, tarragon and pepper, then place in an ovenproof dish. Mix together the breadcrumbs and cheese and sprinkle over the top. Place under the grill (broiler) or bake in the oven at 200°C/400°F/gas mark 6 until the cheese has melted and browned.

Vegetable Lasagne

SERVES 4

425 g/15 oz/1 large can ratatouille
100 g/4 oz/2 cups button mushrooms,
*   sliced*
5 ml/1 tsp mixed dried herbs
6-8 no-need-to-precook lasagne
*   sheets*
20 g/³/₄ oz/3 tbsp plain (all-purpose)
*   flour*
20 g/³/₄ oz/1¹/₂ tbsp butter
300 ml/¹/₂ pt/1¹/₄ cups milk
Salt and freshly ground black pepper
175 g/6 oz/1¹/₂ cups grated Cheddar
*   cheese*

Mix together the ratatouille, mushrooms and herbs. Layer the mixture with the lasagne sheets in a shallow ovenproof dish. Whisk the flour, butter and milk together in a saucepan. Bring to the boil, whisking all the time until thickened. Season to taste and stir in two-thirds of the cheese. Pour over the top of the lasagne. Sprinkle with the remaining cheese. Bake in the oven at 190°C/375°F/gas mark 5 for 35–40 minutes.

Baked Bean Lasagne

SERVES 4

15 ml/1 tbsp olive oil
1 onion, chopped
2 garlic cloves, crushed
225 g/8 oz/4 cups button mushrooms, sliced
400 g/14 oz/1 large can baked beans
30 ml/2 tbsp tomato ketchup (catsup)
45 ml/3 tbsp soy sauce
Pinch of chilli powder
Freshly ground black pepper
6-8 no-need-to-precook lasagne sheets
20 g/³/₄ oz/3 tbsp plain (all-purpose) flour
20 g/³/₄ oz/1¹/₂ tbsp butter
300 ml/¹/₂ pt/1¹/₄ cups milk
175 g/6 oz/1¹/₂ cups grated Cheddar cheese
Salt

Heat the oil in a large pan and fry (sauté) the onion and garlic for about 4 minutes until softened. Add the mushrooms and cook for 2 minutes. Stir in the beans, ketchup, soy sauce, chilli powder and pepper. Layer the bean mixture and lasagne sheets in a shallow ovenproof dish, finishing with a layer of lasagne. Whisk the flour, butter and milk

together in a saucepan. Bring to the boil, whisking all the time until thickened. Stir in two-thirds of the cheese and season with a little salt and pepper. Pour over the top of the lasagne. Sprinkle with the remaining cheese. Bake in the oven at 190°C/375°F/gas mark 5 for 35–40 minutes.

Dolmas

SERVES 4

12 large cabbage leaves
350 g/12 oz/3 cups cooked chopped mixed vegetables
400 g/14 oz/1 large can chopped tomatoes
1 red chilli, seeded and chopped
1 garlic clove, crushed
15 ml/1 tbsp tomato purée (paste)
Salt and freshly ground black pepper

Cook the leaves in boiling salted water for about 5 minutes until just tender. Drain. Place a large spoonful or two of the vegetables on each leaf at one end and roll over to make a parcel, turning in the edges as you go. Arrange in a single layer in an ovenproof dish. Mix together the remaining ingredients and pour over. Bake in the oven at 180°C/350°F/gas mark 4 for 30 minutes until piping hot and the liquid is slightly reduced.

Onion and Apple Crumble

SERVES 4

3–4 eating (dessert) apples
2 onions, sliced
5 ml/1 tsp dried sage
Pinch of grated nutmeg
Salt and freshly ground black pepper
50 g/2 oz/¹/₂ cup plain (all-purpose)
flour
50 g/2 oz/¹/₄ cup butter or margarine
Fresh breadcrumbs

Grease an ovenproof dish. Arrange alternating layers of apple and onion in the dish, seasoning with sage, nutmeg, salt and pepper as you go. Rub the flour and fat together until the mixture resembles breadcrumbs. Stir in the breadcrumbs and sprinkle over the dish. Bake in the oven at 200°C/400°F/gas mark 6 for about 30 minutes until the filling is soft and the topping golden.

Baked Bean Loaf

SERVES 4

400 g/14 oz/1 large can baked beans
1 small onion, finely chopped
50 g/2 oz/1 cup breadcrumbs
30 ml/2 tbsp tomato ketchup
(catsup)
1 egg
5 ml/1 tsp yeast extract
5 ml/1 tsp mixed dried herbs
Salt and freshly ground black pepper

Mix together all the ingredients. Pour into a greased and lined 450 g/1 lb loaf tin. Bake in the oven at 180°C/350°F/gas mark 4 for 30 minutes or until firm. Turn out, remove the paper and serve cut in slices.

Lentil Pud

SERVES 4

175 g/6 oz/1 cup green or brown
lentils, soaked overnight
1 garlic clove, crushed
175 g/6 oz/1¹/₂ cups grated Cheddar
cheese
15 ml/1 tbsp tomato ketchup
(catsup)
10 ml/2 tsp sweet pickle
Dash of soy sauce
Salt and freshly ground black pepper

Drain the lentils, place in a pan with fresh water, bring to the boil, then simmer for about 45 minutes until tender. Drain. Add the garlic, two-thirds of the cheese, the ketchup, pickle, soy sauce and salt and pepper. Turn into a greased ovenproof dish and sprinkle with the remaining cheese. Bake in the oven at 200°C/400°F/gas mark 6 for 20 minutes until golden.

Vegetable Crumble

SERVES 4

450 g/1 lb courgettes (zucchini),
sliced
15 ml/1 tbsp olive oil
1 red (bell) pepper, sliced
100 g/4 oz/2 cups button mushrooms,
sliced
200 g/7 oz/1 small can tomatoes
2 garlic cloves, crushed
1 onion, chopped
5 ml/1 tsp dried marjoram
Salt and freshly ground black pepper
175 g/6 oz/1¹/₂ cups grated Cheddar
cheese
100 g/4 oz/2 cups fresh breadcrumbs

Cook the courgettes in boiling salted water for 5 minutes. Drain. Heat the oil and fry (sauté) the remaining vegetables, the marjoram and seasoning for about 10 minutes until softened. Stir in the courgettes. Spoon the vegetables into a shallow ovenproof dish. Mix together the cheese and breadcrumbs and sprinkle over the top. Bake in the oven at 200°C/400°F/gas mark 6 for about 25 minutes until heated through and golden brown.

Swede and Potato Pie

SERVES 4

450 g/1 lb potatoes, sliced
450 g/1 lb swede, sliced
45 ml/3 tbsp milk
Freshly ground black pepper
175 g/6 oz/1¹/₂ cups grated mature
*   Cheddar cheese*
65 g/2¹/₂ oz ready-salted crisps
*   (potato chips), lightly crushed*
Baked beans in tomato sauce

Cook the vegetables in boiling, salted water for about 15 minutes until tender. Drain well then mash together. Stir in the milk and pepper. Spoon into an ovenproof dish. Mix together the cheese and crisps and sprinkle over the top. Bake in the oven at 200°C/400°F/gas mark 6 for 15 minutes until crisp and golden. Serve with baked beans.

Nut Roast

SERVES 4

150 g/5 oz/1¹/₄ cups chopped mixed
*   nuts*
75 g/3 oz/1¹/₂ cups fresh breadcrumbs
1 small onion, chopped
15 ml/1 tbsp soy sauce
2.5 ml/¹/₂ tsp dried thyme
5 ml/1 tsp lemon juice
25 g/1 oz/2 tbsp butter or margarine
5 ml/1 tsp sunflower oil
5 ml/1 tsp yeast extract
150 ml/¹/₄ pt/²/₃ cup water

Mix together all the ingredients in a bowl, dissolving the yeast extract in the water before adding it to the mixture. Press gently into a greased 450 g/1 lb loaf tin. Bake in the oven at 190°C/375°F/gas mark 5 for 30–40 minutes until crisp on top and hot in the centre. Turn out and serve sliced.

Speedy Stuffed Peppers

SERVES 4

4 red or green (bell) peppers
1 packet savoury rice, any flavour
Olive oil

Remove the stem, core and seeds of the peppers. Cook the rice as directed on the packet. Stuff the rice into the peppers and drizzle with a little oil. Bake in the oven at 200°C/400°F/gas mark 6 for 20 minutes or until tender.

Cheaty Vegetable Pie

SERVES 4

225 g/8 oz/2 cups plain (all-purpose)
*   flour*
Pinch of salt
100 g/4 oz/¹/₂ cup margarine
60 ml/4 tbsp water
175 g/6 oz/1¹/₂ cups chopped mixed
*   vegetables*
400 g/14 oz/1 large can mushroom
*   soup*
5 ml/1 tsp mixed dried herbs
Milk

Mix together the flour and salt. Rub in the margarine until the mixture resembles breadcrumbs. Stir in the water a little at a time until the mixture forms a soft but not sticky dough. Knead on a lightly floured surface until smooth. Roll out two-thirds of the dough and use to line a 20 cm/8 in pie dish. Heat the vegetables in a pan of water for a few minutes, then drain. Mix with the soup and herbs and pour into the pastry-lined dish. Roll out the remaining pastry and lay over the top, sealing the edges together with a little water. Knock up and flute with the back of a knife. Brush the top with milk. Place on a baking sheet. Bake in the oven at 180°C/350°F/gas mark 4 for 30 minutes until golden brown on top and piping hot.

Broccoli Flan

SERVES 4

100 g/4 oz shortcrust pastry (basic
*   pie crust)*
100 g/4 oz small broccoli florets
2 eggs
150 ml/¹/₄ pt/²/₃ cup milk
Salt and freshly ground black pepper
100 g/4 oz/1 cup grated Cheddar
*   cheese*

Roll out the pastry and use to line an 18 cm/7 in flan tin (pie pan). Cook the broccoli in boiling water for 2 minutes, then drain. Mix with the remaining ingredients and pour into the pastry case (shell). Place on a baking sheet. Bake in the oven at 190°C/375°F/gas mark 5 for about 20–30 minutes until the filling is firm. Serve hot or cold.

Photograph opposite: **Broccoli and Roquefort tagliatelle (page 161)**

VEGETABLE SIDE DISHES

If you are serving plainly cooked meat or fish, an exciting vegetable accompaniment can transform the meal. There are lots of clever garnishing ideas to brighten up basic cooked vegetables too.

Fruity Cabbage

SERVES 4

15 ml/1 tbsp oil
1 cabbage, shredded
1 onion, chopped
1 garlic clove, crushed
1 cooking (tart) apple, peeled and chopped
10 ml/2 tsp lemon juice
Salt and freshly ground black pepper

Heat the oil and gently fry (sauté) the cabbage, onion and garlic for about 5 minutes until just soft. Add the apple, lemon juice, salt and pepper. Cover and cook over a low heat for 10–15 minutes, stirring occasionally. Serve hot.

Fried Aubergines

SERVES 4

2 aubergines (eggplants), sliced
Salt
25 g/1 oz/¹/₄ cup plain (all-purpose) flour
1 garlic clove, crushed
Oil for shallow-frying

Put the aubergine slices in a colander and sprinkle with salt. Leave for 30 minutes. Rinse and dry on kitchen paper. Mix together the flour, some salt and the garlic. Coat the aubergines in the seasoned flour. Heat the oil and fry (sauté) the aubergines until crisp and brown on both sides. Drain on kitchen paper.

Creamy Peas

SERVES 4

175 g/6 oz/1¹/₂ cups frozen peas
300 ml/¹/₂ pt/1¹/₄ cups crème fraîche
5 ml/1 tsp sugar
Salt and freshly ground black pepper
10 ml/2 tsp chopped mint

Cook the peas in boiling salted water for 5 minutes. Drain and return to the pan. Add the remaining ingredients and toss over a gentle heat.

Pasta with Vegetable Ribbons

SERVES 4

225 g/8 oz tagliatelle
1 carrot
1 courgette (zucchini)
15 g/¹/₂ oz/1 tbsp butter

Cook the pasta according to the packet directions. Meanwhile, pare the carrot and courgette into ribbons with a potato peeler. Add the carrot ribbons and then the courgette for the last minute of the pasta cooking time. Drain, toss in butter and serve.

***Photograph opposite:* French beans with feta and sun-dried tomatoes (page 209) and Spiced bulgar with pine nuts (page 213)**

Crunchy Cauliflower with Coriander Sauce

SERVES 4

75 g/3 oz/¹/₃ cup butter
2 thick slices bread, finely diced
1 onion, chopped
1 garlic clove, crushed
5 ml/1 tsp ground cumin
2 courgettes (zucchini), diced
*1 small cauliflower, cut into tiny
    florets*
*150 ml/¹/₄ pt/²/₃ cup double (heavy)
    cream*
*15 ml/1 tbsp chopped coriander
    (cilantro)*
Salt and freshly ground black pepper

Melt 50 g/2 oz/¹/₄ cup of the butter in a frying pan (skillet) and fry (sauté) the bread cubes until crisp and golden. Drain on kitchen paper. Melt the remaining butter in a saucepan, add the onion and garlic and fry gently for 2 minutes. Add the cumin and fry for 1 minute. Add the courgettes, stir gently, then cover, reduce the heat and simmer for 5 minutes until the courgettes are just tender. Meanwhile, cook the cauliflower in boiling salted water for 4–5 minutes until just tender. Drain. Add the cauliflower to the courgette mixture. Stir in the cream, coriander and seasoning. Heat through. Just before serving, sprinkle with the croûtons.

Artichoke Bake

SERVES 4

*400 g/14 oz/1 large can artichoke
    hearts, drained*
*250 ml/8 fl oz/1 cup Basic
    Mayonnaise (see page 229)*
1 garlic clove, crushed
5 ml/1 tsp chopped basil
5 ml/1 tsp white wine vinegar
Salt and freshly ground black pepper
*75 g/3 oz/³/₄ cup grated Parmesan
    cheese*
25 g/1 oz/¹/₂ cup fresh breadcrumbs

Arrange the artichokes in a shallow ovenproof dish. Mix together the mayonnaise, garlic, basil, vinegar, salt and pepper and pour over the artichokes. Mix together the cheese and breadcrumbs and sprinkle over the top. Bake in the oven at 200°C/400°F/gas mark 6 for 20–25 minutes until golden.

Celery and Beans in Soured Cream

SERVES 4

6 celery sticks
450 g/1 lb French beans
60 ml/4 tbsp olive oil
*150 ml/¹/₄ pt/²/₃ cup soured (dairy
    sour) cream*
15 ml/1 tbsp caraway seeds
Salt and freshly ground black pepper

Cut the celery into pieces the same size as the beans. Cook the celery and beans in boiling water for about 6 minutes until just tender, then drain well. Heat the oil and fry (sauté) the vegetables quickly for 2 minutes. Stir in the soured cream and caraway seeds and season with salt and pepper.

Mushrooms in Balsamic Vinegar

SERVES 4

450 g/1 lb button mushrooms
30 ml/2 tbsp lemon juice
Salt and freshly ground black pepper
150 ml/¹/₄ pt/²/₃ cup balsamic
  vinegar
120 ml/4 fl oz/¹/₂ cup olive oil
4 garlic cloves, crushed
15 ml/1 tbsp chopped capers
45 ml/3 tbsp chopped parsley

Place the mushrooms and lemon juice in a pan and season with salt and pepper. Just cover with water, bring to the boil, then simmer for about 5 minutes until tender. Drain. Meanwhile, bring the vinegar, oil and garlic to the boil in a separate pan. Simmer for 20 minutes. Pour the hot marinade over the mushrooms, then leave to cool. Add the capers and parsley and season to taste.

Sweet Glazed Shallots

SERVES 4–6

450 g/1 lb small shallots
50 g/2 oz/¹/₄ cup butter or
  margarine, melted
60 ml/4 tbsp golden (light corn)
  syrup

Peel the shallots, then place in a pan, cover with water and bring to the boil. Simmer for 4 minutes, then drain thoroughly. Arrange in a shallow roasting tin (pan) and pour over the butter or margarine. Drizzle with syrup. Cook in the oven at 200°C/400°F/gas mark 6 for about 20 minutes, stirring occasionally, until the onions are tender and golden.

Courgette Ribbons Vinaigrette

SERVES 4

450 g/1 lb courgettes (zucchini)
30 ml/2 tbsp olive oil
5 ml/1 tsp white wine vinegar
1 garlic clove, crushed
15 ml/1 tbsp chopped parsley
Salt and freshly ground black pepper

Use a potato peeler to cut long thin ribbons off the courgettes. Place 2–3 ribbons on top of each other, then thread on to soaked wooden skewers, folding them backwards and forwards concertina-style. Whisk together the oil, vinegar, garlic, parsley, salt and pepper. Brush over the courgettes. Grill (broil) for about 8–10 minutes, turning and basting frequently.

Grilled Fennel with Caraway

SERVES 4

4 fennel bulbs, thickly sliced
40 g/1¹/₂ oz/3 tbsp butter or
margarine, melted
15 ml/1 tbsp caraway seeds
Salt and freshly ground black pepper
50 g/2 oz/¹/₂ cup grated Parmesan
  cheese

Cook the fennel in boiling water for about 6 minutes until just tender. Drain well. Place on foil on a grill (broiler) rack. Brush with butter, sprinkle with caraway seeds and season with salt and pepper. Grill (broil) for about 2 minutes on each side until lightly browned. Transfer to a serving dish and sprinkle with Parmesan before serving.

Grilled Leeks with Basil Butter

4 leeks
30 ml/2 tbsp olive oil
4 tomatoes, halved
2 garlic cloves, crushed
15 ml/1 tbsp lemon juice
Salt and freshly ground black pepper
40 g/1¹/₂ oz/3 tbsp butter or
margarine, softened
15 ml/1 tbsp chopped basil

Trim the leeks and cut them in half lengthways. Place on foil on a grill (broiler) rack. Brush with olive oil, then grill (broil) for about 3 minutes on each side until just soft and lightly browned. Add the tomatoes to the rack and grill for the last 2 minutes. Transfer for a serving dish and sprinkle with half the garlic, the lemon juice and a little salt and pepper. Meanwhile blend the butter or margarine with the remaining garlic and the basil and season with salt and pepper. Dot over the vegetables and return to the grill for a few moments until bubbling.

Grilled Onions with Basil Butter

Prepare as for Grilled Leeks with Basil Butter but substitute 4 peeled, halved onions for the leeks and grill (broil) for about 6 minutes on each side.

Mushroom and Banana Kebabs

225 g/8 oz button mushrooms
2 red (bell) peppers, cut into chunks
1 large courgette (zucchini), cut
into chunks
1 firm banana, cut into chunks
Salt and freshly ground black pepper
Freshly grated nutmeg
50 g/2 oz/¹/₄ cup butter or
margarine, melted

Thread the vegetables and banana alternately on to soaked wooden skewers. Place on a grill (broiler) rack. Season with salt and pepper, sprinkle with nutmeg and brush well with butter or margarine. Grill (broil) gently for about 15 minutes, brushing and basting regularly, until the pepper and courgette are tender.

Sherried Mushroom Kebabs

450 g/1 lb large mushrooms
120 ml/4 fl oz/¹/₂ cup olive oil
Salt and freshly ground black pepper
25 g/1 oz/2 tbsp butter, melted
30 ml/2 tbsp dry sherry
30 ml/2 tbsp chopped flatleaf
parsley

Toss the mushrooms in the oil with plenty of pepper until the oil is absorbed. Thread the mushrooms on to soaked wooden skewers. Grill (broil) the kebabs for about 8 minutes, turning frequently until crispy. Meanwhile, mix together the butter, sherry and parsley and season with salt and pepper. Arrange the kebabs in a shallow serving dish and pour over the flavoured butter. Serve straight away.

Chestnut Mushroom Parcels

SERVES 4

450 g/1 lb chestnut mushrooms,
sliced
2 spring onions (scallions), chopped
2 garlic cloves, crushed
45 ml/3 tbsp olive oil
15 ml/1 tbsp balsamic vinegar
15 ml/1 tbsp chopped parsley
Salt and freshly ground black pepper
4 tomatoes, sliced
15 ml/1 tbsp chopped basil

Place the mushrooms in 4 squares of foil. Sprinkle with the spring onions and garlic. Whisk together the oil and vinegar, stir in the parsley and season with salt and pepper. Pour over the mushrooms. Top with tomato slices and the basil. Fold the foil over the filling and twist the foil at the top to seal. Bake in the oven at 200°C/400°F/gas mark 6 for about 20 minutes until cooked through. Serve in the parcels so each person unwraps their own.

Spiced Herb Onions

SERVES 4

450 g/1 lb/4 cups button (pearl)
onions
45 ml/3 tbsp chopped parsley
45 ml/3 tbsp finely chopped spring
onions (scallions)
5 ml/1 tsp mixed dried herbs
2.5 ml/¹/₂ tsp mustard powder
Few drops of chilli sauce
Salt and freshly ground black pepper
225 g/8 oz/1 cup butter or
margarine, softened

Place the onions in a roasting tin (pan). Mix together the remaining ingredients (a food processor is a quick way to do this). Spread over the onions and bake in the oven at 200°C/400°F/gas mark 6 for about 20–30 minutes or until tender and bubbling.

Red Onions with Bacon

SERVES 4

4 red onions, cut into wedges
4 streaky bacon rashers (slices),
quartered
30 ml/2 tbsp olive oil
Salt and freshly ground black pepper
15 ml/1 tbsp chopped parsley

Thread the onions and bacon alternately on soaked wooden skewers. Brush with oil and season with salt and pepper. Grill (broil) for about 10 minutes, turning frequently and brushing with more oil if necessary. Serve sprinkled with parsley.

Grilled Garlic Peppers

SERVES 4

3 red, yellow or green (bell) peppers
90 ml/6 tbsp olive oil
1 garlic clove, crushed
5 ml/1 tsp dried thyme
Pinch of cayenne

Cut the peppers into quarters or large strips. Place on a sheet of foil on the grill (broiler) rack. Mix the remaining ingredients together and brush over the peppers. Grill (broil) for about 10 minutes until tender, turning occasionally and brushing with the flavoured oil as necessary.

Sage and Onion Tomatoes

SERVES 4

4 large tomatoes, halved
Salt and freshly ground black pepper
1 onion, finely chopped
50 g/2 oz/1 cup fresh breadcrumbs
5 ml/1 tsp chopped sage
100 g/4 oz/1 cup strong cheese,
  grated

Scoop out the seeds from the tomato halves and season the insides with salt and pepper. Place in a roasting tin (pan). Mix the onion with the breadcrumbs and sage and season with salt and pepper. Pile the stuffing mixture into the tomato halves and top the tomatoes with the cheese. Bake in the oven at 200°C/400°F/ gas mark 6 for 20–30 minutes until golden and bubbling.

Carrots with Orange and Cardamom

SERVES 4–6

750 g/1¹/₂ lb baby carrots, topped
  and tailed
150 ml/¹/₄ pt/²/₃ cup thick plain
  yoghurt
Juice of large 1 orange
3 green cardamoms, crushed
30 ml/2 tbsp olive oil
Salt

Steam the carrots for 10–12 minutes until just tender. Turn them into a deep dish. Mix the yoghurt, orange juice, cardamoms and olive oil with a pinch of salt and quickly stir the mixture into the carrots. Serve lukewarm.

Zingy Carrots and Courgettes

SERVES 4

15 ml/1 tbsp sunflower oil
25 g/1 oz/2 tbsp butter
2 courgettes (zucchini), grated
2 carrots, grated
2 garlic cloves, crushed
Grated rind of 1 lime
Salt and freshly ground black pepper
Juice of ¹/₂ lime
5 ml/1 tsp dried thyme

Heat the oil and butter in a large frying pan (skillet). Add the grated vegetables and garlic and fry (sauté) for 2 minutes. Add the lime rind and season to taste. Stir in the juice and thyme and continue to cook for a further 5–6 minutes. Serve hot.

Buttered Carrots and Parsley

SERVES 4

8 carrots, sliced
25 g/1 oz/2 tbsp butter
15 ml/1 tbsp chopped parsley
Salt and freshly ground black pepper

Boil the carrots until just tender. Drain and return to the pan. Toss in the butter until melted. Add the parsley and a little salt and pepper and toss again before serving.

Thyme and Parsley Carrots

SERVES 4

450 g/1 lb carrots, thinly sliced
5 ml/1 tsp light brown sugar
25 g/1 oz/2 tbsp butter
5 ml/1 tsp chopped thyme
10 ml/2 tsp chopped parsley

Boil the carrots in water with the sugar added until tender. Drain off the liquid, stir in the butter and herbs, toss gently and serve hot.

Orange Ginger Carrots

SERVES 4

450 g/1 lb carrots, thinly sliced
10 ml/2 tsp caster (superfine) sugar
5 ml/1 tsp cornflour (cornstarch)
1.5 ml/¹/₄ tsp salt
1.5 ml/¹/₄ tsp ground ginger
75 ml/5 tbsp orange juice
15 g/¹/₂ oz/1 tbsp butter

Cook the carrots until almost tender but still with a little 'bite'. Drain. Combine the sugar, cornflour, salt, ginger and orange juice. Pour over the carrots and cook over a low heat until boiling. Add the butter, remove from the heat, toss well and serve.

Turkish Fried Carrots

SERVES 4

450 g/1 lb carrots, sliced, lightly
*   cooked and cooled*
15 ml/1 tbsp flour
Salt and freshly ground black pepper
30 ml/2 tbsp olive oil
300 ml/¹/₂ pt/1¹/₄ cups plain yoghurt
Good pinch of garam masala
A little chopped mint

Spread the carrots on to kitchen paper to dry. Toss them in the flour, seasoned with salt and pepper, and shake off any surplus. Fry (sauté) in the oil until golden brown. Season to taste. Keep warm on a serving dish. Put the yoghurt into a small pan and heat very gently. Pour over the carrots, sprinkle on the garam masala and garnish with a little chopped mint.

No-nonsense Ratatouille

SERVES 4

1 small aubergine (eggplant), sliced
3 courgettes (zucchini), sliced
1 onion, sliced
1 green (bell) pepper, sliced
4 tomatoes, chopped
45 ml/3 tbsp olive oil
15 ml/1 tbsp tomato purée (paste)
30 ml/2 tbsp red wine or water
2.5 ml/¹/₂ tsp dried oregano
Salt and freshly ground black pepper

Put the prepared vegetables in a large pan with the olive oil. Cook, stirring, for 5 minutes until they begin to soften. Blend the tomato purée with the wine or water and add to the pan with the oregano and seasoning. Cover and simmer for 15 minutes, stirring occasionally, until the vegetables are just tender.

Creamy Courgette Bake

SERVES 4

450 g/1 lb courgettes, grated
5 ml/1 tsp salt
5 ml/1 tsp caster (superfine) sugar
10 ml/2 tsp tarragon vinegar
Butter, for greasing
1 egg, beaten
300 ml/¹/₂ pt/1¹/₄ cups double
(heavy) cream
6 basil leaves, torn
15 ml/1 tbsp grated Parmesan
cheese

Toss the courgettes with the salt, sugar and vinegar. Cover and leave in a cool place for several hours. Drain the courgettes very well, squeezing them to get rid of all the juice – this is very important. Put them in a lightly buttered shallow ovenproof dish and fluff them up with a fork. Beat the egg lightly with the cream, the basil leaves and the Parmesan. Pour over the courgettes. Bake in the oven at 200°C/400°F/gas mark 6 for about 20 minutes until the custard is set around the edges and still slightly creamy in the centre.

Courgette Patties

SERVES 4

275 g/10 oz courgettes (zucchini),
grated
40 g/1¹/₂ oz/¹/₃ cup plain (all-
purpose) flour
2 eggs, lightly beaten
2.5 ml/¹/₂ tsp salt
Freshly ground black pepper
25 g/1 oz/2 tbsp butter
30 ml/2 tbsp oil

Mix the courgettes with the flour, eggs, salt and a pinch of pepper to form a batter. Put spoonfuls of the batter in hot butter and oil to form patties about 5 cm/2 in diameter. Flatten each one slightly with the back of a spoon. Cook for about 4 minutes on each side until golden brown and crusty. Drain on kitchen paper and keep warm. Keep frying (sautéing) the patties until all the batter is used up, adding more oil to the pan if needed. Serve hot.

Note: To serve as a starter, accompany the patties with flavoured Mayonnaise (see page 229).

Scalloped Spuds

SERVES 4

Butter, for greasing
450 g/1 lb potatoes, sliced
1 onion, sliced
Salt and freshly ground black pepper
100 g/4 oz/1 cup grated Cheddar
cheese
1 egg
150 ml/¹/₄ pt/²/₃ cup milk

Grease a shallow ovenproof dish with butter and layer the potatoes and onion in the dish, seasoning with salt and pepper as you go. Beat together the cheese, egg and milk and pour over the vegetables. Bake in the oven at 180°C/350°F/gas mark 4 for about 1¹/₂ hours until tender throughout and browned on top.

Tomato Potatoes

450 g/1 lb potatoes, halved
400 g/14 oz/1 large can chopped
  tomatoes
25 g/1 oz/¹/² cup fresh breadcrumbs
50 g/2 oz/¹/² cup grated Cheddar
  cheese

Cook the potatoes in boiling salted water for about 10 minutes until just soft. Drain and arrange in an ovenproof dish. Pour over the tomatoes and bake in the oven at 180°C/350°F/gas mark 4 for 15 minutes. Mix together the breadcrumbs and cheese and sprinkle over the top. Return to the oven or place under a hot grill (broiler) for a few minutes until the cheese is brown and bubbling.

Sesame Potatoes

750 g/1¹/² lb potatoes, scrubbed and
  halved
30 ml/2 tbsp olive oil
30 ml/2 tbsp sesame seeds
Coarse sea salt

Put the potatoes in a roasting tin (pan). Toss in the oil and sprinkle with the sesame seeds and salt. Bake in the oven at 190°C/375°F/gas mark 5 for 1–1¹/² hours until golden and tender.

Bombay Potatoes

5 ml/1 tsp ground coriander
  (cilantro)
Pinch of turmeric
Pinch of chilli powder
60 ml/4 tbsp water
30 ml/2 tbsp sunflower oil
100 g/4 oz/1 cup finely chopped
  onion
Pinch of cardamom seeds
5 ml/1 tsp dried fenugreek (methi)
leaves
2 tomatoes, finely chopped
5 ml/1 tsp sugar
5 ml/1 tsp salt
1 large potato, quartered and boiled

Mix together the ground spices in a cup with 15 ml/1 tbsp of the water. Heat the oil and fry (sauté) the onion until golden brown. Add the spice mix from the cup, plus the cardamom seeds and fenugreek leaves and fry for 1 minute. Add the tomato, sugar and salt and cook until the tomatoes go mushy. Add the remaining water and the potato and coat well with the sauce. Heat through for 3–4 minutes.

Tandoori Cauliflower

SERVES 4

1 small cauliflower, cut into florets
30 ml/2 tbsp tandoori spice mix
15 ml/1 tbsp lemon juice
150 ml/¹/₄ pt/²/₃ cup plain yoghurt

Cook the cauliflower in boiling water for 5 minutes. Drain and arrange in an ovenproof dish. Mix together the remaining ingredients and pour over the cauliflower. Leave for 1 hour to marinate. Cook the cauliflower in the oven at 200°C/400°F/gas mark 6 for 30 minutes until soft and slightly blackened.

Cauliflower with Almonds

SERVES 4

1 large cauliflower, cut into florets
Salt
50 g/2 oz/¹/₂ cup flaked almonds
50 g/2 oz/¹/₄ cup unsalted (sweet) butter

Boil or steam the cauliflower until almost tender but not soft. Drain, if necessary, and season very lightly with salt, if liked. Fry (sauté) the almonds in the butter until brown. Spoon over the cooked cauliflower and serve.

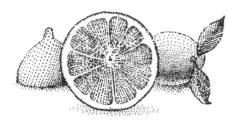

Cauliflower Sautéed with Coriander

SERVES 2–4

1 small cauliflower
¹/₂ onion, finely chopped
30 ml/2 tbsp olive oil
5 ml/1 tsp coriander (cilantro) seeds, crushed
Salt and freshly ground black pepper
15 ml/¹/₂ oz/1 tbsp butter
1 small garlic clove, crushed

Separate the cauliflower into small florets. Do not wash, but wipe if necessary. Soften the onion in the oil in a large frying pan (skillet). Turn up the heat, add the cauliflower florets and keep turning them. After 2 minutes add the crushed coriander seeds and continue cooking for about 5 minutes. Season, add the butter and garlic and cook for a further 1–2 minutes until golden brown but still crunchy.

Cauliflower Fritters

SERVES 4

1 small cauliflower, cut into florets
A little plain (all-purpose) flour
1 packet batter mix
Oil for deep-frying

Cook the cauliflower in boiling salted water for about 5 minutes until almost tender. Drain well and dry on kitchen paper. Dust with flour. Make up the batter according to the packet directions for a coating batter. Drop the cauliflower in the batter, then deep-fry the florets, a few at a time, in hot oil until crisp and golden. Drain well on kitchen paper before serving.

Potato Pudding

SERVES 4

900 g/2 lb potatoes, peeled and
grated
1 egg, beaten
Salt and freshly ground white pepper

Mix together the potatoes, egg, salt and pepper and place in a greased ovenproof dish. Bake in the oven at 180°C/350°F/gas mark 4 for about 1 hour until soft in the centre and crisp on top.

Potch

SERVES 4

225 g/8 oz carrots, diced
225 g/8 oz swede (rutabaga), diced
25 ml/1 oz/2 tbsp butter or
margarine
Salt and freshly ground black pepper

Cook the carrots and swede in boiling water for about 10 minutes until tender. Drain and mash with the butter of margarine. Season to taste with salt and pepper. Spoon the mixture into an ovenproof dish and bake in the oven at 200°C/400°F/gas mark 6 for 10 minutes until a crust forms on the top.

Bubble and Squeak

SERVES 4

450 g/1 lb/2 cups cooked mashed
potato
225 g/8 oz/2 cups cooked brussels
sprouts or cabbage
Salt and freshly ground black pepper
Butter or margarine for frying

Mix together the potato and greens (or you can use other leftover vegetables). Season generously with salt and pepper. Heat the butter or margarine in a large frying pan (skillet). Add the vegetable mixture to the pan and press into a pancake shape. Cook until browned on the underside, then turn over and brown the other side.

Note: This is a traditional recipe for using up leftovers. Quantities are not really important, just use whatever you have.

Lemon Potatoes

SERVES 4

900 g/2 lb potatoes, cubed
50 g/2 oz/¹/₄ cup butter
1 onion, finely chopped
Grated rind and juice of 1 lemon
30 ml/2 tbsp chopped parsley
Salt and freshly ground black pepper

Cover the potatoes with cold water, bring to the boil, simmer for 3 minutes and drain. In the empty pan, melt the butter, add the onion and fry (sauté) until soft but not brown. Stir in the lemon rind and juice, parsley, salt and pepper. Return the potatoes to the pan and toss gently to coat in the mixture. Put into a shallow ovenproof dish (they can be left like this all day in a cool place). Bake in the oven at 190°C/375°F/gas mark 5 for about 1 hour until golden brown and crispy on top.

Classic Potatoes with Cream

QUANTITIES TO SUIT TASTE

This is a combination of various potato recipes cooked in the oven with cream. It is delicious with any plain meat or fish dish which requires a moist vegetable. You can make as little or as much as you like – allow at least 1 potato per person.

Slice the potatoes thinly and sprinkle with salt. Leave for 5–10 minutes, then squeeze out the excess water. Butter a shallow ovenproof dish and rub it with a halved garlic clove. Layer the potatoes in the dish, sprinkle with nutmeg and freshly ground black pepper between each layer and pour enough single (light) cream to reach the top layer. Top with dots of butter. Bake uncovered at 130°C/250°F/gas mark 1 for at least 1 hour (preferably longer).

To microwave: Cover with microwave film and cook on low for 30 minutes (at least), depending on the power of your microwave. If ready early just remove them from the oven and reheat later. Grill (broil) the potatoes until golden brown on top before serving.

Note: If making a larger quantity, use a larger shallow dish. Do not be tempted to make the layers too deep, or it will take too long to cook through.

Parsnips with Cream

QUANTITIES TO SUIT TASTE

Prepare as for Classic Potatoes with Cream substituting sliced parsnips for sliced potatoes. There is no need to sprinkle with salt and leave to stand.

Swedish Potatoes

SERVES 4

750 g/1¹/₂ lb new potatoes, scraped
15 ml/1 tbsp olive oil
25 g/1 oz/2 tbsp butter
40 g/1¹/₂ oz/¹/₃ cup plain (all-
    purpose) flour
300 ml/¹/₂ pt/1¹/₄ cups milk
5 ml/1 tsp dried dill (dill weed)
5 ml/1 tsp dill seeds
15 ml/1 tbsp finely chopped parsley
Salt and freshly ground black pepper
30 ml/2 tbsp lemon juice

Place the potatoes in a pan of boiling, lightly salted water. Add the oil. Bring back to the boil and cook until the potatoes are tender. Drain and keep warm. Melt the butter in a saucepan and blend in the flour. Gradually add the milk, stirring constantly. Add the dried dill and dill seed. Cook, stirring, until it starts to thicken, then add the parsley, seasoning and lemon juice. Beat the sauce well and add the potatoes. Heat through for 2 minutes, then turn into a warmed dish and serve. This dish is excellent served with smoked fish.

Sugar-browned Potatoes

SERVES 4–6

900 g/2 lb small potatoes, cooked
    and drained
25 g/1 oz/2 tbsp caster (superfine)
sugar
50 g/2 oz/¹/₄ cup unsalted (sweet)
    butter

Rinse the potatoes in cold water and dry on kitchen paper. Melt the sugar and butter in a frying pan (skillet) until golden. Add the potatoes and continue cooking over a low heat, shaking the pan gently until the potatoes are evenly glazed and golden brown. Serve hot.

Antibes Potatoes

SERVES 2 OR 3

450 g/1 lb potatoes, scrubbed
Oil for roasting
Salt and freshly ground black pepper
15 ml/1 tbsp chopped mixed herbs
(parsley, oregano, thyme and
*   tarragon are good)*

Cut the potatoes into big chips and boil them until they are nearly cooked. Drain and put into a roasting tin (pan). Drizzle over enough oil to just coat the chips. Season with salt, pepper and herbs. Toss lightly. Bake in the oven 230°C/450°F/gas mark 8 for about 20 minutes until golden brown.

Galettes

SERVES 6

900 g/2 lb old potatoes
900 g/2 lb celeriac (celery root)
1 garlic clove, crushed
Grated nutmeg
Salt and freshly ground black pepper
75 g/3 oz/¹/₃ cup butter, melted
A few parsley sprigs

Thinly slice the potatoes and celeriac, preferably in a food processor or with a mandolin. Grease and line two 20 cm/8 in sandwich tins (pans) with baking parchment. Layer the sliced vegetables with the garlic, nutmeg and seasoning.

Press down firmly after each layer. Pour about half of the melted butter over each tin. Cover with foil and bake at 230°C/450°F/gas mark 8 for 1¹/₄ hours until the vegetables are tender when tested with a skewer. Turn out on to serving dishes and garnish with parsley.

Note: This also makes a good light meal with salad.

Baked Sliced Potatoes

SERVES 4

4 potatoes, thinly sliced
45 ml/3 tbsp olive oil
5 ml/1 tsp salt
2.5 ml/¹/₂ tsp freshly ground black pepper
2.5 ml/¹/₂ tsp mixed dried herbs

Mix the potatoes with the remaining ingredients. Cook in the oven in a large flat dish for about 20–30 minutes at 220°C/425°F/gas mark 7, until the potatoes are crispy at the edges.

Stir-fried Vegetables

Stir-fried vegetables, especially a combination of vegetables, makes a lovely bright accompaniment to many dishes, not just Chinese ones. Choose any mixture: carrots, celery, (bell) peppers, mushrooms, cucumber, courgettes (zucchini), etc. Cut into even-sized strips or slices. Remember to keep the oil hot and use only enough to cover the base of the pan. Work quickly and, starting with the firmest vegetables, toss in the oil then add the next, finishing with the softest. Add a dash of soy sauce and sherry, a pinch of sugar, ground ginger, salt and pepper.

Garlic Cabbage

SERVES 4

1 small head of cabbage
2 garlic cloves, finely sliced
50 g/2 oz/¹/₄ cup unsalted (sweet)
butter
2.5 ml/¹/₂ tsp salt
1.5 ml/¹/₄ tsp freshly ground black
pepper
1 red (bell) pepper, thinly sliced

Quarter the cabbage, cut out and discard the core, and then slice thinly. Add the cabbage and garlic to the melted butter and fry (sauté) for about 1 minute. Cover the pan and cook very gently for about 15 minutes so that the cabbage is cooked, but still crisp. Season with the salt and pepper. Garnish with thinly sliced red pepper.

Mushroom and Wild Rice Pilaff

SERVES 6

1 large onion, chopped
750 g/1¹/₂ lb mushrooms, sliced
1 garlic clove, crushed
60 ml/4 tbsp sunflower oil
225 g/8 oz/1 cup long-grain rice
30 ml/2 tbsp wild rice
600 ml/1 pt/2¹/₂ cups vegetable
stock
5 ml/1 tsp mixed dried herbs
Salt and freshly ground black pepper

Fry (sauté) the onion, mushrooms and garlic in the oil. When the onion is soft, add the long-grain and wild rice and stir around to absorb the flavours. Pour in the stock, add the herbs and seasoning. Cover and simmer for about 20 minutes so that the liquid is absorbed and the rice is just tender. Fluff up with a fork and serve.

Creamed Spinach

SERVES 6

50 g/2 oz/¹/₄ cup unsalted (sweet)
butter
1 kg/2¹/₄ lb frozen spinach,
thawed and drained
2 garlic cloves, crushed
Grated nutmeg
Salt and freshly ground black pepper
120 ml/4 fl oz/¹/₂ cup double (heavy)
cream

Melt the butter, add the spinach, garlic, plenty of nutmeg, a little salt and a good grinding of pepper. Gradually add the cream (more or less will be needed depending on how well you have drained the spinach – add enough to give the spinach a creamy consistency). Gently heat through and serve.

Orange-glazed Turnips

SERVES 4

750 g/1¹/₂ lb baby turnips, peeled
75 g/3 oz/¹/₃ cup butter
30 ml/2 tbsp sugar
1 large red onion, cut into wedges
2 oranges, peeled and cut into
segments
A few snipped chives

Cook the turnips in boiling salted water for 10 minutes or until tender. Drain. Melt the butter and stir in the sugar, cooking gently until dissolved. Add the turnips and cook for 6–8 minutes over a high heat, stirring now and then. Add the onion and oranges and cook for a further 5 minutes. Serve hot, garnished with snipped chives.

Broccoli with Garlic and Mustard Seeds

900 g/2 lb broccoli, cut into equal sized florets
10 ml/2 tsp yellow mustard seeds
75 ml/5 tbsp olive oil
2–3 garlic cloves, crushed
2.5 ml/¹/₂ tsp salt
Lemon juice

Steam the broccoli until just tender, then rinse immediately in cold water. Fry (sauté) the mustard seeds in the oil. When they start popping, add the garlic, stirring once. Add the broccoli and the salt. Stir gently to mix and cook until heated through and glistening. Add a good squeeze of lemon juice, toss gently and serve.

Brussels Sprouts with Almonds

450 g/1 lb sprouts
25 g/1 oz/¹/₄ cup flaked almonds
25 g/1 oz/2 tbsp butter
15 ml/1 tbsp olive oil
Freshly ground black pepper

Trim the sprouts and cut a small cross in the stalks. Boil them in salted water for 5 minutes, if they are young – increase the time if they are older. Meanwhile, fry (sauté) the almonds until golden in the butter and oil. Season with the pepper. Drain the sprouts, pour the almonds and butter sauce over them, toss gently and serve.

French Beans with Onions and Garlic

450 g/1 lb French (green) beans, topped and tailed
1 small onion, very finely chopped
25 g/1 oz/2 tbsp butter
1 garlic clove, crushed

Cook the beans in boiling, lightly salted water until just tender. Meanwhile, fry (sauté) the onion in the butter until soft but not brown. Add the garlic and cook for a further 30 seconds. Do not allow to brown. Drain the beans and toss with the onion mixture before serving.

French-style Green Beans

450 g/1 lb French (green) beans
2 rashers (slices) streaky bacon, cut into pieces
25 g/1 oz/2 tbsp butter
6 spring onions (scallions), chopped
8 outside lettuce leaves, shredded
Salt and freshly ground black pepper
Pinch of sugar
Chopped mint or parsley

Par-boil the beans, then drain. Cook the bacon in the butter. Add the spring onions, beans, lettuce, seasoning and sugar. Cover and continue cooking, stirring occasionally, until the beans are tender. Serve garnished with mint or parsley.

French-style Peas

SERVES 4

Prepare as for French-style Green Beans (see page 207) but substitute frozen peas for the green beans. There is no need to par-boil them before adding to the bacon and butter.

Fried Peas and Garlic

QUANTITIES TO SUIT TASTE

Fry (sauté) frozen peas in plenty of butter. After 2 minutes add a little sugar, lots of black pepper and crushed garlic to taste. Cover and cook gently for about 5 minutes until the peas are tender.

Artichoke and Potato Bake

SERVES 3–6

750 g/1¹/₂ lb potatoes, thinly sliced
400 g/14 oz/1 large can artichoke
* bottoms, drained and thinly*
* sliced*
2 garlic cloves, crushed
30 ml/2 tbsp chopped thyme
Salt and freshly ground black pepper
150 ml/¹/₄ pt/²/₃ cup double (heavy)
* cream*
450 ml/³/₄ pt/2 cups milk
25 g/1 oz/2 tbsp unsalted (sweet)
* butter*

Layer the potatoes and artichokes with the garlic, thyme and seasoning in a shallow ovenproof dish, finishing with a layer of potato slices. Mix the cream and milk together and pour over the top of the layers. Dot with the butter. Bake in the oven for 1¹/₂–1³/₄ hours at 180°C/350°F/gas mark 4 until the potatoes are tender and most of the liquid has been absorbed.

Broccoli and Potato Casserole

SERVES 4

150 ml/¹/₄ pt/²/₃ cup double (heavy)
* cream*
75 g/3 oz Gruyère (Swiss) cheese,
* grated*
Salt and freshly ground black pepper
225 g/8 oz broccoli florets, cooked
until just tender
750 g/1¹/₂ lb potatoes, boiled and
* sliced*

Mix the cream with half the cheese and add pepper and salt to taste. Place the broccoli and then the potatoes in a shallow flameproof dish. Top with the cream mixture and then the remaining cheese. Cook under a hot grill (broiler) for about 5 minutes until the top is bubbling and golden brown.

Re-fried White Beans

SERVES 3 OR 4

425 g/15 oz/1 large can haricot
* (navy) beans, drained, rinsed and*
* drained again*
60 ml/4 tbsp olive oil
2 garlic cloves, crushed
Salt and freshly ground black pepper
Chopped coriander (cilantro) or
* parsley*

Put all the ingredients except the coriander or parsley into a shallow frying pan (skillet) and mash lightly. Cook over a low heat, stirring to blend all together. When heated through, continue cooking for a further 5–6 minutes so that the beans become a bit mushy. Serve garnished with chopped coriander or parsley.

Traditional Re-fried Beans

SERVES 3 OR 4

30 ml/2 tbsp olive oil
425 g/15 oz/1 large can pinto beans,
drained and mashed
10 ml/2 tsp chopped oregano
1 garlic clove, crushed (optional)
Salt and freshly ground black pepper
Grated Cheddar cheese

Heat the oil in a large frying pan (skillet). Add the beans, oregano, garlic, if using, and a little salt and pepper. Cook, stirring, until very thick and piping hot. Sprinkle with cheese before serving.

French Beans with Feta and Sun-dried Tomatoes

SERVES 6

350 g/12 oz French (green) beans,
topped and tailed
50 g/2 oz sun-dried tomatoes, sliced
100 g/4 oz Feta cheese, crumbled
Freshly ground black pepper and a
little salt
15 ml/1 tbsp oil from the tomatoes

Cook the beans in boiling, salted water until just tender. Drain and return to the pan. Toss together with the remaining ingredients over a gentle heat. Serve immediately.

Soy Garlic Beans

SERVES 4

450 g/1 lb French (green) beans,
topped and tailed
15 ml/1 tbsp sunflower oil
15 g/¹/₂ oz/1 tbsp butter
2 garlic cloves, chopped
15 ml/1 tbsp soy sauce
Pinch of caster (superfine) sugar
250 ml/8 fl oz/1 cup water

Fry (sauté) the beans in the oil and butter for 3 minutes. Sprinkle the garlic, soy sauce and sugar over the beans and pour over the water. Bring to the boil and boil rapidly until the liquid has evaporated. Serve at once.

Baked Fennel and Tomatoes

SERVES 4

6 garlic cloves
30 ml/2 tbsp olive oil, plus extra for
roasting
750 g/1¹/₂ lb fennel bulbs, thickly
sliced
60 ml/4 tbsp plain (all-purpose)
flour
450 g/1 lb tomatoes, cut into
quarters
10 ml/2 tsp granulated sugar
Salt and freshly ground black pepper
10 ml/2 tsp dried thyme

Fry (sauté) the garlic in the measured oil until browned and transfer to a casserole dish (Dutch oven). Coat the fennel with flour and fry until golden. Add a little more oil and the tomatoes, sugar and seasoning. When bubbling, turn into the dish with the garlic. Sprinkle with the thyme, cover and cook in the oven for 1 hour at 180°C/350°F/gas mark 4.

Festive Sweet and Sour Onions

SERVES 6

1 kg/2¹/₄ lb button (pearl) onions,
*   peeled*
450 ml/³/₄ pt/2 cups passata (sieved
*   tomatoes)*
100 g/4 oz/¹/₂ cup light brown sugar
30 ml/2 tbsp olive oil
60 ml/4 tbsp red wine vinegar
2.5 ml/¹/₂ tsp dried thyme
Freshly ground black pepper

Blanch the onions for 10 minutes in boiling salted water. If you are using a bag of frozen onions, then this blanching is not necessary. Drain and tip into a shallow ovenproof dish. Mix all the other ingredients together and pour over the onions. Bake in the oven at 180°C/350°F/ gas mark 4 for 1 hour, basting occasionally.

Mustard Turnips

SERVES 6

900 g/2 lb baby turnips, peeled
50 g/2 oz/¹/₄ cup unsalted (sweet)
*   butter*
150 ml/¹/₄ pt/²/₃ cup chicken stock
5 ml/1 tsp light brown sugar
Salt and freshly ground black pepper
10 ml/2 tsp French mustard
30 ml/2 tbsp finely chopped parsley

Fry (sauté) the turnips in the butter, coating them well. Continue to cook over a moderate heat for about 10 minutes so that they turn an even golden colour, like roast potatoes. Add the stock, sprinkle with sugar and season to taste. Bring to the boil, reduce the heat, cover and simmer for 20 minutes, shaking occasionally, until tender. Remove them from the pan and stir the mustard into

the pan juices, adding more sugar or seasoning if necessary. Return the turnips to the pan, reheat them and swirl around to coat in the buttery glaze. Serve garnished with the parsley.

Onion Bhaji

SERVES 4

75 g/3 oz/²/₃ cup gram (besan) or
*   plain (all-purpose) flour*
5 ml/1 tsp chilli powder
Good pinch of turmeric
5 ml/1 tsp mustard powder
5 ml/1 tsp salt
Oil for deep-frying
15 ml/1 tbsp chopped coriander
*   (cilantro) leaves*
2 onions, halved and thinly sliced

Beat together the gram flour and enough water (about 75 ml/5 tbsp) to make a stiffish batter. Add the chilli powder, turmeric, mustard and salt and beat thoroughly until smooth. Leave to stand for 30 minutes. Heat the oil until hot. Put the coriander leaves and onions in the batter and, using your hands, shape into golf ball-sized rough balls.Cook them about four at a time in the hot oil over moderate heat for about 5 minutes until golden.

Potato Bhaji

SERVES 4

Prepare as for Onion Bhaji but omit the onion and dip 1 large potato, cut into thin slices, into the batter and fry (sauté) as for the onion balls.

Simple Pilau

SERVES 4

175 g/6 oz/³/₄ cup basmati rice
15 ml/1 tbsp sunflower oil
1 onion, finely chopped
400 ml/14 fl oz/1³/₄ cups water
Good pinch of garam masala
2.5 cm/1 in piece cinnamon stick
50 g/2 oz/¹/₂ cup frozen peas
5 ml/1 tsp salt

Wash the rice and soak for 30 minutes, then drain. Heat the oil and fry (sauté) the onion until dark reddish-brown. Add about 50 ml/2 fl oz/3¹/₂ tbsp of the water and boil for a few minutes to bring out the colour of the onion. Add the garam masala, cinnamon, peas, rice and salt. Add the remaining water and bring to the boil. Lower the heat to moderate and cook until the water has evaporated completely. Cover and leave to rest for about 5 minutes, then fluff up with a fork.

Potato Pakora

SERVES 4

100 g/4 oz/1 cup gram (besan) or
*   plain (all-purpose) flour*
Good pinch of chilli powder
Good pinch of ground cumin
Good pinch of turmeric
5 ml/1 tsp salt
Oil for deep-frying
1–2 potatoes, cut into 5 mm/¹/₄ in
*   thick slices*

Put the flour, spices and salt in a bowl. Add enough water to make a batter just a little thicker than double (heavy) cream. Heat the oil. Dip the potato slices in the batter and then fry them gently in the hot oil for 3–4 minutes until cooked through and golden. Drain on kitchen paper.

Vegetable Pakora

SERVES 4

15 ml/1 tbsp pomegranate seeds
15 ml/1 tbsp coriander (cilantro)
*   seeds*
2 onions, thinly sliced
400 g/14 oz/1 large can chopped
*   tomatoes*
450 g/1 lb potatoes, grated
1 egg, beaten
50 g/2 oz/¹/₂ cup finely chopped
*   coriander*
7 green chillies, seeded and finely
chopped
1 small green (bell) pepper, finely
chopped
350 g/12 oz/3 cups gram (besan) or
*   plain (all-purpose) flour*
Oil for deep-frying

Crush the pomegranate and coriander seeds roughly. Put all the ingredients in a large bowl and mix well by hand. If the mixture is very dry add 15–30 ml/1–2 tbsp water. Heat the oil. Take small spoonfuls of the mixture and drop gently into the hot oil. Cook for about 3 minutes until golden. Drain on kitchen paper.

Quick and Easy Fresh Pasta

3 eggs
275 g/10 oz/2¹/₂ cups strong plain
(bread) flour
Flour for dusting
Salt
15 ml/1 tbsp olive oil or a knob of
butter

Break the eggs into a food processor and run the machine for 30 seconds. Add the flour and blend for a further 30 seconds or until the mixture forms a soft but not sticky dough. Turn out on to a floured board and knead until the dough is smooth and elastic, adding a little more flour if getting sticky. Wrap in a polythene bag and leave for 30 minutes to rest. On a large floured surface, roll out and stretch the dough, rolling away from you and giving it a quarter turn or so every so often until it is thin enough to almost see through and hanging over the edge of the work surface. For shapes, cut now (see below); for tagliatelle, cover with a cloth and leave for 15 minutes before cutting.

To Shape:

Cannelloni/Lasagne: Cut the rolled dough into oblongs 10 × 13 cm/4 x 5 in. Boil in lightly salted water for 1 minute, then place in a bowl of cold water with 5 ml/1 tsp oil added. Drain on a damp cloth.

Farfalle: Cut the rolled dough into 5 cm/2 in squares with a fluted pastry wheel. Pinch the squares together diagonally across the middle to form butterflies or bows.

Maltagliate: This literally means 'badly cut'. Simply cut the rolled dough into small triangles about the size of a thumb nail. Use mainly in soups.

Pappardelle: Cut the rolled dough with a plain or fluted cutter into strips 2 cm/³/₄ in wide.

Ravioli: Cut dough in half and roll out each half to a similar sized square or rectangle. Put teaspoonfuls of the chosen filling in a mound at regular intervals in rows across one sheet of dough. Brush all round each mound with water. Lay the second sheet on top and press down gently between each mound. Use a fluted pastry wheel to cut between the filling down the length and then across the width to form little cushions of filled pasta.

Tagliatelle: Roll up the rested sheet of pasta like a Swiss (jelly) roll. Cut into slices about 5 mm/¹/₄ in thick. Unroll and drape over a clean cloth on the back of a chair (or clothes horse) while you cut the rest.

Note: If you are a pasta fanatic, you could buy a pasta machine to roll and cut the dough into professional-looking shapes. The best ones, in my opinion, are chrome-plated with stainless steel rollers.

To cook: Allow 100 g/4 oz/1 cup pasta per person Bring a large pan of lightly salted water to the boil. Add 15 ml/1 tbsp olive oil or a knob of butter to the pasta and cook for about 4 minutes until almost tender but not soggy (al dente). Drain and use as required.

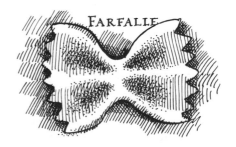
FARFALLE

Spiced Bulgar with Pine Nuts

SERVES 4

60 ml/4 tbsp olive oil
1 onion, finely chopped
1 garlic clove, finely chopped
30 ml/2 tbsp pine nuts
150 g/5 oz/scant 1 cup bulgar
Salt and freshly ground black pepper
600 ml/1 pt/2¹/₂ cups vegetable stock
30 ml/2 tbsp raisins
Pinch of ground coriander (cilantro)
Pinch of ground cinnamon

Heat half the oil and gently fry (sauté) the onion until beginning to soften. Add the garlic and pine nuts and continue to fry until the onion is soft. Stir in the bulgar and remaining oil, season with salt and pepper and stir well together. Add the stock and remaining ingredients, cover and bring to the boil. Simmer for about 15 minutes until all the stock is absorbed. If serving hot, stand the pan in a warm place for about 30 minutes until the bulgar is soft and swollen. Fluff up with a fork before serving. If serving cold, simply leave covered until cold then chill, if liked, until ready to serve.

Dhal

SERVES 4

175 g/6 oz/1 cup red lentils
1 onion, chopped
2 garlic cloves, crushed
15 ml/1 tbsp turmeric
15 ml/1 tbsp ground cumin
15 ml/1 tbsp ground coriander
  (cilantro)
10 ml/2 tsp paprika
600 ml/1 pt/2¹/₂ cups vegetable stock

Put all the ingredients into a saucepan and bring to the boil. Skim the surface, then simmer for 20–30 minutes until very mushy, stirring frequently to stop it sticking to the bottom of the pan. Add a little more water while cooking if the lentils become too dry.

Vegetable Rice

SERVES 4

175 g/6 oz/³/₄ cup long-grain rice
600 ml/1 pt/2¹/₂ cups vegetable stock
75 g/3 oz/³/₄ cup frozen mixed
  vegetables

Cook the rice in the stock for 15 minutes until tender. Add the vegetables for the last 5 minutes of the cooking time.

Spicy Fried Rice

SERVES 4

25 g/1 oz/2 tbsp butter or margarine
1 onion, finely chopped
5 ml/1 tsp turmeric
5 ml/1 tsp ground cumin
5 ml/1 tsp ground coriander
  (cilantro)
175 g/6 oz/1¹/₂ cups cooked long-
  grain rice

Melt the butter or margarine and fry (sauté) the onion until soft. Add the spices and stir-fry for 2 minutes, without allowing the spices to burn. Stir in the rice and stir-fry for 5 minutes until heated through.

Lemon Rice

SERVES 4

*350 g/12 oz/1¹/₂ cups basmati or
other long-grain rice*
450 ml/³/₄ pt/2 cups water
1 garlic clove, crushed
*10 ml/2 tsp grated lemon grass or
lemon rind*
10 ml/2 tsp turmeric
50 g/2 oz/¹/₂ cup creamed coconut
Salt and freshly ground black pepper

If you are using basmati rice, wash then soak in cold water for 30 minutes. Drain. Place the rice, water, garlic, lemon grass or lemon rind and turmeric in a saucepan, bring to the boil, then simmer for 15 minutes until just tender, stirring frequently. Stir in the coconut and season with salt and pepper.

Creamy Peas Crecy Style

SERVES 4

225 g/8 oz/2 cups frozen peas
60 ml/4 tbsp olive oil
1 bunch of watercress
30 ml/2 tbsp chopped basil leaves
120 ml/4 fl oz/¹/₂ cup crème fraîche
Grated nutmeg
Salt and freshly ground black pepper

Gently stew the peas in the olive oil in a covered saucepan for 4 minutes, stirring occasionally. Don't have the heat too high or you will fry (sauté) rather than stew them. Add the remaining ingredients, seasoning to taste, stir well and simmer for a further 2–3 minutes.

Spring Onion and Mushrooms with Soy Sauce

SERVES 4

1 bunch of spring onions (scallions)
15 ml/1 tbsp oil
450 g/1 lb button mushrooms
60 ml/4 tbsp lemon juice
30 ml/2 tbsp soy sauce
Salt and freshly ground black pepper

Cut the spring onions, green and white parts, into 2.5 cm/1 in pieces. Heat the oil in a pan. Add the spring onions and mushrooms and fry (sauté) for 3 minutes. Add the lemon juice, soy sauce, and a little salt and pepper. Simmer for 4 minutes, stirring gently, until cooked and bathed in the juices.

Curried Coconut Cauliflower

SERVES 4

1 garlic clove, crushed
*300 ml/¹/₂ pt/1¹/₄ cups canned
coconut milk*
*50 g/2 oz/¹/₂ cup desiccated
(shredded) coconut*
15 ml/1 tbsp curry powder
10 ml/2 tsp lemon juice
Pinch of cayenne
Salt and freshly ground black pepper
1 cauliflower, cut into florets

Place the garlic, coconut milk, coconut and curry powder in a pan, bring to the boil, then simmer for 15 minutes, stirring occasionally. Remove from the heat and add the lemon juice, cayenne, salt and pepper. Transfer to a dish and add the cauliflower, stirring to coat it well. Simmer gently for about 10 minutes until the cauliflower is tender, stirring occasionally to prevent sticking.

Cheese Courgettes

SERVES 4

4 courgettes (zucchini), thinly sliced
2 garlic cloves, crushed
30 ml/2 tbsp olive oil
5 ml/1 tsp dried oregano
Salt and freshly ground black pepper
100 g/4 oz Emmental (Swiss) cheese,
  sliced

Arrange the courgettes in 4 pieces of foil. Sprinkle with garlic and olive oil, then with oregano, salt and pepper. Lay the cheese on top. Seal the parcels and bake in the oven at 200°C/400°F/gas mark 6 for 20 minutes until the courgettes are tender and the cheese has melted.

Sweet Potatoes with Nutty Butter

SERVES 4

4 sweet potatoes
100 g/4 oz/¹/₂ cup butter or
  margarine
5 ml/1 tsp clear honey
Grated rind and juice of 1 orange
25 g/1 oz/¹/₄ cup walnuts, chopped
Pinch of mustard powder
Salt and freshly ground black pepper

Pierce the skin of the potatoes and cook them in the oven at 200°C/400°F/gas mark 6 for about 1 hour until soft. Melt all the remaining ingredients together in a pan and keep hot. Slit open the potatoes and spoon over the flavoured butter. Serve straight away.

Spinach-stuffed Mushrooms

SERVES 4

8 large mushrooms, peeled
30 ml/2 tbsp butter or margarine
15 ml/1 tbsp sunflower oil
1 onion, chopped
2 garlic cloves, chopped
225 g/8 oz frozen spinach, thawed
and drained
90 ml/6 tbsp vegetable stock
Salt and freshly ground black pepper
100 g/4 oz/¹/₂ cup curd (smooth
  cottage) cheese
45 ml/3 tbsp dried breadcrumbs
50 g/2 oz/¹/₂ cup freshly grated
  Parmesan cheese

Remove the stems from the mushrooms and chop them finely. Heat the butter or margarine and oil and fry (sauté) the onion and garlic until soft. Stir in the mushroom stalks, spinach and stock and season well with salt and pepper. Remove from the heat and stir in the cheese. Place the mushroom caps stem-side up on foil on a grill (broiler) rack. Pile the spinach mixture on top. Sprinkle with breadcrumbs and cheese. Grill (broil) for about 10 minutes until cooked through and bubbling.

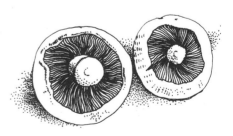

Italian-style Artichokes

SERVES 4

*400 g/14 oz/1 large can artichoke
    hearts, drained*
15 ml/1 tbsp white wine vinegar
15 ml/1 tbsp chopped fresh basil
1 garlic clove, crushed
*100 g/4 oz/1 cup freshly grated
    Parmesan cheese*
Salt and freshly ground black pepper

Slice the artichokes thickly and arrange them in 4 squares of foil. Sprinkle with the remaining ingredients. Seal the parcels and place on a baking sheet. Bake in the oven at 200°C/400°F/gas mark 6 for about 15 minutes until the vegetables are heated through and the cheese has melted.

Barbecued Sweetcorn with Lime and Chilli Butter

SERVES 4

4 corn on the cob
175 g/6 oz/³/4 cup butter, softened
45 ml/3 tbsp lime juice
30 ml/2 tbsp chilli powder
Salt

Leave the sweetcorn in the husks. Soak in cold water for at least 20 minutes. Beat together the butter, lime juice and chilli powder and season to taste with salt. Add more chilli powder if you wish. Roll into a sausage shape and chill. Drain the corn and barbecue in the husks for about 20 minutes until the husks are evenly browned. Remove from the grill and carefully take off the husks and silks. Serve with the flavoured butter, cut in slices. Alternatively, remove the husks and boil the cobs in salted water for 15–20 minutes until tender. Drain and serve with the flavoured butter.

Nutty Celeriac

SERVES 4

1 celeriac (celery root)
15 ml/1 tbsp white wine vinegar
90 ml/6 tbsp oil
50 g/2 oz/¹/2 cup ground walnuts

Peel the celeriac and cut into 2.5 cm/ 1 in slices. Boil for about 10 minutes until just tender. Drain well and place in a roasting tin (pan). Mix together the remaining ingredients and brush over the celeriac. Leave to stand if possible for about 30 minutes. Bake in the oven at 200°C/400°F/gas mark 6 for about 30 minutes until golden.

Baked Chicory

SERVES 4

4 chicory (Belgian endive) heads
30 ml/2 tbsp oil
*25 g/1 oz/2 tbsp butter or margarine,
    melted*
30 ml/2 tbsp chopped mixed herbs
Salt and freshly ground black pepper

Cut a cone-shaped core out of the base of each chicory head, then slice in half lengthways. Place in a roasting tin (pan). Mix together the remaining ingriediednts and brush over the chicory. Bake in the oven at 200°C/400°F/gas mark 6 for about 40 minutes, until golden and tender.

SALADS AND DRESSINGS

The great thing with salads is that there is no real 'right' way of making them. Don't worry if you don't have some of the ingredients; replace them with something else or just forget them!

Caesar Salad Special

SERVES 4

15 g/¹/₂ oz/1 tbsp butter
1 egg, beaten
75 g/3 oz/¹/₃ cup soft cheese with
garlic and herbs
45 ml/3 tbsp milk
15 ml/1 tbsp olive oil
10 ml/2 tsp lemon juice
1 cos (romaine) lettuce
50 g/2 oz/1 small can anchovies,
drained and chopped
8 French bread slices, fried (sautéed)
in a little olive oil
Tomato wedges

Melt the butter in a pan. Add the egg and scramble lightly over a gentle heat. Remove from the heat and leave to cool. Whisk the cheese with the milk, oil and lemon juice until smooth. Tear the lettuce into neat pieces. Place in a salad bowl. Add the egg and anchovies, pour over the dressing and toss. Arrange the slices of French bread around the edges of the bowl and garnish with tomato wedges.

Sicilian Salad

SERVES 4

225 g/8 oz dwarf green beans,
cooked whole
225 g/8 oz/2 cups baby new potatoes,
cooked
4 tomatoes, quartered
3 hard-boiled (hard-cooked) eggs,
quartered
1 small onion, sliced into rings
6 black or green olives
45 ml/3 tbsp olive oil
15 ml/1 tbsp wine vinegar
Salt and freshly ground black pepper
Crisp lettuce
75 g/3 oz goat's cheese, diced
Crusty bread

Cut the beans and potatoes into two or three pieces. Place in a bowl with the remaining ingredients except the lettuce, cheese and bread, and toss lightly. Pile on to a bed of lettuce and scatter the cheese over. Serve with crusty bread.

Seafood Sicilian Salad

SERVES 4

Prepare as for Sicilian Salad but add 185 g/6¹/₂ oz/1 small can tuna, drained and flaked and 75 g/3 oz/³/₄ cup peeled prawns (shrimp) with the vegetables and eggs. Omit the cheese, if preferred.

Salad Alice

SERVES 4

1 lettuce, leaves separated
350 g/12 oz/1 small can pineapple
cubes, drained
1 grapefruit, segmented
50 g/2 oz/¹/₂ cup hazelnuts, chopped
45 ml/3 tbsp olive oil
10 ml/2 tsp lemon juice
Salt and freshly ground black pepper

Place the lettuce leaves in a large bowl. Add the fruit and nuts. Whisk together the oil and lemon juice and pour over the salad. Season with salt and pepper and toss well. Chill before serving.

Frozen Cheese Salad

SERVES 4

100 g/4 oz/¹/₂ cup cottage cheese
100 ml/3¹/₂ fl oz/6¹/₂ tbsp evaporated
milk
Pinch of snipped chives
Salt and freshly ground black pepper
Lettuce
Nutty Burgers (see page 159)
Pitta bread

Mix the first four ingredients together and press gently into a freezer container. Cover and freeze until firm. Cut into slices and serve with lettuce, Nutty Burgers and pitta bread.

Orange and Cucumber Salad

SERVES 4

225 g/8 oz/1 cup cottage cheese
2 oranges, segmented
¹/₂ cucumber, sliced
45 ml/3 tbsp olive oil
15 ml/1 tbsp lemon juice

Mix together all the ingredients and chill before serving.

Potato Salad

SERVES 4

750 g/1¹/₂ lb new potatoes, cut into
bite-sized pieces
1 hard-boiled (hard-cooked) egg,
chopped (optional)
15 ml/1 tbsp chopped parsley
15 ml/1 tbsp mayonnaise
5 ml/1 tsp made mustard
5 ml/1 tsp white wine vinegar
Freshly ground black pepper

Simmer the potatoes in boiling water for about 15 minutes until just cooked but still firm. Drain and leave to cool. Mix together the remaining ingredients and add to the potatoes. Stir together well. Chill (preferably overnight to develop the flavour) before serving.

Simple Pasta Salad

SERVES 4

100 g/4 oz/1 cup pasta shapes
1 garlic clove, crushed
90 ml/6 tbsp olive oil
5 ml/1 tsp tomato purée (paste)
Salt and freshly ground black pepper
Pinch of dried tarragon
5 ml/1 tsp wine vinegar

Cook the pasta in boiling salted water until just tender. Drain and leave to cool. Put all the remaining ingredients into a screw-topped jar and shake well to mix. Pour over the pasta and toss together well. Chill before serving.

TV Supper Special

225 g/8 oz/2 cups ruote or other
  pasta
4 tomatoes, chopped
¹/₄ cucumber, diced
175 g/6 oz Cheddar cheese, cubed
320 g/12 oz/1 large can sweetcorn
(corn), drained
45 ml/3 tbsp olive oil
15 ml/1 tbsp lemon juice
5 ml/1 tsp Dijon mustard
1.5 ml/¹/₄ tsp salt
Freshly ground black pepper

Cook the pasta according to the packet directions. Drain, rinse with cold water and drain again. Put the tomatoes, cucumber and cheese in a bowl with the sweetcorn and mix gently. Add the pasta and mix again. Whisk the remaining ingredients together and pour over. Toss lightly. Add an extra grinding of black pepper. Chill, if liked, before serving.

Oriental Green Bean and Peanut Salad

250 g/9 oz/1 packet soba noodles or
  Chinese egg noodles
225 g/8 oz thin green beans
90 ml/6 tbsp peanut butter
30 ml/2 tbsp caster (superfine)
  sugar
150 ml/¹/₄ pt/²/₃ cup dashi (available
  from Asian food shops) or
  vegetable stock
30 ml/2 tbsp soy sauce

Cook the noodles according to the packet directions. Drain and leave to cool. Top and tail the beans, cut into 2.5 cm/1 in lengths, then cook in boiling, salted water for 5 minutes until just tender. Drain, rinse with cold water and drain again. Blend the peanut butter, sugar, stock and soy sauce together in a bowl. Add the beans. Add to the cold cooked noodles, toss well and serve straight away.

Eastern Rice Salad

175 g/6 oz/³/₄ cup long-grain rice
2.5 ml/¹/₂ tsp salt
10 ml/2 tsp turmeric
50 g/2 oz/¹/₃ cup raisins
1 banana, sliced
50 g/2 oz/¹/₂ cup creamed coconut,
  grated
1 red (bell) pepper, diced
30 ml/2 tbsp sweetcorn (corn)
2.5 ml/¹/₂ tsp dried tarragon
A few chunks of fresh or canned
  pineapple

Cook the rice in boiling salted water with the turmeric for about 15 minutes until tender. Drain and leave to cool. Mix the rice with the remaining ingredients and toss well. Chill before serving.

Chinese Bean Sprout Salad

4 pineapple rings, diced
400 g/14 oz/1 large can
  bean sprouts, drained and rinsed
100 g/4 oz/¹/₂ cup tofu, diced
1 quantity Sweet and Sour Dressing
  (see page 232)

Mix together the pineapple, bean sprouts and tofu. Pour over the dressing and toss well. Chill before serving.

Sunshine Rice Salad

175 g/6 oz/³/₄ cup long-grain rice
5 ml/1 tsp turmeric
225 g/8 oz/1 small can pineapple in
*   juice*
200 g/7 oz/1 small can sweetcorn
*   (corn), drained*
5 ml/1 tsp dried tarragon
15 ml/1 tbsp lemon juice
5 ml/1 tsp soy sauce
15 ml/1 tbsp oil
Salt and freshly ground black pepper

Cook the rice in boiling salted water with the turmeric for about 15 minutes until tender. Drain and leave to cool. Mix together all the remaining ingredients and pour over the cooled rice. Toss together well. Chill before serving.

Feta Bulgar Salad

225 g/8 oz/1¹/₃ cups bulgar
1 bunch of spring onions (scallions),
*   chopped*
2 eating (dessert) apples, chopped
75 g/3 oz Feta cheese, crumbled
50 g/2 oz/¹/₂ cup cashew nuts
30 ml/2 tbsp chopped parsley
10 ml/2 tsp chopped tarragon
60 ml/4 tbsp olive oil
15 ml/1 tbsp wine or cider vinegar
30 ml/2 tbsp lemon juice
30 ml/2 tbsp freshly ground black
*   pepper*
30 ml/2 tbsp chopped mint
Plain yoghurt (optional)

Soak the bulgar in boiling water for 30 minutes, then leave to cool. Mix together all the ingredients, except the yoghurt, in a large bowl and toss together well. Top with plain yoghurt, if liked, before serving.

Tabbouleh

Prepare as for Feta Bulgar Salad but omit the apples, cheese, cashew nuts and tarragon and add 1–2 garlic cloves, crushed, 450 g/1 lb tomatoes, chopped and ¹/₂ cucumber, chopped.

Egg Mayonnaise

3 hard-boiled (hard-cooked) eggs
30 ml/2 tbsp mayonnaise
Pinch of paprika or dried dill
Salt and freshly ground black pepper
Lettuce leaves
Tomato slices

Mash the eggs in a bowl. Stir in the mayonnaise, paprika or dill, salt and pepper. Chill before serving piled on lettuce leaves and garnished with tomato slices.

Mediterranean Egg Mayonnaise

Prepare as for Egg Mayonnaise but add 1 diced canned pimiento cap to the mixture and decorate with a lattice of canned anchovy fillets.

Waldorf Salad

1 eating (dessert) apple, diced
2 bananas, sliced
Lemon juice
50 g/2 oz/¹/₂ cup walnuts, chopped
4 celery sticks, sliced
45 ml/3 tbsp mayonnaise
Lettuce leaves

Place the fruit in a bowl and toss in a little lemon juice. Add the nuts and celery and gently mix together. Add the mayonnaise and toss together well. Chill before serving piled on a bed of lettuce.

Grape and Pear Salad

100 g/4 oz/1 cup seedless (pitless)
    black grapes
2 pears, diced
100 g/4 oz Lancashire cheese, cubed
45 ml/3 tbsp grape or apple juice
Dash of soy sauce
15 ml/1 tbsp olive oil

Mix together the fruit and cheese. Whisk together the juice, soy sauce and olive oil. Pour over the salad and chill before serving.

Hot Lentil Salad

400 g/14 oz/1 large can lentils
45 ml/3 tbsp oil
175 g/6 oz streaky bacon, rinded and
    diced
15 ml/1 tbsp red wine vinegar
5 ml/1 tsp mild mustard
Salt and freshly ground black pepper
15 ml/1 tbsp chopped parsley

Warm the lentils gently in a pan. Meanwhile, heat a little of the oil and fry (sauté) the bacon pieces until crisp. Blend the remaining oil with the wine vinegar and mustard to make a vinaigrette. Season with salt and pepper. Drain the lentils, mix with the bacon and blend with the dressing. Season again with salt and pepper to taste. Sprinkle with parsley and serve hot.

Artichoke and Sun-dried Tomato Salad

400 g/14 oz/1 large can artichoke
    hearts, drained
8 sun-dried tomatoes
12 black olives, stoned (pitted)
45 ml/3 tbsp pine nuts, toasted
30 ml/2 tbsp chopped basil
45 ml/3 tbsp lemon juice
60 ml/4 tbsp olive oil
Salt and freshly ground black pepper

Cut the artichoke hearts into quarters and place in a bowl. Cut the tomatoes into julienne strips and add to the artichokes with the olives, pine nuts and basil. Blend together the lemon juice and olive oil and season with salt and pepper. Pour over the salad and toss together well.

Aubergine Salad

2 tomatoes, cut into strips
1 red (bell) pepper, cut into strips
1 onion, cut into rings
30 ml/2 tbsp white wine vinegar
30 ml/2 tbsp dry sherry
90 ml/6 tbsp sunflower oil
5 ml/1 tsp sesame oil
Pinch of caster (superfine) sugar
Salt and freshly ground black pepper
1 aubergine (eggplant)
30 ml/2 tbsp lemon juice

Mix the tomatoes, pepper and onion in a salad bowl. Mix together the vinegar, sherry, 15 ml/1 tbsp of the oil, the sesame oil, sugar, salt and pepper. Pour over the salad and leave to marinate. Cut the aubergine into thin strips and toss in the lemon juice to prevent discolouring. Heat the remaining oil and fry (sauté) the aubergine for about 8 minutes until lightly browned. Drain on kitchen paper and leave to cool. Mix the aubergine into the salad and toss together gently.

Colourful Salad

1 green (bell) pepper, cut into strips
2 hard-boiled (hard-cooked) eggs,
*   quartered*
5 cm/2 in piece cucumber, thinly
*   sliced*
2 tomatoes, cut into wedges
8 stoned (pitted) black olives
8 stoned (pitted) green olives
5 ml/1 tsp capers
45 ml/3 tbsp Vinaigrette Dressing
*   (see page 231)*
Salt and freshly ground black pepper

Put the prepared salad ingredients in a bowl and pour over the vinaigrette. Toss together gently, then season with salt and pepper.

Coleslaw

2 large carrots, grated
1/2 white cabbage, shredded
1/2 small onion, grated
90 ml/6 tbsp olive oil
30 ml/2 tbsp mayonnaise
1.5 ml/1/4 tsp made English mustard
Freshly ground black pepper
15 ml/1 tbsp white wine vinigar

Mix together the vegetables. Place the remaining ingredients in a screw-topped jar and shake well to mix. Pour the dressing over the vegetables and mix well.

Crispy Fruit Coleslaw

1/2 small white cabbage, finely
*   shredded*
1 onion, grated
1 carrot, grated
1 eating (dessert) apple, grated
50 g/2 oz/1/3 cup raisins or sultanas
*   (golden raisins)*
150 ml/1/4 pt/2/3 cup mayonnaise
15–30 ml/1–2 tbsp milk
Salt and freshly ground black pepper

Place the cabbage in a large bowl with the onion, carrot, apple and raisins or sultanas and mix well. Thin the mayonnaise with a little milk and season with salt and pepper. Pour over the salad and toss well together.

Red Cabbage Salad

1 eating (dessert) apple, cut into
chunks
30 ml/2 tbsp lemon juice
225 g/8 oz red cabbage, shredded
1 orange, peeled and cut into
chunks
50 g/2 oz/¹/₃ cup sultanas (golden
raisins)
60 ml/4 tbsp orange juice
15 ml/1 tbsp clear honey
60 ml/4 tbsp olive oil
Salt and freshly ground black pepper
1 banana

Toss the apple in 10 ml/2 tsp of the lemon juice in a salad bowl. Add the cabbage, orange and sultanas. Whisk together the orange juice and remaining lemon juice, honey and oil. Season with salt and pepper. Pour over the salad and toss well together. Leave to stand for 2 hours. Just before serving, slice the banana and add it to the salad. Toss again and adjust the seasoning to taste.

Greek Potato Salad

450 g/1 lb new potatoes, cooked and
diced
225 g/8 oz tomatoes, chopped
1 onion, finely chopped
50 g/2 oz/¹/₃ cup black olives
45 ml/3 tbsp Basic Mayonnaise (see
page 229)
30 ml/2 tbsp plain yoghurt
Salt and freshly ground black pepper

Carefully mix together the potatoes, tomatoes, onion and olives. Mix together the mayonnaise and yoghurt and season with salt and pepper. Pour the dressing over the salad and toss well. Chill before serving.

Cucumber and Walnut Salad

350 g/12 oz cucumber, sliced
8 radishes, thinly sliced
1 green (bell) pepper, chopped
2 spring onions (scallions), chopped
50 g/2 oz/¹/₂ cup walnuts, chopped
15 ml/1 tbsp chopped parsley
5 ml/1 tsp chopped thyme
60 ml/4 tbsp soy sauce
15 ml/1 tbsp olive oil
15 ml/1 tbsp lemon juice
2.5 ml/¹/₂ tsp ground ginger
15 ml/1 tbsp clear honey, warmed
60 ml/4 tbsp water

Mix together the cucumber, radishes, pepper, spring onions and walnuts. Whisk together the remaining ingredients. Pour the dressing over the salad and toss together well.

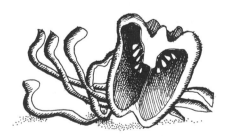

Feta and Cucumber Salad

SERVES 4
---

1 cucumber
225 g/8 oz Feta cheese, crumbled
45 ml/3 tbsp chopped mint
15 ml/1 tbsp caster (superfine) sugar
90 ml/6 tbsp olive oil
45 ml/3 tbsp white wine vinegar
Salt and freshly ground black pepper

Slice the cucumber very thinly, using a mandolin, if possible. Arrange in a shallow serving dish and sprinkle with the cheese and mint. Sprinkle over the sugar. Whisk together the oil, vinegar and seasoning. Pour over the salad and leave to stand for 1 hour before serving.

Regatta Rice Ring

SERVES 4
---

175 g/6 oz/³/₄ cup long-grain rice
100 g/4 oz/1 cup frozen diced mixed
  vegetables
30 ml/2 tbsp olive oil
15 ml/1 tbsp red wine vinegar
Salt and freshly ground black pepper
2 ripe pears, diced
175 g/6 oz Cheddar cheese, diced
1 Florence fennel bulb, chopped,
  reserving the fronds
45 ml/3 tbsp plain yoghurt
Garlic Bread (see page 290)

Cook the rice and mixed vegetables in plenty of boiling, lightly salted water for 10 minutes. Drain, rinse thoroughly with cold water and drain again. Add the oil, vinegar and a little salt and pepper to the rice and vegetables and toss well. Spoon the mixture into a 1.5 litre/2¹/₂ pt/6 cup oiled ring mould (mold). Press down and chill while making the filling. Mix the pears with the cheese and fennel. Gently fold in the yoghurt and

season lightly. Place a serving plate over the ring mould. Invert, give a good shake and remove the mould. Pile the cheese mixture in the centre, garnish with the fennel fronds and serve with garlic bread.

Bacon, Egg and Avocado Salad

SERVES 4
---

4 eggs
10 ml/2 tsp lemon juice
4 streaky bacon rashers (slices)
2 avocados
225 g/8 oz mixed salad leaves
  (including radiccio or Lollo Rosso)
60 ml/4 tbsp olive oil
20 ml/4 tsp wine vinegar
Salt and freshly ground black pepper
Onion rings
Croûtons (see page 17)
Hot Herb Loaf (see page 290)

Poach the eggs in gently simmering water with half the lemon juice for about 3 minutes until the whites are set but the yolk is still soft (or longer if you like them hard). Carefully lift out with a draining spoon and place in a bowl of cold water. Grill (broil) or dry-fry the bacon rashers until crisp. Cut into pieces with scissors. Halve, peel and slice the avocados, discarding the stones (pits). Toss in the remaining lemon juice. Put the salad leaves in a bowl, add the avocado and bacon and toss in the oil, vinegar and a little salt and pepper. Transfer to individual serving bowls. Lift the eggs out of the water and put one in each bowl. Garnish with the onion rings and Croûtons and serve with Hot Herb Loaf.

Photograph opposite: **Artichoke and sun-dried tomato salad (page 221)**

Sausage Salad

SERVES 4–6

4 slices white bread, cubed
45 ml/3 tbsp oil
8 thick sausages, cooked and sliced
2 × 300 g/2 × 11 oz/2 × large cans
Mexican sweetcorn (corn with
bell peppers), drained
425 g/15 oz/1 large can butter
beans, drained
$^1/_2$ cucumber, diced
1 garlic clove, crushed
150 ml/$^1/_4$ pt/$^2/_3$ cup plain yoghurt or
soured (dairy sour) cream
15 ml/1 tbsp snipped chives

Fry (sauté) the cubes of bread in the hot oil until golden. Drain on kitchen paper. Mix the sausages with the corn, butter beans and cucumber. Chill until ready to serve. Mix the garlic with the yoghurt or soured cream and chives. Chill. Just before serving, add the fried bread to the salad and toss. Pile on to serving plates and add a spoonful of the creamy dressing on top. Serve immediately.

Salt Beef and Potato Salad

SERVES 4–6

175 g/6 oz/1$^1/_2$ cups cooked salt
beef, cubed
750 g/1$^1/_2$ lb cold potatoes, cut into
chunks
1 small red (bell) pepper, diced
$^1/_4$ cucumber, diced
200 g/7 oz/1 small can sweetcorn
(corn), drained
60 ml/4 tbsp olive oil
30 ml/2 tbsp wine vinegar
2.5 ml/$^1/_2$ tsp Dijon mustard
2.5 ml/$^1/_2$ tsp caster (superfine) sugar
Salt and freshly ground black pepper
A few onion rings

Put the meat and the vegetables in a large salad bowl. Blend together the oil, vinegar, mustard, sugar and a little salt and pepper and pour over the meat and vegetables. Toss well. Garnish with onion rings and serve.

Chicken Hawaii

SERVES 4

1 fresh pineapple
175 g/6 oz/1$^1/_2$ cups cooked long-
grain rice
175 g/6 oz/1$^1/_2$ cups cooked chicken
meat, diced
200 g/7 oz/1 small can Mexican
sweetcorn (corn with bell
peppers), drained
30 ml/2 tbsp mayonnaise
Salt and freshly ground black pepper
Lettuce
Tomato wedges

Cut the green top off the pineapple about 5 cm/2 in down from the stalk. Loosen the flesh with a serrated knife. Scoop out into a bowl, leaving the shell intact. Roughly chop the fruit, discarding any tough core. Drain off the excess juice. Add the rice, chicken, sweetcorn and mayonnaise. Mix well and season to taste. Pile the mixture back into the pineapple shell placed on a serving plate on a bed of lettuce. Put the green top back on as a 'lid'. Spoon any mixture that won't fit in the shell around the edge. Garnish with tomato wedges.

Photograph opposite: **Pitta pocket cooler (page 239)**

Rosy Chicken Salad

SERVES 4–6

1.5 kg/3 lb whole ready-cooked
chicken
150 ml/¹/₄ pt/²/₃ cup mayonnaise
15 ml/1 tbsp milk
15 ml/1 tbsp tomato purée (paste)
5 cm/2 in piece cucumber, finely
diced
50 g/2 oz/¹/₂ cup blanched whole
almonds
15 g/¹/₂ oz/2 tbsp butter or margarine
1.5 ml/¹/₄ tsp chilli powder
1.5 ml/¹/₄ tsp mixed (apple pie) spice
Lettuce

Joint the chicken into six pieces and carve the breast. Alternatively, cut all the meat off the bones, discard the skin and leave the meat in chunky pieces. Blend the mayonnaise, milk, tomato purée and cucumber together. Fry (sauté) the almonds in the butter or margarine until golden brown. Sprinkle with spices and toss well. Drain on kitchen paper. Arrange the chicken attractively on a bed of lettuce. Spoon the mayonnaise mixture over and scatter with the almonds.

Mozzarella and Cherry Tomato Vinaigrette

SERVES 4

225 g/8 oz Mozzarella cheese, finely
diced
350 g/12 oz/3 cups cherry tomatoes,
quartered
16 basil leaves, torn if liked
250 ml/8 fl oz/1 cup olive oil
30 ml/2 tbsp red wine vinegar
Freshly ground black pepper
A little coarse sea salt

Put all the ingredients except the salt, adding lots of black pepper, in a bowl. Toss lightly and chill for 30 minutes. Sprinkle with salt just before serving.

Wild Rice Salad

SERVES 4

450 ml/³/₄ pt/2 cups vegetable stock
100 g/4 oz/¹/₂ cup wild rice
175 g/6 oz/³/₄ cup long-grain rice
400 g/14 oz/1 large can red
pimientos, drained and chopped
60 ml/4 tbsp oil
30 ml/2 tbsp red wine vinegar
5 ml/1 tsp Worcestershire sauce
Salt and freshly ground black pepper

Bring the stock to the boil. Add the wild rice, return to the boil, cover and simmer gently for 15 minutes. Add the long-grain rice, cover again and simmer for about 20 minutes until all the rice is cooked. If there is any liquid left, uncover and boil until absorbed. Leave to cool. Stir in the pimiento. Mix together the oil, vinegar, Worcestershire sauce, salt and pepper. Pour over the salad and toss together well.

Pasta Niçoise

SERVES 4

*175 g/6 oz/1¹/₂ cups conchiglie
(pasta shells)*
*225 g/8 oz/2 cups French (green)
beans, topped, tailed and cut into
three*
*2 hard-boiled (hard-cooked) eggs,
roughly chopped*
*1 small onion, sliced and separated
into rings*
4 tomatoes, diced
*185 g/6¹/₂ oz/1 small can tuna in oil,
drained, reserving the oil*
*50 g/2 oz/1 small can anchovies,
drained and cut into thin slivers*
90 ml/6 tbsp olive oil
30 ml/2 tbsp red wine vinegar
Salt and freshly ground black pepper
Cos (romaine) lettuce leaves
Chopped parsley
A few black olives

Cook the pasta in boiling salted water for 10 minutes until just tender. Add the beans half-way through cooking. Drain, rinse with cold water and drain again. Place in a bowl with the remaining ingredients except the lettuce, parsley and olives, and season lightly with salt and lots of black pepper. Toss very gently so as not to break up the tuna too much. Pile on to a bed of lettuce and garnish with parsley and olives.

Mexican Avocado Salad

SERVES 4

225 g/8 oz green tagliatelle
*2 ripe avocados, peeled and stoned
(pitted)*
30 ml/2 tbsp lemon juice
30 ml/2 tbsp Worcestershire sauce
5 ml/1 tsp grated onion
2.5 ml/¹/₂ tsp chilli powder
60 ml/4 tbsp olive oil
Salt and freshly ground black pepper
*5 cm/2 in piece cucumber, finely
diced*
2 tomatoes, seeded and chopped
¹/₂ red (bell) pepper, diced
A little extra olive oil
A few tortilla chips, roughly crushed

Cook the tagliatelle according to the packet directions. Drain, rinse with cold water and drain again. Mash the avocados in a bowl with the lemon juice. Beat in the Worcestershire sauce, onion and chilli powder. Beat in the oil a little at a time to form a mayonnaise-type mixture. Season to taste with salt and lots of pepper. Fold in the cucumber, tomatoes and diced pepper. Chill for up to 1 hour. Toss the tagliatelle in a little extra olive oil. Pile on serving plates. Top with the avocado mixture and sprinkle with crushed tortilla chips.

Curried Chicken and Pasta Mayonnaise

SERVES 4

175 g/6 oz/1¹/₂ cups wholewheat
  penne pasta
60 ml/4 tbsp mayonnaise
30 ml/2 tbsp mango chutney
10 ml/2 tsp curry paste
175 g/6 oz/1¹/₂ cups cooked chicken,
  roughly chopped
Mixed salad leaves
Paprika
Lemon wedges

Cook the pasta according to the packet directions. Drain, rinse with cold water and drain again. Blend the mayonnaise in a bowl with the chutney and curry paste. Fold in the pasta and cooked chicken and chill until ready to serve on a bed of salad, garnished with paprika and lemon wedges.

Prawn Cocktail Bows

SERVES 4

175 g/6 oz/1¹/₂ cups farfalle (pasta
  bows)
150 ml/¹/₄ pt/²/₃ cup mayonnaise
15 ml/1 tbsp tomato ketchup
  (catsup)
15 ml/1 tbsp single (light) cream
10 ml/2 tsp horseradish cream
6 stuffed olives, chopped
1 hard-boiled (hard-cooked) egg,
  finely chopped
1 small green (bell) pepper, finely
  chopped
175 g/6 oz/1¹/₂ cups peeled prawns
  (shrimp)
Shredded lettuce
Snipped chives

Cook the pasta according to the packet directions. Drain, rinse with cold water and drain again. Mix the mayonnaise with the tomato ketchup, cream and horseradish in a large bowl. Add the pasta and all the remaining ingredients except the lettuce and chives and toss well but lightly. Chill until ready to serve on a bed of shredded lettuce, garnished with chives.

Warm Tomato and Herb Pasta Salad

SERVES 4

175 g/6 oz/1¹/₂ cups pasta twists
225 g/8 oz/4 cups wholemeal
  breadcrumbs
12 tomatoes, chopped
4 thyme sprigs, chopped
45 ml/3 tbsp chopped basil
45 ml/3 tbsp chopped parsley
Salt and freshly ground black pepper
120 ml/4 fl oz/¹/₂ cup olive oil
3 garlic cloves, crushed
Freshly grated Parmesan cheese

Cook the pasta according to the packet directions. Drain, rinse briefly in cold water and drain again. Meanwhile, dry-fry the breadcrumbs in a large frying pan (skillet), tossing all the time until crisp but not brown. Mix the tomatoes, herbs, a little salt and lots of pepper in a bowl. Add the cooked, warm pasta. Heat the oil in a frying pan, add the breadcrumbs and garlic and fry until golden brown. Add to the bowl and toss well. Serve straight away, sprinkled with Parmesan cheese.

Basic Mayonnaise

SERVES 4

1 egg
1 egg yolk
30 ml/2 tbsp lemon juice
15 ml/1 tbsp white wine vinegar
2.5 ml/¹/₂ tsp mustard powder
Salt and freshly ground black pepper
375 ml/13 fl oz/1¹/₂ cups sunflower or
  olive oil

Using a blender or whisk, blend together the egg, egg yolk, lemon juice, vinegar, mustard, salt and pepper. Add a little of the oil and whisk again. Gradually add the remaining oil a little at a time, whisking or blending continuously until the mayonnaise thickens and emulsifies. Store in the fridge for up to 3 weeks in a screw-topped jar.

Blue Cheese Mayonnaise

SERVES 4

Take 250 ml/8 fl oz/1 cup Basic (or bought) Mayonnaise and add 40 g/1¹/₂ oz/¹/₃ cup crumbled blue cheese. Beat well.

Blushing Mayonnaise

SERVES 4

Take 250 ml/8 fl oz/1 cup Basic (or bought) Mayonnaise and add 60 ml/4 tbsp grated beetroot (red beet). Sprinkle with caraway seeds before serving.

Curried Mayonnaise

SERVES 4

Blend 15 ml/1 tbsp curry powder into 250 ml/8 fl oz/1 cup Basic (or bought) Mayonnaise. Add 1 crushed garlic clove and a good squeeze of lemon juice. For a sweeter version add 15 ml/1 tbsp mango chutney.

Green Herb Mayonnaise

SERVES 4

Add 30 ml/2 tbsp chopped mixed herbs (parsley, chives and marjoram are good) to 250 ml/8 fl oz/1 cup Basic (or bought) Mayonnaise.

Tarragon Mayonnaise

SERVES 4

Add 30 ml/2 tbsp chopped tarragon and 1 small crushed garlic clove to 250 ml/8 fl oz/1 cup Basic (or bought) Mayonnaise. Spike with lemon juice to taste.

Light Mayonnaise

SERVES 4

Blend equal quantities of Basic (or bought) Mayonnaise with fromage frais or plain yoghurt. Use as is or blend in salt and pepper and a little wine or herb vinegar, then 1–2 sieved hard-boiled (hard-cooked) eggs.

229

Carrot and Orange Salad

SERVES 4

Coarsely grate 4 or 5 carrots and season with lots of freshly ground black pepper. Then dress in a simple Vinaigrette Dressing (see page 231), or with 45 ml/3 tbsp orange juice mixed with 15 ml/1 tbsp lemon juice.

Mixed Bean Salad

SERVES 4

Dress a rinsed and drained 425 g/ 15½ oz/1 large can of mixed pulses with French Dressing (see page 231) and sprinkle with fresh herbs.

Tomato and Chive Salad

Layer sliced tomatoes with a sprinkling of sugar and snipped chives, then spoon over some Vinaigrette Dressing (see page 231). Leave for 1 hour before serving, if time.

Easy Rice Salad

Mix cooked long-grain rice with a selection of: chopped onion or spring onion (scallion), cooked peas, chopped mushrooms or (bell) peppers. Leave without a dressing, moisten with Vinaigrette Dressing (see page 231), or blend a little curry powder into 45 ml/3 tbsp of Basic Mayonnaise (see page 229) and stir gently into the rice salad.

Tuna and Pasta Salad

Cook small pasta shapes in chicken stock instead of water. Drain well. Mix with chunks of canned tuna and diced canned pimientos, season well with salt and pepper and dress with a little Vinaigrette Dressing (see page 231).

Mixed Green Salad

Go for contrast in flavours and textures and risk unusual combinations. You can choose from: little gem, lambs' lettuce, oakleaf, lollo rosso, lollo blanco, dandelion, spinach leaves, cos, Chinese leaves (stem lettuce), curly endive (frissé) – the possibilities are almost endless! Toss in French Dressing (see page 231) just before serving.

Special Potato Salad

To a basic potato salad of boiled new or chopped potatoes with Basic Mayonnaise (see page 229), add chopped spring onions (scallions), freshly snipped chives, a spoonful of soured (dairy sour) cream, some chopped black or green olives, or a few chopped canned anchovies.

Tzaziki

Mix finely diced cucumber, drained on kitchen paper to remove excess moisture, into Greek yoghurt with a little clear honey and season with salt and freshly ground black pepper. Add a crushed garlic clove, if liked. Sprinkle with plenty of chopped fresh mint and serve as a salad or a dip.

Jewel Salad

Mix drained canned sweetcorn (corn) with chopped drained canned pimientos, a chopped tomato and a few chopped mushrooms. Dress with a Vinaigrette Dressing (see right).

Feta and Onion Salad

Toss cubes of Feta cheese with sliced onions and tomatoes and dress with olive oil and black pepper.

Winter Salad

Mix walnuts and sliced eating (dessert) apples with salad leaves and Gran's Dressing (see page 232).

Super Special Salad

Sprinkle salad leaves with chopped nuts, chopped herbs, crumbled cheese, crisply fried pieces of bacon and slivers of canned smoked mussels and toss in a little Vinaigrette Dressing (see right).

French Dressing

SERVES 4

45 ml/3 tbsp white wine vinegar
120 ml/4 fl oz/¹/₂ cup olive oil
5 ml/1 tsp Dijon mustard
1 garlic clove, crushed (optional)
5 ml/1 tsp caster (superfine) sugar
Salt and freshly ground black pepper

Shake all the ingredients together well in a screw-topped jar. Store in the fridge.

Provençale Dressing

SERVES 4

Add 15 ml/1 tbsp chopped tarragon and 15 ml/1 tbsp chopped parsley to the basic French Dressing.

Olive Dressing

SERVES 4

Add 30 ml/2 tbsp chopped black or green olives (or half and half) to the basic French Dressing.

Piquant Dressing

SERVES 4

Add 10 ml/2 tsp chopped capers, 10 ml/2 tsp chopped gherkins (cornichons) and 15 ml/1 tbsp snipped olives to the basic French Dressing.

Vinaigrette Dressing

SERVES 4

30 ml/2 tbsp white wine vinegar
90 ml/6 tbsp olive oil
Salt and freshly ground black pepper
15 ml/1 tbsp snipped chives
Dash of lemon juice

Shake all the ingredients together well in a screw-topped jar. Chill before serving.

Soy Dressing

SERVES 4

60 ml/4 tbsp soy sauce
15 ml/1 tbsp lemon juice
15 ml/1 tbsp oil
20 ml/4 tsp clear honey
2.5 ml/¹/₂ tsp ground ginger
60 ml/4 tbsp water

Blend all the ingredients together well.

Thousand Island Dressing

SERVES 4

15 ml/1 tbsp tomato purée (paste)
15 ml/1 tbsp each chopped red and green (bell) pepper
1 gherkin (cornichon), chopped
1 hard-boiled (hard-cooked) egg, chopped
150 ml/¹/₄ pt/²/₃ cup Basic Mayonnaise (see page 229)

Blend the ingredients together well. Use as a salad dressing or dip.

Sweet and Sour Dressing

SERVES 4

120 ml/4 fl oz/¹/₂ cup pineapple juice
5 ml/1 tsp soy sauce
2.5 ml/¹/₂ tsp tomato purée (paste)
Freshly ground black pepper to taste

Mix together all the ingredients and chill before serving.

Gran's Dressing

SERVES 4–6

15 ml/1 tbsp light brown sugar
5 ml/1 tsp made English mustard
150 ml/¹/₄ pt/²/₃ cup single (light) cream or evaporated milk
Malt vinegar
Salt and freshly ground black pepper

Mix the sugar with the mustard and cream or evaporated milk until it dissolves. Whisk in vinegar and salt and pepper to taste. Store in a screw-topped jar in the fridge for up to 2 weeks. Use as an alternative to mayonnaise.

SNACKS

When you fancy a quick bite, the usual sandwich doesn't always hold much appeal. Here are some imaginative snacks to quash the hunger pangs and make you drool!

Croque Madame

SERVES 1

2 slices bread, well buttered
40 g/1¹/₂ oz/3 tbsp grated Cheddar
  cheese
¹/₂ small onion, sliced and separated
  into rings
5 ml/1 tsp chopped sage
Oil for shallow-frying

Sandwich the slices of bread together, buttered sides out, with the cheese, onion (rings) and the sage. Fry (sauté) or grill (broil) until golden on both sides. Serve straight away, cut into quarters.

Devilled Mushrooms

SERVES 2

1 small onion, finely chopped
15 ml/1 tbsp oil
175 g/6 oz button
  mushrooms
2 tomatoes, skinned if liked, and
  chopped
10 ml/2 tsp tomato ketchup (catsup)
10 ml/2 tsp Worcestershire sauce
1–2 drops Tabasco sauce
Hot buttered toast

Cook the onion in the oil for 2 minutes until softened. Add the mushrooms and tomatoes and cook, stirring, for 2 minutes. Add the remaining ingredients except the toast and simmer for 5 minutes or until the mushrooms are just cooked. Serve on hot buttered toast.

Macaroni Masterpiece

SERVES 2

4 streaky bacon rashers (slices)
100 g/4 oz/1 cup quick-cook
  macaroni
100 g/4 oz Red Leicester cheese,
  grated
5 ml/1 tsp Worcestershire sauce
Salt and freshly ground black pepper
25 g/1 oz/2 tbsp butter, melted
Snipped chives

Grill (broil) or dry-fry (sauté) the bacon until crisp, them cut into pieces. Meanwhile, cook the macaroni according to the packet directions, drain and return to the pan. Add the cheese, Worcestershire sauce, a little seasoning and the butter. Toss well until creamy. Pile on to warm serving plates and serve sprinkled with the bacon and chives.

Potato Crisps

Salt
Clean potato peelings

Sprinkle a thin layer of salt on a baking sheet. Spread the potato peelings over the top and bake in the oven at 200°C/400°F/ gas mark 6 for about 20 minutes until crispy. Toss and serve warm or cold.

Melting Crescent

SERVES 1

1 croissant
2 slices salami
1 Emmental or Gruyère (Swiss)
*   cheese slice*
Tomato slices

Split the croissant almost in half and fill with folded salami and cheese slices. Place under a moderate grill (broiler) until the cheese melts, turning once. Serve straight away garnished with tomato slices.

Garlic and Herb Crescent

SERVES 4

Prepare as for Melting Crescent but fill the croissant with a good layer of soft cheese with garlic and herbs and a little chopped red (bell) pepper instead of salami and cheese before grilling (broiling).

Cheese and Mushroom Croissants

SERVES 2–4

4 croissants
215 g/7¹/₂ oz/1 small can creamed
mushrooms
50 g/2 oz/¹/₂ cup grated Cheddar
*   cheese*

Carefully slit each croissant without breaking apart if necessary. Spread the creamed mushrooms inside and pack in the cheese. Grill (broil), turning once, until the cheese has melted and the croissants are crisp and hot through. Take care not to burn. Alternatively, heat as for Pizza Rolls (see page 238). Serve straight away.

Cheese and Tomato Pan Pizza

SERVES 1 OR 2

100 g/4 oz/1 cup self-raising (self-
rising) flour
Pinch of salt
45 ml/3 tbsp sunflower oil
227 g/8 oz/1 small can chopped
*   tomatoes, drained*
50 g/2 oz/¹/₂ cup grated Cheddar
*   cheese*
1.5 ml/¹/₄ tsp dried oregano
A few black olives

Mix the flour, salt and 30 ml/2 tbsp of the oil in a bowl. Add enough cold water to form a firm dough and knead gently. Roll or press out to a round to roughly fit the base of a frying pan (skillet). Heat the remaining oil in the frying pan, add the dough and fry (sauté) until the base is golden brown. Turn over and spread with the tomatoes. Top with the cheese and sprinkle with the oregano. Garnish with a few olives. Cover with a lid or foil and cook over a gentle heat for 5 minutes until the cheese is melting. Place under a hot grill (broiler) to brown the top.

Ham and Mushroom Pan Pizza

SERVES 1 OR 2

Prepare as for Cheese and Tomato Pan Pizza but add 4 button mushrooms, sliced and fried (sautéed) in a little butter first, and 1 chopped slice of ham to the pizza before topping with cheese.

Piperade

15 ml/1 tbsp olive oil
15 g/¹/₂ oz/1 tbsp butter
2 onions, sliced
2 green (bell) peppers, sliced
4 large tomatoes, quartered
1 garlic clove, crushed
4 eggs, beaten
Salt and freshly ground black pepper

Heat the oil and butter in a large frying pan (skillet). Add the prepared vegetables and garlic and fry (sauté) gently for 5 minutes, stirring, until soft. Add the eggs, season and cook, lifting and stirring gently, until set. Serve straight from the pan.

Somerset Rarebit

SERVES 1 OR 2

175 g/6 oz/1¹/₂ cups grated Cheddar
*   cheese*
5 ml/1 tsp made English mustard
30 ml/2 tbsp cider
2 slices toast

Put all the ingredients except the toast in a small pan. Heat gently, stirring until the cheese has melted and the mixture is well blended. Spoon on to toast and serve.

Quick Cheese Fondue

SERVES 2–4

Double the quantity of cheese, mustard and cider in Somerset Rarebit. Add 15 ml/1 tbsp Kirsch, if liked, and serve with cubes of French bread to dip in.

Spicy Potato Cakes

SERVES 2

225 g/8 oz potatoes, grated
1 small onion, grated
2.5 ml/¹/₂ tsp garam masala
1.5 ml/¹/₄ tsp chilli powder
1 egg, beaten
5 ml/1 tsp plain (all-purpose) flour
Salt and freshly ground black pepper
30 ml/2 tbsp sunflower oil
Mango chutney

Mix the potato, onion, spices, egg, flour and seasoning together. Heat the oil in a frying pan (skillet) and fry (sauté) tablespoonfuls of the mixture until golden brown underneath. Turn over and fry the other sides for 4–5 minutes in all. Serve hot with mango chutney.

Tortilla

SERVES 2

1 large potato, finely diced
1 small onion, chopped
15 ml/1 tbsp olive oil
15 ml/1 tbsp chopped parsley
Salt and freshly ground black pepper
4 eggs, beaten

Put the potato, onion and oil in a frying pan (skillet) and fry (sauté) for 4 minutes, stirring, until the potato is almost cooked. Add the parsley, a little seasoning and the eggs. Cook gently, lifting and stirring at first until the egg has almost set. Place under a hot grill (broiler) to brown and set the top. Serve hot or cold, cut into wedges.

Dutch Cheesy Bread

SERVES 4

1 small uncut loaf
225 g/8 oz Edam cheese, sliced
Sweet pickle

Slice the loaf but not right through, so that each slice is still attached at the bottom. Put a slice of cheese and a spoonful of pickle between each slice. Wrap the loaf in foil. Bake in the oven at 220°C/425°F/gas mark 7 for 15–20 minutes or until crisp and the cheese has melted.

French Cheesy Bread

SERVES 4

Prepare as for Dutch Cheesy Bread but substitute Brie for the Edam and tomato slices for the sweet pickle.

English Cheesy Bread

SERVES 4

Prepare as for Dutch Cheesy Bread but substitute Cheddar for the Edam and slices of pickled onion for the sweet pickle.

Hot Tuna and Garlic Bread

SERVES 4

2 garlic cloves, crushed
150 g/5 oz/²/₃ cup butter
15 ml/1 tbsp chopped parsley
185 g/6¹/₂ oz/1 small can tuna,
    drained
Squeeze of lemon juice
1 French stick

Mash together the garlic, butter, parsley and tuna. Add lemon juice to taste. Slice the bread thickly, without cutting right through the bottom. Spread each side of the slices with the garlic and tuna butter. Wrap the loaf in foil and bake in the oven at 200°C/400°F/gas mark 6 for 20 minutes. Serve hot.

Hash Browns

SERVES 4

45 ml/3 tbsp oil
1 onion, chopped
450 g/1 lb potatoes, finely diced
Salt and freshly ground black pepper
Fried eggs

Heat the oil and fry (sauté) the onion over a low heat for 5 minutes until soft. Remove from the pan with a draining spoon. Add the potatoes to the pan and fry for 10–15 minutes until golden on the outside and soft inside. Return the onions to the pan, stir and season well with salt and pepper. Press down firmly and cook until piping hot. Serve topped with fried eggs.

Eggy Bread

SERVES 2–4

4 eggs
Dash of milk
Salt and freshly ground black pepper
6 slices bread
Oil for shallow-frying

Beat the eggs with the milk and salt and pepper. Cut each slice of bread into quarters and dip into the egg mixture until completely coated. Heat the oil and fry (sauté) the soaked bread until browned on both sides. Sprinkle with salt and serve hot.

Super Sausage Rolls

MAKES 8

*350 g/12 oz shortcrust pastry (basic
    pie crust)*
Corn relish
A little plain (all-purpose) flour
450 g/1 lb/4 cups pork sausagemeat
Beaten egg, to glaze

Roll out the pastry to a 46 × 18 cm/
18 × 7 in rectangle. Spread with
relish to within 2.5 cm/1 in of the long
edges but right out to the shorter sides.
With floured hands, roll the sausagemeat
to 46 cm/18 in long. Place on the centre
of the pastry. Brush the edges of the pastry
with water, then fold over the sausage and
press the edges well together to seal.
Knock up and flute with the back of a knife.
Cut into 8 pieces and place on a baking
sheet. Brush with beaten egg and bake in
the oven at 200°C/400°F/gas mark 6 for
30 minutes until golden and cooked
through.

Potato Cakes

SERVES 4

5 ml/1 tsp oil
1 onion, chopped
*225 g/8 oz/1 cup cold mashed
    potato*
15 ml/1 tbsp mixed dried herbs
*50 g/2 oz/¹/₂ cup grated Cheddar
    cheese*
Salt and freshly ground black pepper
5 ml/1 tsp paprika
*50 g/2 oz/¹/₂ cup plain (all-purpose)
    flour*
Oil for shallow-frying

Heat the oil and fry (sauté) the onion
over a low heat for 5 minutes. Mix
together the onion, potato, herbs, cheese,
salt, pepper and paprika. Shape the
mixture into flat cakes and dust with flour.
Heat the oil and fry the cakes for about 8
minutes until browned on both sides.
Drain on kitchen paper.

Cheese Pâté

SERVES 4

*100 g/4 oz/1 cup grated Cheddar
    cheese*
*100 g/4 oz mature Stilton cheese,
    crumbled*
25 g/1 oz/2 tbsp butter
45 ml/3 tbsp white wine or stock
Salt and freshly ground black pepper

Mash all the ingredients together to
make a smooth paste. Press into a
dish and cover with foil. Chill before
serving with warm toast or crackers.

Cheese Crunchies

SERVES 4

8 slices bread
Butter
Yeast extract
100 g/4 oz/¹/₂ cup cream cheese
50 g/2 oz/2 cups cornflakes, crushed

Make the bread, butter and yeast
extract into sandwiches, then cut
them into 2.5 cm/1 in cubes. Spread each
cube with cream cheese on all sides, then
toss in the cornflakes. Serve.

Pizza Rolls

SERVES 4

4 soft rolls
225 g/8 oz/1 small can chopped
*   tomatoes, drained*
5 ml/1 tsp dried oregano
Grated Mozzarella or Cheddar
*   cheese*

Cut a slit in the top of each roll, not quite through. Gently pull away some of the soft filling to leave a thick shell. Divide the tomatoes between the rolls. Sprinkle with the herbs and fill up with cheese. Wrap each roll in foil and steam in a steamer or colander over a saucepan of boiling water for 10 minutes until the cheese has melted. Alternatively, bake in the oven at 220°C/425°F/gas mark 7 for 10 minutes.

Note: You can heat these Pizza Rolls in the microwave. Put in a microwave-safe dish with a lid. Do not wrap in foil. Microwave for 2 minutes, rearrange and cook a little longer depending on the power output of your model. Do not overcook or they will be tough.

Salmon Tartare Sandwiches

MAKES 4 ROUNDS

75 g/3 oz/^{1}/$_3$ cup butter or margarine
100 g/4 oz/1 small can pink salmon,
*   drained*
30 ml/2 tbsp tartare sauce
15 ml/1 tbsp chopped parsley
Salt and freshly ground black pepper
8 slices bread

Put the butter in a bowl and mash with a fork. Discard the bones and skin from the fish and mash into the butter with the tartare sauce, parsley and a little salt and pepper. Spread over the slices of bread and sandwich together in pairs. Cut off the crusts, if liked. Cut into triangles and serve.

Orange and Cream Cheese Deckers

MAKES 3 ROUNDS

6 slices bread
200 g/7 oz/scant 1 cup low-fat soft
*   cheese*
300 g/11 oz/1 small can mandarin
*   oranges, drained*
Cress or lettuce
Freshly grated black pepper

Spread the bread with the cheese. Top half the slices with the oranges, then cress or shredded lettuce leaves. Season with pepper, then sandwich together with the remaining bread slices. Cut and serve.

Pitta Packets

SERVES 4

300 ml/^{1}/$_2$ pt/1^1/$_4$ cups vegetable
*   stock*
225 g/8 oz leeks, sliced
1 small apple, chopped
6 radishes, chopped
4 button mushrooms, sliced
10 ml/2 tsp grated fresh root ginger
Salt and freshly ground black pepper
60 ml/4 tbsp olive oil
15 ml/1 tbsp white wine vinegar
Pinch of mustard powder
4 pitta breads

Bring the stock to the boil in a pan, add the leeks and simmer for 10 minutes until soft. Drain and leave to cool. Mix together the leeks, apple, radishes, mushrooms and ginger. Season with salt and pepper. Blend together 45 ml/3 tbsp of the oil, the wine vinegar and mustard and sprinkle over the vegetables. Slit the pitta breads lengthways down one side and fill with the vegetable mixture. Brush the outsides with the remaining oil and wrap the breads individually in foil. Grill (broil) or heat on a barbecue for about 6 minutes, turning once.

Pitta Pocket Cooler

SERVES 1

2.5 cm/1 in piece cucumber, chopped
15 ml/1 tbsp cooked lamb, sliced
15 ml/1 tbsp plain yoghurt
1.5 ml/¹/₄ tsp dried mint
Salt and freshly ground black pepper
1 pitta bread
Shredded lettuce
1 tomato, sliced

Mix the cucumber, lamb, yoghurt and mint together. Season to taste. Warm the pitta bread briefly under the grill (broiler) or in a toaster if liked. Make a slit along one edge to form a pocket. Fill with lettuce, then add the yoghurt mixture and a sliced tomato.

Dill Squares

SERVES 1 OR 2

2 slices bread
Butter
1 large dill pickle, sliced
50 g/2 oz/¹/₂ cup grated Cheddar cheese

Toast the bread and spread with butter. Top with the slices of pickle, then the cheese. Place under a hot grill (broiler) until golden and bubbling. Serve hot.

Eggy Baguette

SERVES 1 OR 2

1 small French stick
Butter
2 eggs
1.5 ml/¹/₄ tsp mixed dried herbs
Salt and freshly ground black pepper

Warm the French stick in the oven, or under the grill (broiler), turning frequently, or for a short time in the microwave. Cut a slit along the length and butter the inside. Meanwhile, beat the eggs and add 30 ml/2 tbsp water, the herbs and some salt and pepper. Beat well. Heat an omelette pan and add a knob of butter. When sizzling, pour in the egg mixture. Lift and stir the egg until set. Fold in three. Slide inside the French stick and cut in half, if liked.

Waffle Dagwoods

SERVES 2

4 frozen potato waffles
2 eggs
Butter or oil
2 ham slices
Shredded lettuce

Grill (broil) or fry (sauté) the waffles according to packet directions. Fry (sauté) the eggs in a little butter or oil until cooked. Place a slice of ham on each of 2 waffles. Top each with an egg and some shredded lettuce. Top with a second waffle and try to eat!

Fish Fingers American Style

SERVES 2

8 fish fingers
2 soft baps
2 processed cheese slices
30 ml/2 tbsp tartare sauce
Shredded lettuce

Grill (broil), fry (sauté) or microwave the fish fingers. Split the rolls and lay 4 fish fingers in each roll. Top with a slice of cheese and flash under a hot grill (broiler) to melt the cheese. Top with the tartare sauce and lettuce, then close the lids of the rolls. Serve.

Ploughman's Grill

SERVES 1 OR 2

2 slices bread
25 g/1 oz/2 tbsp butter
50 g/2 oz/¹/₂ cup grated Cheddar
* cheese*
2 pickled onions, chopped
1 tomato, sliced

Toast the bread on both sides. Meanwhile, mash the butter with the cheese and pickled onions. Spread over the toast and top with the tomato slices. Grill (broil) until golden and bubbling. Serve hot.

Toasted Turkey and Cranberry Sandwiches

SERVES 4

8 slices granary bread, buttered
175 g/6 oz/1¹/₂ cups cooked turkey,
* chopped*
15 ml/1 tbsp cranberry sauce
30 ml/2 tbsp mayonnaise
Salt and freshly ground black pepper

Lay 4 of the slices of bread buttered-side down on a board. Mix the turkey, cranberry and mayonnaise with a little salt and pepper and spread over the bread, not quite to the edges. Top with the remaining slices, buttered sides up. Cook as for Toasted Baked Bean and Cheese Sandwiches (see page 241).

Pitta Salad

SERVES 1

1 pitta bread
15 ml/1 tbsp shredded lettuce
2 tomato slices
2 cucumber slices
Filling suggestions: 15 ml/1 tbsp
* tuna; chopped ham; mashed*
* pilchard; sliced corned beef;*
* chopped frankfurter; salami or*
* hard-boiled (hard-cooked) egg*
10 ml/2 tsp mayonnaise

Toast or microwave the pitta until just puffed up. Split along one long edge to form a pocket. Add the shredded lettuce, tomato and cucumber and any other suggested filling. Finish with mayonnaise.

Naan Tiffin

SERVES 4

2 naan breads
225 g/8 oz/1 small can pease
* pudding*
10 ml/2 tsp curry paste
30 ml/2 tbsp mango chutney
Lemon juice
Shredded lettuce (optional)

Grill or microwave the naans according to the packet directions. Heat the pease pudding with the curry paste in a saucepan or the microwave until hot through, stirring occasionally. Spread the mixture over the surface of the naans. Spread the chutney over and sprinkle on lemon juice to taste. Add the shredded lettuce, if liked. Fold in halves, then cut into handy sized wedges. Wrap in kitchen paper and eat in the fingers.

Saucy Ham and Eggs

SERVES 2

1 bunch of watercress, chopped
15 g/¹/₂ oz/1 tbsp butter or
  margarine
15 g/¹/₂ oz/2 tbsp plain (all-purpose)
  flour
150 ml/¹/₄ pt/²/₃ cup milk
Salt and freshly ground black pepper
2 eggs
5 ml/1 tsp lemon juice or vinegar
2 ham slices
2 toast slices, buttered

Put the watercress, fat, flour and milk in a saucepan. Whisk over a moderate heat until thickened and smooth. Season to taste. Poach the eggs in water with the lemon juice or vinegar added for 3–5 minutes to the consistency you like. Put a ham slice on each of the slices of toast. Top with a poached egg. Spoon the hot watercress sauce over and serve straight away.

Omelette in the Fingers

SERVES 2–4

4 eggs
60 ml/4 tbsp cold water
Salt and freshly ground black pepper
5 ml/1 tsp mixed dried herbs
Butter
290 g/10¹/₂ oz/1 small can asparagus
  spears, drained

Beat one egg in a bowl with 15 ml/1 tbsp of the water, a little salt and pepper and 1.5 ml/¹/₄ tsp of the herbs. Heat a little butter in an omelette pan. Pour in the egg and fry (sauté), lifting the edge and letting the uncooked egg run underneath until set. Transfer to a plate and leave to cool while making the remaining three omelettes in the same way. Divide the asparagus spears between the omelettes. Roll up and serve.

Toasted Baked Bean and Cheese Sandwiches

SERVES 4

8 slices bread, buttered
20 ml/4 tsp brown table sauce
400 g/14 oz/1 large can baked beans
  in tomato sauce
50 g/2 oz/¹/₂ cup grated Cheddar
  cheese

Lay 4 slices of the bread buttered-side down on a board. Spread lightly with the brown sauce. Divide the beans between the centres of the sandwiches and spread out, not quite to the edges, all round. Sprinkle on the cheese. Top with the remaining bread slices, buttered-sides up. Place in a sandwich toaster and cook in the normal way, or place on a grill (broiler) rack with a cooling rack pressed firmly over the top. Grill (broil) until the tops are golden brown. With oven-gloved hands, invert the grill rack so the cake rack is on the bottom and return to the grill to toast the other sides. Alternatively, fry (sauté) in a frying pan, pressing down firmly from time to time with a fish slice, until the bases are golden, then carefully turn over and brown the other sides.

Toasted Curried Chicken Sandwiches

SERVES 4

8 slices wholemeal bread, buttered
20 ml/4 tsp mango or peach chutney
100 g/4 oz/1 cup cooked chicken,
*   chopped*
30 ml/2 tbsp mayonnaise
5–10 ml/1–2 tsp curry paste
Salt and freshly ground black pepper

Lay 4 slices of bread buttered-side down on a board. Spread with the chutney. Mix the chicken with the mayonnaise and curry paste to taste. Season lightly. Spread over the bread, not quite to the edges. Top with the remaining slices, buttered sides up. Cook as for Toasted Baked Bean and Cheese Sandwiches (see page 241).

Cheese and Sausage Burgers

SERVES 4

450 g/1 lb/4 cups pork sausagemeat
2.5 ml/¹/₂ tsp dried sage
4 Baby Bel cheeses, rinded
15 ml/1 tbsp oil
Tomato relish
4 burger buns

Knead the sausagemeat and sage together, then shape into 8 small flat cakes. Place a Baby Bel cheese in the centre of each of 4 cakes, then top with the remainder, pressing the edges well together to seal. Brush with oil, then grill (broil) or shallow-fry in the oil for 4–5 minutes on each side, turning once, until crisp, golden and cooked through. Drain on kitchen paper. Spread with a little tomato relish and serve in the buns.

Barking Mad Hot Dogs

SERVES 4

25 g/1 oz/2 tbsp butter
10 ml/2 tsp yeast extract
1 large onion, chopped
425 g/15 oz/1 large can of 8 hot-dog
*   sausages*
8 finger rolls, warmed
45 ml/3 tbsp tomato ketchup
*   (catsup)*

Melt the butter in a small saucepan. Add the yeast extract and onion and fry (sauté) for 2 minutes, stirring. Cover and cook gently for 5 minutes or until the onions are tender. Remove the lid and boil quickly until the liquid has evaporated. Meanwhile, heat the hot dogs according to the instructions. Split the rolls and spread one cut surface with ketchup. Spoon in the onion mixture. Add a hot dog to each and serve straight away.

Egg and Mushroom Milk Toasts

SERVES 4

4 large flat mushrooms
50 g/2 oz/¹/₄ cup butter
1 garlic clove, chopped
Salt and freshly ground black pepper
4 size 4 eggs
10 ml/2 tsp lemon juice
4 slices round milk bread
A little extra butter
Chopped parsley

Peel the mushrooms and remove and discard the stalks. Melt the butter in a frying pan (skillet), add the mushrooms, sprinkle with the garlic and season lightly. Fry (sauté) for 2 minutes, then cover with a lid, reduce the heat and cook for about 5 minutes until just tender. Meanwhile, poach the eggs in gently simmering water with the lemon juice added. Toast the bread and spread with a little butter. Place on serving plates. Top each with a mushroom, then a poached egg and sprinkle with chopped parsley.

German Open Toasties

SERVES 4

4 slices multi-grain bread
Butter
10 ml/2 tsp German mustard
4 slices Westphalian ham
50 g/2 oz/¹/₂ cup grated Tilsit or
*   Cheddar cheese*
4 gherkins (cornichons)

Toast the bread on both sides. Spread one side lightly with butter, then mustard. Top each with a slice of ham, then cover with cheese. Grill (broil) until the cheese has melted. Meanwhile, cut 3 slices in each gherkin from the tip almost through to the stem end. Gently open out to form fans. Lay one on top of each toast and serve straight away.

Mushroom Cottage Pittas

SERVES 4

25 g/1 oz/2 tbsp butter
1 small onion, finely chopped
50 g/2 oz/1 cup button mushrooms,
*   sliced*
225 g/8 oz/1 cup cottage cheese with
*   chives*
2 tomatoes, finely chopped
Salt and freshly ground black pepper
4 pitta breads
Shredded lettuce

Melt the butter in a pan and add the onion and mushrooms. Fry (sauté), stirring for 5 minutes. Stir in the cheese and tomatoes and season to taste. Heat through, gently. Meanwhile, grill (broil) the pittas briefly until they start to puff up. Make a slit along one edge of each to form a pocket. Spoon in the warm cheese mixture, add some shredded lettuce and serve straight away.

Spicy Sardine and Bean Pittas

SERVES 4

120 g/4¹/₂ oz/1 small can sardines in
*   tomato sauce*
1 small garlic clove, crushed
1 small fresh red chilli, seeded and
*   finely chopped, or 1.5 ml/¹/₄ tsp*
*   chilli powder*
225 g/8 oz/1 small can butter beans,
*   drained and mashed*
Salt and freshly ground black pepper
4 wholemeal pitta breads
Shredded lettuce
Cucumber slices

Mash the sardines, preferably including the bones. Add the garlic, chilli and mashed beans and season to taste. Grill (broil) the pittas briefly until they begin to puff up. Make a slit along one side of each to form a pocket. Spoon in the sardine mixture and add some shredded lettuce and cucumber slices.

Herby Egg Pittas

SERVES 4

15 g/¹/₂ oz/1 tbsp butter
4 eggs
30 ml/2 tbsp milk
15 ml/1 tbsp chopped parsley
15 ml/1 tbsp snipped chives
Salt and freshly ground black pepper
4 wholemeal pitta breads
Tomato ketchup (catsup)

Melt the butter in a small saucepan. Beat in the eggs and milk. Stir in the herbs and season lightly. Cook over a gentle heat, stirring all the time until scrambled but still creamy. Grill (broil) the pittas briefly until they begin to puff up. Split along one edge and spread the inside with ketchup. Spoon in the eggs and serve straight away.

Cheese and Pineapple Toasts

SERVES 4

4 slices bread
Butter
225 g/8 oz/1 small can pineapple
    slices
4 slices Leerdammer or Gruyère
    (Swiss) cheese
1 tomato, cut into 4 slices
Dried basil

Toast the bread on both sides. Butter lightly. Top each with a pineapple slice, then a slice of cheese and top with a tomato slice. Sprinkle the tomato with a pinch of dried basil. Grill (broil) until the cheese melts. Serve straight away.

Wheaty Potato Pizza

SERVES 2–4

225 g/8 oz/1 cup cooked mashed
    potato
75 g/3 oz/³/₄ cup wholemeal flour
2.5 ml/¹/₂ tsp salt
Milk
Oil for shallow-frying
45 ml/3 tbsp tomato purée (paste)
2.5 ml/¹/₂ tsp dried oregano
75 g/3 oz/³/₄ cup grated Cheddar
    cheese

Mix the potato with the flour, salt and enough milk to form a firm dough. Roll out on a lightly floured surface to a round the size of the base of the frying pan (skillet). Heat a little of the oil in the pan and fry (sauté) the pizza base until golden underneath. Slide out on to a plate. Heat a little more oil in the pan, then invert the pizza base into the pan, browned side up. Spread with the tomato purée, sprinkle with oregano, then cheese. Fry for 2 minutes or until golden on the other side, then place under a hot grill (broiler) until the cheese melts and bubbles.

Any Time Breakfast Pizza

SERVES 2–4

Prepare as for Wheaty Potato Pizza, but cut the cooked pizza into quarters and top each wedge with a grilled (broiled) bacon rasher (slice) and a fried egg.

SAUCES, DIPS AND SAVOURY BUTTERS

Here is a wide variety of delicious recipes to brighten barbecues, add excitement to plain-cooked meat, fish, vegetables or pasta, and jazz up salads and cold meats.

Basic White Sauce

SERVES 4

25 g/1 oz/¹/₄ cup plain (all-purpose) flour
300 ml/¹/₂ pt/1¹/₄ cups milk
25 g/1 oz/2 tbsp butter or margarine
Salt and freshly ground black pepper

Whisk the flour and milk in a saucepan until smooth. Add the butter or margarine and whisk over a moderate heat until boiling and thickened. Cook, whisking for 2 minutes. Season to taste.

Basic Cheese Sauce

SERVES 4

Prepare as for Basic White Sauce but add 75 g/3 oz/³/₄ cup grated Cheddar cheese to the thick sauce and stir until melted. 5 ml/1 tsp made mustard may also be added for a stronger flavour.

Quick Italian-style Tomato Sauce

SERVES 4

1 onion, chopped
1 garlic clove, crushed
15 ml/1 tbsp oil
400 g/14 oz/1 large can chopped tomatoes
15 ml/1 tbsp tomato paste (purée)
Salt and freshly ground black pepper
2.5 ml/¹/₂ tsp dried oregano

Fry (sauté) the onion and garlic in the oil for 2 minutes to soften. Add the remaining ingredients, bring to the boil and simmer for 10 minutes until pulpy. Use as required.

Cocktail Sauce

SERVES 4

60 ml/4 tbsp mayonnaise
30 ml/2 tbsp plain yoghurt
15 ml/1 tbsp tomato ketchup (catsup)
10 ml/2 tsp horseradish cream
Salt and freshly ground black pepper

Blend all the ingredients together until smooth. Store in a screw-topped jar in the fridge for up to 1 week. Use as required to brighten up cold fish, chicken or vegetables, or serve as a dip.

Fresh Tomato Sauce

SERVES 4

45 ml/3 tbsp oil
1 onion, finely chopped
1 celery stick, finely chopped
1 carrot, finely chopped
2 garlic cloves, crushed
1.5 kg/3 lb ripe tomatoes, chopped
45 ml/3 tbsp water
Pinch of sugar
15 ml/1 tbsp chopped basil or
*   parsley*
1 bay leaf
Salt and freshly ground black pepper

Heat the oil and fry (sauté) the onion, celery, carrot and garlic for a few minutes over a low heat until soft but not brown. Add the remaining ingredients and bring to a simmer. Cover and simmer gently for about 20 minutes, stirring occasionally, until the tomatoes are reduced to a pulp. Discard the bay leaf. Purée the sauce, if you want a smooth texture. Serve hot with pasta, blend into mayonnaise to make a dip, or serve as a side dressing for simple grilled vegetables.

Spicy Orange and Tomato Sauce

SERVES 4

100 g/4 oz/¹/₂ cup butter
250 ml/8 fl oz/1 cup tomato purée
*   (paste)*
250 ml/8 fl oz/ 1 cup white wine
*   vinegar*
45 ml/3 tbsp horseradish sauce
45 ml/3 tbsp light brown sugar
60 ml/4 tbsp orange juice
30 ml/2 tbsp lemon juice
15 ml/1 tbsp Worcestershire sauce
Salt

Simmer all the ingredients for about 30 minutes, stirring occasionally, until thick. Serve warm or cold with chicken or strongly flavoured fish such as mackerel.

Deep South Sauce

SERVES 4

250 ml/8 fl oz/1 cup tomato purée
*   (paste)*
1 garlic clove, crushed
150 ml/¹/₄ pt/²/₃ cup white wine
*   vinegar*
75 g/3 oz/²/₃ cup light brown sugar
75 ml/5 tbsp oil
30 ml/2 tbsp Worcestershire sauce
15 ml/1 tbsp mustard powder
15 ml/1 tbsp lemon juice
Salt and freshly ground black pepper

Place all the ingredients in a pan and bring to the boil. Simmer gently for 15 minutes, stirring occasionally. Leave to stand for 2 hours, if possible, before serving hot or cold. Serve with robust vegetables such as potatoes or fennel.

Yoghurt and Mint Sauce

SERVES 4

60 ml/4 tbsp plain yoghurt
5 ml/1 tsp bottled mint sauce
5 ml/1 tsp sugar

Mix together all the ingredients. Serve with kebabs, samosas or pakoras.

Yoghurt and Mustard Sauce

SERVES 4

60 ml/4 tbsp plain yoghurt
5 ml/1 tsp mustard powder
5 ml/1 tsp sugar

Mix together all the ingredient Serve with kebabs, samosas or pakoras.

Cooked Barbecue Sauce

SERVES 4

50 g/2 oz/¹/₄ cup butter or margarine
1 onion, chopped
5 ml/1 tsp tomato purée (paste)
30 ml/2 tbsp red wine vinegar
30 ml/2 tbsp light brown sugar
10 ml/2 tsp mustard powder
30 ml/2 tbsp Worcestershire sauce
150 ml/¹/₄ pt/²/₃ cup water

Melt the butter or margarine and fry (sauté) the onion until soft. Add the remaining ingredients, stirring together over a low heat until well blended. Bring to the boil, then simmer for 10 minutes. Serve warm or cold.

All-purpose Barbecue Sauce

SERVES 4

15 ml/1 tbsp lemon juice
15 ml/1 tbsp red wine (or other) vinegar
30 ml/2 tbsp tomato ketchup (catsup)
15 ml/1 tbsp Worcestershire sauce
30 ml/2 tbsp golden (light corn) syrup

Mix all the ingredients together until thoroughly blended. Store in a screw-topped jar in the fridge for up to 1 month. Serve as a side sauce with grilled (broiled) meat or fish or use as a baste.

Garlic and Herb Sauce

SERVES 4

15 ml/1 tbsp cornflour (cornstarch)
300 ml/¹/₂ pt/1¹/₄ cups milk
15 g/¹/₂ oz/1 tbsp butter or margarine
85 g/3¹/₂ oz/scant ¹/₂ cup soft cheese with garlic and herbs, cut into pieces
Salt and freshly ground black pepper

Whisk the cornflour with a little of the milk in a saucepan until smooth. Stir in the remaining milk. Add the butter or margarine. Bring to the boil, stirring until thickened. Add the cheese and continue stirring over a gentle heat until blended. Season with salt and pepper and use as required with fish, vegetables or white meat.

Guacamole

SERVES 4

2 stoned (pitted) avocados, peeled and mashed
1 garlic clove, crushed
30 ml/2 tbsp lemon juice
15 ml/1 tbsp olive oil
2.5 ml/¹/₂ tsp ground coriander (cilantro)
A few drops of Tabasco sauce
Salt and freshly ground black pepper

Purée all the ingredients in a food processor. Taste, and adjust the seasoning as you prefer.

Creamy Tarragon Sauce

SERVES 4

15 ml/1 tbsp butter or margarine
15 ml/1 tbsp plain (all-purpose)
  flour
250 ml/8 fl oz/1 cup milk
30 ml/2 tbsp chopped tarragon
Salt and freshly ground black pepper
45 ml/3 tbsp single (light) cream

Melt the butter or margarine, then stir in the flour and cook over a very low heat for 1 minute, stirring. Remove from the heat and stir in the milk until well blended. Return to a low heat and bring to the boil, stirring, then simmer gently for 2 minutes. Stir in the tarragon, season well with salt and pepper and blend in the cream. Serve with vegetable burgers or patties.

Piquant Mustard Sauce

SERVES 4

250 ml/8 fl oz/1 cup white wine
  vinegar
175 ml/6 fl oz/³/₄ cup made mustard
¹/₂ onion, finely chopped
4 garlic cloves, crushed
75 ml/5 tbsp water
60 ml/4 tbsp tomato purée (paste)
15 ml/1 tbsp paprika
2.5 ml/¹/₂ tsp cayenne
Salt and freshly ground black pepper

Gently simmer all the ingredients for about 20 minutes, stirring occasionally, until the onion is soft and the sauce thick. Serve warm or cold with grilled (broiled) meats or oily fish.

Indonesian Hot Peanut Sauce

SERVES 4

120 ml/4 fl oz/¹/₂ cup water
120 ml/4 fl oz/¹/₂ cup white wine
  vinegar
50 g/2 oz/¹/₄ cup sugar
100 g/4 oz/¹/₂ cup peanut butter
30 ml/2 tbsp grated fresh root
  ginger
1 garlic clove, crushed
45 ml/3 tbsp soy sauce
15 ml/1 tbsp chopped coriander
  (cilantro)
Pinch of cayenne
Salt
15 ml/1 tbsp sesame oil

Boil the water, vinegar and sugar for 5 minutes, stirring to dissolve the sugar. Remove from the heat and leave to cool. Purée the mixture with all the remaining ingredients except the oil in a blender or food processor until smooth. Blend in the oil. Serve warm with chicken or chicken kebabs.

Quick Chinese Sauce

SERVES 4

250 ml/8 fl oz/1 cup hoisin sauce
120 ml/4 fl oz/¹/₂ cup rice wine or
  white wine vinegar
2–3 garlic cloves, crushed
60 ml/4 tbsp soy sauce
15 ml/1 tbsp chopped fresh root
  ginger
5 ml/1 tsp anise

Simmer all the ingredients gently for 10 minutes. Serve hot or warm with chicken or pork. Store in the fridge for several weeks in an airtight jar.

Treacly Apple Sauce

50 g/2 oz/¹/₄ cup butter or margarine
1 onion, finely chopped
1 eating (dessert) apple, peeled and
finely chopped
450 ml/³/₄ pt/2 cups apple juice
30 ml/2 tbsp black treacle
(molasses)
15 ml/1 tbsp Worcestershire sauce
15 ml/1 tbsp cider vinegar
5 ml/1 tsp ground cinnamon

Melt the butter or margarine and fry (sauté) the onion until soft. Stir in the remaining ingredients until well blended. Bring to the boil, then simmer for about 25 minutes until thickened, stirring regularly. Serve warm. Especially good with pork or duck.

Tuna Dip

185 g/6¹/₂ oz/1 small can tuna,
drained
60 ml/4 tbsp mayonnaise
45 ml/3 tbsp plain yoghurt
15 ml/1 tbsp tomato ketchup
(catsup)
5 ml/1 tsp lemon juice
1.5 ml/¹/₄ tsp chilli powder
Freshly ground black pepper

Put the tuna in a bowl and break up with a wooden spoon. Beat in the remaining ingredients until well blended. Turn into a small bowl and chill until ready to serve.

Middle Eastern Dip

440 g/15¹/₂ oz/1 large can chick
peas (garbanzos), drained
1 garlic clove, crushed
90 ml/6 tbsp olive oil
15 ml/1 tbsp lemon juice
Salt and freshly ground black pepper
A little extra olive oil
Dried mint

Put the chick peas and garlic in a blender or food processor and run the machine until they are smooth. Gradually add the oil in a thin stream, keeping the machine running. Add the lemon juice and season with salt and pepper. Turn into a small bowl, drizzle a little olive oil over and sprinkle with dried mint.

Brandied Blue Cheese Dip

100 g/4 oz blue cheese, grated or
crumbled
50 g/2 oz/¹/₄ cup butter or margarine
100 g/4 oz/¹/₂ cup cream cheese
90 ml/6 tbsp crème fraîche
1 shallot, finely chopped
30 ml/2 tbsp chopped parsley
45 ml/3 tbsp brandy
A few drops of Worcestershire sauce
Pinch of sugar
Salt and freshly ground black pepper

Blend all the ingredients together well and chill before serving.

Minted Soured Cream Dip

SERVES 4

250 ml/8 fl oz/1 cup soured (dairy sour) cream
30 ml/2 tbsp chopped mint
Salt and freshly ground black pepper

Blend the ingredients together well, seasoning to taste with salt and pepper. Serve as a dip or a salad dressing.

Tomato Dip

SERVES 4

200 g/7 oz/1 small can tomatoes, drained and chopped
45 ml/3 tbsp tomato purée (paste)
15 ml/1 tbsp chopped basil
A few drops of Worcestershire sauce
Salt and freshly ground black pepper

Blend all the ingredients together well, seasoning to taste with Worcestershire sauce, salt and pepper. Serve as a dip or a salad dressing.

Herb and Lemon Dip

SERVES 4

250 ml/8 fl oz/1 cup crème fraîche
60 ml/4 tbsp chopped parsley
60 ml/4 tbsp chopped dill (dill weed)
30 ml/2 tbsp snipped chives
15 ml/1 tbsp lemon juice
Salt and freshly ground black pepper

Blend all the ingredients together well, seasoning to taste with salt and pepper. Serve as a dip or a salad dressing.

Raita

SERVES 4

150 ml/¹/₄ pt/²/₃ cup plain yoghurt
15 ml/1 tbsp chopped mint
1.5 ml/¹/₄ tsp salt
1.5 ml/¹/₄ tsp sugar
5 cm/2 in piece cucumber, finely chopped
5–10 ml/1–2 tsp milk

Mix together all the ingredients, adding just enough milk to make the mixture creamy but not too runny. Chill before serving.

Cheese and Gherkin Dip

SERVES 4

250 ml/8 fl oz/1 cup plain yoghurt
75 g/3 oz strong cheese, grated
2 gherkins (cornichons), chopped
Salt and freshly ground black pepper

Blend all the ingredients together well, seasoning to taste with salt and pepper.

Ginger Dip

SERVES 4

90 ml/6 tbsp oil
15 ml/1 tbsp soy sauce
15 ml/1 tbsp lemon juice
1 garlic clove, crushed
2.5 ml/¹/₂ tsp grated fresh root ginger

Mix together all the ingredients well. Serve with barbecued or grilled (broiled) meats, poultry or fish.

Yoghurt and Blue Cheese Dip

SERVES 4

150 ml/¹/₄ pt/²/₃ cup plain yoghurt
15 ml/1 tbsp soft blue cheese
5 ml/1 tsp chopped fresh dill
(dill weed)

Mix together all the ingredients and chill before serving as a dip or salad dressing.

Peanut Dip

SERVES 4

60 ml/4 tbsp peanut butter
30 ml/2 tbsp olive oil
5 ml/1 tsp lemon juice
5 ml/1 tsp soy sauce
Pinch of dried tarragon

Mix together all the ingredients and chill before serving. Serve as a dip or salad dressing.

Chilli Yoghurt Dip

SERVES 4

60 ml/4 tbsp plain yoghurt
1.5 ml/¹/₄ tsp chilli powder
Pinch of salt
Pinch of sugar

Mix together all the ingredients and chill before serving as a dip or salad dressing.

More Dip Ideas

Mandarin and Almond Dip: mix 120 ml/ 4 fl oz/¹/₂ cup Basic Mayonnaise (see page 229) with 300 g/11 oz/1 small can mandarins, drained, 2.5 ml/¹/₂ tsp curry powder, 25 g/1 oz/¹/₄ cup chopped almonds and 5 ml/1 tsp lemon juice.

Cream Cheese and Avocado Dip: purée the flesh of an avocado with a garlic clove, 225 g/8 oz/1 cup cream cheese, 15 ml/1 tbsp lemon juice and 15 ml/1 tbsp snipped chives.

Flavour mayonnaise or fromage frais, or cream cheese, or thick plain yoghurt (or a combination) to taste with one of the following: grain mustard, chopped herbs, crushed garlic, chopped gherkins (cornichons), tomato chutney and a few drops of Worcestershire sauce, cayenne, chilli or curry powder.

Interesting Crudités

You need a choice of fresh and crunchy vegetables or biscuits to serve with your dips. Here are some ideas.

A bowl of raw vegetables cut into thin julienne strips makes a colourful table centrepiece and the perfect accompaniment to a selection of dips. Go for all the old favourites – carrot, cucumber, celery, (bell) peppers – but don't ignore other vegetables that give you a more unusual selection. Try cauliflower florets, baby carrots, sugarsnap peas, mangetout (snow peas), chicory (Belgian endive), different mushrooms or pieces of lightly cooked asparagus.

Fruits also offer an interesting variety. Try pieces of star fruit, pear, apple, melon, pineapple, firm peach or apricot.

Tortilla chips, corn chips and strips of pitta bread are also great for dipping. Try fingers of toast rubbed with a cut clove of garlic. Don't forget grissini, cheese straws, melba toast or crackers. Finger-shaped croûtons of bread fried until golden with a crushed clove of garlic have a wonderful flavour and texture too.

Spinach and Cashew Nut Paste for Pasta

SERVES 4–6

350 g/12 oz young spinach leaves
100 g/4 oz/1 cup grated Pecorino
 cheese
100 g/4 oz/1 cup cashew nuts
2 garlic cloves, crushed
30 ml/2 tbsp lemon juice
250 ml/8 fl oz/1 cup olive oil
Salt and freshly ground black pepper

Chop the spinach in a blender or food processor. Add the cheese, nuts, garlic and lemon juice and run the machine until well blended. Add the olive oil in a thin stream, with the machine running all the time, until a smooth paste if formed. Season lightly with salt and pepper. If the sauce is too thick, add a little hot water. Store in a screw-topped jar in the fridge for up to 3 weeks. Add to hot cooked pasta and toss well until it melts.

Pesto Sauce

SERVES 4

14 large basil leaves
2 garlic cloves, chopped
5 ml/1 tsp coarse sea salt
15 ml/1 tbsp pine nuts, toasted
30 ml/2 tbsp freshly grated
 Parmesan cheese
45 ml/3 tbsp olive oil
Freshly ground black pepper

Place the basil leaves in a blender or food processor with the garlic and salt and run the machine until they form a purée. Add the nuts and cheese and blend until smooth, scraping the mixture from the sides as necessary. Gradually add the oil a drop at a time until the mixture becomes a thick green sauce. Alternatively, you can pound the ingredients in a pestle and mortar. Add a good grinding of pepper. Store in a screw-topped jar in the fridge for up to 3 weeks. Toss with pasta, until it melts, or use as required.

Almond and Herb Paste for Pasta

SERVES 4

100 g/4 oz/¹/₂ cup butter
50 g/2 oz/¹/₂ cup ground almonds
20 ml/4 tsp freshly grated Parmesan
 cheese
45 ml/3 tbsp chopped parsley
15 ml/1 tbsp snipped chives
10 ml/2 tsp chopped sage
Salt and freshly ground black pepper

Mash the butter with the almonds. Work in the cheese and herbs and season well. Add to hot cooked pasta and toss over a gentle heat until melted.

Bagna Cauda

SERVES 4–6

75 ml/5 tbsp walnut oil
75 ml/5 tbsp olive oil
3 garlic cloves, finely chopped
50 g/2 oz/1 small can anchovy
 fillets, drained and chopped
25 g/1 oz/2 tbsp unsalted (sweet)
 butter
1 tomato, seeded and chopped
45 ml/3 tbsp double (heavy) cream
 (optional)
Salt

Heat the oils in a saucepan. Add the garlic and fry (sauté) until golden. Reduce the heat, add the anchovies and cook gently, stirring, until they have 'melted' into the oil. Stir in the butter until melted. Add the tomato and cream, if using, and heat through. Taste and add salt if necessary. Serve as a dip with crudités, or as a dressing for hot pasta.

Tapenade

SERVES 4–6

250 ml/8 fl oz/1 cup olive oil
225 g/8 oz/1¹/₃ cups stoned (pitted) black olives
225 g/8 oz/1¹/₃ cups stoned (pitted) green olives
3 garlic cloves
75 g/3 oz parsley
2 × 50 g/2 × 2 oz/2 small cans anchovies, drained
60 ml/4 tbsp capers, drained
45 ml/3 tbsp lemon juice
Freshly ground black pepper

Put all the ingredients, including a good grinding of pepper, in a food processor or blender. Run the machine until a smooth paste is formed. Stop the machine and scrape down the sides from time to time. Store in a screw-topped jar in the fridge for up to 3 weeks. Use to toss hot pasta or to spread on slices of Ciabatta or French bread.

Sun-dried Tomato Paste for Pasta

SERVES 4–6

350 g/12 oz/3 cups sun-dried tomatoes, drained, reserving the oil
Olive oil
150 g/5 oz/1¹/₄ cups freshly grated Parmesan cheese
75 g/3 oz/³/₄ cup chopped mixed nuts
45 ml/3 tbsp chopped parsley
3 garlic cloves

Put the tomatoes in a blender or food processor. Make up the reserved tomato oil to 375 ml/13 fl oz/1¹/₂ cups with the olive oil. Add the oil to the blender with the remaining ingredients. Run the machine until the mixture forms a smooth paste, stopping the machine and scraping down the sides from time to time. If the paste is too thick, add a little hot water. Store in a screw-topped jar in the fridge for up to 3 weeks. Add to hot pasta and toss until melted.

Pimiento and Olive Paste

SERVES 4–6

400 g/14 oz/1 large can pimientos, drained
2 garlic cloves
300 ml/¹/₂ pt/1¹/₄ cups olive oil
75 g/3 oz/³/₄ cup stuffed olives
50 g/2 oz/¹/₂ cup freshly grated Parmesan cheese
60 ml/4 tbsp parsley
30 ml/2 tbsp lemon juice
Salt and freshly ground black pepper

Put all the ingredients except salt and pepper in a food processor or blender. Run the machine until the mixture forms a paste. Stop the machine and scrape down the sides from time to time. Taste and season with a little salt and lots of black pepper. Store in a screw-topped jar for up to 3 weeks. Toss with hot pasta or spread on slices of toasted French bread and grill (broil) until melted.

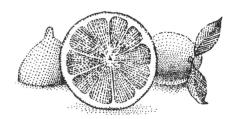

253

Garlic Butter

SERVES 4

1 garlic clove, crushed, or 5 ml/1 tsp
garlic purée (paste) or granules
75 g/3 oz/¹/₃ cup butter, softened
Freshly ground black pepper

Mash the garlic and butter and add a good grinding of pepper. Either spread in French bread or rolls, wrap in foil and bake until crisp and melted, or shape into a roll on a piece of baking parchment, roll up and chill. Cut into slices to top plain cooked meat or fish.

Garlic and Herb Butter: Add 5 ml/1 tsp mixed dried herbs to Garlic Butter.

Herb Butter: Omit the garlic and add 10 ml/2 tsp mixed dried herbs to plain butter and continue as above.

Tomato Butter: Add 15 ml/1 tbsp tomato purée (paste) to plain or Garlic Butter. Mash thoroughly to mix continue as above.

Anchovy Butter: Add 10 ml/2 tsp anchovy essence (extract) to plain butter. Continue as above.

Curry Butter: Add 5 ml/1 tsp curry paste to plain or Garlic Butter. Mash thoroughly to mix. Continue as above.

Black Butter

SERVES 4–6

175 g/6 oz/³/₄ cup unsalted (sweet)
butter
3 garlic cloves, finely chopped
175 g/6 oz/1¹/₂ cups freshly grated
Parmesan cheese
Salt a·l freshly ground black pepper

Put the butter in a frying pan (skillet) and melt over a moderate heat. When the butter starts to foam, add the garlic and continue cooking for about 1 minute until the butter begins to turn brown.

Immediately remove from the heat or it will burn. Stir in the Parmesan and a little salt and pepper. Either use immediately or cool and store in the fridge until required. Use to toss with hot pasta or dot on grilled (broiled) fish.

Tarragon and Garlic Butter

SERVES 4

100 g/4 oz/¹/₂ cup butter, softened
30 ml/2 tbsp chopped tarragon
1 garlic clove, crushed
Freshly ground black pepper

Mash the butter, tarragon, garlic and a good grinding of pepper. Shape into a roll on a sheet of greaseproof (waxed) paper or clingfilm (plastic wrap). Roll up and chill. Use to toss with hot pasta or sliced to garnish grilled (broiled) fish or meat.

HOT DESSERTS

For many people the crowning glory of the meal is the dessert. And after a simple main course, there is nothing nicer than a steaming, rich pudding which smells sensational and tastes superb.

Caramel Apples

SERVES 4

50 g/2 oz/¹/₄ cup butter
4 eating (dessert) apples, sliced
50 g/2 oz/¹/₄ cup light brown sugar
2.5 ml/¹/₂ tsp mixed (apple pie) spice
25 g/1 oz/2 tbsp sultanas (golden raisins)
25 g/1 oz/¹/₄ cup walnuts or pecans, chopped
Whipped cream or Greek-style yoghurt

Melt the butter in a frying pan (skillet). Add the apples and sprinkle with sugar. Fry (sauté), tossing occasionally, for about 3 minutes until the sugar has melted. Add the sultanas and nuts and toss gently. Serve with whipped cream or Greek-style yoghurt.

Frinklies

SERVES 4

50 g/2 oz/¹/₄ cup soft margarine
50 g/2 oz/¹/₄ cup caster (superfine) sugar
2 eggs
50 g/2 oz/¹/₂ cup plain (all-purpose) flour
150 ml/¹/₄ pt/²/₃ cup milk
Warm jam (conserve) or clear honey
Icing (confectioners') sugar

Beat the fat, sugar, eggs and flour together, then stir in the milk. (Do not worry if the mixture curdles.) Spoon into 12 sections of a greased bun tin (muffin pan). Bake in the oven at 200°C/400°F/gas mark 6 for about 15–20 minutes until set and golden. They will sink when they are taken out of the oven – but don't worry, they're supposed to! Arrange three frinklies slightly overlapping on each serving plate. Spoon a little warmed jam or clear honey over and dust with icing sugar before serving.

Drunken Pears

SERVES 4

15 ml/1 tbsp light brown sugar
5 ml/1 tsp lemon juice
300 ml/¹/₂ pt/1¹/₄ cups red wine
4 pears, peeled

Dissolve the sugar and lemon juice in the wine over a gentle heat. Cut a slice off the bottom of the pears so that they stand upright and remove the core from the base. Stand them in a dish and pour over the wine. Cover with foil or a lid. Bake in the oven at 160°C/325°F/gas mark 3 for 30 minutes. Serve hot, or cool then chill.

Jalousie

SERVES 6–8

225 g/8 oz puff pastry (paste),
thawed if frozen
Black cherry jam (conserve)
Milk to glaze
Icing (confectioners') sugar, sifted
Whipped cream

Cut the pastry in half and roll out one half to a rectangle about 20 × 25 cm/ 8 × 10 in. Transfer to a dampened baking sheet. Roll out the other half to the same size. Dust with a little flour, then fold in half, lengthways. Make a series of cuts along the folded edge to within 2.5 cm/1 in of the open edge (like the paper lanterns you made as a child). Spread the uncut rectangle generously with jam, leaving a 2.5 cm/1 in border all round. Brush the edges with water, then carefully unfold the cut rectangle and lay over the top, pressing the edges well together to seal. Bake in the oven at 220°C/425°F/gas mark 7 for about 15 minutes until golden and puffy. Dust with icing sugar and serve warm with whipped cream.

Pear and Ginger Strudels

SERVES 4

2 ripe pears, chopped
2 pieces stem ginger in syrup,
chopped
4 filo pastry (paste) sheets
20 g/³/₄ oz/1¹/₂ tbsp butter, melted

Mix the pears and ginger together. Brush the filo sheets with a little butter, fold in half and brush lightly with a little more butter. Divide the mixture between the sheets of pastry, putting it in the middle of one edge. Fold the pastry either side over the filling, then roll up.

Brush with any remaining butter. Transfer to a lightly buttered baking sheet and bake in the oven at 190°C/375°F/gas mark 5 for 10–15 minutes until golden. Serve warm with a little syrup from the ginger jar spooned over.

Apple Strudels

SERVES 4

Prepare as for Pear and Ginger Strudels but substitute 1 cooking (tart) apple for the pears. Omit the ginger and add 40 g/1¹/₂ oz/3 tbsp granulated sugar, 25 g/1 oz/2 tbsp sultanas (golden raisins) and 5 ml/1 tsp ground cinnamon.

Fruit Parcels

MAKES ABOUT 8

8 filo pastry (paste) sheets (approx)
75 g/3 oz/¹/₃ cup butter, melted
410 g/14¹/₂ oz/1 large can peach or
pear halves, drained, reserving
the juice
450 g/1 lb jar mincemeat

For each parcel, brush a filo sheet pastry with a little butter. Fold in half and brush again. Place a peach or pear half in the centre of each pastry sheet and top with a spoonful of mincemeat. Draw the pastry up over the filling and pinch together to form a parcel. Transfer to a buttered baking sheet and brush the pastry with a little more melted butter. Prepare the remaining parcels the same way. Bake in the oven at 200°C/400°F/gas mark 6 for about 15 minutes until golden brown. Serve hot or cold with a little of the reserved juice.

Photograph opposite: **Plum and almond clafoutie (page 263)**

Blackberry and Apple Crumble

SERVES 4

450 g/1 lb cooking (tart) apples,
peeled and chopped
15 ml/1 tbsp granulated sugar
45 ml/3 tbsp water
175 g/6 oz/1¹/₂ cups blackberries
100 g/4 oz/1 cup plain (all-purpose)
flour
Pinch of salt
50 g/2 oz/¹/₄ cup margarine
50 g/2 oz/¹/₄ cup light brown sugar
2.5 ml/¹/₂ tsp ground cinnamon

Put the apples into a saucepan with the sugar and water. Heat gently, stirring occasionally, until the apples are pulpy. Remove from the heat and stir in the blackberries. Pour into an ovenproof dish. Mix the flour and salt, then rub in the margarine until the mixture looks like crumbs. Stir in the sugar and cinnamon. Sprinkle over the fruit. Bake in the oven at 190°C/375°F/gas mark 5 for 20 minutes or until the top is golden brown. Serve with custard.

Pear and Chocolate Rolls

SERVES 6

410 g/14¹/₂ oz/1 large can pears,
drained, reserving the juice
50 g/2 oz/¹/₂ cup chocolate chips
6 filo pastry (paste) sheets
Butter, melted
15 ml/1 tbsp cocoa (unsweetened
chocolate) powder
15 ml/1 tbsp cornflour (cornstarch)
Sugar to taste

Chop the pears and mix with the chocolate chips. Lay a filo sheet on a board. Brush with a little melted butter. Fold in half and brush lightly again. Spoon a sixth of the pear mixture along the centre of one long edge. Fold in the side edges, then roll up. Place on a buttered baking sheet. Brush lightly with butter again. Repeat with the remaining pastry and filling. Bake in the oven at 200°C/400°F/gas mark 6 for about 15 minutes or until golden. Meanwhile, make the sauce. Make the reserved pear juice up to 300 ml/¹/₂ pt/1¹/₄ cups with water. Blend a little with the cocoa and cornflour in a saucepan. Stir in the remainder. Bring to the boil and cook for 2 minutes until thickened. Sweeten to taste with sugar. Serve the rolls hot with a little of the chocolate sauce spooned over.

Toffee Plum Charlotte

SERVES 4

50 g/2 oz/¹/₄ cup butter
225 g/8 oz/1 cup light brown sugar
15 ml/1 tbsp lemon juice
4 thick slices bread, crusts
removed, cubed
450 g/1 lb ripe plums, quartered
and stoned (pitted)
Thick cream

Melt the butter in a large heavy-based frying pan (skillet). Add the sugar and stir over a gentle heat until the sugar has dissolved. Add the lemon juice. Gently fold the bread through the toffee mixture until completely coated. Add the plums, cover and cook for about 5 minutes until the fruit is soft. Serve hot or chilled with thick cream.

Photograph opposite: **Ginger rhubarb crisp (page 275)**

Rice Pudding

SERVES 4

100 g/4 oz/¹/₂ cup short-grain rice
1.2 litres/2 pts/5 cups milk
50 g/2 oz/¹/₄ cup sugar
Pinch of grated nutmeg
15 g/¹/₂ oz/1 tbsp butter or margarine

Put the rice and half the milk into a saucepan. Bring to the boil, then simmer for 20–25 minutes until the milk is nearly all absorbed. Add all the remaining ingredients except the margarine, then pour into a greased ovenproof dish. Dot with margarine. Bake in a preheated oven at 150°C/300°F/gas mark 2 for about 1¹/₂ hours. Serve hot or cold.

Chocolate Rice Pudding

SERVES 4

Prepare as for Rice Pudding but add 25 g/1 oz/¹/₄ cup cocoa (unsweetened chocolate) powder to the milk.

Fruity Rice Pudding

SERVES 4

Prepare as for Rice Pudding but add 75 g/3 oz/¹/₂ cup mixed dried fruit and 2.5 ml/¹/₂ tsp mixed (apple pie) spice with the rice.

Apple Muesli

SERVES 4

2 cooking (tart) apples, peeled and
*   chopped*
225 g/8 oz/2 cups blackberries
15 ml/1 tbsp lemon juice
15 ml/1 tbsp light brown sugar
*   (optional)*
150 g/5 oz/1¹/₄ cups muesli
Crème fraîche

Simmer the fruit in the lemon juice and a little water until soft. Add the sugar, if using; if you prefer a sharper taste, leave it out. Place in a flameproof dish and cover with the muesli. Sprinkle a little sugar on top, if liked. Place under a low grill (broiler) for 10 minutes until the muesli is golden. Serve with crème fraîche.

Strawberry Baked Apples

SERVES 4

4 cooking (tart) apples
Strawberry jam (conserve)
Light brown sugar
Water

Remove the cores from the apples and cut a line around the centre of the apples to prevent the skin splitting. Stand them in an ovenproof dish. Fill the holes with jam and sprinkle with a little sugar. Add about 2.5 cm/1 in of water to the bottom of the dish. Bake in the oven at 180°C/350°F/gas mark 4 for about 1 hour or until tender but still holding their shape. Serve hot with custard.

258

Fruit and Nut Baked Apples

SERVES 4

Prepare as for Strawberry Baked Apples but omit the jam and fill the centres with chopped nuts and sultanas (golden raisins). Spoon a little golden (light corn) syrup over instead of sugar.

Chocolate Bananas

SERVES 4

4 bananas, unpeeled
4 chocolate squares

Make a slit in the skin along each banana. Poke a chunk of chocolate into the hole and close the skin around it. Bake in the oven at 200°C/400°F/gas mark 6 for 10 minutes until the chocolate has just started to melt.

Pineapple Fritters

SERVES 4

225 g/8 oz/2 cups plain (all-purpose)
* flour*
5 ml/1 tsp baking powder
Pinch of salt
300 ml/¹/₂ pt/1¹/₄ cups water or milk
16 pineapple rings
A little plain (all-purpose) flour
Oil for deep-frying
Maple or golden (light corn) syrup
Ice cream

Put the flour, baking powder and salt into a bowl and make a well in the centre. Gradually pour in the liquid, whisking to make a smooth, thick batter. Dip the pineapple rings in flour, then in the batter. Deep-fry the rings in hot oil until crispy and golden. Serve hot with maple or golden syrup and ice cream.

Apple Fritters

SERVES 4

Prepare as for Pineapple Fritters but substitute 4 eating (dessert) apples, peeled, cored and thickly sliced, for the pineapple.

Pear Fritters

SERVES 4

Prepare as for Pineapple Fritters but use 4 just-ripe pears, peeled, cored and quartered, instead of the pineapple.

Honey Bread Pudding

SERVES 4

8 slices bread, crusts removed
25 g/1 oz/2 tbsp butter or margarine
45 ml/3 tbsp honey
3 eggs
450 ml/³/₄ pt/2 cups milk
15 ml/1 tbsp caster (superfine)
* sugar*

Spread the bread the with butter or margarine and honey, cut into halves and layer in an ovenproof dish. Mix together the eggs, milk and sugar and pour over the bread. Leave to soak for 30 minutes, if possible. Bake in the oven at 180°C/350°F/gas mark 4 for about 40 minutes until firm. Serve cut into pieces.

Fruit and Spice Bread Pudding

SERVES 4

Prepare as for Honey Bread Pudding but substitute 25 g/1 oz/2 tbsp granulated sugar for the honey and add 75 g/3 oz/¹/₂ cup mixed dried fruit in layers with the bread. Use the caster sugar to sprinkle on top of the cooked pudding.

Grilled Grapefruit

2 grapefruit, halved
60 ml/4 tbsp light brown sugar
Vanilla ice cream

Cut round the edge of each grapefruit half between the flesh and pith. Separate each segment from the membrane on either side with a serrated knife. Sprinkle each half with sugar. Place under a hot grill (broiler) for 3 minutes until the sugar has gone sticky. Put a scoop of ice cream on top of each and serve straight away.

No-effort Crumble

SERVES 3 OR 4

410 g/14¹/₂ oz/1 large can fruit,
drained reserving juice
2 Weetabix
15 ml/1 tbsp light brown sugar
50 g/2 oz/¹/₄ cup butter or
margarine, melted
2.5 ml/¹/₂ tsp ground ginger,
cinnamon or mixed (apple pie)
spice
Cream or custard

Put the fruit in a 1 litre/1³/₄ pt/4¹/₄ cup ovenproof dish. Crumble the cereal and mix with the sugar, butter or margarine and spice. Sprinkle over the fruit, pressing down lightly. Bake in the oven at 190°C/375°F/gas mark 5 for about 15 minutes until crisp. Serve warm with cream or custard.

Peach and Raisin Crisp

SERVES 6

2 × 410 g/2 × 14¹/₂ oz/2 large cans
peach slices, drained, reserving
juice
75 g/3 oz/¹/₂ cup raisins
25 g/1 oz/2 tbsp margarine
50 g/2 oz/¹/₂ cup plain (all-purpose)
flour
25 g/1 oz/2 tbsp caster (superfine)
sugar
100 g/4 oz/1 cup Original Oat
Crunch cereal
Custard

Put the fruit in the base of a 1.2 litre/2 pt/5 cup ovenproof dish. Sprinkle the raisins over. Rub the fat into the flour until the mixture resembles breadcrumbs. Stir in the sugar and Original Oat Crunch. Spoon the crumble over the fruit and press down lightly. Bake in the oven at 190°C/375°F/gas mark 5 for about 35 minutes until golden and crisp. Serve hot with custard and the reserved juice.

Raspberry Baked Alaska

SERVES 4

1 Swiss (jelly) roll
3 egg whites
175 g/6 oz/³/₄ cup caster (superfine)
sugar
8 scoops raspberry ripple ice cream
6 glacé (candied) cherries
6 angelica 'leaves'

Slice the Swiss roll and arrange in a single layer on an ovenproof plate. Whisk the egg whites until stiff. Whisk in half the sugar and continue whisking until stiff and glossy. Fold in the remaining sugar with a metal spoon. Just before serving, pile the ice cream in a mound on top of the Swiss roll. Cover completely with the meringue. Decorate with the cherries and angelica and bake in the oven at 230°C/450°F/gas mark 8 for 2 minutes until the meringue is just turning golden. Serve immediately.

Rhubarb and Custard Charlotte

SERVES 4 OR 5

25 g/1 oz/2 tbsp butter, melted
4 slices bread, buttered
1 individual carton custard
550 g/1¼ lb/1 very large can rhubarb, drained, reserving the juice
30 ml/2 tbsp light brown sugar

Grease a 1.2 litre/2 pt/5 cup ovenproof dish with half the butter. Line the dish with 2½ slices of the bread. Spread the custard in the base, then top with the fruit. Dice the remaining bread, toss in the remaining butter and the sugar and spoon over. Bake in the oven at 200°C/400°F/gas mark 6 for about 40 minutes until golden. Serve with the reserved juice.

Pineapple Floating Islands

SERVES 4

50 g/2 oz/¼ cup butter
100 g/4 oz/½ cup caster (superfine) sugar
25 g/1 oz/¼ cup cornflour (cornstarch)
300 ml/½ pt/1¼ cups milk
150 ml/¼ pt/⅔ cup single (light) cream
440 g/15½ oz/1 large can crushed pineapple, drained, reserving the juice
4 size 1 eggs, separated

Beat the butter and 50 g/2 oz/¼ cup of the sugar until light and fluffy and blend in the cornflour. Warm the milk and cream but do not boil. Pour into the butter mixture. Return to the pan and cook, stirring, until thickened. Put the pineapple in the base of a 1.5 litre/2½ pt/6 cup ovenproof dish. Pour the custard over. Whisk the egg whites until stiff, add 40 g/1½ oz/3 tbsp of the sugar and whisk again until glossy. Put 4 spoonfuls of meringue on top of the custard to make the 'islands' and sprinkle with the remaining sugar. Bake in the oven at 150°C/300°F/gas mark 2 for 30 minutes or until the meringues are lightly golden. Serve hot or cold with the reserved pineapple juice.

Pineapple Upside-down Pudding

SERVES 6

15 g/½ oz/1 tbsp butter
30 ml/2 tbsp light brown sugar
225 g/8 oz/1 small can pineapple slices, drained, reserving the juice
Glacé (candied) cherries, halved
Angelica 'leaves'
1 packet sponge cake mix
Egg and water, according to packet directions

Liberally butter a 20 cm/8 in round sandwich tin (pan) or other ovenproof dish. Sprinkle the sugar over the base, then top with the pineapple rings. Place a halved glacé cherry, cut side up, in the centre of each ring and in the gaps around. Decorate with angelica leaves in the gaps. Make up the sponge mixture according to the packet directions. Spoon over the fruit. Bake in the oven at 190°C/375°F/gas mark 5 for 20 minutes until risen and the centre springs back when pressed. Leave to cool slightly in the tin, then loosen the edges and turn out on to a serving plate. Serve with the juice.

No-fuss Bakewell-type Tart

SERVES 6

175 g/6 oz shortcrust pastry (basic
*   pie crust)*
30–45 ml/2–3 tbsp raspberry jam
*   (conserve)*
1 packet sponge cake mix
Egg and water, according to packet
*   directions*
Almond essence (extract)
Flaked almonds

Roll out the pastry and use to line a 20 cm/8 in flan dish (pie pan) set on a baking sheet. Spread the jam over the base. Make up the sponge according to the packet directions. Add a few drops of almond essence. Spread over the jam. Scatter with almonds. Bake for 20–30 minutes at 190ºF/375ºF/gas mark 5 until the pastry is cooked and the sponge springs back when pressed. Serve warm or cold.

Raspberry Brulée

SERVES 4

225 g/8 oz/2 cups raspberries
150 ml/¹/₄ pt/²/₃ cup double (heavy)
*   cream*
150 ml/¹/₄ pt/²/₃ cup thick plain
*   yoghurt*
Light brown sugar

Arrange the raspberries in a shallow flameproof dish. Whip the cream and yoghurt together until softly peaking. Spread over the fruit. Sprinkle liberally with sugar so it covers the top completely. Place under a very hot grill (broiler) until the sugar melts. Serve straight away.

Strawberry Brulée

SERVES 4

Prepare as for Raspberry Brulée but use sliced strawberries instead of raspberries.

Peach or Nectarine Brulée

SERVES 4

Prepare as for Raspberry Brulée but use 3 or 4 ripe peaches or nectarines, peeled, stoned (pitted) and sliced, instead of raspberries.

Surprise Cherry Pancakes

SERVES 4

1 packet batter mix or 1 quantity
*   Basic Pancake Mix (see page 267)*
200 g/7 oz/scant 1 cup low-fat soft
*   c   h   e   e   s   e*
425 g/15 oz/1 large can cherry pie
*   filling*
30 ml/2 tbsp water
15 ml/1 tbsp lemon juice
45 ml/3 tbsp cherry brandy or kirsch

Make up the batter into 8 pancakes as directed. Spread each with a little of the cream cheese and fold into quarters. Heat the pie filling, water and lemon juice in a large frying pan (skillet). When bubbling, add the pancakes one at a time, bathing each in sauce and pushing it to one side before adding the next. Pour over the cherry brandy or kirsch. Set alight straight away and shake the pan until the flames subside. Serve immediately.

Pear and Cinnamon Clafoutie

SERVES 4–6

410 g/14¹/₂ oz/1 large can pears,
  drained, reserving the juice
Butter for greasing
1 packet batter mix or 1 quantity
  Basic Pancake Mix (see page 267)
5 ml/1 tsp ground cinnamon
Icing (confectioners') sugar for
  dusting

Lay the pears in a buttered shallow ovenproof dish. Make up the batter according to the packet directions. Pour over. Sprinkle with the cinnamon. Bake in the oven at 200°C/400°F/gas mark 6 for about 30 minutes until risen and golden. Dust with sifted icing sugar before serving with the juice.

Plum and Almond Clafoutie

SERVES 4–6

Prepare as for Pear and Cinnamon Clafoutie but substitute canned red plums for the pears and sprinkle with 15 ml/1 tbsp flaked almonds instead of the cinnamon.

Melon and Grapes with Camembert

SERVES 6

1 cantaloupe melon
1 honeydew melon
¹/₂ small watermelon
225 g/8 oz/2 cups seedless (pitless)
  grapes
90 ml/6 tbsp fromage frais
1 Camembert cheese
50 g/2 oz/¹/₂ cup toasted almonds

Cut the melons into wedges, discarding the seeds and peel, and arrange on serving plates. Arrange the grapes on top. Place a spoonful of fromage frais at the side of each plate. Cut the Camembert into 6 wedges and place on a piece of foil on the grill (broiler) rack. Grill (broil) for about 45 seconds on each side until warm and slightly runny. Place on top of the fruits. Sprinkle with the flaked almonds and serve at once.

Bananas Foster

SERVES 4

40 g/1¹/₂ oz/3 tbsp butter or
  margarine, melted
45 ml/3 tbsp light brown sugar
Pinch of ground cinnamon
Pinch of grated nutmeg
4 bananas, halved lengthways
Vanilla ice cream
60 ml/4 tbsp chopped mixed nuts

Mix the fat with the sugar, cinnamon and nutmeg. Brush the mixture over the bananas. Place on a sheet of foil on the grill (broiler) rack. Grill (broil) for about 5 minutes until soft and brown. Spoon into a serving dish and top with ice cream and the nuts.

Pears with Liqueur Cream

SERVES 4

4 Pears
40 g/1¹/₂ oz/3 tbsp butter or
**   margarine, melted**
100 g/4 oz/¹/₂ cup light brown sugar
225 g/8 oz/1 cup fromage frais
250 ml/8 fl oz/1 cup double
(heavy) or whipping cream,
**   whipped**
250 ml/8 fl oz/1 cup plain yoghurt
90 ml/6 tbsp coffee liqueur
Pinch of grated nutmeg

Peel and core the pears and slice thickly or cut into wedges. Mix the melted butter or margarine and 30 ml/2 tbsp of the sugar and brush over the pears. Arrange on a piece of foil on a grill (broiler) rack. Grill (broil) for about 5 minutes until golden and hot through. Blend together the fromage frais, cream, remaining sugar, yoghurt, liqueur and nutmeg. Place the pears on serving plates and top with the liqueur cream.

Orange Chestnut Kebabs

SERVES 4

225 g/8 oz/1 cup drained canned
**   chestnuts**
50 g/2 oz/4 tbsp butter or margarine,
**   melted**
10 ml/2 tsp grated orange rind
15 ml/1 tbsp light brown sugar
150 ml/¹/₄ pt/²/₃ cup double (heavy)
**   or whipping cream, whipped**

Thread the chestnuts on to soaked wooden skewers. Mix the butter with the orange rind and brush over the chestnuts. Grill (broil) for about 5 minutes, turning frequently and brushing with the flavoured butter. Sprinkle with sugar and serve with whipped cream.

Gingered Melon

SERVES 4

1 honeydew melon
15 ml/1 tbsp finely chopped
**   crystallised ginger**
30 ml/2 tbsp finely chopped fresh
**   root ginger**
120 ml/4 fl oz/¹/₂ cup dry white wine
5 ml/1 tsp ground cinnamon
Pinch of sugar
Pinch of salt
Brandy snaps
Whipped cream

Peel the melon, then cut into wedges. Mix the crystallised and root ginger, wine, cinnamon, sugar and salt in a pan and bring to the boil. Add the melon wedges and simmer for 2 minutes. Drain the melon, reserving the liquid in a pan, and place on warm serving plates. Boil the liquid until syrupy and spoon over the melon. Serve with brandy snaps and whipped cream.

Almond Pear Flan

SERVES 6

225 g/8 oz shortcrust pastry (basic
pie crust)
75 g/3 oz/¹/₃ cup unsalted (sweet)
**   butter**
75 g/3 oz/¹/₃ cup caster (superfine)
**   sugar**
75 g/3 oz/³/₄ cup ground almonds
25 g/1 oz/¹/₄ cup plain (all-purpose)
**   flour**
1 egg, beaten
1 egg yolk
2 ripe pears, peeled and cut into
**   even slices**
30 ml/2 tbsp apricot jam (conserve)

Line a 25 cm/10 in flan dish (pie pan) with the pastry and leave to chill while preparing the filling. Beat together the butter and sugar until light and fluffy. Mix in the ground almonds, flour, beaten egg and egg yolk. Turn into the flan dish, level with a spatula and place the pear slices over this, pressing them down slightly. Bake in the oven at 180°C/350°F/gas mark 4 for 45–50 minutes, until the flan is golden and firm to the touch. Bring the jam to the boil with 15 ml/1 tbsp of water in a small pan, stirring with a wooden spoon. Remove from the heat and sieve, then use to glaze the flan while still warm.

Chocolate and Pear Pie

SERVES 8

---

750 g/1¹/₂ lb puff pastry (paste)
75 g/3 oz/¹/₃ cup unsalted (sweet)
  butter
75 g/3 oz/¹/₃ cup caster (superfine)
  sugar
1 egg
150 ml/¹/₄ pt/²/₃ cup soured (dairy
  sour) cream
100 g/4 oz/1 cup self-raising (self-
  rising) flour
2.5 ml/¹/₂ tsp ground ginger
15 ml/1 tbsp cocoa (unsweetened
  chocolate) powder
25 g/1 oz/¹/₄ cup ground almonds
425 g/15 oz/1 large can pear halves,
  drained, reserving the juice
Milk or cream, to glaze
Caster (superfine) sugar, for
  sprinkling

Cut the pastry in 2 pieces and roll each out to form a circle, one measuring 20 cm/8 in in diameter, the other 23 cm/ 9 in. Place the smaller circle on a greased baking sheet. Beat together the butter and sugar until pale and fluffy, then beat in the egg and stir in the cream, flour, ginger, cocoa and almonds. Spread this mixture on to the pastry, leaving a small border all round the edge. Top with the pears. Brush the border of the pastry with a little milk or cream. Place the larger pastry circle on top and press the pastry edges together to seal. Knock up with the back of a knife. Mark the top with a sharp knife to decorate and brush all over with milk or cream. Sprinkle with sugar and bake in the oven at 200°C/400°F/gas mark 6 for 40–45 minutes. Serve warm.

Meringue Peaches

SERVES 4

---

4 canned peach halves
1 trifle sponge square
30 ml/2 tbsp orange liqueur
1 egg white
50 g/2 oz/¹/₄ cup caster (superfine)
  sugar
25 g/1 oz/¹/₄ cup flaked almonds
Icing (confectioners') sugar for
  dusting

Dry the peaches on kitchen paper and place hollow-side up on a greased baking sheet. Cut the trifle sponge into quarters and place a piece in each hollow. Drizzle the liqueur over. Whisk the egg white until stiff, then gradually whisk in the sugar. Using a teaspoon, top the peaches with the meringue and sprinkle with the almonds. Bake in the oven at 200°C/400°F/gas mark 6 until the meringue is pale golden brown. Lightly dust with icing sugar and serve at once.

Caramelised Pear Pizza

225 g/8 oz puff pastry (paste)
15 ml/1 tbsp butter, softened
200 g/7 oz/scant 1 cup caster
(superfine) sugar
3 ripe pears, peeled, cored and
sliced
30 ml/2 tbsp Mascarpone cheese
Single (light) cream or vanilla ice
cream

Roll out the pastry to form a 25 cm/ 10 in circle, place on a dampened baking sheet and bake in the oven at 190°C/375°F/gas mark 5 for about 6 minutes until lightly golden. Remove from the oven and set aside while making the topping. Melt the butter in a frying pan (skillet), then add the sugar, stirring. When this mixture starts to turn golden, add the pear slices and keep tossing them over a high heat until they are caramelised. Add a little water if they start to stick (be careful of any spluttering). Arrange the pears over the pastry and dot with the Mascarpone cheese. Bake in the oven at the same temperature as before for about 15 minutes, until the pastry is well risen and the pears are golden brown. Serve warm with a jug of cream or vanilla ice cream.

Caramelised Cinnamon Apple Pizza

Prepare as for Caramelised Pear Pizza but substitute eating (dessert) apples for the pears and sprinkle with 5 ml/1 tsp ground cinnamon after dotting with the cheese.

Valentine Apples

450 g/1 lb puff pastry (paste)
Beaten egg, to glaze
Icing (confectioners') sugar
175 g/6 oz white marzipan
2 crisp green eating (dessert) apples
25 g/1 oz/2 tbsp butter, melted
45 ml/3 tbsp caster (superfine)
sugar
Pouring cream

Make 2 heart-shaped templates, one measuring 10 cm/4 in at its widest point and the other 2 cm/1 in smaller all round. Roll out the pastry and, using the larger template, cut out 6 hearts. Place on a dampened baking sheet and brush with beaten egg. Dust the work surface with icing sugar and roll out the marzipan. Using the smaller template, cut out 6 hearts and place these on top of the pastry hearts. Peel, core and slice the apples and arrange 3 or 4 slices on each heart in a fan shape. Brush with melted butter and sprinkle over the caster sugar. Bake in the oven at 220°C/425°F/gas mark 7 for 15 minutes until the pastry is golden and the apples are caramelised. Serve warm with cream.

Crêpes Suzette

SERVES 4

*1 packet batter mix or 1 quantity
   Basic Pancake Mix (see page 267)*
25 g/1 oz/2 tbsp butter
45 ml/3 tbsp light brown sugar
60 ml/4 tbsp orange juice
15 ml/1 tbsp lemon juice
*45 ml/3 tbsp orange liqueur or
   brandy*

Make up the batter into 8 pancakes as directed. Melt the butter in a large frying pan (skillet). Add the sugar and stir over a gentle heat until it dissolves. Add the fruit juices. Stir well to dissolve the caramel (about 3–4 minutes). Fold the pancakes into quarters. Place one in the pan, spoon over the juices, then push to one side. Continue until all the pancakes are in the pan and bathed in juices. Pour over the liqueur or brandy, set alight straight away, and shake the pan until the flames subside. Serve immediately.

Bananas with Brandy Caramel

SERVES 6

5 cm/2 in piece of cinnamon stick
15 ml/1 tbsp juice of orange
15 ml/1 tbsp light brown sugar
6 bananas
30 ml/2 tbsp orange liqueur
4 Mars Bars
30 ml/2 tbsp brandy

Put the cinnamon, orange juice and sugar in a pan over a low heat so the sugar dissolves. Thickly slice the bananas diagonally and add to the pan. Cook for 5 minutes, adding the liqueur half-way through cooking. Discard the cinnamon. Chop the Mars Bars finely, put into another pan and melt on a very low heat, adding enough water to keep runny. Add the brandy, stir until blended and serve over the bananas.

Basic Pancake Mix

MAKES 8

*100 g/4 oz/1 cup plain (all-purpose)
   flour*
Pinch of salt
300 ml/¹/₂ pt/1¹/₄ cups milk
1 egg, beaten
15 g/¹/₂ oz/1 tbsp butter, melted
Oil or extra butter for frying

Whisk the flour, salt, milk and egg to a smooth batter. Add the melted butter to the mixture. Melt a knob of butter or a little oil in a frying pan (skillet). Pour in just enough mixture to cover the bottom of the pan and cook until just brown underneath. Toss or turn over and cook the other side. Repeat to make 8 pancakes. Serve as a sweet with sugar and lemon juice, or as a savoury course (see individual recipes).

Caribbean Bananas

1 orange
45 ml/3 tbsp cocoa (unsweetened
  chocolate) powder
45 ml/3 tbsp light brown sugar
Pinch of ground cinnamon
45 ml/3 tbsp rum or orange liqueur
4 bananas
Whipped cream or fromage frais

Cut 4 slices from the orange for decoration. Grate the rind and squeeze the juice from the remainder into a frying pan (skillet). Add the cocoa powder, sugar and cinnamon and heat gently until the sugar melts. Add the rum or orange liqueur. Peel the bananas and cut into chunky pieces. Add to the pan. Spoon over the sauce, cover with foil or a lid and cook gently for 4 minutes or until the bananas are just cooked but still hold their shape. Spoon into serving dishes, decorate with orange slices and serve hot or cold with whipped cream or fromage frais.

Bananas with Hot Lemon Butter Sauce

50 g/2 oz/¹/₄ cup butter
75 g/3 oz/¹/₃ cup light brown sugar
30 ml/2 tbsp lemon juice
300 ml/¹/₂ pt/1¹/₄ cups Greek-style
  plain yoghurt
4 bananas
Toasted flaked almonds

Put the butter, sugar and lemon juice in a small pan. Heat gently, stirring, until the sugar has dissolved. Simmer for one minute. Divide the yoghurt between 4 sundae glasses. Top with sliced banana. Spoon the sauce over and decorate with toasted almonds. Serve straight away.

The Best Custard Tart

175 g/6 oz shortcrust pastry (basic
  pie crust)
2 eggs
150 ml/¹/₄ pt/²/₃ cup milk
425 g/15 oz/1 large can custard
25 g/1 oz/2 tbsp caster (superfine)
  sugar
Grated nutmeg

Roll out the pastry and use to line a 20 cm/8 in flan dish (pie pan) set on a baking sheet. Beat the eggs with the milk, then stir in the remaining ingredients except the nutmeg. Pour into the flan case (pie shell). Sprinkle a little nutmeg over, then bake in the oven at 190°C/375°F/gas mark 5 for about 40 minutes until set. Serve warm or cold.

Zabaglione

2 eggs
25 g/1 oz/2 tbsp caster (superfine)
  sugar
45 ml/3 tbsp Marsala or sweet sherry
Sponge fingers

Put the eggs, sugar and Marsala or sherry in a deep bowl over a pan of hot water. Whisk until thick and creamy – a hand-held electric mixer is easiest, but a balloon whisk will give a larger volume. Pour the Zabaglione into glasses and serve straight away with sponge fingers.

COLD DESSERTS

Cold desserts tend to fall into two categories. Either they can be made well in advance, then forgotten about until you are ready to serve them, or they can be thrown together at the very last minute. Whatever the recipe, if you want to decorate with piped whipped cream, you can 'cheat' and use one of the aerosol cans of cream to pipe whirls or stars. But only squirt it on at the last moment as it will gradually lose its fluffiness.

Blackberry and Apple Layer

SERVES 4–6

450 g/1 lb cooking (tart) apples, sliced
100 g/4 oz/1 cup blackberries
Sugar
4 trifle sponge cakes
30 ml/2 tbsp cider or apple juice
150 ml/¹/₄ pt/²/₃ cup whipping cream
300 ml/¹/₂ pt/1¹/₄ cups vanilla-flavoured thick yoghurt

Put the apples in a pan. Choose a few blackberries for decoration, then add the remainder to the pan with 15 ml/1 tbsp water. Cover and cook gently for about 5 minutes until just soft and the juice has run. Sweeten to taste. Crumble the trifle sponges into a glass serving bowl. Add the fruit, drizzle cider or apple juice over. Leave to cool. Whip the cream and fold in the yoghurt. Spread over the fruit and decorate with reserved blackberries, if liked.

Chocolate-dipped Delights

SERVES 4

175 g/6 oz/1¹/₂ cups plain (semi-sweet) chocolate
4 ripe nectarines or peaches, sliced
150 ml/¹/₄ pt/²/₃ cup sweetened whipped cream or crème fraîche
A little grated chocolate (optional)

Melt the chocolate in a bowl over a pan of hot water or in the microwave. Dip the fruit in the chocolate to come half-way up each slice. Arrange on serving plates in a starburst pattern and put a spoonful of sweetened whipped cream or crème fraîche in the middle. Top this with a little grated chocolate, if liked.

Fool-proof Chocolate Mousse

SERVES 6

4 eggs, separated
200 g/7 oz/1³/₄ cups plain (semi-
sweet) chocolate
75 ml/5 tbsp strong hot coffee
2.5 ml/¹/₂ tsp vanilla essence
(extract)
A little whipped cream and drinking
(sweetened) chocolate powder

Whisk the egg whites until stiff. Break the chocolate up and put into a food processor or blender. Run the machine until completely crushed. Add the hot coffee and blend until smooth. Add the yolks and vanilla essence and blend for about 1 minute. Pour the chocolate mixture slowly over the whites and fold in lightly but thoroughly. Spoon into individual dishes or a large serving dish and chill for about 1 hour. Top with whipped cream and a sprinkling of drinking chocolate powder.

Boozy Chocolate Mousse

SERVES 6

200 g/7 oz/1³/₄ cups plain (semi-
sweet) chocolate
3 eggs, separated
15 ml/1 tbsp brandy
150 ml/¹/₄ pt/²/₃ cup whipping cream
Coursely grated chocolate

Melt the chocolate over a pan of hot water or in the microwave. Beat in the egg yolks and brandy. Whisk the egg whites first and then the cream in separate bowls until peaking (this means you do not have to wash the beaters in between). Fold the cream, then the egg whites, into the mixture. Turn into a serving dish, sprinkle with grated chocolate and chill until ready to serve.

Coffee Cream Cheese Italienne

SERVES 6

15 ml/1 tbsp instant coffee powder
15 ml/1 tbsp water
225 g/8 oz/1 cup cream cheese
100 g/4 oz/¹/₂ cup icing
(confectioners') sugar, sifted
A few chopped walnuts
Thin ginger biscuits (cookies)

Blend the coffee and water together until dissolved. Gradually beat into the cream cheese with the icing sugar. Turn into a small glass dish, sprinkle with walnuts and chill before serving with thin ginger biscuits.

Fresh Fruit Platter with Raspberry Sauce

SERVES 6

225 g/8 oz/2 cups raspberries
thawed, if frozen
25 g/1 oz/2 tbsp icing
(confectioners') sugar
15 ml/1 tbsp lemon juice
A selection of sliced fresh fruits, e.g.
star fruit, mango, pawpaw,
strawberries, kiwifruit
Ratafias

Purée the raspberries with the sugar and lemon juice in a blender or processor, then pass through a sieve to remove the seeds. Spoon a little of the sauce on to each of 6 serving plates. Arrange slices of fruit attractively around. Serve with ratafias.

Greek Yoghurt Surprise

SERVES 4

100 g/4 oz/²/₃ cup dried no-need-to-
soak apricots, chopped
30 ml/2 tbsp brandy
450 ml/³/₄ pt/2 cups Greek-style
plain yoghurt
Clear honey

Mix the apricots and brandy together and place in 4 glass dishes. Spoon on the yoghurt, then top with a layer of clear honey.

Lemon Dream

SERVES 6

1 egg white
75 g/3 oz/¹/₃ cup caster (superfine)
sugar
150 ml/¹/₄ pt/²/₃ cup double (heavy)
cream
Grated rind and juice of 1 lemon
300 ml/¹/₂ pt/1¹/₄ cups thick plain
yoghurt
Crystallised (candied) violets or
lemon slices
Angelica 'leaves'

Whisk the egg white until stiff, then whisk in half the sugar. Whip the cream, lemon rind and juice and the remaining sugar until softly peaking. Gently whisk or fold in the yoghurt. Finally fold in the egg white with a metal spoon. Spoon into 6 wine goblets and chill, if liked. Just before serving, top each with a crystallised violet or lemon slice and an angelica 'leaf'.

Mango Fool

SERVES 4

1 mango
45 ml/3 tbsp lemon juice
15 ml/1 tbsp caster (superfine)
sugar
425 g/15 oz/1 large can custard
150 ml/¹/₄ pt/²/₃ cup whipped cream
Angelica 'leaves'

Peel and cut all the flesh off the mango stone (pit). Purée in a blender or processor with the lemon juice and sugar. Fold in the custard and half the cream. Spoon into 4 wine goblets. Decorate each with a swirl of remaining whipped cream and an angelica leaf. Eat within 2 hours.

Melon Glacé

SERVES 4

2 small ogen, cantaloupe, galia or
charentais melons
4 scoops vanilla ice cream
30 ml/2 tbsp ginger wine

Cut the melons into halves, scoop out and discard the seeds (pits). Place in 4 individual serving dishes. Add a scoop of ice cream to the cavity in the centre of each and spoon ginger wine over. Serve straight away.

Minted Melon and Raspberries

SERVES 6

1 honeydew melon
225 g/8 oz/2 cups raspberries
12 mint leaves
50 g/2 oz/¹/₄ cup granulated sugar
Mint sprig

C ut the melon in half, remove the seeds, then scoop out the flesh with a melon baller. Alternatively, peel the melon and dice the flesh. Mix with the raspberries in a glass serving dish. Put the mint leaves on a board with the sugar and chop finely. Sprinkle over the fruit and chill until ready to serve, decorated with a mint sprig.

Orange Raffles

SERVES 6

6 oranges
3 trifle sponges
30 ml/2 tbsp sherry
250 ml/8 fl oz/1 cup double (heavy)
*   or whipping cream*
Few drops of vanilla essence
*   (extract)*
30 ml/2 tbsp caster (superfine)
*   sugar*
Toasted flaked almonds

C ut off and discard the rounded ends of the oranges (they will stand up better on the stalk end) and scoop out the flesh with a serrated knife. Chop fairly finely and place in a bowl with any juice. Crumble in the trifle sponges and add the sherry. Mix well and spoon back into the orange shells. Whip the cream with the sugar and vanilla until softly peaking. Pipe or swirl on top of each orange. Sprinkle with nuts and chill until ready to serve.

Pink Grapefruit Cheesecake

SERVES 6

200 g/7 oz/1³/₄ cups chocolate
*   digestive biscuits (Graham*
*   crackers), crushed*
50 g/2 oz/¹/₄ cup butter, melted
500 g/1 lb 2 oz/2¹/₄ cups curd
*   (smooth cottage) cheese*
40 g/1¹/₂ oz/3 tbsp icing
*   (confectioners') sugar, sifted*
Grated rind and juice of 1 pink
*   grapefruit*
15 ml/1 tbsp lemon juice
50 g/2 oz/¹/₂ cup ground almonds
A little grated chocolate

M ix the biscuits and butter and press into a lightly buttered 18–20 cm/7–8 in flan dish (pie pan). Beat the cheese, sugar, grapefruit rind and juice, lemon juice and almonds together. Spoon over the biscuit base. Top with a little grated chocolate and chill until firm.

Sparkling Nectarines

SERVES 4

4 nectarines
¹/₂ bottle sparking medium-sweet
*   wine, chilled*

H alve and slice the nectarines, discarding the stones (pits). Divide between 4 champagne cups or wine goblets. Chill. Just before serving, top up with chilled sparkling wine. Eat the fruit with a spoon, then sip the wine.

Sparkling Strawberries

SERVES 4

Prepare as for Sparkling Nectarines but use 225 g/8 oz/2 cups sliced strawberries and sparkling rosé wine.

Strawberry and Peach Romanoff

SERVES 6

225 g/8 oz strawberries, sliced
4 peaches, stoned (pitted) and sliced
15 ml/1 tbsp caster (superfine) sugar
30 ml/2 tbsp peach or orange liqueur
45 ml/3 tbsp orange juice, freshly squeezed
Whipped cream

Put the prepared fruit in a glass bowl. Sprinkle with the sugar and pour over the liqueur and orange juice. Leave to stand for 20–30 minutes before serving with whipped cream.

Banana Flan

SERVES 4

Raspberry jam (conserve)
1 × 18 cm/7 in sponge flan case (pie shell)
3 or 4 bananas, sliced
15 ml/1 tbsp lemon juice
250 ml/8 fl oz/1 cup whipping cream, whipped

Spread the jam over the flan case, then arrange the bananas on top, squashing them gently. Sprinkle with lemon juice to taste, cover with the cream and chill before serving.

Tropicana Delight

SERVES 4

1 fresh pineapple
75 g/3 oz/¹/₂ cup fresh dates, quartered and stoned (pitted)
2 small bananas, sliced
25 g/1 oz/2 tbsp light brown sugar
45 ml/3 tbsp apple juice
45 ml/3 tbsp dark rum

Cut the top off the pineapple about 4 cm/1¹/₂ in from the leaves and reserve to use as a lid. Scoop out the pineapple flesh with a serrated knife, leaving the skin intact. Chop the flesh, discarding any hard core. Put in a bowl with the dates and bananas. Toss lightly. Blend the sugar, apple juice and rum together until the sugar has dissolved. Add to the bowl and toss well. Spoon the fruit and juice back into the pineapple shell, replace the lid and chill before serving.

Strawberry Syllabub

SERVES 6

350 g/12 oz strawberries, hulled
100 g/4 oz/¹/₂ cup caster (superfine) sugar
15 ml/1 tbsp lemon juice
150 ml/¹/₄ pt/²/₃ cup dry white wine
300 ml/¹/₂ pt/1¹/₄ cups double (heavy) cream

Purée the fruit in a blender or processor. Put the remaining ingredients in a bowl and whisk until softly peaking. Fold in the strawberry purée gently with a metal spoon. Spoon into 6 wine goblets. Chill before serving.

273

Soft Fruit Cheese

SERVES 4

225 g/8 oz/2 cups soft fruit such as
strawberries or raspberries
225 g/8 oz/1 cup low-fat soft cheese
15 ml/1 tbsp sugar
5 ml/1 tsp lemon juice

Mash the berries, then stir in the remaining ingredients. Mix with a fork until fairly smooth. Chill before serving.

Quark Dessert

SERVES 4

1 packet fruit jelly (jello)
450 ml/³/₄ pt/2 cups water
100 g/4 oz/¹/₂ cup quark

Make up the jelly with the water and chill until on the point of setting. Whisk in the quark and chill until set.

Quick Trifle

SERVES 4

1 Swiss (jelly) roll, sliced
200 g/7 oz/1 small can peach slices
1 packet raspberry jelly (jello)
1 packet Peach Dessert Whip
Milk (according to packet)

Arrange the Swiss roll slices in the bottom of a dish. Drain the peaches, reserving the juice, and spoon the fruit over the Swiss roll. Make up the jelly, using the fruit juice instead of some of the water. Pour over the sponge and fruit and chill for a few hours until set. Make up the dessert whip with milk, according to the packet directions 1 hour before serving and spoon over the trifle. Chill again until ready to serve.

The Ubiquitous Trifle

SERVES 4

4 trifle sponges
300 g/11 oz/1 small can strawberries
30 ml/2 tbsp sherry
425 g/15 oz/1 large can custard
150 ml/¹/₄ pt/²/₃ cup whipping cream
Flaked almonds

Crumble the sponges into the base of a glass serving dish. Empty the contents of the can of strawberries over and crush well. Sprinkle the sherry over the top. Spoon on the custard, then spread the lightly whipped cream on the top. Sprinkle with almonds and chill until ready to serve.

Summer Pudding

SERVES 4

900 g/2 lb/4 cups soft fruit such as
raspberries, blackberries and
blackcurrants
Pinch of ground cinnamon
100–175 g/4–6 oz/¹/₂–³/₄ cup light
brown sugar
8 slices white bread, crusts removed

Stew the fruit with the cinnamon and sugar to taste until the fruit is just soft and the juices have run. Cut the bread, if necessary, to line a large pudding basin, covering the bottom and sides and reserving a slice for the top. Pour in the fruit and cover with the reserved bread. Press down lightly with a small plate and weigh down with a can. Chill overnight. It is ready to eat when the fruit juice has soaked through the bread. Turn out of the bowl and serve with custard or ice cream.

Summer Pudding All Year!

SERVES 6

5–6 slices white bread, crusts
    removed
500 g/18 oz packet frozen summer
fruits, thawed
75 g/3 oz/¹/₃ cup caster (superfine)
sugar
Yoghurt or whipped cream

Line a 900 ml/1¹/₂ pt/3³/₄ cup pudding basin with 4–5 slices of the bread. Stew the fruit with the sugar for 3 minutes. Turn into the basin. Top with the remaining bread, cutting to fit so there are no gaps. Stand the basin on a plate, cover with a saucer and weigh down. Chill overnight. Turn out and serve with yoghurt or cream.

Ginger Rhubarb Crisp

SERVES 4

225 g/8 oz rhubarb, chopped into
    small pieces
25 g/1 oz/2 tbsp light brown sugar
25 g/1 oz/¹/₄ cup plain (all-purpose)
    flour
15 ml/1 tbsp water
25 g/1 oz/2 tbsp margarine
6 ginger biscuits (cookies), crushed
Double (heavy) or clotted cream, to
    serve
Extra brown sugar for sprinkling

Cook the rhubarb in a saucepan with the sugar, flour, water and margarine for about 10 minutes until pulpy. Cool. Press the crushed biscuits into the bottom of a dish or individual serving bowls. Chill. Pour the cold rhubarb on to the biscuits and top with the cream and a little sugar. Chill well before serving.

Peach Fool

SERVES 4

410 g/14¹/₂ oz/1 large can peach
    slices, drained, reserving the juice
425 g/15 oz/1 large can custard
150 ml/¹/₄ pt/²/₃ cup plain yoghurt
Glacé (candied) cherries

Liquidise or purée the peaches in a blender or food processor. Fold in the custard until well blended. Fold in the yoghurt to give a marbled effect. Spoon into glasses. Chill. Top each with a glacé cherry and a little of the reserved juice just before serving.

Chocolate Ripple Ring

SERVES 6

45 ml/3 tbsp chocolate hazelnut
    spread
30 ml/2 tbsp coffee liqueur
1 litre/1³/₄ pts/4¹/₄ cups soft-scoop
    chocolate ice cream
Whipped cream
Grated chocolate

Blend the chocolate spread with the liqueur until smooth. Turn the ice cream into a bowl. Mash with a fork then quickly fold in the chocolate mixture to form ripples. Pack into a 1 litre/1³/₄ pt/ 4¹/₄ cup ring mould (mold). Wrap and freeze until firm. Dip the base of the mould into hot water, then loosen the edge with a warmed knife. Turn out on to a serving plate and decorate with whipped cream in the centre and grated chocolate.

Mock Rum Babas

100 g/4 oz/¹/₂ cup granulated sugar
150 ml/¹/₄ pt/²/₃ cup water
30 ml/2 tbsp rum or rum essence
    (extract) and water
6 ring doughnuts
Whipped cream
Chopped nuts

Dissolve the sugar in the water. Boil for 5 minutes until syrupy. Stir in the rum. Prick the doughnuts all over with a skewer and spoon the rum syrup over them. Leave to soak in well. Fill the centres with whipped cream, decorate with nuts and chill, if time, before serving.

Lemon Velvet

1 packet lemon meringue pie filling
    mix
300 ml/¹/₂ pt/1¹/₄ cups water
Grated rind and juice of 1 lemon (or
    a little bottled lemon juice)
150 ml/¹/₄ pt/²/₃ cup cold milk
1 packet Dream Topping mix
Crystallised (candied) lemon slices

Blend the pie mix with the water. Bring to the boil, stirring until thickened. Stir in the lemon rind and juice and leave to cool. Put the cold milk in a bowl. Add the Dream Topping and whisk until thick and fluffy. Fold into the cold lemon mixture. Pile into 4 glasses and decorate each with a crystallised lemon slice before serving.

Chocolate Cups

150 ml/¹/₄ pt/²/₃ cups whipping
    cream
30 ml/2 tbsp chocolate hazelnut
    spread
15ml/1 tbsp brandy, sherry, rum or
    whisky
6 ready-made chocolate shells
Toasted chopped hazelnuts or glacé
    (candied) cherries
Any fresh or drained canned fruit

Whip the cream and fold in the chocolate spread and brandy, sherry, rum or whisky. Spoon into the chocolate shells and swirl the tops with a teaspoon. Alternatively, put the mixture into a piping bag and pipe it into the cases. Sprinkle with chopped nuts or add a halved glacé cherry to each. Chill until ready to serve. Place on serving plates and arrange slices of fruit attractively at the side of each cup.

Coffee Nut Delight

1 packet egg custard or crème
    caramel mix
15 ml/1 tbsp instant coffee powder
600 ml/1 pt/2¹/₂ cups milk
1 small packet peanut brittle
    (about 50 g/2 oz)
150 ml/¹/₄ pt/²/₃ cup thick plain
    yoghurt or fromage frais

Whisk the custard mix and coffee into the milk. Bring to the boil and boil for 2 minutes as directed. Cool slightly, then pour into a glass serving dish. Leave to cool completely, then chill until set. Put the peanut brittle in a bag and crush with a rolling pin. Just before serving, spread the yoghurt or fromage frais over the coffee custard and sprinkle with the crushed peanut brittle.

Note: If you are using a crème caramel mix, drizzle the sachet of caramel over the yoghurt or fromage frais before adding the peanut brittle.

Peach Melba Meringues

SERVES 6

6 meringue nests
200 g/7 oz/scant 1 cup low-fat soft cheese
410 g/14¹/₂ oz/1 large can peach halves, drained
300 g/11 oz/1 small can raspberries

Put the nests on 6 serving plates. Spoon a little soft cheese into each and spread gently. Top each with a peach half, rounded side up. Drain the raspberries and sieve the fruit. Thin to a pouring consistency with a little of the juice. Just before serving, drizzle a little raspberry purée attractively over each filled meringue nest so it runs down on to the plate.

Apricot and Ginger Flan

SERVES 4

175 g/6 oz/1¹/₂ cups ginger biscuits (cookies), crushed
50 g/2 oz/¹/₄ cup butter, melted
¹/₂ can apricot pie filling
170 g/6 oz/1 small can evaporated milk, chilled
Glacé (candied) cherries
Angelica 'leaves'

Mix the biscuit crumbs with the butter and press into the base and sides of an 18 cm/7 in flan dish (pie pan). Chill until firm. Sieve or liquidise the pie filling to form a smooth purée. Whip the evaporated milk until thick and fluffy. Gradually whisk in the purée and spoon into the flan case (pie shell). Decorate with cherries and angelica and chill until ready to serve.

Ice Cream with Boozy Apricot Sauce

SERVES 4

Sieve or liquidise ¹/₂ a can of apricot pie filling, then heat it through with 15 ml/1 tbsp orange liqueur or apricot brandy. Put 2–3 scoops of vanilla ice cream in 4 sundae dishes. Pour the hot sauce over and serve straight away with fantail wafers.

Apricot Nut Crunch

SERVES 6

410 g/14¹/₂ oz/1 large can apricots
1 packet orange jelly (jello)
25 g/1 oz/2 tbsp butter
15 ml/1 tbsp golden (light corn) syrup
15 ml/1 tbsp chopped nuts
50 g/2 oz/2 cups corn or bran flakes
150 ml/¹/₄ pt/²/₃ cup thick plain yoghurt or whipped cream

Drain the fruit, reserving the juice. Sieve or liquidise the fruit. Make the juice up to 450 ml/³/₄ pt/2 cups with water. Dissolve the jelly in a little of this liquid in the microwave or in a saucepan over a gentle heat. Stir in the remainder. Stir in the fruit purée and turn into a glass dish. Chill to set. Melt the butter with the syrup. Add the nuts and lightly crushed cereal. Mix gently. Spread the yoghurt or cream on top of the apricot mixture. Top with the cereal mixture and chill again until ready to serve.

Italian Cassata

SERVES 6

1 litre/1³/₄ pts/4¹/₄ cups soft-scoop vanilla ice cream
50 g/2 oz/¹/₂ cup grated chocolate
50 g/2 oz/¹/₂ cup maraschino cherries, drained and chopped, reserving 1 for decoration

Put the ice cream into a bowl. Quickly mash in the chocolate and cherries until just blended. Don't overmix or the ice cream will start to melt. Pack into a 1 litre/1³/₄ pt/4¹/₄ cup pudding basin, cover and freeze until firm. To serve, loosen the edge with a knife warmed under hot water. Turn out on to a serving place, put a cherry on top and serve straight away.

Honey Nut Bomb

SERVES 6

1 litre/1³/₄ pts/4¹/₄ cups soft-scoop vanilla ice cream
Grated rind and juice of 1 lemon
45 ml/3 tbsp clear honey
50 g/2 oz/¹/₂ cup toasted nuts, chopped
Crystallised (candied) lemon slices

Put the ice cream into a bowl. Quickly fold in the lemon rind and juice, honey and nuts, to give a marbled effect. Don't overmix or the ice cream will start to melt. Pack into a 1 litre/1³/₄ pt/4¹/₄ cup pudding basin, cover and freeze until firm. To serve, loosen the edge with a knife warmed under hot water, turn out and serve straight away, decorated with crystallised lemon slices.

Caribbean Cooler

SERVES 6

1 litre/1³/₄ pts/4¹/₄ cups soft-scoop chocolate ice cream
2 bananas, mashed with lemon juice
25 g/1 oz/2 tbsp crystallised (candied) or stem ginger, chopped
Grated chocolate

Put the ice cream into a bowl. Quickly work in the bananas and ginger until just mixed. Don't over mix or the ice cream will start to melt. Pack into a 450 g/1 lb loaf tin. Wrap and freeze until firm. To serve, stand the base of the tin briefly in hot water. Loosen the edge with a knife and turn out. Decorate with grated chocolate and serve cut into slices.

Rum and Raisin Mountain

SERVES 6

50 g/2 oz/¹/₃ cup raisins
30 ml/2 tbsp rum
1 litre/1³/₄ pts/4¹/₄ cups soft-scoop vanilla ice cream
2 or 3 meringues, crushed
Whipped cream

Put the raisins in a bowl. Add the rum and leave to soak for at least 1 hour. Mash the soaked raisins into the ice cream with the crushed meringues. Work quickly to prevent the ice cream from melting. Pack into a 1 litre/1³/₄ pt/4¹/₄ cup pudding basin. Cover and freeze until firm. To serve, loosen the edge with a warmed knife. Turn out on to a serving plate and pile whipped cream on top. Serve immediately.

Black Forest Rice

410 g/14¹/₂ oz/1 large can cherry pie
*   filling*
425 g/15 oz/1 large can chocolate
*   rice pudding*
170 g/6 oz/1 small can cream
Grated chocolate or drinking
*   (sweetened) chocolate powder*

L ayer the cherry pie filling and
chocolate rice in 4 glasses. Drain the
whey off the cream and pipe or spoon a
swirl of cream on top of each. Sprinkle
with grated chocolate or drinking
chocolate powder. Chill before serving.

Chocolate lemon Flan

225 g/8 oz/2 cups chocolate
*   digestive biscuits (Graham*
*   crackers), crushed*
100 g/4 oz/¹/₂ cup butter, melted
150 ml/¹/₄ pt/²/₃ cup double (heavy)
*   or whipping cream*
200 g/7 oz/1 small can sweetened
*   condensed milk*
90 ml/6 tbsp lemon juice
Grated chocolate

M ix the biscuit crumbs with the
butter and press into the base and
sides of a 20 cm/8 in flan dish (pie pan).
Chill until firm. Whip the cream until softly
peaking. Fold in the condensed milk and
lemon juice. Turn into the flan case (pie
shell). Chill, preferably overnight, then
decorate with grated chocolate before
serving.

Blackcurrant Mousse

1 packet blackcurrant jelly (jello)
300 g/11 oz/1 small can
*   blackcurrants*
170 g/6 oz/1 small can evaporated
milk, chilled
Whipped cream

D issolve the jelly in 150 ml/¹/₄ pt/
²/₃ cup boiling water. Stir in the juice
from the can of blackcurrants and chill
until on the point of setting. Meanwhile,
whisk the evaporated milk until thick and
fluffy. When the jelly is the consistency of
egg white, whisk in the milk. Pour into 4
glasses and chill until set. Top with
whipped cream, then scatter the
blackcurrants over.

Speedy Strawberry Cheesecake

23 cm/9 in medium sponge flan case
*   (pie shell)*
200 g/7 oz/scant 1 cup low-fat soft
*   cheese*
50 g/2 oz/¹/₄ cup caster (superfine)
sugar
2.5 ml/¹/₂ tsp vanilla essence
*   (extract)*
150 ml/¹/₄ pt/²/₃ cup whipped cream
425 g/15 oz/1 large can strawberry
*   pie filling*

P ut the flan case on a serving plate.
Beat the cheese with the sugar and
vanilla, then fold in the whipped cream.
Spoon into the flan case and spread
evenly. Chill until fairly firm. Spread the
pie filling over and chill again before
serving.

Mandarin and Chocolate Cheesecake

SERVES 6

50 g/2 oz/¹/₄ cup butter, melted
200 g/7 oz/1³/₄ cups chocolate
* digestive biscuits (Graham*
* crackers), crushed*
350 g/12 oz/1 small can mandarin
* oranges*
15 g/¹/₂ oz/1 tbsp powdered gelatine
225 g/8 oz/1 cup Mascarpone cheese
2 eggs, separated
75 g/3 oz/¹/₃ cup caster (superfine)
* sugar*
150 ml/¹/₄ pt/²/₃ cup crème fraîche
or soured (dairy sour) cream
30 ml/2 tbsp orange liqueur
Grated rind and juice of 1 tangerine
Grated chocolate

Mix together the butter with the biscuit crumbs and press into the base of a 20 cm/8 in flan dish (pie pan) or springform cake tin (pan). Leave to chill while making the filling. Drain the mandarins, reserving the juice. Finely chop the fruit. Sprinkle the reserved mandarin juice over the gelatine and leave to soften. Beat together the cheese, egg yolks, 50 g/2 oz/¹/₄ cup of the sugar, the crème fraîche and the liqueur until smooth. Heat the gelatine slowly until it dissolves completely, then stir into the cheese mixture. Fold in the tangerine rind and juice and mandarin pieces. Whisk the egg whites until stiff and then whisk in the remaining sugar. Fold this into the cheese mixture and spoon over the biscuit base. Chill for 3–4 hours to set before decorating with grated chocolate.

Chocolate Amaretti Creams

SERVES 4

4 amaretti biscuits (cookies),
* crushed*
250 g/9 oz/2¹/₄ cups plain (semi-
* sweet) chocolate*
30 ml/2 tbsp glycerine
30 ml/2 tbsp amaretto liqueur
150 ml/¹/₄ pt/²/₃ cup double (heavy)
* cream*
Single (light) cream

Line the bases of 4 ramekin dishes (custard cups) with greaseproof (waxed) paper and divide the crushed amaretti biscuits between the dishes. Gently melt the chocolate with the glycerine and liqueur in the microwave or in a bowl over a pan of hot water and allow to cool slightly. Whip the double cream until softly peaking. Stir 30 ml/2 tbsp into the chocolate mixture to soften it, then add the rest and fold in until well blended. Pour into the ramekins and level the surfaces. Chill for at least 45 minutes. To serve, run a knife around the edge of each ramekin, cover with a serving plate and invert on to the plate. Remove the paper and serve with a jug of single cream.

Meringue Fruit Crush

SERVES 6

450 ml/³/₄ pt/2 cups double (heavy)
* cream*
350 g/12 oz soft summer fruits
175 g/6 oz/1¹/₂ cups lightly crushed
* meringues*
50 g/2 oz/¹/₃ cup toasted hazelnuts
or almonds
Grated chocolate

Whip the cream until it forms soft peaks. Layer the fruits, meringue and nuts in 6 glasses, finishing with a layer of cream. Decorate with grated chocolate and chill to allow the flavours to develop and the meringues to soften slightly before serving.

Caledonian Mousse

SERVES 6

30 ml/2 tbsp whisky
30 ml/2 tbsp ginger marmalade
Finely grated rind of 1/2 lemon
15 ml/1 tbsp lemon juice
30 ml/2 tbsp caster (superfine) sugar
300 ml/1/2 pt/1 1/4 cups double (heavy) cream
2 egg whites
Brandy snaps

Put the whisky, marmalade, lemon rind, juice and sugar into a bowl and leave for 15 minutes. Stir the cream into this mixture until blended and then beat until thick. Whisk the egg whites until stiff, fold into the whipped cream mixture and spoon into individual dishes. Chill for 30 minutes before serving with brandy snaps.

Strawberry Crunch

SERVES 6

300 ml/1/2 pt/1 1/4 cups double (heavy) cream
25 g/1 oz/2 tbsp caster (superfine) sugar
350 g/12 oz strawberries
6 amaretti biscuits (cookies), roughly crushed

Whip the cream and sugar until stiff. Chop the strawberries, reserving 6 whole ones for decoration. Fold the crushed biscuits and chopped strawberries into the cream. Pile into individual dishes. Decorate with the reserved strawberries and serve.

Raspberry Crunch

SERVES 6

Prepare as for Strawberry Crunch but substitute raspberries for the strawberries and lightly crush rather than chop them. Substitute brandy snaps for the amaretti biscuits.

White Chocolate Mousse

SERVES 6

225 g/8 oz white chocolate
25 g/1 oz/2 tbsp unsalted (sweet) butter
5 eggs, separated
Mixed white and dark grated chocolate

Gently melt the chocolate with the butter in a microwave or in a bowl over a pan of hot water. Gradually add the egg yolks. Whisk the egg whites until stiff and fold the chocolate mixture into the whites. Pour into 6 ramekins (custard cups) and chill until set. Decorate with a sprinkling of white and dark grated chocolate before serving.

Brandy Snap Baskets

SERVES 8

50 g/2 oz/¹/₄ cup unsalted (sweet)
butter
50 g/2 oz/¹/₄ cup caster (superfine)
sugar
30 ml/2 tbsp golden (light corn)
syrup
50 g/2 oz/¹/₂ cup plain (all-purpose)
flour
2.5 ml/¹/₂ tsp ground ginger
5 ml/1 tsp brandy
Finely grated rind of ¹/₂ lemon
Fresh fruits and/or ice cream

Line 2 baking sheets with baking
parchment. Melt the butter, sugar and
syrup together over a low heat. Remove
from the heat. Sift in the flour and ginger,
and add the brandy and lemon rind. Mix
thoroughly with a wooden spoon and leave
to cool for 1–2 minutes. Drop the mixture
on to the baking sheets using 10 ml/2 tsp
at a time and spacing at 10 cm/4 in
intervals. Bake in the oven at 180°C/
350°F/gas mark 4 for 7–10 minutes or
until the snaps are bubbly, golden brown
and lacy in texture. Remove from the oven
and quickly mould round inverted
individual dishes, then cool on a wire rack.
Fill with fresh fruit and/or scoops of ice
cream just before serving.

Frozen Coffee Crunch Soufflés

SERVES 4

2 egg whites
175 g/6 oz/³/₄ cup caster (superfine)
sugar
7.5 ml/1¹/₂ tsp instant coffee powder
7.5 ml/1¹/₂ tsp boiling water
15 ml/1 tbsp Grand Marnier
375 ml/13 fl oz/1¹/₂ cups double
(heavy) cream
12 amaretti biscuits (cookies),
crushed
Icing (confectioner's) sugar for
dusting
4 toasted almonds

Prepare 4 ramekins (custard cups)
with greaseproof (waxed) paper
collars to stand 5 cm/2 in above the rims.
Tie securely just under the rim with string.
Whisk the egg whites until stiff. Dissolve
the sugar in 90 ml/6 tbsp of water in a
saucepan and boil for 3 minutes without
stirring. Pour this caramel on to the egg
whites in a thin stream, whisking at high
speed until cool. Dissolve the coffee in the
boiling water and stir in the liqueur. Whisk
into the meringue. Whip the cream until
softly peaking and fold into the egg
mixture. Pour into the ramekins until they
are half full and sprinkle with a thick layer
of crushed amaretti biscuits. Continue
with the soufflé mixture pouring to 2.5 cm/
1 in above the rims. Freeze for at least 2
hours, then remove the collars and coat
the raised edges with the remaining
biscuits, dust with icing sugar and top with
a toasted almond before serving. Leave
to stand in the fridge for 20 minutes to
soften before serving.

Tiramisu

SERVES 6

250 g/9 oz/good 1 cup Mascarpone
* cheese*
4 eggs, separated
60 ml/4 tbsp caster (superfine)
* sugar*
10 ml/2 tsp strong coffee
100 g/4 oz/1 cup plain (semi-sweet)
* chocolate, cut into small pieces*
120 ml/4 fl oz/¹/₂ cup weak coffee
90 ml/6 tbsp amaretto or coffee
* liqueur*
20 sponge fingers
Drinking (sweetened) chocolate
* powder*

Whisk the cheese and egg yolks together and gradually add the sugar. Pour in the strong coffee and mix thoroughly. Whisk the egg whites until stiff and fold into the cheese mixture. Add the chocolate pieces and stir gently into the mixture. Mix together the weak coffee and liqueur, then dip in half the sponge fingers one at a time, and use to line the bottom of a serving dish. Pour in half the cheese mixture, then dip the remaining fingers in the liqueur coffee mixture and place on top of the cheese layer. Pour over the remaining cheese mixture, tap the dish down lightly to help settle the layers. Chill until ready to serve. Just before serving, dust with drinking chocolate powder.

Almost Tiramisu

SERVES 6

4 trifle sponges
150 ml/¹/₄ pt/²/₃ cup strong black
* coffee*
1 packet egg custard or crème
* caramel mix*
450 ml/³/₄ pt/2 cups milk
15–30 ml/1–2 tbsp brandy or coffee
* liqueur*
150 ml/¹/₄ pt/²/₃ cup whipped cream
15 ml/1 tbsp drinking (sweetened)
* chocolate powder*

Break up the sponges and place in a shallow round glass dish. Add the coffee and leave to soak. Make up the egg custard or crème caramel mix with the milk. Leave to cool slightly, then stir in the brandy or coffee liqueur. Carefully pour over the sponge and chill until set. Cover with whipped cream and dust with chocolate powder.

Note: If you use crème caramel mix, reserve the sachet of caramel to drizzle over yoghurt and fresh bananas as another dessert.

Whisky Oranges with Atholl Brose Cream

200 g/7 oz/scant 1 cup granulated
sugar
150 ml/¹/₄ pt/²/₃ cup water
120 ml/4 fl oz/¹/₂ cup whisky
8 oranges
450 ml/³/₄ pt/2 cups double (heavy)
cream
45 ml/3 tbsp clear honey

Stir the sugar and water over a low heat until the sugar dissolves. Bring to the boil and simmer for 2 minutes. Remove from the heat, add 75 ml/5 tbsp of the whisky and leave to cool. Thinly pare the rind of 1 orange and cut into thin strips. Boil in water for 2 minutes. Drain, rinse with cold water and drain again. Remove all the remaining rind and pith from the oranges and cut into segments, cutting between the membranes. Put these segments into a bowl and pour the syrup over. Whip the cream until softly peaking. Put the honey and remaining whisky into a bowl and stir until well blended. Gradually whisk into the cream until thick. Chill until ready to serve. Spoon the oranges and syrup into 8 bowls and top with the Atholl Brose cream. Sprinkle with the reserved orange rind before serving.

Brandy Chocolate Roulade

Oil for greasing
175 g/6 oz/1¹/₂ cups plain (semi-
sweet) chocolate
30 ml/2 tbsp hot water
5 size 1 eggs, separated
175 g/6 oz/³/₄ cup caster (superfine)
sugar
150 ml/¹/₄ pt/²/₃ cup double (heavy)
cream
150 ml/¹/₄ pt/²/₃ cup soured (dairy
sour) cream
30 ml/2 tbsp brandy
Caster (superfine) sugar for dusting
Coarsely grated chocolate

Line a 23 × 33 cm/9 × 13 in Swiss roll tin (jelly roll pan) with grease-proof (waxed) paper, cut large enough to extend slightly above the sides. Oil lightly. Melt the chocolate and stir in the hot water. Whisk in the egg yolks. Whisk the egg whites until stiff and fold into the chocolate mixture. Pour into the prepared tin. Bake in the oven at 200°C/400°F/gas mark 6 for 15 minutes. Leave to cool for 2 hours. Whip the double cream until softly peaking, then fold in the soured cream and brandy. When the roulade is cold invert it on to grease-proof paper, dusted with caster sugar. Remove the lining from its base and trim the edges. Spread the filling over, roll up and decorate with grated chocolate.

Scarlet Salad

225 g/8 oz/2 cups redcurrants
225 g/8 oz/2 cups raspberries
225 g/8 oz/2 cups small sweet
strawberries
60 ml/4 tbsp caster (superfine)
sugar
15 ml/1 tbsp lemon juice
30 ml/2 tbsp orange juice
6 amaretti biscuits (cookies),
crushed

Layer the fruits and sugar in a large bowl. Add the lemon and orange juice, cover and chill for several hours. Pile the fruit and their scarlet juices into glasses for serving and top with crushed amaretti biscuits – no cream is needed.

Cookie Log

200 g/7 oz/1 small packet chocolate
chip cookies
45 ml/3 tbsp port
45 ml/3 tbsp brandy
450 ml/³/₄ pt/2 cups whipped cream
Grated chocolate or toasted flaked
almonds

Dip the biscuits in the port and brandy and sandwich together with ³/₄ of the cream. Use the rest of the cream to cover the biscuit log. Decorate with the chocolate or almonds. Chill for at least 3 hours before serving, so that the cookies start to soften and the cream begins to absorb the boozy chocolate flavour.

Chocolate Mallow Pie

200 g/7 oz/1³/₄ cups chocolate
digestive biscuits (Graham
crackers), crushed
75 g/3 oz/¹/₃ cup butter, melted
100 g/4 oz/1 cup plain (semi-sweet)
chocolate
20 marshmallows (pink and white)
30 ml/2 tbsp water
1 egg, separated
300 ml/¹/₂ pt/1¹/₄ cups double
(heavy) cream, whipped
A little extra whipped cream

Mix the biscuits and butter together and use to line an 18 cm/7 in flan dish (pie pan). Melt the chocolate with the marshmallows and water. Cool slightly, then stir in the egg yolk and leave to cool. Whisk the egg white until stiff and fold into the chocolate mixture with the whipped cream. Pour on to the biscuit base and chill until set. Decorate with a little extra cream before serving.

Ginger Orange Log

Prepare as for Cookie Log but substitute gingernuts for the cookies and orange liqueur for the brandy. Add the finely grated rind of ¹/₂ an orange to the cream and thinly pare the remainder and cut into thin shreds for decoration instead of the chocolate or nuts.

Norwegian Cream

9 eggs, separated
175 g/6 oz/³/₄ cup caster (superfine)
sugar
20 g/³/₄ oz/1¹/₂ tbsp gelatine
30 ml/2 tbsp orange juice
Jam (conserve)
Whipped cream
Grated chocolate

Whisk the egg whites until stiff. Add the sugar and whisk again until peaking. Whisk the yolks, fold in the whites. Dissolve the gelatine in the orange juice in a bowl over a pan of hot water (or in the microwave). Fold into the eggs. Turn into a large shallow dish and chill until set. When set, spread jam on the top. Spread whipped cream over. Decorate with grated chocolate.

Apple and Orange Brulée

175 ml/6 fl oz/³/₄ cup crème fraîche
or half yoghurt, half double
(heavy) cream
2 small eating (dessert) apples,
cored and diced
2 small oranges, rinded and
chopped
100 g/4 oz/¹/₂ cup light brown or
granulated sugar

Mix all the ingredients together except the sugar and place in a shallow flameproof dish. Chill well. If using brown sugar, spread on top of the fruit mixture and put under a hot grill (broiler) for about 2 minutes until the sugar caramelises. Chill until needed. Alternatively, add a drop of water to the granulated sugar, put in the microwave in a heatproof dish and cook on high until it forms a light yellow toffee. Pour over the fruit mixture and chill until needed. To serve, bring to the table straight from the fridge and bang the toffee with a metal spoon. This cracks the top and makes it easy to serve.

Oranges with Yoghurt Sauce

4 oranges, peeled
Salt and freshly ground black or
white pepper
Roasted cumin seeds, finely crushed
Cayenne
250 ml/8 fl oz/1 cup plain yoghurt
20 ml/4 tsp caster (superfine) sugar
5 ml/1 tsp finely grated fresh root
ginger

Cut each orange into 5–6 slices and then each slice in half again crosswise. Sprinkle one side very lightly with salt, pepper, cumin and cayenne. Arrange slightly overlapping slices in a circle, leaving a gap in the middle. Cover and chill. Blend the yoghurt with the sugar, ginger and a pinch each of salt, pepper, cumin and cayenne until smooth and creamy. Just before serving, put a dollop of this mixture in the centre of the oranges.

Crêpes with Chocolate Cream

SERVES 4

4 strawberries
30 ml/2 tbsp Kirsch
150 ml/¹/₄ pt/²/₃ cup whipping cream
30 ml/2 tbsp drinking (sweetened)
chocolate powder
30 ml/2 tbsp grated chocolate
4 crêpes
Icing (confectioners') sugar

Wash the strawberries but do not hull. Cut diagonally through the strawberries in several places just to the calyx so they fan out. Soak in the kirsch until needed. Whip the cream with the drinking chocolate powder and grated chocolate adjusting the amounts to suit your own tastes. Open out the crêpes and spread with this chocolate mixture, roll up and top each with a strawberry. Dust with icing sugar and serve.

Kiwi Pavlova

SERVES 8

4 egg whites
225 g/8 oz/1 cup caster (superfine)
sugar
15 ml/1 tbsp cornflour (cornstarch)
1.5 ml/¹/₄ tsp vanilla essence (extract)
10 ml/2 tsp vinegar
Whipped cream
Sliced kiwi fruit

Whisk the egg whites until stiff. Whisk in the sugar gradually, then the remaining ingredients except the cream and kiwi fruit. Spoon in a large circle on baking parchment on a baking sheet. Bake in the oven at 150°C/300°F/gas mark 2 for 1¹/₂ hours. When cool fill the centre with whipped cream and sliced kiwifruit.

Strawberry Pavlova

SERVES 8

Prepare as for Kiwi Pavlova but use 175 g/6 oz/1¹/₂ cups halved small strawberries instead of kiwifruit.

Lemon Curd Mousse

SERVES 6

7.5 ml/1¹/₂ tsp powdered gelatine
3 eggs, separated
100 g/4 oz/¹/₂ cup caster (superfine)
sugar
Grated rind and juice of 2 small
lemons
65 g/2¹/₂ oz/good ¹/₄ cup butter
Grated chocolate

Sprinkle the gelatine on to 30 ml/2 tbsp of water and leave to soften. Whisk the egg yolks with all but 25 g/1 oz/2 tbsp of the sugar, until thick and pale. Put the lemon juice, rind and butter in a saucepan and bring to the boil. Add the soaked gelatine and put into a food processor or blender and run the machine for 1¹/₂–2 minutes with the yolk mixture. Whisk the egg whites until just peaking. Whisk in the remaining sugar and fold in the hot lemon mixture. Turn into individual glass serving dishes and chill for 4–6 hours before serving. Sprinkle with grated chocolate.

Orange Curd Mousse

SERVES 6

Prepare as for Lemon Curd Mousse but use the grated rind and juice of 1 large orange instead of 2 lemons.

Banoffee Pie

350 g/12 oz/1 large can sweetened condensed milk
200 g/7 oz/1³/₄ cups plain biscuits (cookies), crushed
50 g/2 oz/¹/₄ cup butter, melted
3 bananas
300 ml/¹/₂ pt/1¹/₄ cup double (heavy) cream
30 ml/2 tbsp caster (superfine) sugar
15 ml/1 tbsp instant coffee powder
Drinking (sweetened) chocolate powder or grated chocolate

Put the unopened can of milk in a saucepan of boiling water. Simmer for at least 3 hours, keeping the tin submerged all the time. Allow to cool in the water. (I boil a few at a time and have them in the pantry ready to use when I need them.) Make the base by mixing the crumbs with the melted butter and press into a flan dish (pie pan). Chill until firm. Spread the cold caramelised milk on to the base. Top with sliced bananas. Whip the cream, sugar and coffee powder together and pipe on to the bananas. Top with grated chocolate or chocolate powder. Chill until ready to serve.

Tom's Chocolate Gateau

SERVES 6

175 g/6 oz/1¹/₂ cups plain (all-purpose) flour
175 g/6 oz/³/₄ cup granulated sugar
50 g/2 oz/¹/₂ cup cocoa (unsweetened chocolate) powder
2.5 ml/¹/₂ tsp salt
5 ml/1 tsp bicarbonate of soda (baking soda)
5 ml/1 tsp vanilla essence (extract)
15 ml/1 tbsp cider vinegar
120 ml/4 fl oz/¹/₂ cup sunflower oil
250 ml/8 fl oz/1 cup water
Black cherry jam (conserve)
Whipped cream
Grated chocolate

Grease and line a 20 cm/8 in round cake tin (pan). Combine the flour, sugar, cocoa, salt and bicarbonate of soda. Make a well in the centre and add the vanilla, vinegar and oil and gradually stir in the water. Mix until blended, but do not overmix. Turn into the prepared tin. Bake in the oven at 190°C/375°F/gas mark 5 for 40 minutes. Leave to cool in the tin on a wire rack for 10 minutes, then turn out and leave to cool. When cold, split in two and fill with jam and whipped cream. Also spread cream on the top and sprinkle with grated chocolate.

Photograph opposite: **Banana and walnut loaf (page 299)**

Crème Caramel

175 g/6 oz/³/₄ cup granulated sugar
60 ml/4 tbsp cold water
6 egg yolks
15 ml/1 tbsp caster (superfine)
  sugar
750 ml/1¹/₄ pts/3 cups single (light)
  cream
5 ml/1 tsp vanilla essence (extract)

Put the granulated sugar in a pan with the cold water. Heat gently until the syrup is clear, then boil without stirring until it turns a golden caramel colour. Pour into 6 ramekins (custard cups) and leave to cool. Beat the egg yolks with the caster sugar and put in a bowl over a pan of simmering water with the cream and vanilla essence. Cook gently until the cream thickens, whisking gently. Pour through a sieve (strainer) into the ramekins. Chill until cold and set. You can either turn them out or eat as they are.

Gulab Jamun

100 g/4 oz/1 cup dried milk powder
  (non-fat dairy milk)
25 g/1 oz/¹/₄ cup plain (all-purpose)
  flour
5 ml/1 tsp baking powder
25 g/1 oz/2 tbsp margarine
1 egg, beaten
5 ml/1 tsp milk
Oil for deep-frying
200 g/7 oz/scant 1 cup sugar
2 whole green cardamoms
30 ml/2 tbsp rose water

Place the milk powder, flour and baking powder in a bowl. Rub in the margarine and add the egg and milk. Mix to a soft dough and divide into 16 pieces. Using the palms of your hands, shape into small very smooth balls. Deep-fry in hot oil for about 5 minutes until dark golden brown. Remove from the oil and drain on kitchen paper. Boil the sugar in 750 ml/ 1¹/₄ pts/3 cups water with the cardamoms for 10 minutes to make a syrup. Remove from the heat and add the sponge balls. Leave to cool, then add the rosewater. Leave to soak in the syrup for at least 3– 4 hours.

Photograph opposite: **Chewy apricot bars (page 305)**

QUICK BREADS AND SIMILAR BAKES

A delicious array of breads and scones from simple loaves to savoury accompaniments and fruity tea-time treats.

Garlic Bread

SERVES 6

100 g/4 oz/¹/₂ cup butter
1–2 garlic cloves, crushed
1 small French stick

Blend together the butter and garlic. Cut the French stick into 12 slices, not quite slicing through the bottom crust to keep the loaf intact. Spread the butter mixture between the slices and over the top. Wrap in foil and bake in the oven at 200°C/400°F/gas mark 6 for about 15 minutes until the crust feels crisp but the centre is still soft.

Garlic Rolls

SERVES 6

Spread the butter mixture in 6 white or wholemeal rolls or bagels. Wrap in foil, shiny side in. Bake as above or grill (broil) for 15 minutes, turning once.

Herby Pittas

SERVES 6

3 pitta breads
65 g/2¹/₂ oz/scant ¹/₃ cup butter
30 ml/2 tbsp chopped mixed herbs
(parsley, chives and marjoram
  are good) or 15 ml/1 tbsp mixed
  dried herbs
5 ml/1 tsp garlic salt (optional)

Cut the pittas in half widthwise and split open along the cut edge to form pockets. Mash the butter and herbs together with the garlic salt, if using. Spread inside the pockets. Place under a hot grill (broiler) for 2 minutes on each side until the bread is golden and the butter has melted.

Hot Herb Loaf

SERVES 6

Make double the quantity of herb butter for Herby Pittas. Cut a small French stick into 12 slices, not quite cutting through the bottom crust. Spread the butter mixture between the slices and over the top. Wrap in foil and bake in the oven at 200°C/400°F/gas mark 6 for about 15 minutes until the crust feels crisp when squeezed.

Hot Walnut Bread

50 g/2 oz/¹/₂ cup walnut halves
15 ml/1 tbsp chopped parsley
50 g/2 oz/¹/₄ cup butter
5 ml/1 tsp garlic salt
1 small French stick

Grind the nuts in a blender or food processor. Add the remaining ingredients except the bread and blend well. Cut the French stick into 12 slices, not quite cutting through the bottom crust. Spread the nut mixture between the slices and over the top. Wrap in foil and bake in the oven at 200°C/400°F/gas mark 6 for 15 minutes until the crust feels crisp when squeezed.

Oatmeal Bannocks

175 g/6 oz/1¹/₂ cups wholemeal flour
15 ml/1 tbsp baking powder
2.5 ml/¹/₂ tsp salt
50 g/2 oz/¹/₂ cup fine oatmeal
15 ml/1 tbsp caster (superfine) sugar
25 g/1 oz/2 tbsp margarine
150 g/¹/₄ pt/²/₃ cup water
Butter, to serve

Mix the dry ingredients together, then rub in the margarine. Mix with enough of the water to form a soft but not sticky dough. Knead gently and form into 6 flat cakes about 1 cm/¹/₂ in thick. Cook on a griddle or in a hot non-stick frying pan (skillet) for about 5 minutes on each side, until well risen and golden brown. Serve warm, split and buttered.

Quick Cheese Soda Bread

450 g/1 lb/4 cups plain (all-purpose) flour
10 ml/2 tsp bicarbonate of soda (baking soda)
10 ml/2 tsp cream of tartar
5 ml/1 tsp salt
2.5 ml/¹/₂ tsp mustard powder (optional)
25 g/1 oz/2 tbsp butter or margarine
100 g/4 oz/1 cup grated strong Cheddar cheese
300 ml/¹/₂ pt/1¹/₄ cups milk
Butter, to serve

Sift the dry ingredients into a bowl. Rub in the fat. Stir in the cheese and enough of the milk to form a soft but not sticky dough. Shape into a ball on a lightly floured surface. Transfer to a baking sheet, flatten slightly and mark into quarters with a knife. Bake in the oven at 220°C/425°F/gas mark 7 for 20–25 minutes until risen, golden and the base sounds hollow when tapped. Cool slightly, then break into quarters, slice thickly and butter.

Plain Soda Bread

Prepare as for Quick Cheese Soda Bread but omit the cheese and mustard.

Brown Soda Bread

Prepare as for Quick Cheese Soda Bread but use half wholemeal flour and half plain (all-purpose) flour and omit the cheese and mustard.

Rye Scotch Pancakes

MAKES ABOUT 24

100 g/4 oz/1 cup rye flour
Pinch of salt
10 ml/2 tsp caster (superfine) sugar
2 eggs, separated
300 ml/¹/₂ pt/1¹/₄ cups milk
Oil for frying
Butter and honey, to serve

Mix the flour, salt and sugar together. Add the egg yolks and gradually beat in the milk. Whisk the egg whites until peaking and fold into the batter with a metal spoon. Heat a little oil in a large frying pan (skillet). Pour off excess oil. Put tablespoonfuls of the batter into the pan a few at a time and cook on each side until golden. Keep warm in a clean cloth while cooking the remainder. Serve warm with butter and honey.

White Scotch Pancakes

MAKES ABOUT 24

Prepare as for Rye Scotch Pancakes (above) but use plain (all-purpose) flour instead of rye flour.

Savoury Wholemeal Rolls

MAKES 10

225 g/8 oz/2 cups wholemeal flour
50 g/2 oz/¹/₂ cup plain (all-purpose) flour
20 ml/4 tsp baking powder
1.5 ml/¹/₄ tsp salt
15 g/¹/₂ oz/1 tbsp dried onions, crumbled
2.5 ml/¹/₂ tsp mixed dried herbs
30 ml/2 tbsp sunflower oil
150 ml/¹/₄ pt/²/₃ cup plain yoghurt
Milk

Mix all the dry ingredients together in a bowl. Stir in the oil. Mix with the yoghurt and just enough milk to form a soft but not sticky dough. Knead gently on a lightly floured surface and shape the mixture into 10 balls. Place well apart on a lightly greased baking sheet. Brush with a little milk to glaze, then bake in the oven at 200°C/400°F/gas mark 6 for about 20 minutes until golden brown and the bases sound hollow when tapped.

Yoghurt Bread

MAKES 12

225 g/8 oz/2 cups plain (all-purpose) flour
10 ml/2 tsp baking powder
5 ml/1 tsp salt
5 ml/1 tsp caster (superfine) sugar
1 egg, beaten
45 ml/3 tbsp plain yoghurt
Oil for deep-frying

Sift the flour, baking powder, salt and sugar together in a bowl. Add the egg and yoghurt and mix well to form a soft but not sticky dough. (You may need to add a little water.) Knead for 5 minutes. Divide into 12 balls and roll out each ball into a 13 cm/5 in circle. Heat the oil and when hot add one of the circles. Reduce the heat to moderate. Press the top of the bread down into the oil continuously with a spatula or wooden spoon so that it starts to puff up. Cook on the other side for about 20 seconds or until golden. Drain, and keep warm wrapped in foil in a low oven while you cook the remaining circles. This bread freezes well.

Plain Naan Bread

MAKES 4

450 g/1 lb/4 cups plain (all-purpose) flour
10 ml/2 tsp caster (superfine) sugar
5 ml/1 tsp salt
5 ml/1 tsp baking powder
30 ml/2 tbsp sunflower oil
15 g/¹/₂ oz/1 tbsp easy-blend dried yeast
150 ml/¹/₄ pt/²/₃ cup milk
150 ml/¹/₄ pt/²/₃ cup plain yoghurt
1 egg, beaten

Sift the flour, sugar, salt and baking powder together. Rub in the oil. Add the dried yeast. Warm the milk and yoghurt together, then add the egg. Stir into the dry ingredients. Knead for 5 minutes. Cover and leave to prove in a warm place for about 1 hour until it has doubled in size. Knead the risen dough again for about 1 minute and divide into four equal portions. Lightly flour a work surface and roll each of the balls out into a triangular shape about 18 cm/7 in long and 13 cm/5 in wide. The dough should be about 5 mm/¹/₄ in thick. Heat a heavy frying pan (skillet) until a tiny drop of water sizzles and evaporates almost immediately when dropped in. Take one naan bread and place it flat on your hand. With your other hand carefully coat the entire top surface with cold water. Drop the bread, water-side down, into the hot pan. The bread should stick to the pan. Cook for about 3 minutes over a moderate heat. Place the pan under a hot grill (broiler) until the bread is risen and slightly scorched in places. Remove the bread from the pan with a fish slice. Brush the top with 5 ml/1 tsp melted butter and keep warm wrapped in foil in a low oven, while you cook the remaining naans.

Naan Bread with Caraway

MAKES 4

225 g/8 oz/2 cups plain (all-purpose) flour
5 ml/1 tsp caster (superfine) sugar
5 ml/1 tsp salt
15 ml/1 tbsp sunflower oil
15 g/1 tbsp easy-blend dried yeast
5 ml/1 tsp caraway seeds
30 ml/2 tbsp plain yoghurt
85 ml/3 fl oz/5¹/₂ tbsp warm water

Sift the flour, sugar and salt. Stir in the oil. Add the dried yeast and caraway seeds. Pour in the yoghurt and warm water and knead well for 5 minutes. Cover and leave to prove for 1 hour in a warm place, then continue as for Plain Naan Bread.

Garlic Naan Bread

MAKES 4

Follow the recipe for Plain Naan Bread but mix 2.5 ml/¹/₂ tsp garlic powder with each 5 ml/1 tsp butter before spreading on the cooked bread.

Chapattis

*100 g/4 oz/1 cup chapatti flour or
half wholemeal flour and half
plain (all-purpose) white flour,
mixed together*
5 ml/1 tsp salt

Put the flour and salt in a bowl and add enough cold water to mix to a softish dough. Knead for 5 minutes. Cover and leave to rest for at least 30 minutes. Knead the dough. Divide into four equal portions and roll each into a ball. Roll out each ball on a lightly floured surface into a thin circle about 15–20 cm/6–8 in diameter. Heat a large frying pan (skillet) until hot. Add a chapatti and cook for about 1–2 minutes over moderate heat. Turn over and cook the other side for a further 1–2 minutes. The bread should start to puff up in places (you can help it along by pressing gently with a tea towel rolled up into a ball shape). Remove from the pan and keep warm wrapped in foil in a low oven while you cook the remaining chapattis.

Puri

Follow the recipe for Chapattis but instead of using a dry frying pan (skillet), grease the pan first, then cook the bread for about 1 minute on each side.

Plain Scones

*450 g/1 lb/4 cups self-raising (self-
rising) flour*
10 ml/2 tsp baking powder
75 g/3 oz/¹/₃ cup margarine
300 ml/¹/₂ pt/1¹/₄ cups milk

Mix the flour and baking powder. Rub in the margarine until the mixture resembles breadcrumbs. Gradually add the milk until the mixture forms a dough. Roll out on a floured surface to about 2.5 cm/1 in thick. Cut into circles with a biscuit (cookie) cutter. Place on a greased baking sheet and bake in the oven at 220°C/425°F/gas mark 7 for about 12 minutes until well risen and golden brown.

Sultana Scones

Prepare as for Plain Scones but add 75 g/3 oz/¹/₂ cup sultanas (golden raisins) to the dry ingredients.

Cherry Scones

Prepare as for Plain Scones, but add 50 g/2 oz/¹/₂ cup glacé (candied) cherries, quartered, to the dry ingredients.

Banana Honey Bread

MAKES 1 LOAF

100 g/4 oz/^{1}/$_2$ cup margarine,
softened
100 g/4 oz/^{1}/$_2$ cup light brown sugar
3 bananas, mashed
1 egg, beaten
15 ml/1 tbsp honey
1.5 ml/^{1}/$_4$ tsp ground cinnamon
225 g/8 oz/2 cups self-raising (self-
rising) flour
5 ml/1 tsp baking powder
45 ml/3 tbsp milk

Beat together the margarine and sugar until smooth. Add the bananas, egg, honey and cinnamon. Slowly stir in the flour and baking powder, mixing it well. Stir in the milk. Spoon into a greased 450 g/1 lb loaf tin and bake in the oven at 160ºC/325ºF/gas mark 3 for 1–1^1/$_2$ hours until firm.

Cornmeal Pancakes

MAKES 8–10

100 g/4 oz/1 cup plain (all-purpose)
flour
1.5 ml/^{1}/$_4$ tsp salt
50 g/2 oz/^{1}/$_2$ cup cornmeal
375 ml/13 fl oz/1^1/$_2$ cups water
1 egg, beaten
Oil for greasing

Whisk together all the ingredients except the oil in a bowl until smooth. Heat a small, lightly oiled frying pan (skillet). Add about 45 ml/3 tbsp batter to coat the base thickly. Fry (sauté) over a moderate heat, swirling the pan gently until the pancake is dry but the edges are not brown. Turn over and cook the other side briefly. Keep warm on a plate over a pan of hot water while cooking the remaining pancakes. Serve warm.

Cheese and Ham Scones

MAKES 8

225 g/8 oz/2 cups self-raising (self-
rising) flour
Pinch of salt
5 ml/1 tsp mustard powder
40 g/1^1/$_2$ oz/3 tbsp butter
100 g/4 oz/1 cup grated Cheddar
cheese
50 g/2 oz/^{1}/$_2$ cup cooked ham, finely
chopped
150 ml/^{1}/$_4$ pt/^{2}/$_3$ cup milk

Sift the flour, salt and mustard in a bowl. Rub in the butter and stir in half the cheese and the ham. Mix with enough of the milk to form a soft but not sticky dough. Knead gently on a lightly floured surface. Pat to a round about 18 cm/7 in in diameter. Place on a baking sheet. Mark with a knife into 8 wedges. Brush with a little more milk and sprinkle with the remaining cheese. Bake in the oven at 220ºC/425ºF/gas mark 7 for about 25 minutes until well risen and the base sounds hollow when tapped. Break into wedges for serving.

Potato and Onion Scones

MAKES 8

450 g/1 lb/2 cups cooked mashed potato
40 g/1¹/₂ oz/3 tbsp butter
75 g/3 oz/³/₄ cup self-raising (self-rising) flour
1 small onion, grated
Salt and freshly ground white pepper
15 ml/1 tbsp oil

Mash the potato with 25 g/1 oz/2 tbsp of the butter. Work in the flour and onion. Season well. Knead well on a lightly floured surface. Roll out to a round about 18 cm/7 in across. Cut into 8 wedges. Melt the remaining butter and the oil in a frying pan (skillet). Fry (sauté) the wedges over a moderate heat until golden brown underneath. Turn over and cook the other sides. Drain on kitchen paper. Serve hot.

Easy-make Coffee and Pecan Bread

MAKES 1 LOAF

350 g/12 oz/3 cups wholemeal flour
Good pinch of salt
15 ml/1 tbsp baking powder
50 g/2 oz/¹/₄ cup butter
50 g/2 oz/¹/₄ cup caster (superfine) sugar
75 g/3 oz/³/₄ cup pecan halves, chopped
1 egg
15 ml/1 tbsp instant coffee powder
300 ml/¹/₂ pt/1¹/₄ cups milk

Mix the flour in a bowl with the salt and baking powder. Rub in the butter and stir in the sugar and nuts. Beat the egg and coffee into the milk. Stir into the mixture. When well blended, turn into a greased 900 g/2 lb loaf tin (pan). Bake at 190°C/375°F/gas mark 5 for about 1 hour or until well risen and a skewer inserted in the centre comes out clean. Leave to cool in the tin for 5 minutes, then turn out on a wire rack to cool. Serve sliced and buttered.

Yoghurt Cobbles

MAKES 12

450 g/1 lb/4 cups self-raising (self-rising) flour
2.5 ml/¹/₂ tsp salt
100 g/4 oz/¹/₂ cup butter
15 ml/1 tbsp sugar
150 ml/¹/₄ pt/²/₃ cup plain yoghurt
105 ml/7 tbsp milk
Low-fat soft cheese
Jam (conserve)

Sift the flour and salt into a bowl. Rub in the butter, add the sugar, then stir in the yoghurt and 90 ml/6 tbsp of the milk. Pat out to a round about 2 cm/³/₄ in thick. Cut into rounds using a 6 cm/2¹/₂ in fluted cutter. Place on a baking sheet and brush with the remaining milk. Bake in the oven at 230°C/450°F/gas mark 8 for 12 minutes until well risen, golden and the bases sound hollow when tapped. Serve warm, split and filled with low-fat soft cheese and jam.

Herby Yoghurt Cobbles

MAKES 12

Prepare as for Yoghurt Cobbles but omit the sugar and add 1.5 ml/¹/₄ tsp cayenne and 5 ml/1 tsp mixed dried herbs to the mixture. Serve with soft cheese and pickle.

Cheddar Whorls

MAKES 9

280 g/10 oz/1 small packet white
*   bread mix*
40 g/1¹/₂ oz/3 tbsp butter, softened
30 ml/2 tbsp snipped chives
75 g/3 oz/³/₄ cup grated strong
*   Cheddar cheese*
1 egg, beaten
30 ml/2 tbsp poppy seeds

Make up the bread mix according to the packet directions and knead well. Roll out to a rectangle about 35 × 20 cm/14 × 8 in. Spread lightly with the butter, then sprinkle on the chives, then the cheese. Starting with a long edge, roll up and cut into 9 thick slices. Place in a greased 20 cm/8 in square shallow baking tin (pan). Cover with greased clingfilm (plastic wrap) and leave to rise in a warm place for 20 minutes. Brush with egg, then sprinkle with poppy seeds. Bake in the oven at 220°C/425°F/gas mark 7 for about 15 minutes or until well risen and golden. Turn out on to a wire rack to cool. Separate before eating.

Easy Malt Loaf

MAKES 1 LOAF

225 g/8 oz/2 cups self-raising (self-
*   rising) flour*
50 g/2 oz/¹/₄ cup dark brown sugar
30 ml/2 tbsp golden (light corn)
*   syrup*
50 g/2 oz/¹/₂ cup malted bedtime
*   drink granules*
75 g/3 oz/¹/₂ cup sultanas (golden
*   raisins)*
Milk

Mix all the ingredients with enough milk to form a soft dropping consistency. Turn into a greased 450 g/1 lb loaf tin and bake in the oven at 160°C/325°F/gas mark 3 for 1¹/₂ hours or until well risen and golden and a skewer inserted in the centre comes out clean. Turn out on to a wire rack to cool.

Quick Chelsea Buns

MAKES 9

280 g/10 oz/1 small packet white
*   bread mix*
15 g/¹/₂ oz/1 tbsp butter, melted
50 g/2 oz/¹/₄ cup caster (superfine)
sugar
100 g/4 oz/²/₃ cup mixed dried fruit
*   (fruit cake mix)*
5 ml/1 tsp mixed (apple pie) spice
100 g/4 oz/¹/₂ cup icing
*   (confectioners') sugar*
20 ml/4 tsp water

Make up the bread according to the packet directions and knead well. Roll out to a rectangle about 35 × 20 cm/14 × 8 in. Brush with the butter. Mix the caster sugar, fruit and spice together and sprinkle over. Starting with a long edge, roll up and cut into 9 thick slices. Place in a greased 20 cm/8 in square shallow baking tin (pan). Cover with greased clingfilm (plastic wrap) and leave to rise in a warm place for about 20 minutes. Bake in the oven at 220°C/425°F/gas mark 7 for 15–20 minutes until well risen and golden. Meanwhile, mix the icing sugar and water together to make a thin icing. Spoon over the hot buns and leave until cold before separating.

Speciality Griddle Scones

MAKES ABOUT 16

50 g/2 oz/¹/₄ cup plain (all-purpose)
  flour
5 ml/1 tsp baking powder
Pinch of salt
2 eggs, beaten
15 ml/1 tbsp milk
100 g/4 oz/¹/₂ cup cottage cheese
25 g/1 oz/2 tbsp butter, melted
Oil for shallow-frying

Mix the flour, baking powder and salt in a bowl. Beat in the eggs and milk, then the cheese and butter to form a batter. Heat a little oil in a large frying pan (skillet). Pour off any excess. Drop spoonfuls of the mixture into the pan, well apart, and fry (sauté) until golden brown on each side. Remove from the pan and keep warm while cooking the remainder. Serve warm.

One-rise Brown Bread

MAKES 1 LOAF

225 g/8 oz/2 cups malted brown
  (granary) flour
225 g/8 oz/2 cups wholemeal flour
10 ml/2 tsp easy-blend dried yeast
5 ml/1 tsp salt
15 ml/1 tbsp black treacle (molasses)
300 ml/¹/₂ pt/1¹/₄ cups hand-hot
  water
A little milk, to glaze

Mix the flours with the yeast and salt in a bowl. Stir the treacle into the water, then add to the bowl. Mix to a fairly firm dough, then knead on a lightly floured surface until no longer sticky. Press the dough into a greased 900 g/2 lb loaf tin (pan). Lay a piece of oiled clingfilm (plastic wrap) lightly over the tin and leave in a warm place until the dough reaches the top of the tin. Brush with milk to glaze and bake in the oven at 200°C/400°F/gas mark 6 for 35–40 minutes until the base of the loaf sounds hollow when turned out and tapped. Cool on a wire rack.

Fruity Orange Loaf

MAKES 1 LOAF

225 g/8 oz/2 cups self-raising (self-
  rising) flour
5 ml/1 tsp baking powder
2.5 ml/¹/₂ tsp salt
100 g/4 oz/¹/₂ cup light brown sugar
Grated rind and juice of 1 orange
100 g/4 oz/²/₃ cup sultanas (golden
  raisins)
100 g/4 oz/²/₃ cup stoned (pitted)
  dates, finely chopped
50 g/2 oz/¹/₃ cup currants
50 g/2 oz/¹/₃ cup chopped candied
  mixed peel
2 eggs
250 ml/8 fl oz/1 cup milk
40 g/1¹/₂ oz/3 tbsp butter, melted

Grease and line a 900 g/2 lb loaf tin with greased greaseproof (waxed) paper. Mix the flour, baking powder, salt, sugar and orange rind in a bowl. Stir in the fruits and peel. Beat the orange juice with the eggs and milk and stir into the bowl with the melted butter. Mix to form a soft dough. Spoon into the prepared tin and bake in the oven for 1¹/₂ hours at 180°C/350°F/gas mark 4. Turn out, remove the paper and leave to cool.

Brazilian Bread

350 g/12 oz/3 cups self-raising (self-rising) flour
2.5 ml/¹/₂ tsp mixed (apple pie) spice
50 g/2 oz/¹/₄ cup butter
225 g/8 oz/1 cup light brown sugar
100 g/4 oz/1 cup brazil nuts, chopped
50 g/2 oz/¹/₃ cup raisins
2 eggs, beaten
A little milk

Sift the flour and spice into a bowl. Rub in the butter and stir in the sugar, nuts and raisins. Stir in the eggs and add enough milk to form a sticky dough. Turn into a greased 450 g/1 lb loaf tin and bake in the oven at 180°C/350°F/gas mark 4 for about 45 minutes until risen, golden and firm. Turn out on to a wire rack to cool.

Fruity Breakfast Muffins

300 ml/¹/₂ pt/1¹/₄ cups hot tea
100 g/4 oz/²/₃ cup mixed dried fruit (fruit cake mix)
50 g/2 oz/¹/₄ cup butter
75 g/3 oz/¹/₃ cup light brown sugar
5 ml/1 tsp mixed (apple pie) spice
175 g/6 oz/1¹/₂ cups self-raising (self-rising) wholemeal flour
5 ml/1 tsp baking powder
1 egg, beaten

Mix the tea with the fruit and stir in the butter until melted, then the sugar. Leave to soak until the tea is just lukewarm. Stir in the remaining ingredients. Spoon into 12 sections of a greased bun tin (muffin pan) and bake in the oven at 180°C/350°F/gas mark 4 for about 40 minutes until risen and the centres spring back when pressed. Cool on a wire rack.

Banana and Walnut Loaf

2–3 small, very ripe bananas
5 ml/1 tsp bicarbonate of soda (baking soda)
50 g/2 oz/¹/₄ cup butter, softened
275 g/10 oz/2 cups plain (all-purpose) flour
Grated rind of 1 orange
100 g/4 oz/¹/₂ cup light brown sugar
1 egg
50 g/2 oz/¹/₃ cup walnuts, roughly chopped

Put the bananas and bicarbonate of soda in a food processor or mixer. Run the machine until smooth. Add the butter, flour, orange rind, sugar and egg and run the machine again until well blended. Remove the blade and fold in the nuts. Turn into a greased 900 g/2 lb loaf tin and bake in the oven at 180°C/350°F/gas mark 4 for about 1 hour until risen and golden and a skewer inserted in the centre comes out clean. Turn out on to a wire rack to cool.

Banana and Cherry Loaf

Prepare as for Banana and Walnut Loaf but add 5 ml/1 tsp ground cinnamon with the flour and fold in 50 g/2 oz/¹/₂ cup quartered glacé (candied) cherries instead of walnuts to the mixture before putting in the tin.

CAKES, BISCUITS AND SWEETS

There can be no comparison between bought and home-made cakes, biscuits and sweets. And you may be surprised how easy it is to make your own, either from scratch or by cheating a little! Here is a wide selection for you to try.

All-in-one Cake

MAKES 1 CAKE

175 g/6 oz/1¹/₂ cups self-raising (self-rising) flour
5 ml/1 tsp baking powder
175 g/6 oz/³/₄ cup caster (superfine) sugar
175 g/6 oz/³/₄ cup soft margarine
3 eggs
Jam (conserve)
A little extra caster sugar

Put all the ingredients, except the jam and extra sugar, in a processor and run the machine until the mixture is just blended and smooth, or put in a bowl and beat with a wooden spoon for about 2 minutes until smooth. Do not over-beat. Grease two 18 cm/7 in sandwich tins (pans) and line the bases with baking parchment. Divide the mixture between the tins and level the surfaces. Bake in the oven at 190°C/375°F/gas mark 5 for 20 minutes until risen, golden and the centres spring back when pressed. Turn out on to a wire rack to cool. Remove the paper. Sandwich together with jam and sprinkle with a little extra caster sugar.

Chocolate Cake

MAKES 1 CAKE

Make as for All-in-one Cake but substitute 25 g/1 oz/2 tbsp of the flour with cocoa (unsweetened chocolate) powder. Fill with whipped cream or chocolate spread.

Coffee Cake

MAKES 1 CAKE

Make as for All-in-one Cake but dissolve 15 g/1 tbsp instant coffee in 15 ml/1 tbsp water and add to the basic mix. Sandwich with sweetened cream, flavoured with coffee liqueur or 5 ml/1 tsp coffee granules dissolved in 5 ml/1 tsp water.

Carrot Cake

MAKES 1 CAKE

225 g/8 oz/2 cups self-raising (self-rising) flour
15 ml/1 tbsp baking powder
5 ml/1 tsp mixed (apple pie) spice
150 g/5 oz/²/₃ cup margarine
100 g/4 oz/¹/₂ cup light brown sugar
2 large carrots, grated

Mix the flour, baking powder and spice in a bowl. Melt the margarine and sugar, add to the flour and mix well. Stir in the carrots. Pour into a greased 450 g/ 1 lb loaf tin. Bake in the oven at 160°C/ 325°F/gas mark 3 for 1 hour until a knife inserted into the centre of the cake comes out clean.

No-bake Chocolate Fudge Cake

MAKES 1 CAKE

100 g/4 oz/¹/₂ cup butter or margarine
175 g/6 oz/³/₄ cup icing (confectioners') sugar
15 ml/1 tbsp cocoa (unsweetened chocolate) powder
3 small chocolate fudge finger bars, cut into pieces
175 g/6 oz plain sweet biscuits (cookies), crushed
50 g/2 oz/¹/₂ cup chopped mixed nuts
A little extra sifted icing (confectioners') sugar

Put the butter, sugar, cocoa and fudge fingers in a pan and heat gently, stirring until melted. Add the biscuits and nuts and mix well. Turn into a greased 18 cm/7 in square sandwich tin (pan) and press down well. Leave to cool, then chill until set. Turn out on to a serving plate, dust with a little extra icing sugar and serve cut into fingers.

Pineapple Loaf

MAKES 1 LOAF

350 g/12 oz/3 cups plain (all-purpose) flour
15 ml/1 tbsp baking powder
2.5 ml/¹/₂ tsp bicarbonate of soda (baking soda)
100 g/4 oz/¹/₂ cup light brown sugar
150 g/5 oz/²/₃ cup soft margarine
3 eggs, beaten
30 ml/2 tbsp milk
5 ml/1 tsp ground cinnamon
30 ml/2 tbsp honey
227 g/8 oz/1 small can pineapple drained and chopped

Mix all the ingredients together, adding a little of the pineapple juice if necessary to form a soft, dropping consistency. Pour into a greased 450 g/1 lb loaf tin (pan). Bake on a low shelf in the oven at 180°C/350°F/gas mark 4 for about 1 hour or until firm. Serve warm or cold, cut in slices.

Clotted Cream Buns

MAKES 12

100 ml/3¹/₂ fl oz/6¹/₂ tbsp clotted cream
225 g/8 oz/2 cups self-raising (self-rising) flour
1 egg
100 g/4 oz/¹/₂ cup caster (superfine) sugar
45–60 ml/3–4 tbsp milk

Mix the cream and flour together. Add the remaining ingredients and mix to a soft dough. Shape into about 12 flattened rounds and place on a greased baking sheet. Bake in the oven at 220°C/ 425°F/gas mark 7 for 10–15 minutes. Serve plain, or split and filled with more cream and jam.

Fresh Cream Gâteau In A Hurry

SERVES 6–8

1 packet sponge cake mix
1 egg (according to the packet)
30 ml/2 tbsp raspberry jam
(conserve)
150 ml/¹/₄ pt/²/₃ cup whipping cream
Icing (confectioners') sugar for
dusting

Make up the cake mix according to the packet directions. Divide between two 18 cm/7 in sandwich tins (pans) and bake as directed. Turn out on to a wire rack to cool. Sandwich the cakes together with the jam and whipped cream. Dust the top with icing sugar and chill until ready to serve.

Chocolate Bar Cookies

MAKES ABOUT 20

50 g/2 oz/¹/₄ cup margarine
50 g/2 oz/¹/₄ cup caster (superfine)
sugar
1 egg, beaten
175 g/6 oz/1¹/₂ cups self-raising
(self-rising) flour
2 chocolate bars such as Mars or
Snickers, finely chopped

Melt the margarine in a saucepan. Stir in the sugar and leave to cool slightly. Add the egg, flour and chocolate bars and mix to a lumpy dough. Make about 20 small flat rounds about 4 cm/ 1¹/₂ in diameter and place on a greased baking sheet. Bake in the oven at 190°C/ 375°F/gas mark 5 for 15–20 minutes. Cool on a wire rack.

Cornflake Cakes

MAKES ABOUT 12

75 g/3 oz/¹/₃ cup margarine
75 ml/5 tbsp golden (light corn)
syrup
100 g/4 oz/1 cup drinking
(sweetened) chocolate powder or
45 ml/3 tbsp cocoa (unsweetened
chocolate) powder
100–175 g/4–6 oz/4–6 cups
Cornflakes

Melt the margarine and syrup in a pan. Stir in the chocolate or cocoa. Gradually stir in enough cornflakes so that they are coated in the mixture. Put spoonfuls into paper cases (cupcake papers) and leave to cool and set.

Chocolate Squidge

MAKES 15–20 SQUARES

60 ml/4 tbsp condensed milk
60 ml/4 tbsp drinking (sweetened)
chocolate powder
50 g/2 oz/¹/₄ cup margarine, melted
225 g/8 oz/1 cup icing
(confectioners') sugar

Mix together the milk, drinking chocolate and margarine. Gradually add the icing sugar until the mixture is firm and will absorb no more sugar. Flatten to about 1 cm/¹/₂ in thick and cut into squares. Chill for a few hours.

Flapjacks

100 g/4 oz/¹/₂ cup margarine
75 g/3 oz/¹/₃ cup light brown sugar
60 ml/4 tbsp golden (light corn)
  syrup
275 g/10 oz/2¹/₂ cups rolled oats

Melt the margarine, sugar and syrup in a saucepan over a low heat. Stir in the oats until completely coated. Spoon into a greased shallow baking tin (pan) and spread until about 1 cm/¹/₂ in thick. Bake in the oven at 180°C/350°F/gas mark 4 for about 25 minutes until golden. Leave to cool in the tin, then cut into squares.

Spice is Nice Flapjacks

MAKES 12

75 g/3 oz/¹/₃ cup butter or
  margarine, softened
75 g/3 oz/¹/₃ cup light brown sugar
100 g/4 oz/1 cup rolled oats
5 ml/1 tsp mixed (apple pie) spice

Beat the butter or margarine in a bowl until creamy. Add the sugar, oats and spice and work in until well mixed. Turn into a greased 18 cm/7 in square tin and press down well. Bake in the oven at 220°C/425°F/gas mark 7 for 15–20 minutes until golden. Leave to cool in the tin for 10 minutes, then cut into squares. Leave in the tin until cold before removing.

Rum Truffle Cakes

MAKES 12

30 ml/2 tbsp golden (light corn)
  syrup
25 g/1 oz/2 tbsp butter
30 ml/2 tbsp cocoa (unsweetened
  chocolate) powder
100 g/4 oz/2 cups plain cake crumbs
15 ml/1 tbsp icing (confectioners')
  sugar
Rum essence (extract)
Extra cocoa powder

Melt the syrup, butter and cocoa powder together. Stir in the cake crumbs, sugar and a few drops or rum essence to taste. Roll into 12 small balls. Chill for about 20 minutes, then roll in cocoa powder and place in small paper (petits fours) cases. Store in the fridge.

Peanut Honey Bites

MAKES 12

75 g/3 oz/¹/₃ cup butter or margarine
45 ml/3 tbsp set honey
225 g/8 oz plain biscuits (cookies),
  crushed
5 ml/1 tsp grated lemon rind
45 ml/3 tbsp crunchy peanut butter

Melt the fat with the honey and bring to the boil. Stir in the remaining ingredients and mix well. Press into a greased 18 cm/7 in square sandwich tin (pan) and chill until set. Cut into squares before serving.

Crispy Oatcake Thins

MAKES 8

75 g/3 oz/³/₄ cup medium oatmeal
Salt
1.5 ml/¹/₄ tsp bicarbonate of soda
  (baking soda)
15 g/¹/₂ oz/1 tbsp butter, melted
60 ml/4 tbsp hot water
Oil for greasing

Put all the ingredients except the oil in a bowl and mix to a dough. Turn out on to a surface dusted with oatmeal and pat or roll out thinly to about 25 cm/10 in round. Cut out 8 wedges. Lightly oil a large frying pan (skillet) and heat gently. Cook the oatcakes a few at a time until firm. Turn over carefully so that they don't break and cook for 2–3 minutes more. Cool on a wire rack. Store in an airtight tin. Serve with butter and marmalade or with cheese.

Broken Biscuit Cakes

MAKES 15

100 g/4 oz/¹/₂ cup butter or
  margarine
15 ml/1 tbsp caster (superfine)
  sugar
15 ml/1 tbsp golden (light corn)
  syrup
30 ml/2 tbsp cocoa (unsweetened
  chocolate) powder
225 g/8 oz broken biscuits (cookies),
  crushed
50 g/2 oz/¹/₃ cup sultanas (golden
  raisins)

Melt the fat, sugar, syrup and cocoa in a saucepan until well blended, but do not boil. Stir in the biscuits and sultanas. Press into a greased 28 × 18 cm/11 × 7 in baking tin (pan). Chill until firm, then cut into squares.

Raspberry Oat Squares

MAKES 15

225 g/8 oz/2 cups self-raising (self-
  rising) flour
5 ml/1 tsp salt
175 g/6 oz/³/₄ cup margarine
175 g/6 oz/1¹/₂ cups rolled oats
175 g/6 oz/³/₄ cup caster (superfine)
  sugar
300 g/11 oz/1 small can raspberries

Put the flour and salt in a bowl. Rub in the margarine, then stir in the oats and sugar. Grease a 28 × 18 cm/11 × 7 in baking tin (pan) and press half the mixture into the base. Drain the raspberries and scatter the fruit over the top. Cover with the remaining crumble mixture, pressing down well. Bake in the oven at 200°C/400°F/gas mark 6 for 30 minutes. Leave to cool for 15 minutes, then cut into squares and transfer to a wire rack to cool completely.

Chewy Apricot Bars

175 g/6 oz/1 small can evaporated milk
20 ml/4 tsp clear honey
45 ml/3 tbsp apple juice
50 g/2 oz/¹/₄ cup butter
50 g/2 oz/¹/₄ cup light brown sugar
50 g/2 oz/¹/₃ cup sultanas (golden raisins)
50 g/2 oz/¹/₃ cup raisins
225 g/8 oz/1¹/₃ cups ready-to-eat dried apricots, chopped
100 g/4 oz/1 cup desiccated (shredded) coconut
225 g/8 oz/2 cups rolled oats

Heat the evaporated milk with the honey, apple juice, butter and sugar until melted. Add the remaining ingredients and mix well. Press into a greased 28 × 18 cm/11 × 7 in baking tin (pan). Wrap in clingfilm (plastic wrap) and chill overnight to allow the flavours to develop before cutting into bars.

Cinnamon French Toast

1 egg
30 ml/2 tbsp milk
4 thick slices white bread, crusts removed
25 g/1 oz/2 tbsp butter
30 ml/2 tbsp oil
20 ml/4 tsp caster (superfine) sugar
5 ml/1 tsp ground cinnamon

Beat the egg and milk together. Dip the bread in to coat completely. Heat the butter and oil in a large frying pan (skillet). Fry (sauté) the slices for about 1¹/₂ minutes over a high heat until a deep golden brown. Drain on kitchen paper. Mix the sugar and cinnamon on a flat plate. Dip the bread in the mixture until coated on both sides. Serve straight away, cut into triangles.

Peanut Nibbles

225 g/8 oz plain biscuits (cookies), crushed
100 g/4 oz/¹/₂ cup butter, melted
225 g/8 oz/1 cup crunchy peanut butter
25 g/1 oz/2 tbsp glacé (candied) cherries, chopped
25 g/1 oz/¹/₆ cup currants

Mix all the ingredients together until well blended. Press into a greased 28 × 18 cm/11 × 7 in baking tin (pan). Cover with foil or clingfilm (plastic wrap) and chill until firm before cutting into squares.

Fruit and Fibre Crackles

100 g/4 oz/1 cup plain (semi-sweet) chocolate
50 g/2 oz/¹/₄ cup butter or margarine
15 ml/1 tbsp golden (light corn) syrup
100 g/4 oz/2 cups Fruit and Fibre breakfast cereal

Melt the chocolate in a bowl over a pan of hot water or in the microwave. Beat in the butter or margarine and syrup until smooth, heating a little more if necessary. Stir in the cereal. Pack into paper cases (cupcake papers) and chill until firm.

No-bake Crunchy Bars

MAKES 12–16

175 g/6 oz/³/₄ cup butter or
margarine
50 g/2 oz/¹/₄ cup light brown sugar
30 ml/2 tbsp golden (light corn)
syrup
45 ml/3 tbsp cocoa (unsweetened
chocolate) powder
75 g/3 oz/¹/₂ cup raisins
350 g/12 oz/3 cups Original Oat
Crunch cereal
225 g/8 oz/2 cups plain (semi-sweet)
chocolate

Oil and line the base of an 18 × 28 cm/
7 × 11 in baking tin (pan) with baking
parchment. Melt the butter or margarine,
sugar, syrup and cocoa in a pan. Stir in
the raisins and cereal. Press into the tin.
Melt the chocolate in a pan over hot water
or in a microwave and spread over right
to the corners. Chill until set, cut into
fingers and store in an airtight tin.

Easy-does-it Biscuits

MAKES ABOUT 20

65 g/2¹/₂ oz/5 tbsp soft butter or
margarine
50 g/2 oz/¹/₄ cup caster (superfine)
sugar
5 ml/1 tsp vanilla essence (extract)
100 g/4 oz/1 cup self-raising (self-
rising) flour
Whole blanched almonds or glacé
(candied) cherries, halved

Put all the ingredients in a processor
and run the machine until the mixture
just forms a ball. Alternatively, put in a
bowl and work with a fork or wooden
spoon until the mixture forms a ball.
Shape into walnut-sized balls and place a
little apart on a greased baking sheet (you
may need two). Press down with a fork
dipped in cold water. Bake in the oven at
190°C/375°F/gas mark 5 for about 15
minutes until pale golden. Top each
immediately with a nut or cherry half and
leave for a few minutes to harden, then
transfer to a wire rack to cool.

Muesli Cookies

MAKES ABOUT 30

75 g/3 oz/¹/₃ cup margarine
75 g/3 oz/¹/₃ cup light brown sugar
20 ml/4 tsp golden (light corn)
syrup
5 ml/1 tsp bicarbonate of soda
(baking soda)
75 g/3 oz/³/₄ cup plain (all-purpose)
flour
150 g/5 oz/1¹/₄ cups muesli

Melt the margarine, sugar and syrup
in a pan. Add the bicarbonate of
soda – it will froth up. Stir in the flour and
muesli. Shape into walnut-sized balls and
place a little apart on two greased baking
sheets. Flatten slightly with a fork. Bake
in the oven at 190°C/375°F/gas mark 5
for 8–10 minutes or until golden brown.
Leave to cool for 2 minutes, then transfer
to a wire rack to cool completely.

Quick Rum Truffles

MAKES 12

30 ml/2 tbsp chocolate hazelnut
spread
50 g/2 oz/1 cup cake crumbs
5 ml/1 tsp rum, brandy or sherry
essence (extract)
Cocoa (unsweetened chocolate)
powder, drinking (sweetened)
chocolate powder or chocolate
vermicelli, to coat

Mix the chocolate spread and cake crumbs together until well blended. Add the essence to taste and a little water to give a soft but not sticky consistency. Roll the mixture into small balls, then roll in cocoa, drinking chocolate or vermicelli. Place in small paper (petits four) cases and chill.

Fridge Biscuits

MAKES ABOUT 16

100 g/4 oz/¹/₂ cup soft margarine
100 g/4 oz/¹/₂ cup caster (superfine) sugar
225 g/8 oz/2 cups plain (all-purpose) flour
5 ml/1 tsp baking powder
1 size 4 egg, beaten
5 ml/1 tsp vanilla essence (extract)

In a food processor (or in a bowl using a wooden spoon) work all the ingredients together to form a stiff dough. Shape into a roll and wrap in greaseproof (waxed) paper. Chill for up to 2 weeks until ready to use. Cut into 5 mm/¹/₄ in slices. Place on a baking sheet and bake in the oven at 190°C/375°F/gas mark 5 for 10–12 minutes until golden. Cool on a wire rack.

Cherry Cookies

MAKES ABOUT 16

Prepare as for Fridge Biscuits but knead 50 g/2 oz/¹/₂ cup chopped glacé (candied) cherries into the mixture before shaping into a roll.

Almond Cookies

MAKES ABOUT 16

Prepare as for Fridge Biscuits but substitute almond essence for the vanilla and press a whole blanched almond into each slice before baking.

Ginger Crumblies

MAKES ABOUT 16

Prepare as for Fridge Biscuits, adding 30 ml/2 tbsp ground ginger.

Chocolate Chip Shortbread

MAKES 8 WEDGES

175 g/6 oz/1¹/₂ cups plain (all-purpose) flour
50 g/2 oz/¹/₂ cup caster (superfine) sugar
100 g/4 oz/¹/₂ cup butter
50 g/2 oz/¹/₂ cup chocolate dots or chopped plain (semi-sweet) chocolate

Mix the flour and sugar in a bowl. Rub in the butter. Stir in the chocolate, then knead together. Press into a 20 cm/8 in round on a lightly greased baking sheet. Pinch the edge between the finger and thumb and mark into 8 wedges. Prick with a fork. Bake at 160°C/325°F/gas mark 3 for 25 minutes or until just beginning to colour. Leave to cool, then cut into wedges.

Peanut Cracklies

MAKES 12

50 g/2 oz/¹/₄ cup butter
45 ml/3 tbsp golden (light corn)
*   syrup*
50 g/2 oz/¹/₄ cup caster (superfine)
sugar
60 ml/4 tbsp crunchy peanut butter
25 g/1 oz/¹/₄ cup roasted peanuts,
*   chopped*
75 g/3 oz/3 cups puffed rice cereal

Melt the butter, syrup, sugar and peanut butter in a saucepan. Stir in the nuts and cereal. Spoon into paper cake cases (cupcake papers) and chill until firm.

Raspberry Chewies

MAKES 12

50 g/2 oz/¹/₄ cup butter
45 ml/3 tbsp raspberry jam
*   (conserve)*
50 g/2 oz/¹/₂ cup pink marshmallows
100 g/4 oz/4 cups Cornflakes

Melt the butter, jam and marshmallows in a saucepan, stirring. Stir in the cornflakes and spoon into paper cake cases (cupcake papers). Chill until firm.

Croaties

MAKES ABOUT 18–20

100 g/4 oz/¹/₂ cup butter
100 g/4 oz/15 ml/1 tbsp golden
*   (light corn) syrup*
100 g/4 oz/1 cup self-raising (self-
*   rising) flour*
100 g/4 oz/1 cup rolled oats
2.5 ml/¹/₂ tsp bicarbonate of soda
*   (baking soda)*

Melt the butter and syrup in a saucepan. Stir in the flour, oats and bicarbonate of soda. Beat well. Cool slightly, then shape into small balls and place well apart on greased baking sheets. Flatten slightly. Bake in the oven at 180°C/350°F/gas mark 4 for 15 minutes or until golden. Cool slightly, then transfer to a wire rack.

Seeded Cookies

MAKES ABOUT 18–20

Prepare as for Croaties but add 25 g/1 oz/¹/₄ cup sunflower seeds and 25 g/1 oz/¹/₄ cup sesame seeds to the mixture before shaping.

Chocolate Nibbles

MAKES ABOUT 18–20

Make as for Croaties but shape the mixture into small sausage shapes, press out and spread each with a little chocolate hazelnut spread and top with a sprinkling of rolled oats before baking.

Tutti-frutti Chews

MAKES ABOUT 18–20

Prepare as for Croaties but add 50 g/ 2 oz/¹/₂ cup marshmallows, snipped into small pieces with scissors, and 50 g/ 2 oz/¹/₂ cup multicoloured glacé (candied) cherries, chopped, to the mixture before shaping.

Gaelic Coffee Ring

MAKES 1 CAKE
---

100 g/4 oz/1 cup self-raising (self-rising) flour
2.5 ml/¹/₂ tsp baking powder
100 g/4 oz/¹/₂ cup soft margarine
100 g/4 oz/¹/₂ cup caster (superfine) sugar
2 eggs
30 ml/2 tbsp instant coffee powder
30 ml/2 tbsp hot water
30 ml/2 tbsp whisky
150 ml/¹/₄ pt/²/₃ cup whipped cream
15 ml/1 tbsp toasted flaked almonds

Beat the flour, baking powder, margarine, sugar and eggs together until light and fluffy. Turn into a greased 900 ml/1¹/₂ pt/3³/₄ cup round tin (pan). Level the surface and bake in the oven at 180°C/350°F/gas mark 4 for 25 minutes until risen and golden and the cake springs back when lightly pressed. Turn out on to a wire rack to cool, then transfer to a plate. Blend the coffee with the water and whisky. Spoon over the cake a little at a time until it has all soaked in. Spread the cream all over and sprinkle with the toasted almonds.

Mocha and Walnut Rich Tea Cake

MAKES 1 CAKE
---

100 g/4 oz/¹/₂ cup butter, softened
175 g/6 oz/1³/₄ cup icing (confectioners') sugar, sifted
1 egg, separated
120 ml/4 fl oz/¹/₂ cup hot water
15 ml/1 tbsp instant coffee powder
15 ml/1 tbsp cocoa (unsweetened chocolate) powder
50 g/2 oz/¹/₂ cup walnut halves, finely chopped
2 packets rich tea finger biscuits (cookies)
6 walnut halves

Beat the butter and sugar until smooth. Beat in the egg yolk. Blend the water with the coffee and cocoa until smooth. Add 30 ml/2 tbsp to the sugar mixture and beat until well blended. Whisk the egg white until stiff and fold into the mixture with the walnuts. Dip 10 of the biscuits in the remaining coffee and cocoa and lay side by side in 2 rows on a flat plate. Spread with about one-sixth of the butter icing. Repeat with more layers of dipped biscuits and icing until all the biscuits are used. Spread the remaining icing over the sides and top of the cake and decorate with walnut halves. Chill until ready to serve.

Seed Cake

MAKES 1 CAKE

175 g/6 oz/³/₄ cup butter, softened
175 g/6 oz/³/₄ cup caster (superfine)
* sugar*
225 g/8 oz/2 cups self-raising (self-
* rising) flour*
5 ml/1 tsp baking powder
3 eggs
15 ml/1 tbsp caraway seeds
45 ml/3 tbsp milk

Beat all the ingredients together until smooth. Turn into a greased and lined 20 cm/8 in round deep cake tin (pan). Cook in the oven at 160°C/325°F/gas mark 3 for 1 hour or until risen and golden and a skewer inserted in the centre comes out clean. Leave in the tin for 5 minutes. Turn out on to a wire rack, remove the paper and leave to cool.

No-bake Chestnutty Cake

MAKES 1 CAKE

Melted butter for greasing
30 ml/2 tbsp toasted chopped nuts
100 g/4 oz/¹/₂ cup butter or
* margarine*
100 g/4 oz/¹/₂ cup caster (superfine)
* sugar*
450 g/16 oz/1 large can
* unsweetened chestnut purée*
225 g/8 oz/2 cups plain (semi-sweet)
* chocolate, broken into pieces*
A few drops of almond essence
* (extract)*

Grease and line a 450 g/1 lb loaf tin (pan) with greaseproof (waxed) paper. Brush the paper with melted butter and sprinkle with the nuts. Beat the fat, sugar and purée together until light. Melt the chocolate in a bowl over a pan of hot water or in the microwave. Stir into the mixture with the almond essence. Spoon into the tin, level the surface and chill until firm (preferably overnight). Turn out, remove the paper and serve cut into slices.

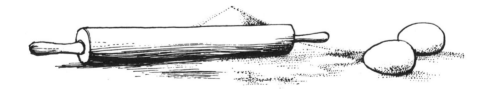

DRINKS

From heady summer cocktails to mulled punches, from soothing pick-me-ups to fruity specials, this section has drinks for every occasion.

HOT PUNCHES

Dr Johnson's Choice

MAKES 8–10 GLASSES

1 bottle red wine
1 small orange, sliced
4 whole cloves
1 small piece cinnamon stick
300 ml/¹/₂ pt/1¹/₄ cups water
50 g/2 oz/¹/₄ cup light brown sugar
30 ml/2 tbsp orange liqueur
30 ml/2 tbsp brandy
Freshly grated nutmeg

Put all the ingredients except the nutmeg in a large pan. Bring slowly to the boil, stirring. Turn off the heat, cover and leave to stand for 5 minutes. Reheat but do not boil. Ladle into goblets and sprinkle with a little grated nutmeg.

Victorian Milk Punch

MAKES 6 SMALL GLASSES

600 ml/1 pt/2¹/₂ cups milk
45 ml/3 tbsp clear honey
Finely grated rind of 1 orange
30 ml/2 tbsp Grand Marnier
Freshly grated nutmeg

Put the milk, honey and orange rind in a pan and heat, stirring, but do not boil. Remove from the heat, stir in the Grand Marnier and serve straight away, dusted with a little nutmeg.

Warming Cider Cup

MAKES 12 MUGS

1 litre/1³/₄ pts/4¹/₄ cups dry cider
75 g/3 oz/¹/₃ cup light brown sugar
2 small pieces cinnamon stick
8 allspice berries
75 ml/5 tbsp calvados
1 red eating (dessert) apple, halved, cored and sliced
1 green eating (dessert) apple, halved, cored and sliced

Pour the cider in a pan with the sugar and spices. Bring just to the boil, turn off the heat and leave to infuse for at least 1 hour. Stir in the calvados, reheat but do not boil. Add the apple slices and serve ladled into pottery mugs.

Cockle Warmer

1 whole lemon
5 whole cloves
Juice of 2 lemons
50 g/2 oz/¹/₄ cup caster (superfine)
sugar
1 bottle ruby port
600 ml/1 pt/2¹/₂ cups water
30 ml/2 tbsp brandy

Stud the lemon with the cloves. Place in a pan with the strained lemon juice, the sugar, port and water. Bring just to the boil, cover, turn off the heat and leave to stand for 5 minutes. Stir in the brandy, reheat but do not boil, and serve straight away.

SUMMER COOLERS

Red Wine Punch

1 bottle of red wine
60 ml/4 tbsp brandy
60 ml/4 tbsp port
600 ml/1 pt/2¹/₂ cups lemonade
1 lemon, sliced
1 apple, sliced
1 orange, sliced
Ice cubes

Mix together all the ingredients except the ice cubes in a large jug or bowl and pour over lots of ice cubes to serve.

White Wine Punch

Prepare as for Red Wine Punch but use a bottle of dry white wine instead of red.

Dry Wine Winner

1 bottle dry white wine, chilled
Juice of 1 small lemon
150 ml/¹/₄ pt/²/₃ cup dry sherry
10 ml/2 tsp caster (superfine) sugar
500 ml/17 fl oz/2¹/₄ cups carbonated
water, chilled

Mix the wine with the lemon, sherry and sugar. Pour into tall glasses and top with carbonated water. Serve straight away.

Somerset Cup

30 ml/2 tbsp sweet red vermouth
30 ml/2 tbsp grenadine syrup
3 drops of Angostura bitters
1 litre/1³/₄ pts/4¹/₄ cups medium-
sweet still cider
Ice cubes

Blend all the ingredients except the ice in a jug. Pour over ice cubes in tall glasses and serve straight away.

Planter's Punch

250 ml/8 fl oz/1 cup dark rum
60 ml/4 tbsp grenadine syrup
450 ml/³/₄ pt/2 cups pure orange
juice
450 ml/³/₄ pt/2 cups pure pineapple
juice
Juice of 1 lemon or lime
Orange and lemon or lime slices
Ice cubes

Mix all the ingredients in a tall jug. Pour into tumblers and serve.

Fruit-of-the-vine Zinger

MAKES 6 GLASSES

*450 ml/³/4 pt/2 cups white grape
  juice, chilled
45 ml/3 tbsp brandy
Pinch of ground ginger
250 ml/8 fl oz/1 cup ginger ale
Crushed ice*

Mix the grape juice, brandy and ginger together in a jug. Just before serving, stir in the ginger ale and pour over crushed ice in small glasses.

Mango Cooler

MAKES 4 GLASSES

*400 g/14 oz/1 large can mango in
  juice
300 ml/¹/2 pt/1¹/4 cups dry white
  wine
250 ml/8 fl oz/1 cup carbonated
  mineral water
30 ml/2 tbsp lime juice
Ice cubes*

Purée the mango with its juice. Mix together with the remaining ingredients in a large jug.

Strawberry Fruit Punch

MAKES 6 GLASSES

*450 g/1 lb strawberries
75 g/3 oz/³/4 cup caster (superfine)
sugar
175 ml/6 fl oz/³/4 cup brandy
1 bottle dry white wine, chilled
Soda water or mineral water*

Slice the strawberries, sprinkle with sugar and pour over the brandy. Leave to stand for at least an hour. Add the white wine and soda or mineral water to taste.

Peach Fruit Punch

MAKES 6 GLASSES

Prepare as for Strawberry Fruit Punch but substitute 4 ripe peaches, stoned (pitted) and sliced, for the strawberries.

CLASSIC COCKTAILS

Mint Julep

MAKES 6 GLASSES

*12 small mint sprigs
30 ml/2 tbsp caster (superfine)
  sugar
Cracked ice
175 ml/6 fl oz/³/4 cup bourbon
  whiskey*

Chop half the sprigs of mint and mix with the sugar. Divide between 6 glasses. Fill the glasses with ice then add the bourbon. Stir with long spoons and top each with a mint sprig.

Daiquiri

MAKES 6 GLASSES

*15 ml/1 tbsp caster (superfine)
  sugar
Juice of 3 limes
175 ml/6 fl oz/³/4 cup white rum
Cracked ice*

Mix the sugar and lime juice until dissolved. Divide between 6 glasses. Pour on the rum and fill with cracked ice.

Champagne Cocktail

MAKES 6 GLASSES

6 small sugar cubes
12 dashes Angostura bitters
1 bottle chilled dry champagme

Place a sugar cube in each of 6 champagne flutes. Add 2 dashes of Angostura bitters to each. Top with champagne and serve straight away without stirring.

Brandy Sour

MAKES 6 GLASSES

175 ml/6 fl oz/³/₄ cup brandy
Juice of 3 lemons
Ice cubes
Carbonated water
6 thin lemon slices

Put the brandy and lemon in a large shaker with ice. Shake well and pour into 6 tall glasses. Top up with carbonated water to taste and decorate the glasses with lemon slices.

FRUITY FAVOURITES

Black Watch

MAKES 6 GLASSES

600 ml/1 pt/2¹/₂ cups red grape juice
30 ml/2 tbsp apple and blackcurrant
    cordial
Ice cubes
Carbonated water

Mix the juice and cordial together. Pour into glasses. Add a few ice cubes, then top up with carbonated water.

Fresh Fruit Refresher

MAKES 10 GLASSES

2 ripe peaches, peeled and stoned
    (pitted)
100 g/4 oz/1 cup raspberries
15 ml/1 tbsp lime juice cordial
300 ml/¹/₂ pt/1¹/₄ cups pure orange
juice
300 ml/¹/₂ pt/1¹/₄ cups pure apple
juice
1 litre/1³/₄ pts/4¹/₄ cups chilled
    lemonade
10 orange slices

Purée the peaches and raspberries in a food processor or blender with the lime cordial and orange juice. Strain into a jug. Stir in the apple juice and top with lemonade. Serve with a slice of orange on the rim of each glass.

Sunset

MAKES 6 GLASSES

Ice cubes
Grenadine syrup
900 ml/1¹/₂ pts/3³/₄ cups pure orange
    juice
Straws

Put ice cubes in 6 tall glasses. Pour in about 2.5 cm/1 in grenadine syrup. Slowly pour orange juice on top. Do not stir. Place a straw in each and serve.

Three-fruit Cocktail

MAKES 6 GLASSES

300 ml/¹/₂ pt/1¹/₄ cups pure orange juice
300 ml/¹/₂ pt/1¹/₄ cups pure grapefruit juice
300 g/11 oz/1 small can crushed pineapple
Ice cubes
Carbonated water

Mix the juices and pineapple together with some ice cubes. Pour into tall glasses and top up with carbonated water. Stir and serve.

AFTER-DINNER SOOTHERS

Egg Nog

MAKES 4 GLASSES

2 eggs, separated
45 ml/3 tbsp icing (confectioners') sugar
45 ml/3 tbsp cognac
600 ml/1 pt/2¹/₂ cups milk
170 g/6 oz/1 small can evaporated milk
4 cinnamon sticks

Whisk the yolks with 15 ml/1 tbsp of the sugar and the cognac. Whisk the egg whites until stiff and whisk in the remaining sugar. Warm the two milks together until almost boiling. Whisk into the yolks, then add the whites and fold in until completely blended. Serve immediately in small thick glasses, with a cinnamon stick as a 'stirrer'.

Golden Tea Punch

SERVES 6

450 ml/³/₄ pt/2 cups ginger ale
300 ml/¹/₂ pt/1¹/₄ cups pineapple juice
250 ml/8 fl oz/1 cup orange juice
250 ml/8 fl oz/1 cup cold strong black tea
90 ml/6 tbsp lime juice
15 ml/1 tbsp clear honey, warmed
Ice cubes

Mix together all the ingredients and serve at once.

Gaelic Coffee

MAKES 4 GLASSES

20 ml/4 tsp light brown sugar
150 ml/¹/₄ pt/²/₃ cup Scotch whisky
300 ml/¹/₂ pt/1¹/₄ cups freshly made strong black coffee
150 ml/¹/₄ pt/²/₃ cup thick double (heavy) cream, chilled

Spoon the sugar into warmed wine goblets or coffee glasses. Divide the whisky between the glasses and stir. Pour on the hot coffee and stir well to dissolve the sugar. Hold a cold teaspoon over the coffee, almost touching it, and slowly pour on a good layer of cream (it should float on the coffee). Serve straight away.

Irish Coffee: Make as for Gaelic Coffee but substitute Irish whisky for the Scotch.

Calypso Coffee: Make as for Gaelic Coffee but substitute dark rum for the whisky.

Caribbean Coffee: Make as for Gaelic Coffee but substitute white rum for the whisky.

French Coffee: Make as for Gaelic Coffee but substitute cognac for the whisky.

Italian Coffee: Make as for Gaelic Coffee but substitute Amaretto for the whisky.

Mocha Speciality: Make as for Gaelic Coffee but substitute chocolate liqueur for the whisky.

Anjou Coffee: Make as for Gaelic Coffee but substitute Cointreau for the whisky.

Chocolate Comfort

MAKES 4 CUPS

75 g/3 oz/³/₄ cup plain (semi-sweet)
*   chocolate, broken into squares*
45 ml/3 tbsp dark rum
30 ml/2 tbsp water
600 ml/1 pt/2¹/₂ cups milk
150 ml/¹/₄ pt/²/₃ cup whipping cream,
*   whipped*
Ground cinnamon
8 chocolate mint, orange or coffee
*   sticks*

Put the chocolate in a pan with the rum and water. Heat gently, stirring, until the chocolate has melted. Blend in the milk and bring almost to the boil. Pour into cups with saucers. Spoon the whipped cream on top and dust with cinnamon. Add 2 chocolate sticks to each saucer and serve straight away.

Banana Whip

SERVES 2

450 ml/³/₄ pt/2 cups milk
1 ripe banana, chopped
2 scoops vanilla ice cream
Ice cubes

Blend the milk, banana and ice cream until frothy in a blender or food processor. Pour into tall glasses and add the ice cubes.

Hawaiian Iced Coffee

SERVES 2–4

300 g/11 oz/1 small can pineapple
in juice
300 ml/¹/₂ pt/1¹/₄ cups milk
15 ml/1 tbsp instant coffee powder
10 ml/2 tsp hot water
2 scoops vanilla ice cream
10 ml/2 tsp demerara sugar
Freshly grated nutmeg

Purée the pineapple pieces and juice in a blender or food processor. Add the milk and process again. Dissolve the coffee in the hot water and add to the blender. Blend until well mixed. Taste and add a little more dissolved coffee if you like. Add the ice cream and process briefly. Pour into a jug or individual glasses and sprinkle with sugar and a little nutmeg.

INDEX